Readings in
Investment Management

Edited by Frank J. Fabozzi
Fordham University

Readings in
Investment Management

1983

RICHARD D. IRWIN, INC.
Homewood, Illinois 60430

© RICHARD D. IRWIN, INC., 1983

All rights reserved. No part of this publication may be reproduced, stored in a retrieval system, or transmitted, in any form or by any means, electronic, mechanical, photocopying, recording, or otherwise, without the prior written permission of the publisher.

ISBN 0-256-02934-2
Library of Congress Catalog Card No. 82-82691

Printed in the United States of America

1 2 3 4 5 6 7 8 9 0 ML 0 9 8 7 6 5 4 3

Preface

This book is designed for use as a supplementary book for an undergraduate or MBA course in investment management. It differs from other readings books in two ways. First, the majority of readings in most books are reprints of articles that have provided the foundation for the development of the present literature. Although instructors would like their students to read the original works, it is unlikely that students will gain an appreciation of the significance of the contribution in an introductory course. In fact, an important consideration in selecting an investment management textbook is the depth and breadth of coverage of the literature. At the introductory level, it is easier to have the textbook set forth the prevailing literature and summarize the contribution of researchers than trying to have students read the original works and recognize the significance of the contributions.

The selection of readings in this book was based on a different criterion. The topics are those that are either not adequately covered or not covered at all in most investment textbooks. In some instances, the lack of coverage may be due to the fact that a topic is too new to have been included in the textbook. The field of investment management has grown dramatically in recent years with the development of new financial contracts and new portfolio strategies, and the willingness of money managers to invest in opportunities outside of the traditional investments such as common stock and bonds. Therefore, it is understandable that authors find it difficult to cover all new developments.

The second way in which this book differs from other readings books is the source of the contributions. Whereas other readings books include articles from academic and professional journals, only one selection in this book is taken from a journal. The other selections are taken from either a Dow Jones-Irwin handbook or adapted from a book written on the topic. Consequently, the selections are written like chapters in a textbook. This makes it easier for the instructor to integrate the readings with the textbook and for students to understand the topic. The grid that appears on page xi suggests how each selection in this book can be assigned as supplementary reading to the chapters of 15 investment management textbooks.

The book is divided into the following five sections:

1. Psychology and Markets
2. Fixed Income Instruments
3. Portfolio Management
4. Options and Financial Futures
5. Tax Shelters, Real Estate, and Venture Capital

The contributors are recognized experts in the area they have written about for this book. Of the 26 contributors, only 3 are not engaged in full-time employment in the investment community. Twelve of the contributors have written or edited at least one book related to the topic they have contributed to this book.

I am indebted to many for their assistance in this project. To all the contributors, I extend my deep thanks and appreciation. The following individuals provided me with guidance in selecting the topics included in this book: Professor Stanley B. Block (Texas Christian University), Professor Geoffrey A. Hirt (Illinois State University), and Professor Robert Klemkosky (Indiana University). Special thanks are extended to Dr. Sylvan Feldstein (Moody's Investors Service), Professor Michael G. Ferri (University of South Carolina), Professor Jack Clark Francis (Bernard M. Baruch College, CUNY), Gary L. Gastineau (Kidder, Peabody & Co., Inc.), Professor Harry Greenfield (Queens College, CUNY), Dr. Robert Kopprasch (Salomon Brothers Inc), and Dean Richard R. West (Amos Tuck School, Dartmouth College) whose advice and friendship have been helpful throughout.

I am grateful to the following publishers for granting me permission to reprint the selections in this book: Addison-Wesley Publishing Company, Inc., Dow Jones-Irwin, Inc., McGraw-Hill Book Company, Random House, Inc., and the *Financial Analysts Journal.*

Frank J. Fabozzi

List of Contributors

Gary L. Bergstrom, Ph.D.: President, Acadian Financial Research, Inc., Boston, Massachusetts.

Peter L. Bernstein: Peter L. Bernstein, Inc., New York, New York, and Editor of *The Journal of Portfolio Management*.

Richard M. Bookstaber, Ph.D.: Associate Professor of Economics and Finance in the Graduate School of Business at Brigham Young University.

Peter E. Christensen: Vice President, The First Boston Corporation.

David N. Dreman: Managing Director, Dreman, Gray & Embry, Inc., New York, New York.

Frank J. Fabozzi, Ph.D., C.F.A., C.P.A.: Professor of Economics, Fordham University.

Sylvan G. Feldstein, Ph.D.: Vice President and Bond Analyst, Moody's Investors Service.

Gary L. Gastineau: Manager, Options Portfolio Service, Kidder, Peabody & Company, New York, New York.

Roy D. Gottlieb: President, Kenroy Inc., Skokie, Illinois.

Alan J. Inbinder, AFLM: President, The Indevco Group, Skokie, Illinois.

John K. Koeneman: Vice President, State Street Bank & Trust Co., Boston, Massachusetts.

Robert W. Kopprasch, Ph.D., C.F.A.: Vice President, Salomon Brothers Inc, New York, New York.

Martin L. Leibowitz, Ph.D.: Managing Director, Bond Portfolio Analysis Group, Salomon Brothers Inc, New York, New York.

Allan M. Loosigian: President, Allan M. Loosigian & Company, Stamford, Connecticut.

Victor Niederhoffer, Ph.D.: Chairman, Niederhoffer, Cross and Zeckhauser, Inc., New York, an investment banking firm that engages in the trade of commodities through its subsidiary, NCZ Commodities.

Alan Joel Patricof: Alan Patricof Associates, New York, New York.

Paul Sack: The Rosenberg Real Estate Equity Funds, San Francisco, California.

Maury Seldin, DBA: Professor of Finance and Real Estate, School of Business Administration, The American University, Washington, D.C.

Martin Siegel: Vice President of International Arbitrage Department, Salomon Brothers Inc, New York, New York.

Marcia Stigum, Ph.D.: President, Stigum & Associates, New York, New York.

Robert E. Swanson, JD: Tax shelter consultant and lawyer with practices in New York City and Ridgewood, New Jersey.

Barbara Mardinly Swanson: Professional writer.

Kenneth J. Thygerson, Ph.D.: Executive Vice President, Western Federal Savings and Loan Association of Colorado and Chairman of the Board, WestAmerica Mortgage Co., Englewood, Colorado.

James R. Vertin, C.F.A.: Senior Vice President, Wells Fargo Investment Advisors, San Francisco, California.

Arthur W. Weimer, Ph.D., LL.D., MAI, CRE: Economic Consultant, United States League of Savings Associations, Washington, D.C.

Richard Zeckhauser, Ph.D.: Professor of Political Economy, Harvard University, Cambridge, Massachusetts and founder of Niederhoffer, Cross, and Zeckhauser, Inc.

Contents

Cross-Index of Readings to Investment Management Textbooks xi
Key to Textbooks xii

section 1
Psychology and Markets 1

1. Psychology and Markets   David N. Dreman 3

section 2
Fixed Income Instruments 25

2. Money Market Instruments   Marcia Stigum 27
3. Investing in Mortgage-Backed Securities   Kenneth J. Thygerson 49
4. Guidelines in the Credit Analysis of General Obligation
   and Revenue Municipal Bonds   Sylvan G. Feldstein 68
5. Early Redemption (Put) Options on Fixed Income Securities
   Robert W. Kopprasch 97

section 3
Portfolio Management 111

6. Passive Equity Management Strategies   James R. Vertin 113
7. Management of Individual Portfolios   Peter L. Bernstein 137
Appendix: Capital Gain and Loss Tax Treatment   Frank J. Fabozzi 149
8. Trends in Bond Portfolio Management   Martin L. Leibowitz 154
9. Bond Portfolio Immunization   Sylvan G. Feldstein,
   Peter E. Christensen, and Frank J. Fabozzi 189
Appendix: Bond Duration   Frank J. Fabozzi 207
10. International Securities Market   Gary L. Bergstrom,
    John K. Koeneman, and Martin J. Siegel 210

section 4
Options and Financial Futures 237

11. Options: Risks and Rewards   Gary L. Gastineau 239
12. The Option Pricing Formula   Richard M. Bookstaber 267

13.	Financial Futures: Hedging Interest-Rate Risk Allan M. Loosigian 282
14.	Market Index Futures Contracts Victor Niederhoffer and Richard Zeckhauser 309
15.	Predictions Fulfilled: The Early Experience of Market Index Futures Contracts Richard Zeckhauser and Victor Niederhoffer 323

section 5
Tax Shelters, Real Estate, and Venture Capital 331

16.	Tax Shelters Robert E. Swanson and Barbara Mardinly Swanson ... 333
17.	Selecting Real Estate Investment Opportunities Maury Seldin and Arthur M. Weimer 348
18.	Land Investment Alan J. Inbinder and Roy D. Gottlieb 362
19.	Management of Real Estate Portfolios Paul Sack 378
20.	Venture Capital Alan Joel Patricof 393

Sources of Readings **403**

Cross-Index of Readings to Investment Management Textbooks

Authors	1 Psychology and Markets	2 Money Market Instruments	3 Investing in Mortgage-Backed Securities	4 Guidelines in the Credit Analysis of Gen. Ob. & Rev. Muni. Bonds	5 Early Redemption (Put) Options on Fixed Income Securities	6 Passive Equity Management Strategies	7 Management of Individual Portfolios	8 Trends in Bond Portfolio Management	9 Bond Portfolio Immunization	10 International Securities Market	11 Options: Risks and Rewards	12 The Option Pricing Formula	13 Financial Futures: Hedging Interest Rate Risk	14 & 15 Market Index Futures Contracts and Predictions Fulfilled	16 Tax Shelters	17 Selecting Real Estate Investment Opportunities	18 Land Investment	19 Management of Real Estate Portfolios	20 Venture Capital
Bellmore/Phillips/Ritchie	–	–	3	–	13	27	27	12	12	–	14	14	–	–	1	–	–	–	–
Christy/Clendenin	–	22	25	6	6	–	–	–	–	26	5	5	22	–	–	25	25	25	–
Cohen/Zinbarg/Ziekel	–	15	15	13	14	6	6	14	14	–	15	15	15	–	15	15	15	15	15
Curley/Bear	–	–	5	–	11	17	18	17	17	–	12	12	12	12	–	–	–	–	–
Francis (1980)	–	1	1	–	8	19	19	–	–	–	16	16	–	–	5	–	–	–	–
Francis (1983)	–	1	1	17	17	–	–	18	18	–	23	23	24	24	7	25	25	25	16
Gitman/Joehnk	–	1	9	9	11	17	5, 17	17	17	–	11	11	12	12	16	15	15	15	18
Hayes/Bauman	–	–	–	13	11	18	21	11	11	–	–	–	–	–	–	–	–	–	–
Hirt/Block	–	–	3	–	12	–	11	11	–	–	13	13	17	17	19	18	18	18	18
Mittra/Gassen	–	2	8	7	17	14	–	–	–	–	18	18	19	19	16	19	19	19	19
Radcliffe	–	2	–	–	12	22	22	9	9	21	12	12	13	13	–	–	–	–	–
Reilly (1979)	–	–	16	16	17	19	19	18	18	22	23	23	–	–	–	2	2	2	–
Reilly (1982)	–	–	14	14	15	20	20	15	15	22	16	16	18	18	–	2	2	2	–
Sharpe	–	11	11	11	12	20	20	12	–	22	16	16	17	17	9	2	2	2	–
Tinic/West	–	–	–	–	13	19	19	19	10	10	15	15	10	10	–	–	–	–	–

Note: — indicates that there is not extensive coverage of topic in textbook. The numbers in the boxes indicate the chapters in the textbooks.

Key to Textbooks

Douglas H. Bellemore, Herbert E. Phillips, and John C. Ritchie, *Investment Analysis and Portfolio Selection: An Integrated Approach* (Cincinnati: South-Western Publishing, 1979).

George A. Christy and John C. Clendenin, *Introduction to Investments,* 7th ed. (New York: McGraw-Hill, 1978).

Jerome B. Cohen, Edward D. Zinbarg, and Arthur Zeikel, *Investment Analysis and Portfolio Management,* 4th ed. (Homewood, Ill.: Richard D. Irwin, 1982).

Anthony J. Curley and Robert M. Bear, *Investment Analysis and Management* (New York: Harper & Row, 1979).

Jack C. Francis, *Investments: Analysis and Management,* 3d. ed. (New York: McGraw-Hill, 1980).

Jack C. Francis, *Management of Investments* (New York: McGraw-Hill, expected copyright date 1983). Cross-index based on preliminary outline reviewed.

Lawrence J. Gitman and Michael D. Joehnk, *Fundamentals of Investing* (New York: Harper & Row, 1981).

Douglas A. Hayes and W. Scott Bauman, *Investments: Analysis and Management,* 3d. ed. (New York: Macmillan, 1976).

Geoffrey Hirt and Stanley Block, *Fundamentals of Investment Management and Strategy* (Homewood, Ill.: Richard D. Irwin, 1983). Cross-index based on preliminary outline reviewed.

Sid Mittra and Chris Gassen, *Investment Analysis and Portfolio Management* (New York: Harcourt Brace Jovanovich, 1981).

Robert C. Radcliffe, *Investment: Concepts, Analysis, and Strategy* (Glenview, Ill.: Scott, Foresman, 1982).

Frank K. Reilly, *Investment Analysis and Portfolio Management* (Hinsdale, Ill.: Dryden Press, 1979).

Frank K. Reilly, *Investments* (Hinsdale, Ill.: Dryden Press, 1982).

William F. Sharpe, *Investments,* 2d. ed. (Englewood Cliffs, N.J.: Prentice-Hall, 1981).

Seha M. Tinic and Richard R. West, *Investing in Securities: An Efficient Markets Approach* (Reading, Mass.: Addison-Wesley Publishing, 1979).

section 1

Psychology and Markets

INTRODUCTION

We often hear market participants refer to a particular security as under or overvalued in the marketplace. What does this mean? According to the principles of security valuation, it means that the present value of the *expected* cash flow that will be produced by the security, when discounted at an interest rate reflecting the risk inherent with holding the security, is significantly different from its market price. The role of the security analyst is to uncover mispriced securities.

In the case of common stock, the value of a share is equal to the present value of the expected dividends.[1] Several stock valuation models have been developed based on different assumptions about the type of dividend stream that is anticipated from the stock being analyzed.

Not all market observers, however, believe that the present value approach is a valid procedure for valuing common stock. Sir John

---

[1] Some market participants believe that earnings rather than dividends should be discounted. However, as explained in most textbooks, Miller and Modigliani have shown that under specified conditions both approaches are equivalent.

Maynard Keynes, for example, viewed this approach as merely a convention. In his book, *The General Theory of Employment, Interest, and Money,* he argued that short-run speculation, not long-run expectations concerning earnings and dividends, is the key determinant of stock prices. Keynes viewed the activity of professional money managers, as follows:

> most of these persons are, in fact, largely concerned, not with making superior long-term forecasts of the probable yield of an investment over its whole life, but with foreseeing changes in the conventional basis of valuation a short time ahead of the general public. They are concerned, not with what an investment is really worth to a man who buys it "for keeps," but with what the market will value it at, under the influence of *mass psychology,* three months or a year hence. ... For it is not sensible to pay 25 for an investment of which you believe the prospective yield to justify a value of 30, if you also believe that the market will value it at 20 three months hence.
>
> Thus the professional investor is forced to concern himself with the anticipation of impending changes, in the news or in the atmosphere, of the kind by which experience shows that the *mass psychology* of the market is most influenced.[2]

The pressure on professional money managers to "perform" in the short-run lends support to Keynes' view that stock prices may be dominated by short-run speculation.

Although textbooks explain the present value approach to stock valuation, little, if any, attention is devoted to the impact of *mass psychology* on stock prices.[3] In Reading 1, David N. Dreman explains the influence of psychology on financial markets and sets forth some general principles that seem to emerge.

---

[2] John Maynard Keynes, *The General Theory of Employment, Interest, and Money* (New York: Harcourt Brace Jovanovich, 1936), pp. 154-55 (emphasis added).

[3] Two recent studies have found fault with the present value approach based on its apparent inability to explain the volatility of stock prices. See Stephen F. LeRoy and Richard D. Porter, "The Present Value Relation: Tests Based on Implied Variance Bounds," *Econometrica,* May 1981, pp. 555-74; and Robert J. Shiller, "Do Stock Prices Move Too Much to be Justified by Subsequent Changes in Dividends?" *American Economic Review,* June 1981, pp. 421-36.

Psychology and Markets*

1   DAVID N. DREMAN
Managing Director
Dreman, Gray & Embry, Inc.
New York, New York

London during the first days of 1524 was a city awaiting its doom. Crowds of anxious people of every social stratum gathered to listen to the numerous astrologers and fortune tellers along bustling thoroughfares. All said the same thing: on February 1 the Thames would suddenly rise from its banks, engulf the entire city, and sweep away 10,000 homes. The vision was described in terrifying detail to increasingly larger throngs.

It had started the preceding June, when a few soothsayers began to bandy about the prophecy, which quickly permeated their ranks. Month after month the warnings were repeated with total assurance, and as time passed, they became accepted by most of the population, even though the Thames had always been the most docile of rivers.

At first, only a handful of families began to leave the city, but as the time grew near, people left in ever-increasing numbers. Long streams of laborers on foot, trailed by their wives and children, tramped the muddy roads to higher ground, 15 to 20 miles away. They were joined by their more prosperous neighbors whose horse-

---

*Adapted from chapter 4, "The Strange World of Reality," from *The New Contrarian Investment Strategy* by David N. Dreman. Copyright © 1982 by David N. Dreman. Reprinted by permission of Random House, Inc.

drawn carts were piled high with possessions. Nobles and clergy followed suit, fleeing to safe country estates. By the middle of January over 20,000 people had departed. London was rapidly becoming a ghost town.

Electing to stay, the prior of Saint Bartholomew's built a towerlike structure on Harrow-on-the-Hill and provisioned it for two months. He also acquired several boats manned by expert rowers—just in case.[1]

When the ill-fated day arrived, some braver souls stayed behind to watch, the soothsayers had predicted that the river would rise slowly, allowing those fleet enough to escape. The hour finally came and, to the consternation of the watchers, nothing happened. The tide quietly ebbed and flowed, and ebbed and flowed as it always had. An awareness slowly spread over the good people that they had been had. Still, to be safe, most stayed up that night and continued their watch.

The next morning, with the Thames continuing to flow peacefully within its banks, the crowd, joined by the returning evacuees, was boiling with fury. Many shouted to throw the pack of soothsayers into the river.

Fortunately, the prophets were prepared. In a clever maneuver—seemingly not lost on present-day chartists—they said they had scrupulously rechecked their calculations the previous night and found a minute error. London was most certainly doomed, the stars were as always undeniably right. But, because of the minor oversight, the great flood would occur in 1624, not 1524. The good townspeople could go home—at least for a while.

This story, whose many variations have been replayed through history, has a great deal more to do with financial markets than you might at first think. Present-day investors employ a variety of tools to formulate investment strategies. Although these tools appear to be practical, they rest on a bed of psychological quicksand. Without understanding how investors form opinions and the psychology that affects their decision making, people's odds are considerably reduced in the marketplace.

A good place to start examining what goes wrong with established investment methods is to observe how groups or crowds affect our ability to exercise independent judgment, even in areas where we think we can be totally objective. In this chapter, we will look at crowd behavior and how it can influence us as investors.

It is important to recognize that people in groups tend to be continually swept by one idea or trend after another. Sometimes, as in the London of 1524, they have no supporting facts and still participate in crowd action that to an impartial observer borders on the

---

[1] Charles Mackay, *Extraordinary Popular Delusions and the Madness of Crowds* (New York: Noonday Press, 1974), p. 421. Originally published in London in 1841 by Richard Bently.

insane. On each occasion most people justify and often enthusiastically back the new thinking. While we can always look back and shake our heads at group folly in the past, it is far harder to remain unaffected by these influences in our own time.

The American Civil Liberties Union (ACLU) considered itself very brave indeed to defend the right to demonstrate of a handful of Nazis in 1978, a group who—though thoroughly repugnant—represented no real threat at the time. But at the height of McCarthyism during the early 1950s, the ACLU was swept along like most people and refused to defend suspected Communists. And while we may laugh at the absurd carryings on of the 17th-century Dutchmen who frantically sold their gold, jewelry, crops, and houses to buy tulip bulbs, investors made remarkably similar decisions in the 1960s and 1970s—only this time in stock rather than tulip markets.[2]

To survive in the marketplace, it is essential to avoid being carried away by the current mood of the crowd. The investor must find some means of being able to withstand the tide—a task anything but simple. It is necessary first to understand exactly how these crowd influences affect investment decisions and why they are so powerful. Armed with this knowledge, you can develop strategies that should not only allow you to resist the pull of current opinion but take advantage of it.

DR. LEBON'S CROWD

The potent force of massed human beings is a phenomenon recognized since antiquity, one often discussed by the philosopher or portrayed by the dramatists. Still, a more scientific analysis of crowd behavior, like many other such philosophical curiosities, was not undertaken until the latter part of the nineteenth century. Only then did rigorous investigation begin.

In 1895 a Frenchman, Gustave LeBon, wrote what continues to rank as one of the most incisive works on mass psychology, *The Crowd*. According to LeBon, "the sentiments and ideas of all persons in a gathering take one and the same direction, and their conscious personality vanishes. A collective mind is formed, doubtless transitory, but presenting very clearly defined characteristics. The gathering has then become . . . a psychological crowd."[3] In such situations, the actions of individuals may be quite different from those the same individuals would consider when alone.

One of the most striking features of the crowd to LeBon was its

---

[2] For a discussion of "tulipmania," see chapters 3 and 4 in David N. Dreman, *Psychology and the Stock Market* (New York: AMACOM, 1977).

[3] Gustave LeBon, *The Crowd* (New York: Viking Press, 1960), pp. 23-24.

great difficulty in separating the imagined from the real. "A crowd thinks in images, and the image itself calls up a series of other images, having no logical connection with the first ... a crowd scarcely distinguishes between the subjective and the objective. It accepts as real the images invoked in its mind, though they most often have only a very distant relation with the observed facts.... Crowds being only capable of thinking in images are only to be impressed by images."[4]

At times, as LeBon saw, the image evokes cruel behavior; the belief in witches and sorcerers sent tens of thousands to the stake in the 16th and 17th centuries, and the "isms" of this century have taken tens of millions of lives. At other times, the image can inspire heroism: the crowd that swept the Bastille; or the Republican crowd that with bare hands stormed the fascist Montana Barracks in Madrid in 1936. With the benefit of hindsight, the image may become droll, as when London was abandoned to the Thames. But, to capture the crowd, the image must always be extremely simple. LeBon believed the individual regresses in a crowd and "descends several rungs in the ladder of civilization. Isolated, he may be a cultivated individual; in a crowd he is a barbarian. He possesses the spontaneity, the violence, the ferocity, and also the enthusiasm and heroism of primitive beings."[5]

LeBon was an astute, if not particularly sympathetic, observer of crowds, and his description of crowd behavior is strikingly applicable to what we can readily discover taking place in financial markets. Certainly all the elements are present: numbers of people, intense excitement, and that essential simple image. Indeed few images are more simple and yet as beguiling as *instant wealth.* Each such image carried the crowd far into the realm of fantasy, and sometimes beyond the boundaries of sanity. Despite the assumption of the rationality and omniscience of investors claimed by our academic friends, the last word on the subject often seems to be the roar of the crowd.

Each time, as LeBon foresaw, the image was not only simple and enticing, but seemingly infallible. And, as he predicted, people lost their individuality. Crowd contagion swept intellectuals, artists, nobles, and businessmen in every period as easily as it did the common people. Actually, those who should have known best often led the way. And so, to see just how strong its pull can be, we might look a little more closely at the behavior of crowds in the marketplace.

THE MISSISSIPPI SCHEME

The French, usually pacesetters in fashion, launched one of the first of the gigantic speculative manias, beginning in 1716. The Mis-

---
[4] Ibid., pp. 41-61.
[5] Ibid., p. 70.

sissippi Company, as the venture was dubbed, resembled in many ways the classic *South Sea bubble,* which was soon to develop on the other side of the Channel.[6]

The central character in the Mississippi Company was John Law, the son of a Scottish banker. A tall, dashing figure, Law had fled to the Continent with a death sentence on his head, the result of his having killed a rival in a duel over a love affair. Having studied banking in Amsterdam, Hamburg, Vienna, and Genoa, Law had a fairly sophisticated understanding of the use of credit. He was able to convince the French regent of the merits of using paper money to lower interest rates, increase employment, and expand business. A national bank was established, which issued paper money up to twice the value of the country's gold and silver. The beginnings proved sound enough, and the bank prospered.

Law's vision, however, was much grander. Two years later, in 1718, he secured the right to the development of the vast Mississippi basin, then a territory of France.

Under Law's orchestration, a gigantic speculative bubble began to take shape. The stock in the new venture was first sold to the public on very attractive terms. Three quarters of the payment could be made in Louis XIV *billets des états* at face value, although this particular currency then traded at an almost 80 percent discount.

To eliminate any doubt as to the prosperity of the scheme, Law promised a dividend of 40 percent of the face value of the stock in the initial year. Using the discounted Louis XIV notes to subscribe, a shareholder would receive 120 percent of his investment in dividends alone in the first 12 months! This, and the lure of the Indies, proved too much. Few were bothered by the fact that the company was just starting and had no assets. Enthusiasm easily checkmated logic; 300,000 applications were made for the first 50,000 shares. Dukes, marquises and comtes, with their duchesses, marchionesses, and comtesses, jostled in the streets with prostitutes and peddlars seeking to subscribe. Some of the nobility took apartments while waiting their turn in order to avoid rubbing shoulders with the "great unwashed" around them.

The demand for the stock seemed inexhaustible. Law issued a steady stream of new shares at progressively higher prices. Only months after the original stock sale, a new issue was offered and was oversubscribed at 5,000 livres—10 times the initial price.

Law was an expert painting the canvas of concept. To make the potential even more dazzling, he acquired the tobacco monopolies, as well as the East China, India, and Africa Companies, and merged them all into the Mississippi Company. Indians were paraded through

---

[6] For a discussion of the classic South Sea bubble, see chapter 3 of Dreman, *Psychology and the Stock Market.*

the streets of Paris, bedecked with gold and silver, to demonstrate the wealth of the territories. Engravings showing Louisianan mountains bursting with gold, silver, and precious stones were widely distributed.

The price rise of the Mississippi Company was breathtaking and in itself became almost hypnotic. "The tendency to look beyond the simple fact of increasing value to the reasons on which it depends greatly diminishes," wrote John Kenneth Galbraith of investor behavior in 1929.[7]

Professor Galbraith's wry observation is as apt for the rue de Quincampoix, where the stock was traded. Large crowds became acclimated to prices working constantly higher—day after day, week after week, and month after month. Previous and now "old-fashioned" standards of value were left far behind.

It was difficult for anyone to escape the scheme's almost irresistible appeal, and few did. At the height of the frenzy in 1720, the Mississippi Company had appreciated 40 times from the initial offering price of 500 livres in 1716. The market price of the shares was now worth 80 times all the gold and silver in France.[8]

The rue de Quincampoix was packed with speculators of all classes. Every available space was used for trading. A cobbler rented his stall to traders for 10 times his normal wages. The rents for houses on the street rose twelve- to sixteenfold from previous levels. Fortunes, naturally, were made—a banker was said to have made 100 million livres, a waiter 30 million. The word *millionaire* came into use for the first time.

The wild speculation took on many of the aspects of a carnival. Tents were erected to trade stock, sell refreshments, and even to gamble. One man set up a roulette wheel in the midst of the packed throng and did a thriving business. The major roads leading to Paris were made almost impassable because of the masses trying to reach the city. Over 300,000 people came from the provinces to participate in the trading!

Law was idolized by the crowd. So great were the surrounding throngs anywhere he went that the prince regent provided him with a

---

[7] John Kenneth Galbraith, *The Great Crash* (Boston: Houghton Mifflin, 1961), p. 9.

[8] Madness perhaps in retrospect, but only a few years ago the experienced senior investment officers of America's largest and most powerful financial institutions did almost exactly the same thing. They decided that there were only 50 or so stocks to buy out of a total of 12,000 public companies, and they bid them up to astronomical prices. Avon Products, for example, was valued for more than the entire U.S. steel industry, although it was dwarfed in size and profitability. At the time, the heads of these institutions, including Morgan Guaranty, Banker's Trust, and Citibank, vigorously defended the course they were following before Congress as "most prudent." As in the case of the Mississippi Company, both expert and average opinion was convinced that they had found the new Golconda. The subsequent performance of some of the more popular stocks is found in Table 1, page 23.

troop of lancers to clear the way. Enormous bribes were paid to his servants to get an interview with him, and even members of the aristocracy had to wait for weeks for an appointment. One lady drove around Paris for three days looking for Law, instructing her coachman to upset the carriage when he was sighted. When at last they tracked him down, the coach was driven into a post. It turned over, and the lady screamed shrilly to attract Law's attention. As Law came to her aid, she confessed the ruse and asked to subscribe to the next stock issue, to which he smilingly obliged.

Although Law exaggerated the opportunities, he did make a genuine effort to develop Louisiana and was successful in increasing French shipping, establishing new industries, and sharply raising French commercial activity. Nevertheless, the soaring prices of the Mississippi Company stock had little to do with the situation. When this awareness began to spread, a panic followed, both in the paper currency and the Mississippi shares.

LeBon was well aware of how swiftly the image guiding the crowd could change. "These image-like ideas," he wrote, "are not connected by any logical bond or analogy or successor, and may take each other's place like the slides of a Magic Lantern."[9] And so they did. The Mississippi shares, which previously represented spectacular riches, now meant doom.

Law attempted to stem the tide. Anticipating Cecil B. DeMille by several centuries, he staged a spectacular in the streets of Paris. Six thousand of the city's poorest inhabitants were pressed into service, given new clothes, picks, and shovels, and marched through the streets, presumably on the way to mine Louisiana gold. However, even this major production stopped the panic for only a few days.

When the Mississippi bubble burst, the aftermath was devastating. First a few investors, then gradually more, and within weeks almost all realized that the speculative frenzy was insane. A desperate rush to sell began, but few buyers could be found. People now focused on the emptiness of the scheme. Rumor again spread through the rue de Quincampoix, this time that the company had few assets and would be forced to omit its dividend entirely.

The image had changed for good. By late 1720 the stock had fallen to 200 livres, some 99 percent below its peak only months before. Law left the country in disgrace and died in obscurity nine years later in Venice. To the end, he loved risk. No longer gambling the economic stakes of one of the two most powerful nations on earth, he was content to wager his few available shillings with passersby on whatever local action moved him.

---

[9] LeBon, *The Crowd,* p. 62.

WHAT IS SOCIAL REALITY?

The vision of the jeweled and powdered French dukes, comtes, and marquises frantically scurrying about the rue de Quincampoix, breathlessly followed by their duchesses, comptesses, and marchionesses, décolletage aheaving, may be amusing, but are there lessons to be learned that also apply to modern markets?

History has shown that group madness need not last for only brief periods. The fear of the flooding of the Thames occurred over many months, the Mississippi bubble was in full bloom for four or five years, and the persecution of witches and sorcerers went on for centuries. In each of these cases, the image created its own reality, reshaping the perceptions, actions, and attitudes of the crowd. How were such strange realities brought into being and nurtured, and why should supposedly rational people succumb so easily to them?

By and large, historians and psychologists are the only people who have pursued the matter. Historians have helped to preserve the important record of these events, and modern psychologists have moved far beyond LeBon in their investigation of what motivates groups. Meanwhile, for most of us as investors, it has been business as usual. Despite all our "progress," the lack of results remains conspicuous. Yet it seems pretty obvious that LeBon's rampaging crowd has not ignored the marketplace either.

If we are to avoid being victimized by crowds, it is important to possess a clear understanding of the forces that drive them. Social psychologists tell us that our beliefs, values, and attitudes can be thought to lie along a continuum. At one extreme are those based on indisputable physical evidence—if I throw a crystal goblet against a wall, it will shatter; or if I point my skis straight down a long, steep slope, it's pretty unlikely I'll reach the bottom intact. Such outcomes, termed physical reality, are abundantly clear and don't require other people's confirmation.

At the other end of the continuum are beliefs and attitudes that, although important to us, lack firm support. What facts are available are sparse and difficult to evaluate. In this category are such questions as the existence of God, whether there is a "best" political system, or, of primary interest here, what a stock or the market is really worth at a point in time.

Psychologists have demonstrated that the vaguer and more complex a situation, the more we rely on other people whose intelligence we respect, both for clarification and as standards against which to judge the correctness of our own views. This helps us reduce the uncertainty we have toward our own beliefs. Most investors, for example, attempting to assimilate many contradictory facts in order to put a value on the Mississippi Company shares, undoubtedly sought the opinions of other intelligent investors to form their own assessments. When people use others as yardsticks against which to determine the correctness of their own views, they are utilizing what psychologists call *social comparison processes*.

We can do this in very commonplace ways, rarely giving it a second thought. I was once in a Middle Eastern restaurant in New York where the men's and ladies' rooms were marked with what to me were unintelligible symbols. I was momentarily puzzled, until a man who obviously knew where he was going strolled confidently through one of the doors, solving my problem. Or consider the case of *The Wall Street Journal* reporter who wrote of a recent dinner he and his wife had with a desert sheik. After the meal, two other distinguished Western guests sat back and belched heartily. The reporter and his wife, guessing that this was the proper sign of approval for the hearty fare, follwed suit with gusto.

Similarly, a speaker may gauge the worth of his talk from the audience's reaction. After one of his speeches, Lincoln, judging from what he thought was the indifferent response of the crowd, turned to a friend and said: "It's a flat failure and the people are disappointed." The speech was the Gettysburg Address.[10]

The greater the anxiety and the more indeterminate the situation appears to be, the more readily we rely on the behavior of others to gauge the proper course, treating much of the information we receive from them as being no less real than if we had directly observed it from physical reality. We thus forget its personal and tentative nature.

The term *social reality* refers to how a group of people perceive reality. As Leon Festinger, who first proposed the theory, described it: "When the dependence upon physical reality is low, the dependence on social reality is correspondingly high. An opinion, attitude, or belief is 'correct, valid, and proper' to the extent that it is anchored in the group of people with similar beliefs, opinions, and attitudes."[11] The ensuing social reality can then be a strange amalgam of objective criteria and crowd fancy. Facts, such as are available, can be twisted or distorted entirely to conform with prevailing opinions.

And this brings us back to the strange aberrations of people in crowds that we have seen in this chapter. In each instance, the information was vague, sometimes complex, and anxiety producing to the people of the time. Few standards existed to help them. Fortune-

---
[10] Carl Sandburg, *Abraham Lincoln: Volume 2, 1861-1864* (New York: Dell Publishing, 1970), p. 410.

[11] Leon Festinger, "A Theory of Social Comparison Processes," *Human Relations* 7 (1954), pp. 117-40.

tellers may have been right in some of their earlier prophecies, establishing their credibility for the new auguries. During the Mississippi scheme one could see the substantial gains made by those who bought early, and that noblemen, confidants of the regent, and shrewd businessmen were buying the stock—most said the price rise was only beginning.

People then as now were uncertain, sometimes anxious, and as a result wanted to compare their opinions with those of other individuals whom they respected. Great numbers were drawn by the need to verify their individual views into conformity with the group's beliefs; the larger the nucleus of the group, the greater the attraction of its beliefs to those who had initially resisted them.

Just how easily people's behavior can be influenced by others in uncertain and even mildly anxiety-producing circumstances can be seen from the following laboratory experiment of S. Schacter's.[12] Subjects were injected with a drug called epinephrine, which temporarily causes heart palpitations and hand shaking. The subjects were told that the drug was a vitamin supplement called "Suproxin." In each case, the subject was placed in a room with a stooge, planted there by the experimenters, who allegedly had also been injected with "Suproxin." With no forewarning, the subject searched for an explanation as his heart beat faster and his hands began to tremble. He started to watch the stooge who, as you can guess, was not inactive. In one case, he behaved lightheartedly, singing, dancing, constructing and flying paper planes, in general acting in a high-spirited, zany way. Other subjects were put in a room with a stooge who was gloomy and morose, made angry remarks, complained about a questionnaire both were filling out, and in a sudden fit of pique, ripped his up.

How did the subjects react? Feeling the effects of the drug, and watching the behavior of the stooges, the great majority adapted behavior patterns to match.

The record outside of the laboratory is not much different. Because there are so few objective guidelines, social reality has always had a merry time in the fashion world, for males and females alike. At the turn of the century, the dictate was for women's hemlines to drag along the ground; in other periods, they were well above the knee. In the late 19th century, to be *au courant* demanded an exceptionally narrow waist (17 or 18 inches), and many a poor woman had her floating rib removed to conform to the dictate. In 1943, so many women tried to imitate the hairdo covering one eye of then-reigning film queen Veronica Lake that, according to United Press International, "the Federal Government branded her a menace to the war

---

[12] S. Schacter and J. E. Singer, "Cognitive, Social, and Psychological Determinants of Emotional States," *Psychological Review* 69 (1962), pp. 379-99.

effort; it claimed too many lady airplane workers imitating her peek-a-boo bob had scalped themselves in the machinery."[13]

Crowd fashions and fads are no different today. Take jogging, for example. It may be healthy—the jury still seems out there—but it has certainly become contagious. It has mainly taken over from the previous physical fitness exercises such as jumping rope (very "in" several years ago, but now advised against by some doctors because it may cause shin splints), yoga, and the RCAF-X4 plan.

Whether it's on a quiet Vermont byway or early morning in Riverside Park, there is a strong likelihood of meeting someone jogging these days. Many a poor middle-aged businessman or matron goes through the motions, panting heavily, tongue hanging out and eyes bulging, all supposedly in the name of physical fitness. Fashionable jogging outfits costing $175 or more are sold at Bergdorf Goodman and Saks Fifth Avenue. And the elegant ladies of the East Side now lunch at expensive restaurants sporting their faultlessly tailored jogging wear never for a moment meant to be sweated in. Perhaps this isn't a fad—but already numbers of books on walking are being readied for release.

Does the same hold true of fashions in the marketplace? Uncertainty, anxiety, lack of objective reality, and sudden and violent shifts in the image of the group are certainly integral to crowd behavior here too. Each interpretation of what was realistic was established and maintained by the consensus of the group. In every mania the group was injected (in a manner not unlike the epinephrine experiment) with an image of spectacular wealth, which changed its behavior. This new social reality was fabricated of the dreams, hopes, and greed of many thousands of investors. Many watching a particular bubble saw as much clearly. Yet most could still believe that things really would be different this time . . .

THE REALITY OF 1962

Let's next stop briefly at the Wall Street of 1962 to examine the workings of social reality on modern investment crowds. Are they any different from those of years past?

After the 1929 crash speculative fervor burned out for a generation. In fact, the Dow didn't break its 1929 high of 381 until November of 1954, at which time the nation was prosperous, industrial activity was increasing, consumer income was rising, as were corporate earnings and dividends. The market, with only a few minor setbacks, continued to work solidly higher through the balance of the decade. "Time," Disraeli wrote, "is the Great Physician." And so it was. A new generation of investors, untutored in the lessons of disas-

---

[13] J. C. Flugel, *The Psychology of Clothes* (New York: Universities Press, 1969).

ter that their parents had learned, was now firmly at the helm. Confident of the future, they were intrigued with the tremendous investment opportunities that were present in this new dynamic economy.

Just as the 18th-century investors were propelled by the unlimited wealth of the New World, so modern investors now saw the possibility of unlimited profits through modern science. Because of these expectations, the major technology companies of the time—IBM, Xerox, Polaroid, and Texas Instruments—commanded towering prices.

Even more striking, when viewed with the hindsight of seventeen years, was the 1961-62 period's enormous similarity to the English South Sea bubble of the early 18th century—in the willingness of people to buy almost any new venture. In 1720, companies that made wheels of perpetual motion or converted gold from lead were in demand. In 1961-62, esoteric technological companies exerted enormous appeal. Whether it was alchemy in the first place or science in the second didn't matter much, as investors understood the prospects of each equally well. The crowd on the cobblestones in Exchange Alley, where the bubble companies traded, or watching the action on luminous electronic tapes in the boardrooms of space-age America behaved the same.

The beginnings, as usual, were sound enough. Many small technological companies sold to the public in the 1950s showed spectacular appreciation. An investment of $1,000 in Control Data when it was first offered in 1958 was worth $121,000 by 1961. The same $1,000 put into Litton Industries in the mid-1950s moved up fiftyfold during that period. Seeing these profits and believing in the unlimited wealth to be gained in anything scientific, investors scrambled to buy the shares of any small company that was being offered to the public for the first time. A frenzied new issues boom took place in 1960 and 1961. All that was required was that the company be in electronics, computers, medical technology, or pharmaceuticals. Any company ending in "ics" or "tron" was enthusiastically bid up. Nytronics, Bristol Dynamics, and Supronics shot to immediate premiums. Some of the gains were spectacular. Dynatronics was issued at 7 and rose to 25 instantly; Risitron Laboratories went from 1 to $3\frac{7}{8}$. Simulmatics, a company incorporated only two years earlier and with a negative net worth of $21,000, was offered at 2 and immediately quoted at 9.

The public appetite for such stocks was almost insatiable. One elderly woman called her broker to buy shares in "Hebrew National Electronics." The broker explained that the company was not in electronics at all, but was a kosher meat packer and processor. She accepted the news with disappointment and a tinge of anger. Several months later, when the stock had also moved up, she again phoned the broker. "They are too in the electronics business!" she said indignantly. "They sell electronic salami slicers."[14]

As the fever spread, new issues were underwritten in many industries outside technology. The boardrooms were filled to overflowing and the talk on commuter trains and in theater lobbies was of hot new issues and the best little underwriting houses.

Promoters, not really very different animals in 1962 from what they had been in 1718, understood the appetites of the crowd and scoured the countryside for acceptable merchandise. "Why go broke, go public," the prospective underwriting client was told. Shopworn goods were rechristened with sparkling new space-age names. Many of the hottest underwriting firms were one- or two-man companies.

The mania was intensified by the underwriter's advertising of the success of their merchandise. One firm, Michael Lomasney and Company, ran an ad that stated that had an investor purchased $1,000 of each of the 16 issues it had underwritten in the past 18 months, he or she would have had $36,800 by September 1961. This was topped by another small underwriting firm, Globus, Inc., with offices, appropriately enough, on Madison Avenue. "If you bought each of Globus' issues," their ad rang, "you would have tripled your money by late 1961." The froth danced higher and higher.

This was, of course, a house of cards, but nobody seemed to notice . . . or care. With money being made at every turn, a stream of how-to literature came off the printing presses. Nicholas Darvas, a gypsy dancer, wrote a book entitled *How I Made Two Million Dollars in the Stock Market.* Another writer published a book modestly promising *How to Make a Killing on Wall Street.*[15]

The realization came, as always, that this was a fool's paradise. By the latter part of 1961, speculative ardor had cooled noticeably. In the sharp break of April-May 1962, a panic enveloped the new bubble companies. While the market recovered in short order and went on to new highs, most of the underwritings traded at pittances of the former values. An SEC study of 500 randomly selected issues offered in the 1950s and early 1960s showed that 12 percent had simply vanished, 43 percent had gone bankrupt, 25 percent were operating at a loss, while only 20 percent displayed any earnings whatever. Of the

---

[14] "Over the Counter: Frantic, Frenetic, Frazzled," *Dun's Review* 92 (August 1968), pp. 32-37.

[15] Even the art world was unable to avoid the get-rich-quick craze. One service—the Art Market Guide and Forecaster—put together an average of 500 artists and called it the AMG index after its own initials. One ad read: "With the art market for paintings up 97 percent since the war—and 65 percent in the last year alone—you can lose immense profits by failing to keep informed of the monetary value of art, present and future." See Robert Sobel, *The Big Board* (New York: Free Press, 1965).

latter, there were only 12 which had any real promise. Social reality had led the crowd down the same strange path in 1962 as it had in 1720.

THE COMPELLINGNESS OF CROWD OPINION

Why do social comparison processes produce an investor consensus that is often so far off the mark? Part of the answer seems to lie in how easily people's opinions are drawn together under conditions of uncertainty.

An excellent experiment to show this was devised by psychologist Muzafer Sherif.[16] Sherif took advantage of the little-known autokinetic light phenomenon. A tiny pinpoint of light beamed for a few seconds in a darkened room appears to move, although in fact it is stationary. Sherif asked his subjects to calculate the extent of the movement as carefully as possible. (Since the light appeared to be moving, the subjects believed it actually did.) With no reference points upon which to anchor judgment in the blackened room, the answers in individual trials ranged from a few inches to 80 feet—the latter subject believed he was in a gymnasium rather than a small room.

After 100 trial sets, the median guess of each subject was recorded. Figure 1 shows that it ranged from approximately one to over eight inches (as the line on the extreme left of both charts indicates). However, when subjects were brought together, the judgments converged. Figure 1(A) indicates the amount of convergence there was in each succeeding 100-test figure with two people present; Figure 1(B) with three. In the latter case, from individual medians varying from under an inch to almost eight inches, the group's convergence by the third 100-set test moved to slightly over two inches.

Sherif added another variable by including a confederate. If the subject has estimated the light moved 20 inches, the confederate might estimate 2. His influence was enormous. By the end of the trials, most subject's estimates came very close to those of the confederate, which remained stable throughout.

Writing of these experiments, psychologist William Samuels noted: "The majority of subjects in such studies indicate little awareness that their perceptions have been manipulated by the estimates of others, for they maintain that they had previously made their own estimates *before the others spoke*. The influence process then may be a rather subtle phenomenon. Partners who are well liked, who have high status, who are reputed to be competent on the judgmental task, or who merely exude self-confidence when announcing their

---

[16] M. Sherif and C. W. Sherif, *Social Psychology* (New York: Harper & Row, 1969), pp. 208-9.

Figure 1
Convergence of Opinion in Light Movement Experiment

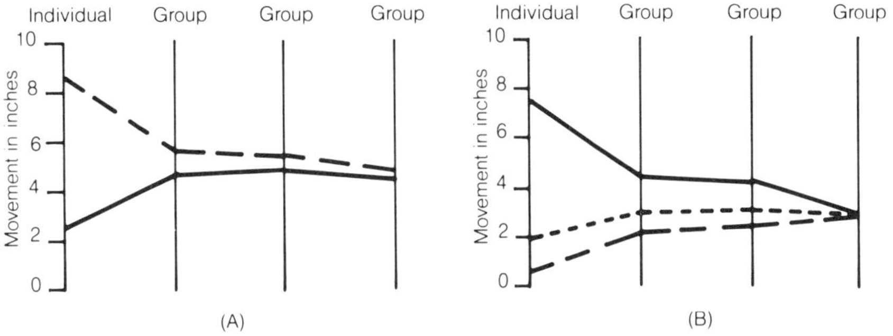

[Two graphs labeled (A) and (B), each with x-axis labels: Individual, Group, Group, Group; y-axis: Movement in inches, 0 to 10]

Source: Muzafer Sherif and Carolyn Sherif, *Social Psychology* (New York: Harper & Row, 1969), pp. 208-209. Copyright © 1969 by Muzafer Sherif and Carolyn W. Sherif.

estimates are all especially effective in influencing a subject's personal norm of movements."[17]

It is also interesting to see how far a naive subject's judgment could be shifted under subtle manipulation—as much as 80 percent or more without pressure of any sort. Because one of the prime features of the stock market is uncertainty, opinions frequently move toward a consensus and, not unlike the autokinetic light experiment, move toward the most authoritative-sounding or most outspoken points of view available at the time—usually those of the experts whose record we already know. Then throw in anxiety, another very powerful force leading toward consensus. During the best of times the stock market is uncertain and difficult, and in its worst moments can induce first-rate terror. People find it natural under such circumstances to take comfort and security in the opinions of savvy, smart money. Small wonder that the consensus of the many appears to be a refuge, not a trap.

Earlier, we saw just how elusive the anchor of objective reality and the concept of value on which it is based actually are. It is not surprising, then, given the nature of the psychological forces at work, that we too can often find ourselves dashing frantically down a rue de Quincampoix, an Exchange Alley, or a Wall Street ... which brings me to the next wild adventure: the "go-go" market of 1967-68.

GOD HAS BEEN GOOD TO SOLITRON DEVICES

The fascinating yet disturbing aspect of financial manias, knowing what we know about social comparison processes, is that few lessons

---
[17] William Samuels, *Contemporary Social Psychology* (Englewood Cliffs, N.J.: Prentice-Hall, 1973), p. 10.

can be learned from the past. The same mistakes made in almost the same fashion inevitably crop up again and again.

Looking back at the bizarre speculative period of a decade ago, one might feel almost as though the clock had stopped at the height of the 1961 enthusiasm and only started ticking again in 1967. Investors resumed the previous speculation at an increasingly intensified pitch, with all memory of the previous crash seemingly erased. Remarkably an even larger new-issues boom commenced, and interest again focused on many of the now familiar technology stocks of 1962—Xerox, Polaroid, Texas Instruments, and IBM.

This was the time when youth took over Wall Street. With youth came changes in the investment game: value was no longer to be found in the stodgy blue chips favored by their elders. The action now was with new issues, growth stocks, and concept stocks. A group of sideburned, flamboyantly dressed young men in their 20s and 30s came to the helm. They were the freewheeling, high-spirited embodiment of the times, who were determined to clear out the dogma, error, and cobwebs of the past. Called "gunslingers," the new breed were out to change the world with the sureness of their instincts and the quickness of their reactions. They believed that rapid moves in and out of stocks led to exceptional results. Often entire portfolios would be turned over two or three times a year. This new style of buying or selling was called "go-go" investing. The sole objective was "performance," which meant achieving higher returns than the market averages and competing gunslingers.

In the deadly competition that soon developed, all benchmarks of fiduciary responsibility were forgotten. Criticism that the new methods were highly speculative was tossed aside, in the words of one gunslinger, "as coming from the cultural alienation of an outdated generation."

On Wall Street a new tide of folk heroes moved in—Gerald Tsai, Fred Carr, Fred Mates, Fred Alger, and John Hartwell, to name a few. They were often treated with awe by the financial press and the public—at the time it seemed with good reason. Gerald Tsai, the initial go-go star, used rapid-fire trading to increase the Fidelity Growth Fund, which he managed, by 65 percent in 1965. Starting his own Manhattan Fund in 1967, he doubled the 20 percent rise in the averages. But Tsai's performance was dull when compared with many of the others. Fred Carr's Enterprise Fund rose 118 percent in that same year as he moved stocks in and out of his portfolio at a breathtaking rate. In one quarter, Enterprise traded 200 companies, more than some staid mutual funds turned over in a decade. In late 1968 the Mates Fund of Fred Mates was up a stunning 158 percent for the year.

Many of the new breed assiduously avoided the major industrial giants, "buggywhip companies," as they were sometimes contemptuously called. At the height of the go-go market in 1968, when numbers of concept companies had gone up twenty five- or even fiftyfold, giant AT&T made an eight-year low. One money manager summed it up in *Forbes:* "Excitement, not solidity, is what makes stocks move now." Again social reality took hold and investors frolicked away, unfettered by the time-tested standards of the past.

The gunslingers bristled with confidence. John Hartwell, who, in 1968, managed $425 million, ignored the prudent policy of wide diversification, stating: "If you have more than half a dozen positions in an account of, say, $500,000, it only means you are not sharp enough to pick winners."[18]

All eyes were focused on relative performance. The winners of the go-go derby would receive large flows of funds from the enthusiastic public, while the losers would have the money quickly taken away. In spite of its excellent record, Gerald Tsai's Manhattan Fund had net redemptions in 1968 as the public moved into better-performing vehicles, such as those of Fred Carr and Fred Mates. As one manager phrased it: "In this market, the crowd is betting on the jockeys, not the horses."

Outstanding fund managers could make a million dollars or more a year, and they lived high—gold faucets in bathrooms, 15-room penthouses on Park Avenue or in the Dakota, and summer homes on the Adriatic. Because of the public's obsession with them, performance rankings became the go-go manager's lifeblood. Fred Alger once flew to Europe to protest to Bernie Cornfeld, then running the vast International Overseas Fund network, that one month he was ranked number two rather than number one because of a typographical error. The mistake was immediately corrected.

Performance was achieved mainly by financial sleight of hand. Substantial gains were made by buying large blocks of thinly traded companies, pushing them higher. Legions of admirers usually followed in the wake of the go-go stars, making the price rise: a self-fulfilling prophecy for a while. Because of their tremendous ability to generate commissions, the major go-go managers would get large blocks of hot new stocks at the issue price, which immediately went to substantial premiums, generating instant profits on their books. The gunslingers would also buy letter stock—stock not authorized to be traded in public markets—at a substantial discount. The discount would often be two thirds or more of the going market price. The fund immediately revalued the stock at a one-third discount from the market, and—voilà—a 100 percent profit.

---

[18] Gilbert Kaplan and Chris Welles, *The Money Managers* (New York: Random House, 1969).

It is a tribute to the power of a speculative frenzy that though these and many other practices were widely known and sometimes criticized at the time, very few people seemed to care how questionable the gains really were. Only the "bottom line" mattered—that the funds were performing well.

The rapid trading of huge blocks of stock made this the golden age of the brokerage firm. Many an institutional salesman who could scarcely distinguish an asset from a liability made six figures a year from his gunslinger clients, and most fully believed they deserved it. One fellow became a brief legend by leaving a $100 tip after a single round of drinks.

The gunslinger's mode of operation was simplicity itself. One merely had to have an exciting story and a record of rapid sales and earnings growth to substantiate it. Almost no attention was paid to how real the earnings actually were. And it was again the day of the black-box operation. Companies in technology were bid up to astronomical prices as investors envisioned futures of limitless growth. The chairman of one small technology company that had multiplied tenfold in price told his annual meeting in 1968: "God has been good to Solitron Devices."

Money managers and clients alike became intoxicated by the gains. One investor, dazzled by the sensational promises of the go-go managers, went to his investment advisor, David Babson, a crusty old New Englander, and told him his objective was no less than 40 to 60 percent a year. For the previous 10 years, Babson had increased his client's money at a not unimpressive 10 percent rate, to $126,000. To illustrate the absurdity of his client's request, Babson showed him that a 40 percent rate of growth would have resulted in this sum becoming $100 million in 20 years, while a 60 percent rate of growth would have made it $1.5 billion!

For those of us playing at the time, and I had come to Wall Street a year or so earlier, it was indeed the golden age. Everywhere the atmosphere was giddy with success. Almost any investment we tried, be it computer service, uranium exploration, or flight safety instruments, worked out and many did spectacularly. With our stocks quadrupling, several going up tenfold, and one over fiftyfold, it was hard not to attribute the gains to our intelligence and surefootedness.

The longer the odds, the more sensational the payout. The favorites went up even more than the Mississippi Company over a similar period of time. With so much money being made so quickly, it was almost impossible not to be sucked into the speculative whirlpool, and not many resisted.

All around us, thousands of professionals wrote research reports condoning the current price movements and recommending a plethora of exciting new opportunities. As experiments have shown, the expert's support of a concept more firmly locks it into place. Very often people are persuaded by a message, not because of its compelling logic but because they consider the communicator an expert.[19] (Thus the old adage of the singer, not the song.) Not only were the experts bullish, but their record of success in the immediate past was good, further enhancing their credibility. Once again, as in the 1920s, everybody talked stocks.

Some authorities became alarmed at the level of speculation. The American Stock Exchange, on which many of the smaller and more speculative companies traded, published a list in February 1969 of 109 speculative companies in which it forbade members to trade for their own accounts.[20] Former SEC chairman Manuel Cohen said at the time: "Frankly, I would have liked the AMEX to have applied the ban to all of its securities." However, most defended the reality of the moment. As one market expert wrote in a major financial magazine:

NEW ENVIRONMENT

I would therefore like to propose the thesis that as the result of all that has been happening in the economy, the world, and the market during the last decade, we are at least in a different—if not a new—era and traditional thinking, the standard approach to the market, is no longer in synchronization with the real world.

Possibly the market ought to be considered as having gone into a sort of orbit in outer space, in the sense that while we can see how we got where we are, we really have never been here before, and therefore cannot be certain of what happens next.[21]

This seems to most clearly summarize the thinking of all investors in all manias. When the 1968 bubble finally burst, it was the most severe crash since 1929. Forty-seven billion dollars, or three times the amount lost on Black Tuesday, 1929, vanished in 30 high fliers alone. Most of the speculative favorites fared even more poorly. National Student Marketing dropped from 140 to 3½, Solitron Devices (whom the Lord apparently no longer favored) from 286 to 10¼, Parvan Dohrman from 142 to 14, and Four Seasons Nursing Homes from 110 to zero! Gone were the performance stocks, along with most of the high-living performance managers.

---

[19] Those interested might see, for example, S. E. Asch, "The Doctrines of Suggestion, Prestige, and Social Psychology," *Psychological Review* 55 (1948), pp. 150-77; and C. I. Hovland, I. I. Janis, and H. H. Kelley, *Communication and Persuasion* (New Haven, Conn.: Yale University Press, 1953).

[20] "Performance in Reverse?" *Forbes,* March 15, 1969.

[21] *Forbes,* October 15, 1968.

NOT VERY DIFFERENT

All manias, though separated by centuries, have had surprisingly similar characteristics. They started in prosperous economies, where people were looking for new investment opportunities and wanted to believe they existed. Each mania had sound beginnings and was based on a simple but intriguing concept. The rise in prices, in every case, became a self-fulfilling prophecy, attracting more and more people into the speculative vortex. Rumor always played a major role, at first of fortunes made and of good things to come, and later in prophecies of doom. In almost every case, the experts were caught up in the speculation, condoning the price rises and predicting much higher levels in the future. At the height of both the 1961 and 1967-68 markets, money managers stated that the valuation standards of the past no longer applied—things really were different this time. And on both occasions, the statements were uttered shortly before the end.

Another point common to all speculative manias is the "greater fool" theory. Some of the more independent or cynical thinkers were not in fact overwhelmed by the consensus thinking of the time. They believed stocks should never have reached the preposterous levels that they had, the crowd really was mad. But they thought it would get madder still. (If a portfolio had gone up sixfold, why not eightfold, or even tenfold?) There would thus be a chance to profit from the folly, which would only become more outrageous. Thus wrote British Member of Parliament James Milner in 1720 after being bankrupted by the South Sea bubble: "I said indeed that ruin must soon come upon us but I owe it came two months earlier than I expected."[22] Not very different was the *Dun's Review* article at the height of the 1968 market, 248 years later: "The overriding question at the moment is: how long can a speculative boom go on? How many months, investors and dealers ask, before we see a repeat of 1962?"[23] Even knowing this, most found it impossible to stop.

As speculation grew more widespread, it became the major topic of the day. In almost every period, credit was abundant and cheap. Near the end, prices rose sharply and turnover increased markedly. Finally, there was a sudden shift in the social reality, resulting in a panic that carried prices far below those initially prevailing. It's also interesting to see the similarity in the declines in each of the speculative manias. As Table 1 shows, all are on the order of 90 percent.

Four general principles seem to emerge from a study of financial speculations. First, an irresistible image of instant wealth is always presented that draws a financial crowd into existence. Second, a

---

[22] Virginia Cowles, *South Sea: The Great Swindle* (London: Crowley Feature, 1960).
[23] *Dun's Review*, August 1968, p. 36.

Table 1
Market Favorites from Different Eras

	High Price	Low Price	Price Decline from High (percent)
Holland, 1637			
Semper Augustis (tulip bulb)	5,500*	50*	99%
England, 1720			
South Sea Company	1,050†	129†	88
France, 1720			
Mississippi Company	18,000‡	200‡	99
1929-32			
Air Reduction	233	31	86
Burroughs	97	6¼	94
Case	467	17	96
General Electric	201	8½	96
General Motors	115	7⅝	94
Montgomery Ward	158	3½	98
1961-62			
AMF	66⅜	10	84
Automatic Canteen	45⅝	9¾	79
Brunswick	74⅞	13⅛	82
Lionel	37⅞	4½	88
Texas Instruments	207	49	76
Transition	42⅜	6¼	85
1967-70			
ITEK	172	17	90
Leasco Data Processing	57	7	88
Ling-Temco-Vought	135	7	95
Litton Industries	104	15	86
National Student Marketing	143	3½	98
University Computing	186	13	93
1971-72			
Avon	140	18⅝	87
Clorox	53	5½	90
Disney	119⅛	16⅝	86
Levitz Furniture	40¼	3⅞	90
MGIC	97⅞	6⅛	94
Polaroid	149½	14⅛	91

*Florins.
†Pounds sterling.
‡Livres.

social reality is created that blinds most people to the dangers of the mania. Opinions converge and become "facts." Experts become leaders approving events and strongly exhorting the crowd on. Overconfidence becomes dominant, and standards of conduct and the experience of many years are quickly forgotten. Third, the LeBon image of the magic lantern suddenly changes and anxiety replaces overconfidence. The distended bubble breaks with an ensuing panic. And fourth, we do not, as investors, learn from past mistakes—things really do seem very different each time, although in fact each set of circumstances was remarkably similar to the last.

As we have seen, even though the investors of the 1960s and 1970s were armed with exacting fundamental tools, these did not save them from behaving in a fashion almost identical to the frenzied English and French centuries earlier.

section 2

Fixed Income Instruments

INTRODUCTION

The money market is a huge and significant part of the U.S. financial system. Each workday, hundreds of billions of dollars of money market instruments are traded. Despite the size of the market and the prominent role the instruments play in providing liquidity for individual and institutional portfolios, textbooks generally devote no more than two or three pages to money market instruments. Coverage is usually limited to a brief description of the more popular instruments. In Reading 2, Dr. Marcia Stigum provides a more thorough treatment of these instruments. In addition to describing the investment characteristics of each instrument, she illustrates key money market calculations that market participants need to know in order to compare yields on the various instruments.

The largest debt market in the United States is the mortgage market. Although trading of mortgages between certain institutions was common, the tremendous growth in secondary mortgage market trading is a relatively recent phenomenon. One of the reasons for this growth is the development of mortgage-backed debt instruments. These instruments are more complex in nature than the typical corporate or government bond. In Reading 3, Dr. Kenneth J. Thygerson explains the major types of mortgage-backed securities issued in the United States and their investment characteristics.

Tax-exempt, fixed income debt instruments, or "municipal bonds" as they are commonly known, come in a variety of types, redemption features, credit risks, and market liquidity. Most recently available information indicates that approximately 37,000 different states, counties, school districts, special districts, and towns have issued municipal bonds. Many investors do not perform their own credit analysis of municipal bonds; instead they rely upon credit risk ratings provided by two major rating agencies—Standard & Poor's Corporation and Moody's Investors Service. However, municipal analysts perform their own credit analysis to assess whether the ratings assigned to an issue are adequate and to discriminate among issues within a given quality rating. Credit analysis has become increasingly important in light of several defaults and bankruptcies by municipal issuers. Most investment management textbooks do not include coverage of how to analyze the credit worthiness of municipal obligations. An excellent overview of the factors that should be considered in the credit analysis of municipal obligations is provided by Dr. Sylvan Feldstein in Reading 4.

The high interest rates that prevailed in the U.S. capital market in the late 70s and early 80s made the cost of borrowing for issuers of even the highest quality rating expensive. To reduce the cost of debt financing for their clients, investment bankers designed offerings to make long-term debt instruments more attractive to investors. Mini-coupon and zero coupon bonds were first offered. These issues were attractive to certain institutional investors who wanted to "lock in" the prevailing rate of interest. Variable rate notes, which were pioneered in 1974, were revived for investors who sought protection against further advances in interest rates. Other features such as warrants to purchase additional bonds from the issuer and early redemption or "put" bonds made their debut. In Reading 5, Dr. Robert W. Kopprasch explains how an early redemption option in a fixed income security can eliminate much of the interest rate risk associated with fixed income securities, and he discusses the factors involved in analyzing and valuing early redemption options.

Money Market Instruments

2   MARCIA STIGUM, Ph.D.
Stigum & Associates, New York

The U.S. money market is a huge and significant part of the nation's financial system in which banks and other participants trade hundreds of billions of dollars every working day. Where those billions go and the prices at which they are traded affect how the U.S. government finances its debt, how business finances its expansion, and how consumers choose to spend or save.

The money market is a wholesale market for low-risk, highly liquid, short-term IOUs. It is a market for various sorts of debt securities rather than equities. The stock in trade of the market includes a large chunk of the U.S. Treasury's debt and billions of dollars worth of federal agency securities, negotiable bank certificates of deposit, bankers' acceptances, municipal notes, and commercial paper. Within the confines of the money market each day, banks, both domestic and foreign, actively trade in multimillion-dollar blocks billions of dollars of Federal funds and Eurodollars, and banks and nonbank dealers are each day the recipients of billions of dollars of secured loans through what is called the *repo market*. State and municipal governments also finance part of their activities in this market.

The heart of the activity in the money market occurs in the trading rooms of dealers and brokers of money market instruments. During the time the market is open, these rooms are characterized by a frenzy of activity. Despite its frenzied and incoherent appearance to the outsider, the money market efficiently accomplishes vital functions every day. One is shifting vast sums of money between banks. This shifting is required because the major money market banks, with the exception of the Bank of America, all need a lot more funds than they obtain in deposits, while many smaller banks have more money deposited with them than they can profitably use internally.

The money market also provides a means by which the surplus funds of cash-rich corporations and other institutions can be funneled to banks, corporations, and other institutions that need short-term money. In addition, in the money market the U.S. Treasury can fund huge quantities of debt with ease. And the market provides the Federal Reserve System (also known as *the Fed*) with an arena in which to carry out open-market operations destined to influence interest rates and the growth of the money supply. The varied activities of money market participants also determine the structure of short-term interest rates, for example, what the yields on Treasury bills of different maturities are and how much commercial paper issuers have to pay to borrow. The latter rate is an important cost to many corporations, and it influences in particular the interest rate that a consumer who buys a car on time will have to pay on the loan. Finally, one might mention that the U.S. money market is becoming increasingly an international short-term capital market. In it the oil imports of the nationalized French electric company, Electricité de France, as well as the oil imports of Japan and a lot of other non-U.S. trade are financed.

Anyone who observes the money market soon picks out a number of salient features. First and most obviously, it is not one market but a collection of markets for several distinct and different instruments. What makes it possible to talk about *the* money market is the close interrelationships that link all these markets. A second salient feature is the numerous and varied cast of participants. Borrowers in the market include foreign and domestic banks, the Treasury, corporations of all types, the Federal Home Loan Banks and other federal agencies, dealers in money market instruments, and many states and municipalities. The lenders include almost all of the above, plus insurance companies, pension funds—public and private—and various other financial institutions. And often standing between borrower and lender is one or more of a varied collection of brokers and dealers.

Another key characteristic of the money market is that it is a wholesale market. Trades are big and the people who make them are almost always dealing for the account of some substantial institution. Because of the sums involved, skill is of the utmost importance and money market participants are skilled at what they do. In effect the market is made by extremely talented specialists in very narrow professional areas. A bill trader extraordinaire may have only vague notions as to what the Euromarket is all about, and the Euro specialist may be equally vague on other sectors of the market.

Another principal characteristic of the money market is honor. Every day traders, brokers, investors, and borrowers do hundreds of billions of dollars of business over the phone and, however a trade may appear in retrospect, people do not renege. The motto of the money market is: *My word is my bond.* Of course, because of the pace of the market, mistakes do occur but no one ever assumes that they are intentional, and mistakes are always ironed out in what seems the fairest way for all concerned.

The most appealing characteristic of the money market is innovation. Compared with our other financial markets, the money market is very unregulated. If someone wants to launch a new instrument or to try brokering or dealing in a new way in existing instruments, he does it. And when the idea is good, which it often is, a new facet of the market is born.

In this chapter we examine money market instruments (negotiable short-term debt securities) in which individuals and business firms invest. Treasury bills, issued by the U.S. Treasury, are the most important class of such securities in the United States, but there are others: commercial paper, bankers' acceptances, and negotiable certificates of deposit.

TREASURY BILLS

Treasury bills (known more familiarly as *T bills* or *bills*) represent about 40 percent of the total marketable securities issued by the Treasury. These securities are held widely by financial business firms, nonfinancial corporations, and, to some extent, by individuals.

All T bills are negotiable, noninterest-bearing securities with an original maturity of one year or less—usually 13, 26, or 52 weeks. Bills are currently offered by the Treasury in denominations of $10,000, $15,000, $50,000, $100,000, $500,000, and $1 million. Bills used to be issued by the Treasury in the form of *bearer certificates.* Accordingly, to prove ownership of a bill, the owner must produce it. The Treasury and the Federal Reserve System then made it possible to hold bills in *book-entry form;* since 1977, the Treasury has offered bills *only* in book-entry form. Exceptions are made, however, for those institutions that are required by law or regulation to hold definitive securities.

Bills are always issued at a discount from face value, with the amount of the discount being determined in bill auctions held by the Fed each time the Treasury issues new bills. At maturity, bills are redeemed by the Treasury for full face value. Thus the investor in bills earns a return because he receives more for his bills at maturity than he paid for them at issue. This return is treated for federal tax purposes as ordinary interest income and, as such, is subject to full federal taxation at ordinary rates; it is, however, specifically *exempt* from state and local taxation.

In addition to normal bill issues, the Treasury periodically issues *tax anticipation bills*. TABs, as they are called, are special-issue T bills that mature on corporate quarterly income tax payment dates and can be used at face value by corporations to pay their tax liabilities.

Determining the Yield on Bills

Bill dealers measure yield on a *bank discount basis;* that is, they quote yield as the percentage amount of the discount on an annualized basis. To illustrate, consider an investor who buys a bill maturing in one year at a price of $9,300 for each $10,000 of face value. The discount on this bill is $700, so yield on a bank discount basis works out to be 7 percent ($700/$10,000). In general, the formula for the yield on a bank discount basis for a bill maturing in one year is as follows:[1]

$$d = \frac{D}{F}$$

where

d = Yield on a bank discount basis
F = Face value in dollars
D = Discount from face value in dollars

Alternatively, if the price in dollars is known, d can be calculated as follows:

$$d = \left(1 - \frac{P}{F}\right)$$

where P is the price in dollars.

---

[1] The formulas presented in this section are derived in Marcia Stigum, *Money Market Calculations: Yields, Break-Evens, and Arbitrage* (Homewood, Ill.: Dow Jones-Irwin, 1981), pp. 27-35.

On a bill maturing in less than one year, the discount is earned more quickly, so to get the correct annualized yield on a bank discount basis, the two general formulas above are modified as follows:

$$d = \frac{D}{F} \times \frac{360}{t_{sm}} \quad \text{or} \quad \left(1 - \frac{P}{F}\right)\frac{360}{t_{sm}}$$

where t_{sm} is the number of days from settlement to maturity. Thus, if the bill selling at \$9,300 had 300 days from settlement to maturity, the annual yield on a bank discount basis would be 8.4 percent, found as follows:

$$d = \frac{\$700}{\$10,000} \times \frac{360}{300} = 8.4\%$$

or equivalently:

$$d = \left(1 - \frac{\$9,300}{\$10,000}\right)\frac{360}{300} = 8.4\%$$

The simple annual interest rate that an investor earns by buying a bill is found as follows:

$$i = \frac{D}{P} \times \frac{365}{t_{sm}}$$

where i is the equivalent simple interest yield. For example, the bill with 300 days from settlement to maturity and which can be purchased for \$9,300 for each \$10,000 of face value, would have an equivalent simple interest yield of 9.16 percent, as shown below:

$$i = \frac{\$700}{\$9,300} \times \frac{365}{300} = 9.16\%$$

Alternatively, given the yield on a bank discount basis (d), the equivalent simple interest yield can be computed, using the following formula:

$$i = \frac{365d}{360 - d\, t_{sm}}$$

Applying this formula to our example, recall that the yield on a bank discount basis is 8.4 percent. We find:

$$i = \frac{365(0.084)}{360 - 0.084(300)} = 9.16\%$$

Notice that the yield on a bank discount basis understates the equivalent simple interest rate that an investor would realize by holding a bill. This holds for all securities offered on a discounted basis.

Table 1
Comparisons at Different Rates and Maturities between Rates of Discount and the Equivalent *Simple Interest* Rates on a 365-Day-Year Basis

Rate of Discount (percent)	Equivalent Simple Interest (percent)		
	30-Day Maturity	182-Day Maturity	364-Day Maturity
4	4.07	4.14	4.23
6	6.11	6.27	6.48
8	8.17	8.45	8.82
10	10.22	10.68	11.27
12	12.29	12.95	13.84
14	14.36	15.28	16.53
16	16.44	17.65	19.35

Moreover, as Table 1 shows, the discrepancy between the two rates is greater the higher the rate of discount (i.e. the higher the yield on a bank discount basis) and the longer the time to maturity.

In the secondary market, bids for and offerings of coupon securities are quoted not in terms of yields (as in the case of discount securities) but in terms of dollar prices.[2] On a coupon quote sheet, however, there is always a number for each security stating what its yield to maturity would be if it were purchased at the quoted asked or offered price. However, the yield to maturity figure on a quote sheet for coupon securities *understates* the effective yield to maturity because it ignores the fact that interest is paid *semiannually*. That is, whatever the investor does with coupon interest, it is worth something to him to get semiannual interest payments rather than a single year-end interest payment.

In converting the yield on a discount security to an add-on interest rate, various approaches are possible. One is to convert to an equivalent simple interest rate as explained previously. However, the "street" in putting together quote sheets takes a slightly different tack. It restates yields on discount securities on a basis that makes them comparable to the yield to maturity quoted on coupon securities. A rate so computed is called a *coupon yield equivalent* or *equivalent bond yield*.

The street's decision to restate bill yields on a coupon yield equivalent basis creates a need to distinguish between discount securities that have six months (182 days) or less to run and those that have more than six months to run. When a coupon security is on its last leg, i.e., when it will mature on the next coupon date and thus offers no opportunity for further compounding, its stated yield to

---

[2] An exception is municipal bonds.

2: Money Market Instruments

maturity equals its yield on a simple interest basis. For this reason, on discount securities with six months or less to run, bond equivalent yield is taken to be the equivalent simple interest rate offered by the instrument. Letting d_b equal the equivalent bond yield, then d_b can be found from the rate of discount (d), or the yield on a bank discount basis, by:

$$d_b = \frac{365 d}{360 - d\, t_{sm}}$$

However, when a discount security has more than six months to maturity, the bond equivalent yield, denoted d_b', is computed by the following formula:

$$d_b' = \frac{\dfrac{-2 t_{sm}}{365} + 2 \sqrt{\left(\dfrac{t_{sm}}{365}\right)^2 - \left(\dfrac{2 t_{sm}}{365} - 1\right)\left(1 - \dfrac{1}{P}\right)}}{\dfrac{2 t_{sm}}{365} - 1}$$

where P is the price per $1 of face value. To illustrate how to use the foregoing formula for a bill with more than six months to run, consider a bill with an asked price of 95.0653 percent of face value and 190 days to run. The equivalent bond yield is 9.95 percent, as shown in the formula:

$$d_b' = \frac{\dfrac{-2(190)}{365} + 2 \sqrt{\left(\dfrac{190}{365}\right)^2 - \left(\dfrac{2(190)}{365} - 1\right)\left(1 - \dfrac{1}{0.950653}\right)}}{\dfrac{2(190)}{365} - 1}$$

$$= 9.95\%$$

Buying Bills

There is no way for an individual to invest in bills unless he has a minimum of $10,000 available or is willing and able to pool his funds with other investors. For an individual with more than $10,000 to invest, it is possible to acquire bills in amounts equal to any multiple of five by buying an appropriate mix of bills in $10,000 and $15,000 denominations. Bills can be purchased from a bank or at auction.

The easiest way for a small investor to acquire bills is to buy them from his bank. If your bank is a major bank in a large financial center, such as Chicago or New York, it may well act as a dealer in government securities; in that case it will sell bills to you directly out of its inventory. If your bank is not a dealer bank, it will purchase the required amount of bills from a larger bank with which it has a correspondent relationship.

If you are willing to put yourself out a little, you can escape the service charge that banks impose on bill purchases by buying bills directly from the Fed during one of the periodic auctions at which the Fed sells new issues of T bills.

Naturally, a small investor can't be expected to arrive panting at the Fed just before the bid window closes with a tender tuned to the morning's developments in the money market. That is no problem, however, since the Fed has made provision for the small investor who is unsophisticated, and, worse still, has no runner at his disposal. To service such investors, the Fed accepts what are called *noncompetitive* bids for amounts up to $500,000 per investor per auction. A person submitting a noncompetitive bid gets his bills at a price equal to the average of the competitive bids accepted by the Treasury. Generally the spread in competitive bids is not very wide, so the noncompetitive bidder does not fare badly.

COMMERCIAL PAPER

Commercial paper, whoever the issuer and whatever the precise form it takes, is an unsecured promissory note with a fixed maturity. In plain English, the issuer of commercial paper (the borrower) promises to pay the buyer (the lender) some fixed amount on some future date. But the issuer pledges no assets—only his liquidity and established earning power—to guarantee that he will make good on his promise to pay. Traditionally, commercial paper resembled in form a Treasury bill; it was a negotiable, noninterest-bearing note issued at a discount from face value and redeemed at maturity for full face value. Today, however, a lot of paper is interest-bearing. For the investor the major difference between bills and paper is that paper carries some small risk of default because the issuer is a private firm, whereas the risk of default on bills is zero for all intents and purposes.

Firms selling commercial paper frequently expect to roll over their paper as it matures; that is, they plan to get money to pay off maturing paper by issuing new paper. Since there is always the danger that an adverse turn in the paper market might make doing so difficult or inordinately expensive, most paper issuers back their outstanding paper with *bank lines of credit;* they get a promise from a bank or banks to lend them at any time an amount equal to their outstanding paper. Issuers normally pay for this service in one of several ways: by holding at their line banks compensating deposit balances equal to some percentage of their total credit lines; by paying an annual fee equal to some small percentage of their outstanding lines; or through some mix of balances and fees.

Issuers of Paper

The large open market for commercial paper that exists in the United States is a unique feature of the U.S. money market. Its origins trace back to the early 19th century, when firms in need of working capital began using the sale of open-market paper as a substitute for bank loans. Their need to do so resulted largely from the unit banking system adopted in the United States. Elsewhere, it was common for banks to operate branches nationwide, which meant that seasonal demands for credit in one part of the country, perhaps due to the movement of a crop to market, could be met by a transfer of surplus funds from other areas to that area. In the United States, where banks were restricted to a single state and more often to a single location, this was difficult. Thus, firms in credit-scarce, high-interest-rate areas started raising funds by selling commercial paper in New York City and other distant financial centers.

Financial and nonfinancial firms (e.g., public utilities, manufacturers, retailers) issue paper. Paper issued by nonfinancial firms, referred to as *industrial paper,* accounts for about 23 percent of all paper outstanding. Such paper is issued, as in the past, to meet seasonal needs for funds and also as a means of interim financing (i.e., to obtain funds to start investment projects that are later permanently funded through the sale of long-term bonds). In contrast to industrial borrowers, finance companies have a continuing need for short-term funds throughout the year; they are now the principal borrowers in the commercial paper market, accounting for roughly 59 percent of all paper.

In the recent years of tight money, bank holding companies have also joined finance companies as borrowers in the commercial paper market. Many banks are owned by a holding company, an arrangement offering the advantage that the holding company can engage in activities in which the bank itself is not permitted. Commercial paper is sold by bank holding companies primarily to finance their nonbank activities in leasing, real estate, and other lines. However, funds raised through the sale of such paper can also be funneled into the holding company's bank, if the latter is pinched for funds, through various devices, such as the sale of bank assets to the holding company.

Issuing Techniques

All industrial paper is issued through paper dealers. Currently there are about eight major paper dealers in the country; their main offices are in financial centers—New York, Chicago, and Boston—but they have branches throughout the country. Also there are a number of smaller regional dealers. Typically, dealers buy up new paper issues directly from the borrower, mark them up, and then resell them to investors. The current going rate of markup is very small, an eighth of 1 percent per annum. Generally, paper issues are for very large amounts, and the minimum round lot in which most dealers sell is $250,000. Thus the dealer market for commercial paper is a meeting ground for big corporate borrowers and for large investors (the latter including financial corporations, nonfinancial corporations, and pension funds).

Finance companies and banks occasionally place their paper through dealers, but most such paper (over 80 percent) is placed directly by the issuer with investors. A big finance company, for example, might place $1 million or more of paper with an insurance company or with a big industrial firm that had a temporary surplus of funds. In addition to these large-volume transactions, some finance companies and banks also sell paper in relatively small denominations directly to small business firms and individual investors, as will be discussed later in this section.

Paper Maturities

Maturities on commercial paper are generally very short—one to three months being the most common on dealer-placed paper. Generally, dealers prefer not to handle paper with a maturity of less than 30 to 45 days because, on paper of such short maturity, their markup (which is figured on a percent *per annum* basis) barely covers costs. However, to accommodate established borrowers, they will do so. Paper with a maturity of more than 270 days is rare because issues of such long maturity have to be registered with the SEC.

Finance companies that place their paper directly with large investors generally offer a wide range of maturities—3 to 270 days. Also they are willing to tailor maturities to the needs of investors and will often accept funds for very short periods, for example for a weekend. Finance companies that sell low-denomination paper to individual investors generally offer maturities ranging from 30 to 270 days on such paper. These companies also issue longer-maturity short-term notes that have been registered with the SEC.

Paper Yields

Some paper bears interest, but much does not. The investor who buys noninterest-bearing paper gets a return on his money because he buys his paper at a discount from face value, whereas the issuer redeems the paper at maturity for full face value. Yields on paper are generally quoted in eighths of 1 percent, for example, at $7\frac{1}{8}$ percent per annum. Paper rates, whether the paper is interest-bearing or not, are quoted on a *bank discount basis,* as in the case of bills.

Bill rates vary over time, rising if business demand for credit increases or if the Fed tightens credit, falling in the opposite cases. The yields offered by paper issuers follow much the same pattern of bill yields except that paper yields are, if anything, even more volatile than bill yields.

The reason paper rates fluctuate up and down in step with the yields on bills and other money-market securities is simple. Paper competes with these other instruments for investors' dollars. Therefore, as yields on bills and other money market securities rise, paper issuers must offer higher rates in order to sell their paper. In contrast, if bill yields and other short-term rates decline, paper issuers can and do ease the rates they offer.

The volatility of paper rates has important consequences for the investor. First, it means that the attractiveness of paper as an investment medium for short-term funds varies over the interest rate cycle. It also means that the rate you get on paper bought today tells you relatively little about what rate you would get if you were to roll over that paper at maturity. Paper yields offered in the future may be substantially higher or lower than today's rates, depending on whether money is tightening or easing.

Risk and Ratings

If you are thinking of buying paper, you should consider not only the *return* it yields, but also whether there is any *risk* that you will not get timely payment on your paper when it matures. Basically there are two situations in which an issuing company might fail to pay off its maturing paper: (1) it is solvent but lacks cash and (2) it is insolvent. How great are the chances that either situation will occur? Fortunately, today the chances are quite small, in fact, negligible, for companies with top-rated paper.

Since the early 1930s, the default record on commercial paper has been excellent. In the case of dealer paper, one reason is that, after the 1920s, the many little borrowers who had populated the paper market were replaced by a much smaller number of large, well-established firms. This gave dealers, who were naturally extremely careful about whose paper they handled, the opportunity to examine much more thoroughly the financial condition of each issuer with whom they dealt.

While the payments record on paper is good, the losses that have occurred make it clear that an individual putting money into paper has the right—more strongly, the responsibility—to ask: How good is the company whose paper I am buying? Because of the investor's very real need for an answer, and because of the considerable time and money involved in obtaining one, rating services have naturally developed. Today a large proportion of dealer and direct paper is rated by one or more of three companies: Standard & Poor's, Moody's, and Fitch.

Paper issuers willingly pay the rating services to examine them and rate their paper, since a good rating makes it easier and cheaper for them to borrow in the paper market. The rating companies, despite the fact that they receive their income from issuers, basically have the interests of the investor at heart for one simple reason: the value of their ratings to investors and thereby their ability to sell rating services to issuers depend on their accuracy. The worth to an issuer of a top rating is the track record of borrowers who have held that rating.

Each rating company sets its own rating standards, but their approaches are similar. Every rating is based on an evaluation of the borrowing company's management and on a detailed study of its earnings record and balance sheet. Just what a rating company looks for depends in part on the borrower's line of business; the optimal balance sheet for a publishing company would look quite different from that of a finance company. Nonetheless, one can say in general that the criteria for a top rating are strong management, a good position in a well-established industry, an upward trend in earnings, adequate liquidity, and the ability to borrow to meet both anticipated and unexpected cash needs.

Since companies seeking a paper rating are rarely in imminent danger of insolvency, the principal focus in rating paper is on *liquidity*—can the borrower come up with cash to pay off his maturing paper? Here what the rating company looks for is ability to borrow elsewhere than in the paper market and especially the ability to borrow short-term from banks. Today, for a company to get a paper rating, its paper must be backed by bank lines of credit.

Different rating firms grade borrowers according to different classifications. Standard & Poor's, for example, rates companies from A for highest quality to D for lowest. It also subdivides A-rated companies into four groups according to relative strength, A-1+ down to A-3. Fitch rates firms F-1 (highest grade) to F-4 (lowest grade). Moody's uses P-1, P-2, and P-3, with P-1 being their highest rating.

BANKERS' ACCEPTANCES

Bankers' acceptances (BAs) are an unknown instrument outside the confines of the money market. Moreover, explaining them isn't easy because they arise in a variety of ways out of a variety of transactions. The best approach is to use an example.

Suppose a U.S. importer wants to buy shoes in Brazil and pay for them four months later, after he has had time to sell them in the United States. One approach would be for the importer to simply borrow from his bank; however, short-term rates may be lower in the open market. If they are, and if the importer is too small to go into the open market on his own, then he can go the bankers' acceptance route.

In that case he has his bank write a letter of credit for the amount of the sale and then sends this letter to the Brazilian exporter. Upon export of the shoes, the Brazilian firm, using this letter of credit, draws a time draft on the importer's U.S. bank and discounts this draft at its local bank, thereby obtaining immediate payment for its goods. The Brazilian bank in turn sends the time draft to the importer's U.S. bank, which then stamps "accepted" on the draft; that is, the bank guarantees payment on the draft and thereby creates an *acceptance.* Once this is done, the draft becomes an irrevocable primary obligation of the accepting bank. At this point, if the Brazilian bank did not want cash immediately, the U.S. bank would return the draft to that bank, which would hold it as an investment and then present it to the U.S. bank for payment at maturity. If, on the other hand, the Brazilian bank wanted cash immediately, the U.S. bank would pay it and then either hold the acceptance itself or sell it to an investor. Whoever ended up holding the acceptance, it would be the importer's responsibility to provide his U.S. bank with sufficient funds to pay off the acceptance at maturity. If the importer should fail for any reason, his bank would still be responsible for making payment at maturity.

Our example illustrates how an acceptance can arise out of a U.S. import transaction. Acceptances also arise in connection with U.S. export sales, trade between third countries (e.g., Japanese imports of oil from the Middle East), the domestic shipment of goods, and domestic or foreign storage of readily marketable staples. Currently most BAs arise out of foreign trade; the latter may be in manufactured goods, but more typically is in bulk commodities, such as cocoa, cotton, coffee, or crude oil, to name a few. Because of the complex nature of acceptance operations, only large banks that have well-staffed foreign departments act as accepting banks.

Bankers' acceptances closely resemble commercial paper in form. They are short-term (270 days or less), noninterest-bearing notes sold at a discount and redeemed by the accepting bank at maturity for full face value. The major difference between bankers' acceptances and paper is that payment on paper is guaranteed by only the issuing company, while payment on bankers' acceptances is also guaranteed by the accepting bank. Thus, bankers' acceptances carry slightly less risk than commercial paper. The very low risk on acceptances is indicated by the fact that to date no investor in acceptances has ever suffered a loss.

Yields on bankers' acceptances are quoted on a bank discount basis, as in the case of commercial paper. Yields on bankers' acceptances closely parallel yields on paper. Also, both rates are highly volatile, rising sharply when money is tight and falling in an equally dramatic fashion when conditions ease. This means that when money is tight, yields on bankers' acceptances are very attractive.

The big banks through which bankers' acceptances originate generally keep some portion of the acceptances they create as investments. The rest are sold to investors through dealers or directly by the bank itself. Major investors in bankers' acceptances are other banks, foreign central banks, and Federal Reserve banks.

Many bankers' acceptances are written for very large amounts and are obviously out of the range of the small investor; certainly this includes all acceptances that pass through the hands of dealers. However, acceptances in amounts as low as $5,000 or even $500 are not uncommon. Some accepting banks offer these low-denomination acceptances to their customers as investments. An individual investing in a $25,000 acceptance may in fact be buying a single small acceptance arising out of one transaction, or he may be buying a bundle of even smaller acceptances, that have been packaged together to form a round-dollar amount. Frequently, bankers' acceptances are available in still smaller odd-dollar amounts. The investor who puts his money into an odd-dollar acceptance should be prepared to experience some difficulty in rolling over his funds. Also the availability of bankers' acceptances varies both seasonally and over the cycle. Generally, availability is greatest when money is tight and banks prefer not to tie up funds in acceptances.

The rates offered on bankers' acceptances, like those on paper, vary from day to day. An easy way to get some idea of the general level of rates on bankers' acceptances and to see how they compare with yields on competing instruments is to check the "Money Rate" quotes in *The Wall Street Journal* or *Barron's* "Economic and Financial Indicators." Rates on bankers' acceptances are normally quoted for maturities of 30, 60, 90, 120, and 180 days. Some dealers quote rates in eighths of 1 percent, but rate quotes to two decimal points are also common.

Since payment on acceptances is guaranteed by both the accepting bank and the ultimate borrower, investing in acceptances exposes an individual to minimal risk. For small acceptances, as for paper, there is no secondary market. Thus an investor who needs cash cannot sell his bankers' acceptance to another investor. However, he can use it as collateral for a bank loan. Also, if his need for cash is really pressing, chances are that the accepting bank will be willing to buy back the acceptance early.

To sum up, bankers' acceptances are little known, but at times very attractive, investment for the small investor.

NEGOTIABLE CERTIFICATES OF DEPOSIT

In the early post-World War II period, when interest rates were low, bankers were not inclined to accept corporate time deposits on which they would have to pay interest. However, in the late 1950s and early 1960s, things changed for several reasons. First, corporate treasurers, who had customarily met their liquidity needs by holding large balances of noninterest-bearing demand deposits, began to manage their money in a more sophisticated manner as short-term rates rose. They switched funds where possible out of demand deposits into liquid, income-yielding, money market instruments, such as T bills and commercial paper. Second, the large New York money market banks, which had historically enjoyed a dominant position on the national banking scene, found that their competitive position was eroding. As a result of industrial decentralization and the rapid growth of population outside the Northeast, their share of total deposits had declined by almost 50 percent between 1940 and 1960.

In response to these trends, the First National City Bank of New York announced in 1961 that it would issue large-denomination *negotiable certificates of deposit* and that a large, well-known government securities dealer, The First Boston Corporation, had agreed to create a secondary market (act as a dealer) in these securities. A negotiable CD is simply a receipt from a bank for funds deposited at that bank for some specified period of time at some specified rate of return.

Negotiable CDs were not a new instrument in 1961; they had been around in small volume for a long time. What made First National City's announcement the beginning of a phenomenal expansion in outstanding CDs was not its willingness to issue this instrument, but rather First Boston's intent to act as a dealer in CDs. To the corporate treasurer looking for liquidity, what is important is not *negotiability* per se, but rather *marketability*. The marketability of an instrument, which is measured in degrees, depends on the existence of a secondary market for that instrument and on the level of activity in that market. Bills and paper are both negotiable, but bills have high marketability whereas paper does not. Thus, corporations typically use bills to provide first-line liquidity, and they use paper and other less liquid instruments to provide second-line liquidity.

Once First National City made its announcement, the other major banks quickly followed suit, and a number of other dealers joined First Boston Corp. in the secondary market. From essentially a zero base in 1961, the volume of negotiable CDs outstanding grew rapidly. Today, the major issuers of negotiable CDs are large nationally known money market banks, principally in New York and Chicago. In addition to these prime borrowers, there are also a number of less well-known regional banks that issue CDs.

Since some investors in Eurodollars wanted liquidity, banks that accepted time deposits in London began to issue Eurodollar CDs. A *Eurodollar CD* resembles a domestic CD except that instead of being the liability of a domestic bank, it is the liability of the London branch of a domestic bank or of a British bank or another foreign bank with a branch in London. Although many of the Eurodollar CDs issued in London are purchased by other banks operating in the Euromarket, a large portion of the remainder are sold to U.S. corporations and other domestic institutional investors. Many Euro CDs are issued through dealers and brokers who maintain secondary markets in these securities.

The Euro CD market is younger and smaller than the market for domestic CDs, but it has grown rapidly since its inception. The most recent development in the Eurodollar CD market is that some large banks have begun offering such CDs through their Caribbean branches.[3]

Foreign banks issue dollar-denominated CDs not only in the Euro market but also in the domestic market through branches established there. CDs of the latter sort are frequently referred to as *Yankee CDs;* the name is taken from Yankee bonds, which are bonds issued in the domestic market by foreign borrowers.

CDs can have any maturity longer than 30 days, and some five- and seven-year CDs have been sold (these pay interest semiannually). Most CDs, however, have an *original maturity* of one to three months. Generally, the CD buyer, who may be attempting to fund a predictable cash need—say, provide for a tax or dividend payment—can select his own maturity date when he makes his deposit.

Until May 1973, the Fed, under Regulation Q, imposed lids on the rates that banks could pay on large-denomination CDs of different maturities. Today these lids are past history, and the general level of yields on negotiable CDs is determined by conditions of demand and supply in the money market. Since holding a CD exposes the investor to a small risk of capital loss (the issuing bank might fail), prime-name negotiable CDs, in order to sell, have to be offered at rates approximately one eighth of a point above the rate on T bills of com-

---

[3] A CD issued, for example, in Nassau is technically a Euro CD because the deposit is held in a bank branch outside the United States.

parable maturity. Of course, in actual practice there is no one CD rate prevailing at any one time. Each issuing bank sets a range of rates for different maturities, normally with an upward-sloping yield curve. On a given day a bank at which loan demand is especially strong, and which therefore needs money, may set rates slightly more attractive than those posted by other banks. Posted rates are not fixed rates; big investors can and do haggle with banks over the rate paid.

Generally, prime-name banks can attract funds more cheaply than other banks, the rate differential being one percentage point or less. Foreign banks pay still higher CD rates. In comparing CD rates with yields on other money market instruments, note that CDs are *not* issued at a discount. It takes $1 million of deposits to get a CD with a $1 million face value. CDs typically pay interest at maturity. Thus rates quoted on CDs correspond to yield in the terms in which the investor normally thinks—what we call *equivalent bond yield.*

Recently banks have introduced on a small scale a new type of negotiable CD, *variable-rate CDs.* The two most prevalent types are six-month CDs with a 30-day *roll* (on each roll date, accrued interest is paid and a new coupon is set) and one-year paper with a three-month roll. The coupon established on a variable-rate CD at issue and on subsequent roll dates is set at some amount (12.5 to 30 basis points, depending on the name of the issuer and the maturity) above the average rate (as indicated by the composite rate published by the Fed) that banks are paying on new CDs with an original maturity equal to the length of the roll period.

We can sum up our discussion of risk, liquidity, and return on negotiable CDs by saying that CDs are slightly riskier than T bills. They are also slightly less liquid since the spread between bid and asked prices is narrower in the bill market than in the secondary CD market, the reason being that in the bill market the commodity traded is homogeneous and buying and selling occur in greater volume.

CDs, however, compensate for these failings by yielding a somewhat higher return than bills do. Euro CDs offer a higher return than domestic CDs. The offsetting disadvantages are that they are less liquid and expose the investor to some extra risk because they are issued outside the United States. Yankee CDs expose the investor to the extra (if only in perception) risk of a foreign name, and they are also less liquid than domestic CDs. Consequently, Yankee CDs trade at yields close to those on Euro CDs. Although variable-rate CDs offer the investor some interest-rate protection, they have the offsetting disadvantage of illiquidity because they trade at a concession to the market. During their last *leg* (roll period) variable-rate CDs trade like regular CDs of similar name and maturity.

Computing the Yield of a CD Given Its Price

Almost all CDs issued in the domestic market have a maturity at issue of less than one year and pay simple interest on a 360-day basis.[4] The rate of interest paid is the coupon rate, and interest is paid at maturity. In the formulas presented for CDs, the following convention will be adopted. Price P is always taken to be price per $1 of face value, with accrued interest, if any, included.[5]

CDs are always quoted, at issue and in the secondary market, in terms of yield on a simple interest basis. The following formula is for the rate of return that a CD offered at a price P will yield an investor:

$$y = \left(\frac{1 + c \frac{t_{im}}{360}}{P} - 1 \right) \frac{360}{t_{sm}}$$

where
- y = Yield on the CD
- c = Coupon rate
- t_{sm} = Days from settlement to maturity
- t_{im} = Days from issue to maturity

For example, suppose that an investor buys a CD that carries a coupon rate of 10 percent and has an original maturity of 90 and a current maturity of 60 days. If the price P is 1.009024, the yield is 9.5 percent, as shown in the formula.

$$y = \left(\frac{1 + 1.100 \frac{90}{360}}{1.009024} - 1 \right) \frac{360}{60} = 0.095$$

There are two points to note about the formula for computing the yield on a CD. First, if a CD is bought on its issue date, then $P = 1$, and the expression for the yield reduces to the coupon rate, c, as would be expected. Second, the fact that CDs pay interest on the basis of a 360-day year should not be forgotten when CD yields are compared with those on other interest-bearing securities, such as government notes and bonds, which pay interest on a 365-day basis. To convert from a 365- to a 360-day basis, the yield on a CD must be multiplied by 1.014.[6] Therefore, getting a year's interest over 360 days is worth 1.4 extra basis points for every 1 percent interest.

---

[4] As noted above, the exceptions are variable-rate CDs and a few long-term issues that have been floated at various times.

[5] The formulas presented in this section are derived in Stigum, *Money Market Calculations*, pp. 71-80.

[6] The conversion factor is found by dividing 365 by 360.

Computing Price Given Yield

Using the formula for the yield on a CD, a formula for the price at which a CD will trade in the secondary market if it is offered at a yield y can be determined. Solving, we have:

$$P = \left(\frac{1 + c \frac{t_{im}}{360}}{1 + y \frac{t_{sm}}{360}} \right)$$

Let's use the CD used to illustrate the yield formula given the price to show how the foregoing formula is applied. The price P is 1.009024, as shown in the following formula:

$$P = \left(\frac{1 + 0.100 \frac{90}{360}}{1 + 0.095 \frac{60}{360}} \right) = 1.009024$$

Breaking Out Accrued Interest

Separating the price P paid for a CD into principal and interest is easily done.

Let

a_i = Accrued interest
t_{is} = Days from issue to settlement

On a CD accrued interest is given by the expression:

$$a_i = c \frac{t_{is}}{360}$$

and

$$\text{Principal per \$1 of face value} = P - c \frac{t_{is}}{360}$$

Applying these formulas to the preceding example, we find that:

$$a_i = 0.10 \frac{30}{360} = 0.083333$$

and

$$\text{Principal} = 1.009024 - 0.083333$$
$$= 1.000691$$

Note that the CD in our example is selling at a premium. This is to be expected since it was traded at a *yield well below* its coupon.

Holding Period Yield

Intuition, which seems to be invariably wrong in money market calculations, suggests that if an investor bought a CD at 10 percent and sold it before maturity at the same rate, he would earn 10 percent over the holding period. In fact, he would earn *less*. The reason is our old friend, compounding. It crops up because interest is not paid by the issuer on the CD until some period after the investor sells it; the CD is priced at sale, however, so that the buyer will earn the offered yield on an amount equal to the principal paid *plus* accrued interest.

Consider first a CD that is bought by an investor at issue and later sold before maturity. The rate of simple interest, i, earned by the investor over the holding period is:

$$i = \left(\frac{1 + c\,\frac{t_{im}}{360}}{1 + y\,\frac{t_{sm}}{360}} - 1 \right) \frac{360}{t_{is}}$$

where

t_{is} = Days from issue to settlement on the sale
y = Rate at which the CD is sold

For example, an investor buys a 90-day CD carrying a 10 percent coupon at issue and sells it 30 days later at a 10 percent yield. The return he earns is not 10 percent but a lower figure, 9.83 percent. The calculation is:

$$i = \left(\frac{1 + 0.10\,\frac{90}{360}}{1 + 0.10\,\frac{60}{360}} - 1 \right) \frac{360}{30} = 9.83\%$$

A Secondary CD

The yield on a CD purchased in the secondary market and sold before maturity can be calculated using a similar but slightly more complex formula as shown in the formula:

$$i = \left(\frac{1 + y_1\,\frac{t_1}{360}}{1 + y_2\,\frac{t_2}{360}} - 1 \right) \frac{360}{t_1 - t_2}$$

where

y_1 = Purchase rate
y_2 = Sale rate
t_1 = Days from purchase to maturity
t_2 = Days from sale to maturity

Sensitivity of Return to Sale Rate and Length of Holding Period

The figures in Table 2 show what return, i, an investor would earn if he sold a 6-month CD purchased at 9 percent after various holding periods and at various rates. Note first the column labeled 9 percent. It shows that if the investor resells his CD at the purchase rate, the return he earns will be higher the longer the holding period is, that is, the closer the sale date is to the date on which the CD matures and accrued interest is paid out.

Table 2
The Rate of Return, i, Earned by an Investor on a 9 Percent, Six-Month CD When Sold at Various Rates after Various Holding Periods (all numbers are percents)

Holding Period (days)	Sale Rate, y				
	11 Percent	10 Percent	9 Percent	8 Percent	7 Percent
30	−0.96	3.84	8.67	13.55	18.46
60	4.82	6.77	8.74	10.71	12.70
90	6.81	7.80	8.80	9.80	10.81
120	7.86	8.36	8.87	9.38	9.88
150	8.59	8.73	8.93	9.14	9.35
179	8.99	8.99	9.00	9.00	9.01

If an investor sells a CD at a rate below the rate at which he bought it, he will receive a capital gain and earn over the holding period a return higher than the yield at which he bought the CD. As the columns labeled 8 percent and 7 percent show, this effect becomes smaller the longer the holding period is. If, conversely, the investor sells his CD at a rate *above* that at which he purchased it, the effect is the opposite and also decreases as the holding period is lengthened.

The reason that the impact of the sale rate on the return earned by the investor diminishes as the holding period increases is: The longer the holding period, the shorter is the time in which the buyer of the CD will earn the rate at which he buys the CD and therefore the smaller will be the impact of that rate on the principal amount he pays for the CD.

Compounding

We have noted that selling a CD before maturity tends to reduce the yield earned by the investor over the holding period. If the investor *fully* reinvests the proceeds (principal *plus* accrued interest) from the sale of the CD, this effect will be offset by the opportunity for compounding of interest earnings created by the sale and subsequent repurchase.

To illustrate, note that an investor who purchased at issue a 182-day CD at 9 percent and sold it 91 days later at 9 percent would earn a yield of 8.80 percent over that period. If he immediately fully reinvested the sale proceeds ($1.022750 per $1 of face value) in a 9 percent, 91-day CD, his total earnings over the 182-day investment period would be identical with what he would have earned if he had held the 182-day, 9 percent CD he originally bought to maturity.

Investing in Mortgage-Backed Securities

3 KENNETH J. THYGERSON, Ph.D.
Executive Vice President,
Western Federal Savings and Loan Association of Colorado and Chairman of the Board of WestAmerica Mortgage Co.

The mortgage market is the largest debt market in the United States. It is not surprising, therefore, that major innovations have been developed for the purpose of broadening the base for mortgage loan investment. Although the secondary market has played a long-standing role as a means of shifting funds from capital surplus to capital deficit areas, major innovations in mortgage securities took place in the decade of the 1970s, when mortgage-backed and secured debt instruments were developed.

A basic objective of these mortgage instrument innovations has been to integrate the bond and mortgage markets. In this way, mortgage loan originators hope to tap the significant sources of investment funds controlled by pension funds, trusts, and insurance companies. Historically, mortgage and bond market participants have not communicated frequently or adequately understood each other's investment needs. The creation of new mortgage instruments in recent years, however, has strengthened the ties between the participants in these two major debt markets.

To the extent that traditional nonmortgage investors are attracted to these new mortgage instruments, the mortgage market is expected to be less vulnerable to cyclic disruptions in the flow of mortgage credit and the overall availability of residential mortgage credit is expected to be increased. In addition, the creation of these new mortgage instruments enhances the liquidity of the mortgage originator's mortgage holdings. This increased liquidity can translate into a freer flow of funds from capital surplus to capital deficit areas and can also bring about lower mortgage rates.

The innovations in mortgage instruments occurred, in large part, with the help of the U.S. government. The National Housing Act of 1968 authorized the creation of the Government National Mortgage Association (GNMA) pass-through security program. (The first GNMA pass-through was issued on February 19, 1970.) This program—to be discussed more fully later—represented the most significant single effort to broaden the base of investor interest in mortgage loans. Because of the complexities of originating and servicing individual mortgage loans, many institutional investors, such as insurance companies, pension funds, and other trusts, found mortgage loan investments less appealing than the more easily marketable and serviceable corporate bonds, municipal bonds, stocks, and government bonds. Thus, in order to broaden the investment base for mortgage investment, efforts had to be made to develop securities backed or secured by mortgage loans which had investment attributes—marketability, reinvestment ease, and minimal servicing requirements—that were more appealing to the many institutional investors who had not traditionally been attracted to mortgages but were very familiar with bonds. The GNMA pass-through security program was the first of numerous efforts which have proved to be a successful means of broadening the investment base for mortgage loans.

Since the inauguration of the GNMA pass-through security program in 1970, a number of other mortgage-backed securities have been developed by quasi-governmental and private institutions servicing the mortgage market. The economic motivation behind each of these mortgage security innovations is similar. It involves the creation of new mortgage-backed and -secured debt instruments with investment attributes that are more appealing than those found in the underlying mortgage loans. Generally speaking, mortgage-backed and -secured bonds are found to have higher liquidity, less default risk, and broader marketability than do the underlying mortgages.

Since 1970, at least six major types of mortgage-backed or -secured debt instruments have been developed and offered in the credit markets. These are: (1) the Government National Mortgage Association pass-through security, (2) the Federal Home Loan Mortgage Corporation (FHLMC) participation certificate, (3) the Federal Home Loan Mortgage Corporation guaranteed mortgage certificate, (4) the private issue mortgage-backed bond, (5) the private issue pass-through certificate, and (6) the industrial development mortgage bond. Four of these six types of mortgage-backed securities are sponsored by federal agencies or quasi-agencies or by state agencies. These include the GNMA pass-through security, the FHLMC participation certificate, the FHLMC guaranteed mortgage certificate, and the state agency-sponsored industrial development mortgage bond. Two of the six types, the mortgage-backed bond and the pass-through certificate, are issued by private mortgage lenders, such as savings and loan associations and commercial banks.

Like the sponsoring organizations, the underlying mortgages which act as security for the instruments differ significantly. The GNMA pass-through securities, for example, use FHA-insured and VA-guaranteed mortgages as collateral. The FHLMC participation certificates normally use conventional residential mortgages as collateral, as do the FHLMC guaranteed mortgage certificates. The private issue mortgage-backed bonds and pass-through certificates normally utilize conventional, FHA, and VA residential mortgages as collateral. The underlying security of the industrial development mortgage bonds, by contrast, is normally commercial mortgages on shopping centers, plants, and other commercial properties.

In addition, the marketability and yields on these securities differ substantially. This is because several of these securities are backed by various government and agency guarantees, whereas others are not.

The investor in mortgage-backed and -secured instruments is concerned with at least these seven major characteristics: (1) the denomination of the securities issued, (2) the marketability and liquidity of the issue, (3) the safety or the susceptibility to default risk of the issue, (4) the means of paying the principal and interest of the issue, (5) the expected average loan life or maturity of the issue, (6) the tax status of the issue, and (7) the relative yield of the issue.

The remainder of this chapter will discuss the background and the investment characteristics of the six major mortgage-backed securities.

GOVERNMENT NATIONAL MORTGAGE ASSOCIATION PASS-THROUGH SECURITIES

The GNMA pass-through security was first issued in 1970 under Section 306(g) of Title III of the National Housing Act. The security represents a share in a pool of FHA and VA mortgages, all of which have the same interest rate and a similar term to maturity. GNMA pools are formed for mobile home loans and multifamily project loans as well as the more common single-family mortgage pools.

The GNMA pass-through security was conceived as a means of attracting institutional money into mortgage investments. By mid-1978, there were over $58 billion of GNMA pass-through securities outstanding. Over two thirds of these were held by investors other than the traditional mortgage-lending thrift institutions.

The major issuers of GNMA pass-throughs are mortgage bankers. Of the approximately 500 issuers, 90 percent are mortgage bankers, the rest mainly thrift institutions. Purchases can be made directly from the issuer, but they are normally made through a dealer. The Ginnie Mae Mortgage-Backed Securities Dealers Association has more than 60 members including most of the large Wall Street investment bankers. Though the minimum denomination certificate is $25,000 of principal at issue, Wall Street trades are usually in blocks of $250,000 or $1 million. Dealers do trade in amounts as small as $25,000, however.

On the GNMA issues backed by single-family mortgages, the contract rate of the underlying mortgages is 50 basis points higher than the coupon rate shown on a GNMA pass-through security. The additional 50 basis points are retained by the mortgage servicer, who receives 44 basis points and pays the Government National Mortgage Association 6 basis points as an insurance fee for the government guarantee. The servicer of the underlying mortgages receives a fee higher than is usual for servicing agreements in the secondary mortgage market because the servicer must pay the scheduled interest and principal payments on the underlying mortgages to the holders of the GNMA pass-through securities, whether or not he actually receives those funds from the pool in a timely manner.

The investor in the GNMA pass-through security receives his pro rata share of the principal and interest payments accruing to the underlying mortgages in the pool. Adding to the appeal of GNMA pass-through securities is the fact that the "full faith and credit" of the U.S. Treasury guarantees that the principal and interest on these securities will be paid to investors on a timely basis. Technically, the GNMA pass-through is referred to as a "modified pass-through" security because payment to security holders is made whether or not the issuer receives his payment from the individual mortgagor. As a result, for all practical purposes the GNMA pass-through security is as safe an investment as a U.S. Treasury bond.

In addition to possessing a high degree of safety, GNMA pass-through securities are characterized by high marketability. This results from the high volume of these issues that is available in the market—over $58 billion of GNMA pass-through securities were outstanding at mid-1978—and the substantial trading in these issues. In some respects, the GNMA pass-through security is the premier mortgage-backed security in the capital market. It has the highest marketability and the greatest safety of all the available types of mortgage-backed securities.

Another desirable feature of the GNMA pass-through is that there

3: Investing in Mortgage-Backed Securities

is now an organized futures market in GNMAs which allows investors to hedge forward purchases and sales of GNMAs. This market, which was established by the Chicago Board of Trade, is one of the more active futures markets that have been established in recent years. The basic contract unit is a principal balance of $100,000 with a stated interest rate of 8 percent. GNMA pass-throughs with other face rates,

Exhibit 1

PROSPECTUS

$ _____

_____% *Modified Pass-Through Mortgage-Backed Securities (Single-Family Mortgages)*
FULLY GUARANTEED AS TO PRINCIPAL AND INTEREST
by
GOVERNMENT NATIONAL MORTGAGE ASSOCIATION
(Backed by the Full Faith and Credit of the United States)
Issued by

GNMA POOL NO.:   ISSUE DATE:
CUSTODIAN: FIRST PAYMENT DUE:
MINIMUM CERTIFICATE AMOUNT: MATURITY DATE:

The above information has been provided by Issuer. Government National Mortgage Association has prepared the balance of the information contained in this Prospectus.

The securities to be issued under this Prospectus provide for timely payment to the registered holder of interest at the specified rate plus scheduled installments of principal. These installments of interest and principal (adjustable) will commence on the 15th day of the month following the month of issue and will continue every month thereafter over the life of the mortgage pool, whether or not such principal and interest shall be collected by the Issuer.

> Timely payment of principal of and interest on the Securities is guaranteed by GNMA pursuant to Section 306(g) of Title III of the National Housing Act. Section 306(g) provides that "The full faith and credit of the United States is pledged to the payment of all amounts which may be required to be paid under any guaranty under this subsection" and an opinion dated December 9, 1969, of an Assistant Attorney General of the United States states that such guarantees under Section 306(g) of mortgage-backed securities of the type offered hereby "constitute general obligations of the United States backed by its full faith and credit."

The Certificates have not been registered under the Securities Act of 1933 since they are exempt from registration.

HUD-1717 (8-71)

however, are delivered in principal amounts which are equivalent to $100,000 of GNMA pass-throughs when calculated at par with an assumed 30-year amortization and a 12-year prepayment.

Prices are quoted as a percentage of par. Consequently, when the cash market yield is 8 percent, an expiring GNMA futures contract trades at about 100. As interest rates rise, the price of the contract falls, so that futures market yields tend to be in harmony with prevailing cash market yields. The minimum fluctuation in the contract price is $\frac{1}{32}$ of 1 percent of par, or $31.25 per contract. Traders can buy or sell contracts for any of four designated "delivery months"— March, July, September, and December.

The GNMA futures market enables mortgage investors to hedge their positions in the cash market. In so doing, they are able to guarantee the price yield of a GNMA pass-through that they contemplate buying or selling in the cash market.

The greatest problem associated with the GNMA pass-through security is the uncertainty regarding the prepayment experience of the underlying mortgages in the pool. It has become conventional in the secondary market for the yield on 30-year GNMA pass-through securities to be quoted as if they were prepaid in 12 years. That is, it is assumed that at the end of 12 years all unpaid principal will be fully paid off and that normal amortization of the mortgage will occur from the date of issue to the end of the 12-year period. Of course, these assumptions run counter to actual experience. Some of the underlying mortgages will prepay earlier than 12 years, thus negating the assumption of normal amortization during the first 12 years; and some of the mortgages will still be outstanding at the end of 12 years, thus negating the assumption of full prepayment of all mortgages at the end of 12 years. As a result, the yield obtained on GNMA pass-through securities can differ from the quoted yields to the extent that the actual prepayment experience does not conform to the assumed prepayment experience.

A copy of the first page of a GNMA pass-through prospectus is shown in Exhibit 1 on page 53.

FEDERAL HOME LOAN MORTGAGE CORPORATION PARTICIPATION CERTIFICATES

The FHLMC participation certificate is a mortgage-backed pass-through security that has many of the same attributes as the GNMA pass-through security. The major difference is that the underlying securities in the participation certificate pool consist of conventional whole loans and conventional loan participations underwritten and purchased by the Federal Home Loan Mortgage Corporation. Over 95 percent of the principal consists of conventional single-family loans; less than 5 percent consists of conventional multifamily loans.

The other major difference is that the FHLMC participation certificate does not include the "full faith and credit" provision of the GNMA pass-through security. The timely payment of interest and the repayment of all principal on participation certificates are guaranteed by the Federal Home Loan Mortgage Corporation, which is not quite as strong a guarantee as the "full faith and credit" protection of the GNMA pass-through security.

Another limitation of the participation certificates is that they are less marketable than the GNMA pass-through securities. This is largely because of the substantially lower volume of participation certificates that is available in the marketplace. Through mid-1978, $10.7 billion in participation certificates had been issued overall since the initial offering in November 1971. Although the volume has grown significantly in recent years, the volume of participation certificates traded in the marketplace is not nearly as great as that of the GNMA pass-through securities.

To encourage a secondary market in participation certificates, the FHLMC stands ready to buy back participation certificates from any holder, provided that the certificates have been registered to that holder for at least 60 days and that the repurchase totals no more than $5 million on any one day. The interest of securities dealers in trading participation certificates has grown, and today a group of dealers distribute all new issues and make a resale market for secondary issues. As a result, a smaller percentage of participation certificates are bought directly from or sold directly to FHLMC.

Yield quotes are available continuously. If a purchase order is made over the phone, a mailed confirmation should arrive within three days. Deferred delivery at the option of FHLMC entitles the purchaser to a commitment fee, depending on how long the deferral period is. Delivery in up to 29 days is considered immediate. As with GNMA pass-throughs, the exact settlement amount is not known until a few days before actual delivery.

The yields of participation certificates, like the yields of GNMA pass-throughs, are quoted on the assumption that the average loan life will be 12 years, which may or may not be reasonable. Thus, uncertainty over the "time" yield and cash flows are present in these investments because the investor receives his pro rata share of mortgage prepayments which do not necessarily conform to the 12-year prepayment assumption.

Because of the lesser guarantee and liquidity of the FHLMC participation certificates as compared to the GNMA pass-throughs, the participation certificates yield slightly higher interest rates than the pass-throughs.

FEDERAL HOME LOAN MORTGAGE CORPORATION GUARANTEED MORTGAGE CERTIFICATES

In February 1975, the Federal Home Loan Mortgage Corporation created a new instrument called the guaranteed mortgage certificate. The purpose of the guaranteed mortgage certificate (GMC) is to encourage institutional investors in the capital markets to purchase mortgage-secured instruments. The GMC was specifically designed to appeal to pension funds, trusts, and insurance companies that find that cash flow certainty and greater freedom from reinvestment problems makes corporate bonds more appealing than the mortgages. Because of the complexity of the GMC, the total amount issued through mid-1978 was only $1.8 billion.

The GMC represents an undivided interest in specific mortgages tailored so as to meet the requirements of institutional investors that dislike the servicing and origination costs and the inconvenience of the monthly principal and interest payments associated with mortgage investments. To do this, the GMC includes these provisions: (1) semiannual payments of interest and annual repayments of principal; (2) minimum annual principal reduction payments according to a predetermined schedule; (3) an unconditional guarantee by the Federal Home Loan Mortgage Corporation of interest payments to the extent of the certificate rate and of the full payment of the principal; and (4) where principal payments—prepayments—exceed the scheduled minimum amounts in a given year, published notice of the amount of principal that will be paid must be given not less than 25 days before principal payment date.

The GMCs have been offered in registered certificate form with initial principal amounts of $100,000, $500,000, and $1,000,000. The maturity of a GMC depends on the maturity of the underlying mortgages in the pool, though FHLMC stands ready to redeem the certificates for the amount of the unpaid principal balance of the underlying mortgages prior to the longest maturity of the mortgages. This latter feature is very appealing to investors, since it gives them the option, usually after 15 to 20 years, to sell the certificates back to the Federal Home Loan Mortgage Corporation for the amount of the unpaid principal of the underlying pool. The investor would be expected to exercise this option if alternative market interest rates exceeded the coupon rate on the GMCs, and vice versa.

The GMC provides the institutional investor with many of the desirable attributes of corporate bonds and fewer of the undesirable attributes of mortgages. Security dealers make a secondary market in GMC public issues. A copy of the first page of the prospectus of a recently issued GMC is shown in Exhibit 2.

3: Investing in Mortgage-Backed Securities

Exhibit 2

PROSPECTUS

$200,000,000

 Federal Home Loan Mortgage Corporation

Guaranteed Mortgage Certificates, Series B 1976

Dated: August 25, 1976   Certificate Rate: 8.375%

> Any Certificate holder may, at his option, require The Mortgage Corporation to purchase his Certificate on September 15, 1996, at the then unpaid principal balance thereof, plus accrued interest, if any. Certificates as to which this option is exercised will have a maximum average weighted life of 10.2 years. Certificates as to which the option is not exercised will have a maximum average weighted life of 10.9 years.

      Interest payable semi-annually each March 15 and September 15, commencing March 15, 1977. Annual principal reduction payable September 15, 1977, and annually thereafter. Fully registered Certificates in initial principal amounts of $100,000, $500,000 and $1,000,000.

      Price 99.125% plus accrued interest, if any, at the Certificate Rate from August 25, 1976

      The Guaranteed Mortgage Certificates ("Mortgage Certificates" or "Certificates") offered hereby will represent undivided interests in specified conventional mortgages and/or participations therein presently owned by the Federal Home Loan Mortgage Corporation ("The Mortgage Corporation" or "FHLMC"). (The aggregate of the undivided interests in such mortgages and participations to be represented by the Certificates are referred to herein as the "Mortgages".)

      FHLMC Guarantee: The Mortgage Corporation unconditionally guarantees payment of interest on the Mortgages to the extent of Certificate Rate and collection of principal on the Mortgages; unconditionally warrants return on the Mortgage Certificates at the Certificate Rate; and unconditionally warrants that until all principal on the Mortgages has been collected, payments of principal on the Mortgages will be sufficient to return to the holders of the Certificates the minimum annual principal reduction payments indicated below (expressed as percentages of the initial principal amounts of the Certificates):

SCHEDULE OF MINIMUM ANNUAL PRINCIPAL REDUCTION PAYMENTS

September 15	% of Initial Principal Amount	September 15	% of Initial Principal Amount	September 15	% of Initial Principal Amount	September 15	% of Initial Principal Amount	September 15	% of Initial Principal Amount
1977	7.5	1983	5.0	1989	3.0	1995	2.5	2001	1.5
1978	7.0	1984	4.5	1990	3.0	1996	2.0	2002	1.5
1979	6.5	1985	4.5	1991	2.5	1997	2.0	2003	1.5
1980	6.0	1986	4.5	1992	2.5	1998	2.0	2004	1.5
1981	6.0	1987	4.0	1993	2.5	1999	2.0	2005	1.0
1982	5.0	1988	3.5	1994	2.5	2000	1.5	2006	1.0

      Since principal payments on the Mortgages could exceed scheduled amounts in a given year, notice of the amount of principal to be paid to each Certificate holder will be published not less than 25 days before each principal payment date.

      Interest and principal reduction payments are payable by check to Certificate holders of record on the February 15 or August 15 next preceding the applicable payment date.

      More complete information regarding the Certificates appears under "Description of Mortgage Certificates" in this Prospectus.

      The Mortgage Certificates are not guaranteed by the United States and do not constitute a debt or obligation of the United States. Interest on the Certificates is not exempt from federal income taxes.

      The Mortgage Certificates do not constitute "qualifying real property loans" within the meaning of Section 593(e) of the Internal Revenue Code.

      The Certificates are not required to be registered under the Securities Act of 1933 and are "exempt securities" within the meaning of the Securities Exchange Act of 1934.

      The Mortgage Corporation has authorized the Office of Finance, Federal Home Loan Banks (Michael Mickett, Acting Director), 320 First Street, N.W., Washington, D. C. 20552 (Telephone 202/376-3485) to act as agent to arrange for the sale of the Mortgage Certificates. It is expected that delivery of Certificates against payment in Federal Funds will be made on or about August 25, 1976.

The date of this Prospectus is August 23, 1976.

PRIVATE ISSUE MORTGAGE-BACKED BONDS

Mortgage-backed and -secured debt instruments have been issued by private lending institutions, such as savings and loan associations and commercial banks. Savings and loan associations have been encouraged to do so by Federal Home Loan Bank Board regulations allowing them to issue mortgage-backed bonds.

A mortgage-backed bond is a debt security with fixed payments of interest and principal and a stated maturity. It differs from a corporate bond in that it is secured by the pledge of mortgage assets. It differs from a pass-through security in that it does not give its purchaser an undivided interest in the mortgage collateral. Unlike pass-through securities, mortgage-backed bonds pay interest twice yearly, and like corporate or government bonds, they return the principal in lump sums. Thus, the cash flow problem (and the problem of principal reinvestment) which falls on the holder of a pass-through security is transferred to the issuer.

Mortgage-backed bonds are a step further removed from the underlying mortgages than pass-through securities. A pool of mortgages serves as collateral, but the cash flow to the holder of the mortgage-backed bond does not depend on the cash flow from the mortgage pool. This is of some benefit to the issuer since older, lower-yielding mortgages can be used as collateral. On the other hand, since the market value of such mortgages is less than par, the pool must be overcollateralized. Because mortgages pay down, however, the pool must be overcollateralized in any event.

The Federal Home Loan Bank Board regulations stipulate that the mortgage-backed bond must have a minimum average life of five years and that the lenders cannot require that the borrowed money be repaid in amounts which exceed 20 percent of the original amount borrowed in any year. Any issue must call for at least five equal annual repayments of principal and must satisfy the average five-year requirement by having a final maturity that is not shorter than seven years. The bonds must have a minimum denomination of $100,000 unless they are sold through brokers and dealers registered with the Securities and Exchange Commission. In that case, they can be offered in denominations as low as $10,000.

The mortgage-backed bond differs from the other types of mortgage-backed securities in that the bondholder does not have a pro rata interest in the underlying mortgage assets. The safety of the mortgage-backed bond is determined in part by the quality and the type of the underlying collateral. The bond is an obligation of a regulated and insured financial institution, which also enhances its quality rating. The quality of the collateral is determined by the types of mortgage loans that make up the collateral—that is, commercial or apartment mortgages, one-four-family conventional mortgages, or one-four-family FHA/VA mortgages—and by the value of the collateral relative to the amount of the borrowing.

The bond-rating services frequently give ratings to mortgage-backed bonds which allow the purchaser to compare the safety of these bonds with that of corporate bonds. These ratings are a significant determinant of the relative interest cost on mortgage-backed bond issues. Standard & Poor's, a primary rating service for mortgage-backed bonds, regards the following as the most important criteria in its ratings: (1) the quality of the mortgages and the credit risk protection built into the pool, (2) the interest rate protection built into the pool, (3) the liquidity of the mortgages, (4) the general creditworthiness of the issuer and its ability to honor its commitment to the pool, and (5) the indenture terms. Most publicly issued mortgage-backed bonds have been granted the top AAA rating.

Mortgage-backed bonds may be offered by an institution through either public offerings or private placements. Large institutional investors are more likely to be interested in private placements, whereas small investors are more likely to be interested in public offerings. Clearly, the marketability of mortgage-backed bonds will be dictated by the size of the issue and the breadth of ownership. Dealers make a market in mortgage-backed bonds.

The popularity of mortgage-backed bonds increased significantly during the real estate recovery of 1975-78. Through mid-1978 an estimated $1.75 billion mortgage-backed bonds were publicly issued. During the same period, an estimated $650 million of mortgage-backed bonds were placed privately. A primary market for these issues has been pension funds, trusts, and insurance companies.

The marketability of mortgage-backed bonds varies significantly, since the size and type of offering for these securities is determined by the individual issuer's preferences. The overcollateralization of most mortgage-backed bonds and the fact that the issuer is a regulated and insured financial institution frequently results in high ratings by the rating services. Thus, yields on mortgage-backed bonds tend to be closer to higher grade corporate debt securities.

A copy of the offering circular summary of a recent mortgage-backed bond issue is shown in Exhibit 3.

PRIVATE ISSUE PASS-THROUGH CERTIFICATES

Unlike the private issue mortgage-backed bond, the private issue pass-through certificate involves pro rata ownership in a specific mortgage pool similar to that of the GNMA pass-through security and the FHLMC participation certificate. The principal difference between the private issue pass-through certificate and the GNMA pass-through or the FHLMC participation certificate is that the private issue pass-through involves no governmental "full faith and credit" or FHLMC guarantee. In some instances, however, the private issue pass-through certificate may include private mortgage insurance coverage on some of its underlying mortgages and/or a blanket pri-

Exhibit 3
Mortgage-Backed Bonds

<table>
<tr><td colspan="2" align="center">Offering Circular Summary
The Bonds</td></tr>
<tr><td>Issuer</td><td>California Federal Savings and Loan Association.</td></tr>
<tr><td>Type of security</td><td>Mortgage-backed bonds.</td></tr>
<tr><td>Amount</td><td>$50,000,000.</td></tr>
<tr><td>Rate of interest</td><td>$9\frac{1}{8}$ percent per annum.</td></tr>
<tr><td>Maturity</td><td>July 15, 1985.</td></tr>
<tr><td>Redemption</td><td>Redeemable in whole or in part at the option of the Association on or after July 15, 1982, at 100% plus accrued interest.</td></tr>
<tr><td>Collateral</td><td>Mortgage notes, either FHA insured or VA guaranteed, secured by deeds of trust (mortgages) on 1 to 4 family dwellings in California. The initial collateral consist of approximately 4,600 such mortgage notes having an aggregate unpaid principal balance of approximately $110,000,000, an average remaining term to maturity of 27 years and a nominal interest rate of 7% per annum.</td></tr>
<tr><td>Discounted value of collateral</td><td>Initially and at least semiannually thereafter, the mortgage notes will be valued on a discounted basis using a discount rate related to certain prevailing mortgage market yields. The initial discount rate is 10.00%.</td></tr>
<tr><td>Initial amount of collateral</td><td>The discounted value of the mortgage notes constituting the initial collateral will not be less than $87,500,000, equal to 175% of the aggregate principal amount of the Series A Bonds to be outstanding.</td></tr>
<tr><td>Maintenance of collateral</td><td>In the event the discounted value of the mortgage notes declines less than 135% of the principal amount of Series A Bonds outstanding on any semiannual valuation date before June 30, 1983, the Association will deposit sufficient additional collateral (which may include government securities) to restore the discounted value thereof to the 135% level, subject to certain regulatory limitations. The required maintenance level will increase to 140% for the period beginning on June 30, 1983, and to 150% for the period beginning on June 30, 1984.</td></tr>
<tr><td>Use of proceeds</td><td>Principally to make loans to finance the construction and purchase of residential properties.</td></tr>
</table>

Source: Printed with the permission of California Federal Savings and Loan Association.

vate mortgage insurance coverage on some portion of the initial aggregate principal amount of the mortgage loans in the pool.

The safety of the pass-through certificate is directly related to the underlying mortgages represented in the mortgage pool. Here the investor will be concerned with the number of mortgages, the average size of the mortgages, the location of the mortgaged properties, the age of the mortgages, and the governmental jurisdiction within which the mortgaged properties are located. All of these factors will affect the default risk, the loan-life, and the prepayment characteristics of the underlying assets.

Apart from the differences noted above between the private issue pass-through certificate and the GNMA pass-through and FHLMC participation certificate, the attributes of private issue pass-through certificates are roughly comparable to those of the GNMA pass-through and the FHLMC participation certificate. Since the pass-through certificate is offered to the investor through a public offering or a private placement, the specific attributes of the issue (size, minimum investment, interest rate, and marketability) will all be dependent on the prospectus stipulations. As with the other pass-through securities, the actual maturity and cash flows will be uncertain, due to the uncertain prepayment experience of the underlying mortgages.

It is too early to assess the general marketability and the relative yields of private issue pass-through certificates. The first issue was offered in 1977. Through mid-1978, a total of $650 million were issued. Securities dealers can be expected to make markets in larger issues.

A summary of a prospectus for a recent public offering of a private issue mortgage-backed pass-through certificate is shown in Exhibit 4.

Exhibit 4

Summary of Prospectus

Title of security	Mortgage-backed pass-through certificates, issuable in series.
Originator and servicer of mortgage loans ...	Bank of America National Trust and Savings Asociation.
Description of security ..	Each certificate represents a fractional undivided interest in one of a number of mortgage pools to be formed by the bank from time to time. A single certificate will initially represent a minimum investment of approximately $25,000. The certificates will be offered in such minimum amounts, or integral multiples thereof, in fully registered form only.
Interest	Passed through monthly at the pass-through rate applicable to each series of certificates, commencing on the 25th day of the month following the month of initial issuance of such certificates. See "Yield Considerations" and "Description of the Certificates."

Exhibit 4 *(concluded)*

Principal (including prepayments)	Passed through monthly, commencing on the 25th day of the month following the month of initial issuance of each series of certificates. See "Maturity and Prepayment Assumptions" and "Description of the Certificates."
The mortgage pools . . .	Pools of conventional fixed-rate mortgage loans secured by single-family residential properties in California, with a loan-to-value ratio at origination (based on the bank's appraisal of the mortgaged property) of 80% or less. Mortgage pools may be formed from time to time in varying sizes, but no mortgage pool will contain less than $5,000,000 aggregate principal amount of mortgage loans. See "The Mortgage Pools."
Mortgage guaranty insurance	Neither the certificates nor the underlying mortgage loans are insured or guaranteed by any governmental agency. The bank will obtain a mortgage guaranty insurance policy for each mortgage pool, limited in scope, covering defaults on the underlying mortgage loans in such pool in an amount equal to 5% of the initial aggregate principal balances thereof. See "Description of Insurance."
Hazard insurance	All of the mortgage loans will be covered by standard hazard insurance policies insuring against losses due to various causes, including fire, lightning, and windstorm. Certain other physical risks which are not otherwise insured against (including earthquakes, mud flows, and floods) will be covered by a special hazard insurance policy to be obtained with respect to each mortgage pool, limited in scope and amount. With respect to each mortgage pool, any hazard losses not covered by either the standard hazard policies or the special hazard insurance policy will not be insured against and will therefore be borne by the holders of certificates of the series evidencing such mortgage pool. See "Description of Insurance."
Tax status	Certificates owned by a "domestic building and loan association" will be considered to represent "loans secured by an interest in real property" within the meaning of Section 7701(a)(19)(C)(v) of the Internal Revenue Code and to represent "qualifying real property loans" within the meaning of Section 593(d) of the Code. See "Tax Aspects."

The foregoing summary is qualified in its entirety by reference to the detailed information appearing elsewhere in this prospectus, and by reference to detailed information with respect to each mortgage pool contained in the supplement to this prospectus to be prepared in connection with each series of certificates.

Source: Bank of America National Trust and Savings Association.

INDUSTRIAL DEVELOPMENT MORTGAGE BONDS

The industrial development mortgage bond is one of the most complicated and least known of the mortgage-backed securities. This bond is an adaptation of the industrial revenue bond. Revenue bonds are limited obligations of political subdivisions of states. They are not, however, backed by the taxing authority of a state or its subdivision. Rather, they are issued by a public body in order to finance private projects and they are secured exclusively by the revenues derived from these projects. Industrial development mortgage bonds involve close cooperation between the investor, the business or industrial issuer, and the state government agency. They are essentially nothing more than a commercial mortgage repackaged into a bond debt instrument.

The interest payments accruing to each type of mortgage-backed security that we have discussed thus far are subject to federal income taxes. The industrial development mortgage bond, by contrast, is tax exempt for federal tax purposes, much like any other state and municipal revenue bond. The tax-exempt status of the industrial development mortgage bond arises where the state has developed a municipal industrial development corporation and uses that corporation to promote commerce and industry and "serve a public purpose." This has generally been interpreted to include shopping centers, industrial parks, warehouses, hospitals, colleges, and arenas, all of which have been financed with industrial development mortgage bonds.

The industrial development mortgage bond is a revenue bond secured by a three-party mortgage. Normally, the mortgagee is the political subdivision which issues the bond, granting it tax-exempt status under Section 103 of the Internal Revenue Code. The commercial or industrial firm and the political subdivision enter into a long-term net lease agreement containing an option to purchase, or into a long-term installment sale contract. The issuer then sells its debt obligation to an underwriter or through a private placement. Typically, the bond is secured by an indenture of mortgage and trust and further secured by an assignment to the lender of the net lease or the installment purchase contract. Once the transaction is completed, the mortgage lender has a first lien on the real estate security.

It is virtually impossible to generalize as to the characteristics of industrial development mortgage bonds. The legal documents needed to perfect the tax-exempt transactions are extremely complex. Basically, the municipality acts initially as a funds conduit between the developer and the lender; and later it acts as a funds conduit between the tenants—under a net lease—and the lender. By performing this role, the municipality can shelter the transaction under its own tax exemption. As a result of this relationship between the municipality and the investor, the investor acquires Municipal Industrial Development Act bonds rather than the mortgage note. However, this difference is somewhat cosmetic since the municipality normally assigns the mortgage loan to the lender as security to cover the bonds. Thus, the holder of the industrial development mortgage bond receives first-lien protection on his investment.

Because the major advantage of the industrial development mortgage bond is its tax-exempt status, careful thought and study are essential before investments are made in such debt instruments. Investors in industrial development mortgage bonds normally require additional protection against the unforeseen elimination of the tax-exempt status of the bond. This can take the form of a clause requiring that in the event that tax-exempt status is lost, the return on the bond be increased to an acceptable taxable equivalent rate or that the bond be called.

The marketability of industrial development mortgage bonds suffers from the highly specialized status of these securities, their generally small issue amounts, and their lack of homogeneity. As a result, they are among the highest yielding tax-exempt securities.

SUMMARY

Recent innovations in mortgage instruments have led to substantial integration of the mortgage and bond markets. These new mortgage instruments have been successful in attracting funds from investment sources not historically tapped by the mortgage borrower. This success dates back to the successful efforts of the federal government in developing the GNMA pass-through security. The specific investment attributes of this instrument provided the basis for other innovations.

The primary innovations of the GNMA pass-through program include the concept of mortgage pooling, the use of insurance and guarantees, the development of mortgage loan servicing arrangements, and the development of an active secondary market to enhance the liquidity of these instruments. Other innovations have built on these accomplishments.

Exhibit 5 summarizes the major investment information relating to mortgage-backed and -secured debt instruments. It is clear from the exhibit that these securities offer appealing investment possibilities for many institutional investors.

Looking to the future, it seems clear that the innovations of the last decade represent only the beginning of more far-reaching changes that can be expected to take place. Because mortgage-backed securities are relatively new to the investment markets, the investor must be aware of the likelihood that additional instruments will be developed and that modifications of the investment characteristics of the existing instruments will be made.

Exhibit 5
The Basic Investment Characteristics of Mortgage-Backed Securities

	GNMA Pass-Through Security	*FHLMC Participation Certificate*	*FHLMC Guaranteed Mortgage Certificate*
Issuer or originator	FHA-approved mortgagee with GNMA approval.	Federal Home Loan Mortgage Corporation.	Federal Home Loan Mortgage Corporation.
Seller	Typically a securities dealer, mortgage banker, or financial institution.	Federal Home Loan Mortgage Corporation or any holder.	Federal Home Loan Mortgage Corporation. Public issues handled through investment banking companies.
Type of security	Share in a pool of FHA or VA mortgages—usually one-four-family loans of similar interest rate and maturity. Minimum pool size is $1 million for one-four-family pools.	Undivided interest in a pool of conventional whole loans or participations underwritten and purchased initially by FHLMC. A typical pool consists of 2,000 to 5,000 mortgages with unpaid principal of $100 million. At least 95 percent of the principal is in single-family loans.	Undivided interest in a pool of specified conventional mortgages and/or participations owned by FHLMC.
Term to maturity	Term of pool usually 30 years for one-four-family pools. Actual maturity subject to loan-life experience of underlying mortgages.	Term of pool determined by maturity of longest maturity mortgage in the pool, usually 30 years. Actual maturity subject to loan-life experience of underlying mortgages.	Term of pool is determined by maturity of longest maturity mortgages in pool, usually 30 years. FHLMC will redeem the GMC prior to maturity, usually after 20 years, at the then unpaid principal balance of the underlying mortgages.
Denomination or typical size	$25,000 minimum denomination in multiples of $5,000. Most securities dealer trades are $250,000 and up.	$100,000, $200,000, $500,000, and $1,000,000.	$100,000, $500,000, and $1,000,000.
Tax status	No preferred tax status.	No preferred tax status.	No preferred tax status.
Relative yield	Generally the highest yielding government security.	Set by FHLMC, generally above comparable GNMA yield.	Comparable to that of high-grade corporation bonds.

Exhibit 5 (concluded)

	GNMA Pass-Through Security	FHLMC Participation Certificate	FHLMC Guaranteed Mortgage Certificate
Guarantee and safety	Backed by the full faith and credit of the U.S. government. Prompt payment of principal and interest guaranteed even if not collected. Prepayments passed through to holders.	Mortgage Corporation guarantees timely payment of interest and repayment of all principal. Prepayments are passed through to holders.	Mortgage Corporation unconditionally guarantees collection of principal and payment of interest to the extent of the certificate rate; unconditionally warrants return on the mortgage certificates at the certificate rate; and unconditionally warrants that until all principal on the mortgages has been collected, payments of principal will be sufficient to return to the holders of the certificates the minimum annual principal reduction payments.
Marketability	Extremely liquid. Securities dealers make a market in GNMAs. More than $1 billion traded monthly.	Freely transferable, and securities dealers make a market in PCs. FHLMC will purchase PCs subject to certain conditions. Bid prices typically one-half point or less below offer price.	Secondary market available for larger public issues through various securities dealers.

	Private Issue Pass-Through Certificate	Private Issue Mortgage-Backed Bond	Industrial Development Mortgage Bond
Issuer or originator	Financial institutions or other holders of mortgages.	Savings and loan associations.	Municipal industrial development corporation.
Seller	For private placement, an investment banker. For a public offering, an SEC-registered dealer.	For private placement, investment banker. For public offering, SEC-registered broker.	Issuer sells its debt obligation to underwriter or privately places it with financial institution pursuant to a bond purchase agreement.

Type of security	Undivided interest in a pool of specified FHA/VA or conventional mortgages. Some conventional mortgages may be privately insured, or a blanket insurance coverage may be used.	Regular bond collateralized by mortgage pool whose principal normally exceeds by a significant amount the amount of the bond issue.	Municipal bond backed by first lien on real estate. Pays down like mortgage.
Term to maturity	Maturity will depend on the maturity of the underlying mortgages in the pool, usually 30 years.	Depends on issue. Usually noncallable for a period of time.	Coincides with mortgage life on underlying real estate.
Denomination or typical size	Depends on issue.	$10,000 minimum if sold via brokers; otherwise large institutional size.	Depends on issue.
Tax status	No preferred tax status.	Subject to all federal and state taxes.	Exempt from federal taxes.
Relative yield	Somewhat above GNMA pass-through securities and FHLMC participation certificates.	Dependent on bond rating.	Depends on issue.
Guarantee and safety	No guarantee. May include a blanket coverage of some proportion of principal by a private mortgage insurer.	No guarantee, but collateral usually FHA/VA guaranteed and sometimes privately issued conventional loans. Issuers are government-regulated and deposit-insured institutions.	None; not a general obligation of the municipality. This revenue bond is secured by an indenture of mortgage or trust and by an assignment of the net lease or the installment purchase contract by the commercial or industrial firm.
Marketability	Secondary market is available for larger public issues through various securities dealers.	Large public issues traded by securities dealers.	No organized market. Dealers may make markets in large issues.

Guidelines in the Credit Analysis of General Obligation and Revenue Municipal Bonds

4

SYLVAN G. FELDSTEIN, Ph.D.*
Vice President and Bond Analyst
Moody's Investors Service

INTRODUCTION

Although historically the degree of safety of investing in municipal bonds has been considered second only to that of U.S. Treasury bonds, beginning in the 1970s there has developed among many investors and underwriters ongoing concerns about the potential default risks of municipal bonds.

The First Influence: Defaults and Bankruptcies

One concern resulted from the well-publicized, billion-dollar general obligation note defaults in 1975 of New York City. Not only were specific investors threatened with the loss of their principal, but also the defaults sent a loud and clear warning to municipal bond investors in general. That warning was that regardless of the supposedly ironclad legal protections for the bondholder, when issuers, such

---

*This reading was written while the author was vice president and analyst at Smith Barney, Harris Upham & Co., Inc. The views expressed here are those of the author and not necessarily those of Moody's Investors Service.

as large cities, have severe budget-balancing difficulties, the political hues, cries, and financial interests of public employee unions, vendors, and community groups may be dominant forces in the initial decision-making process.

This reality was further reinforced by the new federal bankruptcy law, which took effect on October 1, 1979, and which makes it easier for municipal bond issuers to seek protection from bondholders by filing for bankruptcy. One by-product of the increased investor concern is that since 1975 the official statement, which is the counterpart to a prospectus in an equity or corporate bond offering and which is to contain a summary of the key legal and financial security features, has become more comprehensive. As an example, prior to 1975 it was common for a City of New York official statement to be only 6 pages long, whereas for a bond sale in 1981 it was close to 100 pages long.

The Second Influence: Strong Investor Demand for Tax Exemption

The second reason for the increased interest in credit analysis was derived from the changing nature of the municipal bond market. For most of the decade of the 1970s, the municipal bond market was characterized by strong buying patterns by both private investors and institutions. The patterns were caused in part by high federal, state, and local income tax rates. Additionally, as inflation pushed many investors into higher and higher income tax brackets, tax-exempt bonds increasingly became an important and convenient way for sheltering income. One corollary of the strong buyers' demand for tax exemption has been an erosion of the traditional security provisions and bondholder safeguards that had grown out of the default experiences of the 1930s. General obligation bond issuers with high tax and debt burdens, declining local economies, and chronic budget-balancing problems had little difficulty finding willing buyers. Also, revenue bonds increasingly were rushed to market with legally untested security provisions, modest rate covenants, reduced debt reserves, and weak additional-bonds tests. Because of this widespread weakening of security provisions, it has become more important than ever before that the prudent investor carefully evaluate the creditworthiness of a municipal bond before making a purchase.

In analyzing the creditworthiness of either a general obligation or revenue bond, the investor should cover five categories of inquiry. They are questions related to (1) legal documents and opinions, (2) politics/management, (3) underwriter/financial advisor, (4) general credit indicators and economics, and (5) red flags, or danger signals.

The purpose of this chapter is to set forth the general guidelines that the investor should rely upon in asking questions about specific bonds.

THE LEGAL OPINION

The popular notion is that much of the legal work done in a bond issue is boiler plate in nature, but from the bondholder's point of view the legal opinions and document reviews should be the ultimate security provisions. This is because, if all else fails, the bondholder may have to go to court to enforce his or her security rights. Therefore, the integrity and competency of the lawyers who review the documents and write the legal opinions that usually are summarized and stated in the official statements are very important.

The relationship of the legal opinion to the analysis of municipal bonds for both general obligation and revenue bonds is threefold. First, the lawyer should check to determine if the issuer is indeed legally able to issue the bonds. Second, the lawyer is to see that the issuer has properly prepared for the bond sale by having enacted the various required ordinances, resolutions, and trust indentures and without violating any other laws and regulations. This preparation is particularly important in the highly technical areas of determining whether the bond issue is qualified for tax exemption under federal law and whether the issue has not been structured in such a way so as to violate federal arbitrage regulations. Third, the lawyer is to certify that the security safeguards and remedies provided for the bondholders and pledged either by the bond issuer or by third parties, such as banks with letter-of-credit agreements, are actually supported by federal, state, and local government laws and regulations.

General Obligation Bonds

General obligation bonds are debt instruments issued by states, counties, towns, cities, and school districts. They are secured by the issuers' general taxing powers. The investor should review the legal documents and opinion as summarized in the official statement to determine what specific *unlimited* taxing powers, such as those on real estate and personal property, corporate and individual income taxes, and sales taxes, are legally available to the issuer, if necessary, to pay the bondholders. Usually for smaller governmental jurisdictions, such as school districts and towns, the only available unlimited taxing power is on property. If there are statutory or constitutional taxing power limitations, the legal documents and opinion should clearly describe how they impact the security for the bonds.

For larger general obligation bond issuers, such as states and big cities that have diverse revenue and tax sources, the legal opinion should indicate the claim of the general obligation bondholder on the issuer's general fund. Does the bondholder have a legal claim, if necessary, to the first revenues coming into the general fund? This is the case with bondholders of state of New York general obligation bonds. Does the bondholder stand second in line? This is the case with bondholders of state of California general obligation bonds. Or are the laws silent on the question altogether? This is the case for most other state and local governments.

Additionally, certain general obligation bonds, such as those for water and sewer purposes, are secured in the first instance by user charges and then by the general obligation pledge. (Such bonds are popularly known as being double barreled.) If so, the legal documents and opinion should state how the bonds are secured by revenues and funds outside the issuer's general taxing powers and general fund.

Revenue Bonds

Revenue bonds are issued for either project or enterprise financings that are secured by the revenues generated by the completed projects themselves, or for general public-purpose financings in which the issuers pledge to the bondholders tax and revenue resources that were previously part of the general fund. This latter type of revenue bond is usually created to allow issuers to raise debt outside general obligation debt limits and without voter approvals. The trust indenture and legal opinion for both types of revenue bonds should provide the investor with legal comfort in six bond-security areas:

1. The limits of the basic security.
2. The flow-of-funds structure.
3. The rate, or user-charge, covenant.
4. The priority-of-revenue claims.
5. The additional-bonds test.
6. Other relevant covenants.

Limits of the Basic Security. The trust indenture and legal opinion should explain what are the revenues for the bonds and how they realistically may be limited by federal, state, and local laws and procedures. The importance of this is that although most revenue bonds are structured and appear to be supported by identifiable revenue streams, those revenues sometimes can be negatively impacted directly by other levels of government. As an example, the Mineral Royalties Revenue Bonds that the state of Wyoming sold in December 1981 have most of the attributes of revenue bonds. The bonds have a first lien on the pledged revenues, and additional bonds can only be issued if a coverage test of 125 percent is met. Yet the basic revenues, themselves, are monies received by the state from the federal government as royalty payments for mineral production on federal lands. The U.S. Congress is under no legal obligation to continue this aid program. Therefore the legal opinion as summarized in the official statement must clearly delineate this shortcoming of the bond security. The uncertainty of future Congressional actions in the areas of taxation and local government aid clearly make this requirement necessary.

Flow-of-Funds Structure. The trust indenture and legal opinion should explain what the bond issuer has promised to do concerning the revenues received. What is the order of the revenue flows through the various accounting funds of the issuer to pay for the operating expenses of the facility, to provide for payments to the bondholders, to provide for maintenance and special capital improvements, and to provide for debt-service reserves. Additionally, the trust indenture and legal opinion should indicate what happens to excess revenues if they exceed the various annual fund requirements.

The flow of funds of most revenue bonds is structured as *net revenues* (i.e., debt service is paid to the bondholders immediately after revenues are paid to the basic operating and maintenance funds, but before paying all other expenses). A *gross revenues* flow-of-funds structure is one in which the bondholders are to be paid even before the operating expenses of the facility are paid. Examples of gross revenue bonds are those issued by the New York City Metropolitan Transportation Authority. However, although it is true that these bonds legally have a claim to the fare-box revenues before all other claimants, it is doubtful that the system could function if the operational expenses, such as wages and electricity bills, were not paid first.

Rate, or User-Charge, Covenants. The trust indenture and legal opinion should indicate what the issuer has legally committed itself to do to safeguard the bondholders. Do the rates charged only have to be sufficient to meet expenses, including debt service, or do they have to be set and maintained at higher levels so as to provide for reserves? The legal opinion should also indicate whether or not the issuer has the legal power to increase rates or charges upon users without having to obtain prior approvals by other governmental units.

Priority of Revenue Claims. The legal opinion as summarized in the official statement should clearly indicate whether or not others can legally tap the revenues of the issuer even before they start passing through the issuer's flow-of-funds structure. An example would be the Highway Revenue Bonds issued by the Puerto Rico Highway Authority. These bonds are secured by the revenues from the Commonwealth of Puerto Rico gasoline tax. However, under the commonwealth's constitution, the revenues are first subject to being applied to the commonwealth government's own general obligation bonds if no other funds are available for them.

Additional-Bonds Test. The trust indenture and legal opinion should indicate under what circumstances the issuer can issue additional bonds that share equal claims to the issuer's revenues. Usually, the legal requirement is that the maximum annual debt service on the new bonds as well as on the old bonds be covered by the projected net revenues by a specified minimum amount. This can be as low as one times coverage. Some revenue bonds have stronger additional-bonds tests to protect the bondholders. As an example, the state of Florida Orlando-Orange County Expressway Bonds have an additional-bonds test that is twofold. First, under the Florida constitution the previous year's *pledged historical revenues* must equal at least 1.33 times maximum annual debt service on the outstanding and to-be-issued bonds. Second, under the original trust indenture *projected revenues* must provide at least 1.50 times estimated maximum annual debt service on the outstanding and to-be-issued bonds.

Other Relevant Covenants. Lastly, the trust indenture and legal opinion should indicate whether there are other relevant covenants for the bondholder's protection. These usually include pledges by the issuer of the bonds to have insurance on the project (if it is a project-financing revenue bond), to have the accounting records of the issuer annually audited by an outside certified public accountant, to have outside engineers annually review the condition of the capital plant, and to keep the facility operating for the life of the bonds.

In addition to the above aspects of the specific revenue structures of general obligation and revenue bonds, two other developments over the recent past make it more important than ever that the legal documents and opinions summarized in the official statements be carefully reviewed by the investor. The first development involves the mushrooming of new financing techniques that may rest on legally untested security structures. The second development is the increased use of legal opinions provided by local attorneys who may have little prior municipal bond experience. Legal opinions have traditionally been written by recognized municipal bond attorneys.

Legally Untested Security Structures and New Financing Techniques

In addition to the more traditional general obligation bonds, toll road, bridge and tunnel revenue bonds, there are now more nonvoter-approved, innovative, and legally untested security mechanisms. These innovative financing mechanisms include lease-rental bonds, moral obligation housing bonds, take-and-pay power bonds with step-up provisions requiring the participants to increase payments to make up for those that may default, medicaid-backed hospital bonds, commercial bank-backed letter of credit "put" bonds, and tax-exempt commercial paper. What distinguishes these newer bonds from the more traditional general obligation and revenue bonds is that they have no history of court decisions and other case law to firmly protect the rights of the bondholders. For the newer financing mechanisms, the legal opinion should include an assessment of the probable outcome if the bond security were challenged in court. It should be noted, however, that in most official statements this is not provided to the investor.

The Need for Reliable Legal Opinions

For many years before the 1970s, concern over the reliability of the legal opinion was not as important as it is now. As the result of the numerous bond defaults and related shoddy legal opinions in the 19th century, the investment community demanded that legal documents and opinions be written by recognized municipal bond attorneys. As a consequence, over the years a small group of primarily Wall Street-based law firms and certain recognized firms in other financial centers dominated the industry and developed high standards of professionalism.

In the 1970s, however, more and more issuers began to have their legal work done by local law firms, some of whom had little experience in municipal bond work. This development, along with the introduction of more innovative and legally untested financing mechanisms, has created a greater need for reliable legal opinions. An example of a specific concern involves the documents the issuers' lawyers must complete so as to avoid arbitrage problems with the Internal Revenue Service. Legal opinions written entirely by unknown law firms in a few instances raise questions for the investor. On negotiated bond issues, one remedy has been for the underwriters to have their own counsels review the documents and to provide separate legal opinions. If the bond has come to market through a competitive sale, the prudent investor or analyst should carefully review the legal opinion and bond or note indenture before making a conclusion.

THE NEED TO KNOW WHO *REALLY* IS THE ISSUER

Still another general question to ask before purchasing a municipal bond is just what kind of people are the issuers? Are they conscientious public servants with clearly defined public goals? Do they have histories of successful management of public institutions? Have they demonstrated commitments to professional and fiscally stringent operations? Additionally, issuers in highly charged and partisan environments in which conflicts chronically occur between political parties and/or among factions or personalities within the governing bodies are clearly bond issuers to scrutinize closely, and possibly to avoid. Such issuers should be scrutinized regardless of the strength of the surrounding economic environment.

For General Obligation Bonds

For general obligation bond issuers the focus is on the political relationships that exist on the one hand among chief executives, such as mayors, county executives, and governors, and on the other hand their legislative counterparts. Issuers with unstable political elites are of particular concern. Of course, rivalry among political actors is not necessarily bad. What is undesirable is competition so bitter and personal that real cooperation among the warring public officials in addressing future budgetary problems may be precluded. An example of an issuer that was avoided because of such dissension is the city of Cleveland. The political problems of the city in 1978 and the bitter conflicts between Mayor Kucinich and the city council resulted in a general obligation note default in December of that year.

For Revenue Bonds

When investigating revenue bond issuers, it is important to determine not only the degree of political conflict, if any, that exists among the members of the bond-issuing body, but also the relationships and conflicts among those who make the appointments to the body. Additionally, the investor should determine whether the issuer of the revenue bond has to seek prior approval from another governmental jurisdiction before the user-fees or other charges can be levied. If this is the case, then the stability of the political relationships between the two units of government must be determined.

An example of the importance of this information can be seen when reviewing the creditworthiness of the water and electric utility revenue bonds and notes issued by Kansas City, Kansas. Although the revenue bonds and notes were issued by city hall, it was the six-member board of public utilities, a separately elected body, that had the power to set the water and electricity utility rates. In the spring of 1981, because of political dissension among the board members caused by a political struggle between a faction on the board of public utilities and the city commissioners (including the city's finance commissioner), the board refused to raise utility rates as required by the covenant. As a result of the political conflict and confusion, the ratings of the revenue bonds and notes were suspended by both Moody's and Standard & Poor's. The situation only came under control when a new election changed the makeup of the board in favor of those supported by city hall.

In addition to the above institutional and political concerns, for revenue bond issuers in particular an assessment of the technical and managerial abilities of the staff should be made. The professional competency of the staff is a more critical factor in revenue bond analysis than it is in the analysis of general obligation bonds. This is because unlike general obligation bonds, which are secured in the final instance by the full faith and credit and unlimited taxing powers of the issuers, many revenue bonds are secured by the ability of the revenue projects to be operational and financially self-supporting.

The professional staffs of authorities that issue revenue bonds for the construction of nuclear and other public power-generating facilities, apartment complexes, hospitals, water and sewer systems, and other large public works projects, such as convention centers and sports arenas, should be carefully reviewed. Issuers who have histories of high management turnovers, project cost overruns, or little experience should be avoided by the conservative investor, or at least considered higher risks than their assigned credit ratings may indicate. Moreover, it is helpful but not mandatory if revenue bond issuers have their accounting records annually audited by outside certified public accountants, so as to ensure the investor of a more accurate picture of the issuer's financial health.

ON THE FINANCIAL ADVISOR AND UNDERWRITER

Shorthand indications of the quality of the investment are (1) who the issuer selected as its financial advisor, if any, (2) its principal underwriter if the bond sale was negotiated, and (3) its financial advisor if the bond issue came to market competitively. Additionally, since 1975 many prudent underwriters will not bid on competitive bond issues if there are significant credit-quality concerns. Therefore, it is also useful to learn who was the underwriter for the competitive bond sales as well.

Identifying the financial advisors and underwriters is important for two reasons.

The Need for Complete, Not Just Adequate, Investment Risk Disclosures

The first reason relates to the quality and thoroughness of information provided to the investor by the issuer. The official statement, or private placement papers if the issue is placed privately, is usually prepared with the assistance of lawyers and a financial advisor or by the principal underwriter. There are industry-wide disclosure guidelines that are generally adhered to, but not all official statements provide the investor with complete discussions of the risk potentials that may result from either the specific economics of the project or the community settings and the operational details of the security provisions. It is usually the author of this document who decides what to either emphasize or downplay in the official statement. The more professional and established the experience of the author to provide the investor with unbiased and complete information about the issuer, the more comfortable the investor can be with information provided by the issuer and in arriving at a credit-quality conclusion.

The Importance of Firm Reputation for Thoroughness and Integrity

By itself, the reputation of the issuer's financial advisor and/or underwriter should not be the determinant credit-quality factor, but it is a fact the investor should consider. This is particularly the case for marginally feasible bond issues that have complex flow-of-funds and security structures. The securities industry is unique as compared with other industries, such as real estate, in that trading and investment commitments are usually made verbally over the phone with a paper trail following days later. Many institutional investors, such as banks, bond funds, and casualty insurance companies, have learned to judge issuers by the "company" they keep. Institutions tend to be conservative, and they are more comfortable with financial information provided by established financial advisors and underwriters who have recognized reputations for honesty. Individual investors and analysts would do well to adopt this approach as well.

GENERAL CREDIT INDICATORS AND ECONOMIC FACTORS

The last analytical factor is the health or viability of the economics of the bond issuer or specific project financed by the bond proceeds. The economics cover a variety of concerns. When analyzing general obligation bond issuers, one should look at the specific budgetary and debt characteristics of the issuer as well as the general economic environment. For project-financing, or enterprise, revenue bonds, the economics are primarily limited to the ability of the project to generate sufficient charges upon the users to pay the bondholders. These are known as pure revenue bonds.

For those revenue bonds that rely not upon user charges and fees, but instead upon general purpose taxes and revenues, the analysis should take basically the same approach as for general obligation bonds. For these bonds the taxes and revenues diverted to the bondholders would otherwise have gone to the state's or city's general fund.

As examples of such bonds, the New York State Municipal Assistance Corporation for the City of New York Bonds (MAC), secured by general New York City sales taxes and annual state-aid appropriations, and the state of Illinois Chicago School Finance Authority Bonds, secured by unlimited property taxes levied within the city of Chicago, are bonds structured to appear as pure revenue bonds; but in essence they are not. They both incorporate bond structures created to bail out the former, New York City, and the latter, Chicago's board of education, from severe budget deficits. The creditworthiness of these bonds is tied to that of their underlying jurisdictions, which have given or have had portions of their taxing powers and general fund revenues diverted to secure the new revenue-type bailout bonds. Besides looking at the revenue features, the investor therefore must look at the underlying jurisdictions as well.

For General Obligation Bonds

For general obligation bonds, the economics include asking questions and obtaining answers in four specific areas: debt burden, budget soundness, tax burden, and the overall economy.

Debt Burden. Concerning the debt burden of the general obligation bond issuer, some of the more important concerns include the determination of the total amount of debt outstanding and to be issued that is supported by the general taxing powers of the issuer as well as by earmarked revenues. Those general obligation bonds that are secured additionally by earmarked revenues outside the issuer's general taxes are referred to by municipal bond analysts as self-supporting.

For example, general obligation bonds issued by school districts in New York State and certain general obligation bonds issued by the city of New York are general obligations of the issuer and are also secured by state aid to education payments due the issuer. If the issuer defaults, the bondholder can go to the state comptroller and be made whole from the next state-aid payment due the local issuer. An example of another earmarked revenue general obligation bond is the state of Illinois General Obligation Transportation, Series A Bonds. Besides being state general obligations, debt service is secured by gasoline taxes in the state's transportation fund as well.

The debt of the general obligation bond issuer includes, in addition to the general obligation bonds outstanding, unfunded pension liabilities, leases, and "moral obligation" commitments, among others. Key debt ratios that reveal the burden on local taxpayers include determining the per capita amount of general obligation debt as well as the per capita debt of the overlapping or underlying general obligation bond issuers. Other key measures of debt burden include determining what are the amounts and percentages of the outstanding general obligation bonds as well as the outstanding general obligation bonds of the overlapping or underlying jurisdictions to real estate valuations. These numbers and percentages can be compared with Moody's medians as well as with the past history of the issuer to determine whether the debt burden is increasing, declining, or remaining relatively stable.

Budgetary Soundness. Concerning the budgetary operations and budgetary soundness of the general obligation bond issuer, some of the more important questions include how well the issuer over at least the previous five years has been able to maintain balanced budgets and fund reserves. How dependent is the issuer on short-term debt to finance annual budgetary operations? How have increased demands by residents for costly social services been handled? That is, how frugal is the issuer? How well have the public-employee unions been handled? They usually pressure for higher salaries, liberal pensions, and other costly fringe benefits. Clearly, it is undesirable for the pattern of dealing with the constituent demands and public-employee unions to result in raising taxes and drawing down nonrecurring budget reserves. Last, another general concern in the budgetary area is the reliability of the budget and accounting records of the issuer. Are interfund borrowings reported? And who audits the books?

Tax Burden. Concerning the tax burden, it is important to learn two things initially. First, what are the primary sources of revenue in the issuer's general fund? Second, how dependent is the issuer on any one revenue source? If the general obligation bond issuer relies increasingly upon either a property tax, wage and income taxes, or a sales tax to provide the major share of financing for annually increasing budget appropriations, taxes could quickly become so high as to drive businesses and people away. Many larger northern states and cities with their relatively high income, sales, and property taxes appear to be experiencing this phenomenon. Still another concern is the degree of dependency of the issuer on intergovernmental revenues, such as federal or state revenue sharing and grants-in-aid to finance its annual budget appropriations. Political coalitions on the state and federal levels that support these financial transfer programs are not permanent and could undergo dramatic change very quickly. Therefore, a general obligation bond issuer that currently has a relatively low tax burden but receives substantial amounts of intergovernmental monies should be carefully reviewed by the investor. If it should occur that the aid monies are reduced, as has been occurring under many of President Reagan's legislative programs, certain issuers may primarily increase their taxes, instead of reducing their expenditures to conform to the reduced federal grants-in-aid.

Overall Economy. The fourth and last area of general obligation bond analysis concerns the issuer's overall economy. For local governments, such as counties, cities, towns, and school districts, key items include learning the annual rate of growth of the full value of all taxable real estate for the previous 10 years and identifying the 10 largest taxable properties. What kinds of business or activity occur on the respective properties? What percentage of the total property tax base do the 10 largest properties represent? What is the building permit trend for at least the previous five years? What percentage of all real estate is tax exempt, and what is the distribution of the taxable ones by purpose such as residential, commercial, industrial, railroad, and public utility? Last, who are the five largest employers? Concerning the final item, those communities that have one large employer are more susceptible to rapid adverse economic change than communities that have more diversified employment and real estate bases. Additional information that reveals either economic health or decline include determining whether the population of the community over the previous 10 years has been increasing or declining by age, income, and ethnicity and how the monthly and yearly unemployment rates compare with the comparable national averages as well as to the previous history of the community.

For state governments that issue general obligation bonds, the economic analysis should include many of the same questions applied to local governments. In addition, the investor should determine the annual rates of growth on the state level for the previous five years of personal income and retail sales and how much the state has had to borrow from the Federal Unemployment Trust Fund to pay unemployment benefits. This last item is particularly significant for the long-term economic attractiveness of the state, since under current federal law employers in those states with large federal loans in arrears are required to pay increased unemployment taxes to the federal government.

For Revenue Bonds

Airport Revenue Bonds. For airport revenue bonds, the economic questions vary according to the type of bond security involved. There are two basic security structures.

The first type of airport revenue bond is one based upon traffic-generated revenues that result from the competitiveness and passenger demand for the airport. The financial data on the operations of the airport should come from independently audited financial statements going back at least three years. If a new facility is planned, a feasibility study prepared by a recognized consultant should be reviewed. The feasibility study should have two components: (1) a market and demand analysis to define the service area and examine demographic and airport utilization trends and (2) a financial analysis to examine project operating costs and revenues.

Revenues at an airport may come from landing fees paid by the airlines for their flights, concession fees paid by restaurants, shops, newsstands and parking facilities, and from airline apron and fueling fees.

Also, in determining the long-term economic viability of an airport, the investor should determine whether or not the wealth trends of the service area are upward; whether or not the airport is either dependent on tourism or serves as a vital transfer point; whether or not passenger enplanements and air cargo handled over the previous five years have been growing; whether or not increased costs of jet fuel would make such other transportation as trains and automobiles more attractive in that particular region; and whether or not the airport is a major domestic hub for an airline, which could make the airport particularly vulnerable to route changes caused by schedule revisions and changes in airline corporate management.

An example of this last concern can be found in the St. Louis Airport Revenue Bonds issued by the city of St. Louis. The revenues of the airport have been substantially higher than the rate covenant requires. As an example, in 1981 debt service was covered by available revenues 2.52 times, although the rate covenant only required a one-times coverage. On the one hand this appears to show a strong revenue base, but on the other hand the source of the revenues is of concern. At the time of this writing the airport serves as the passenger-transfer hub for both Trans World Airlines and Ozark Airlines, who together are the major users of the airport. Corporate mergers of these companies with others outside the region could result in shifts of flights to other airports, and thus a significant reduction in revenues.

The second type of airport revenue bond is secured by a lease with one or more airlines for the use of a specific facility, such as a terminal or hangar. The lease usually obligates them to make annual payments sufficient to pay the expenses and debt service for the facility. For many of these bonds, the analysis of the airline lease is based upon the credit quality of the lessee airline. Whether or not the lease should extend as long as the bonds are outstanding depends on the specific airport and facility involved. For major hub airports it may be better not to have long-term leases, since without leases fees and revenues can be increased as the traffic grows, regardless of which airline uses the specific facility. Of course, for regional or startup airports, long-term leases with trunk (i.e., major airline) carriers are preferred.

Highway Revenue Bonds. There are generally two types of highway revenue bonds. The bond proceeds of the first type are used to build specific revenue producing facilities, such as toll roads, bridges, and tunnels. For these pure enterprise revenue bonds, the bondholders have claims to the revenues collected through the tolls. The financial soundness of the bonds depends on the ability of the specific projects to be self-supporting. Proceeds from the second type of highway revenue bond generally are used for public highway improvements, and the bondholders are paid by earmarked revenues, such as gasoline taxes, automobile registration payments, and driver's license fees.

Concerning the economic viability of a toll road, bridge, or tunnel revenue bond, the investor should ask a number of questions.

1. What is the traffic history, and how inelastic is the demand? Toll roads, bridges, and tunnels that provide vital transportation links are clearly preferred to those that face competition from interstate highways, toll-free bridges, or mass transit.
2. How well is the facility maintained? Has the issuer established a maintenance reserve fund at a reasonable level to use for such repair work as road resurfacing and bridge painting?
3. Does the issuer have the ability to raise tolls to meet covenant and debt-reserve requirements without seeking approvals from other governmental actors, such as state legislatures and governors? In those few cases where such approvals are necessary, a question to ask is how sympathetic have these other power centers been in the past in approving toll-increase requests?
4. What is the debt-to-equity ratio? Some toll-road, bridge, and tunnel authorities have received substantial nonreimbursable federal grants that have helped to subsidize their costs of construction. This, of course, reduces the amount of debt that has to be issued.
5. What is the history of labor-management relations, and can public employee strikes substantially reduce toll collections?
6. When was the facility constructed? Generally, toll roads financed and constructed in the 1950s and 1960s tend now to be in good financial condition. This is because the cost of financing was much less than it is today. Many of these older revenue bond issuers have been retiring their bonds ahead of schedule by buying them at deep discounts to par in the secondary market.
7. If the facility is a bridge that could be damaged by a ship and made inoperable, does the issuer have adequate "use and occupancy" insurance?

Those few toll-road and bridge revenue bonds that have defaulted have done so because of either unexpected competition from toll-free highways and bridges, poor traffic projections, or substantially higher than projected construction costs. An example of one of the few defaulted bonds is the West Virginia Turnpike Commission's Turnpike Revenue Bond issued in 1952 and 1954 to finance the construction of an 88-mile expressway from Charleston to Princeton, West Virginia. The initial traffic-engineering estimates were overly optimistic, and the construction costs came in approximately $37 million higher than the original budgeted amount of $96 million. Because of insufficient traffic and toll collections, between 1956 and 1979 the bonds were in default. By the late 1970s with the completion of various connecting cross-country highways, the turnpike became a major link for interstate traffic. Since 1979 the bonds have become self-supporting.

Concerning the economics of highway revenue bonds that are not pure enterprise type but instead are secured by earmarked revenues, such as gasoline taxes, automobile registration payments, and driver's license fees, the investor should ask the following questions.

1. Are the earmarked tax revenues based on either state constitutional mandates, such as the state of Ohio's Highway Improvement Bonds, or are they derived from laws enacted by state legislatures, such as the state of Washington's Chapters 56, 121, and 167 Motor Vehicle Fuel Tax Bonds? A constitutional pledge is usually more permanent and reliable.
2. What has been the coverage trend of the available revenues to debt service over the previous 10 years? Has the coverage been increasing, stable, or declining?
3. If the earmarked revenue is a gasoline tax, is it based either on a specific amount of cents per gallon of gasoline sold, or as a percentage of the price of each gallon sold? With greater conservation and more efficient cars, the latter tax structure is preferred because it is not as susceptible to declining sales of gasoline and because it benefits directly from any increased gasoline prices at the pumps.

Hospital Revenue Bonds. Two unique features of hospitals make the analysis of their debt particularly complex and uncertain. The first concerns their sources of revenue, and the second concerns the basic structure of the institutions themselves.

During the past 15 years, the major sources of revenue for most hospitals have been (1) payments from federal (Medicare) and combined federal-state (Medicaid) hospital reimbursement programs and (2) appropriations made by local governments through their taxing powers. It is not uncommon for hospitals to receive at least two thirds of their annual revenues from these sources. From a technical point of view, hospital bonds are structured as revenue bonds, but their major revenues come from payment formulas established through the annual political-legislative conflicts and compromises on the federal, state, and local levels of government. Therefore, while the analysis of these bonds is primarily based on the hospital operation, one must also be aware of outside funding sources. Of course, how well the hospital management markets its services to attract more private-pay patients, how aggressive it is in its third-party collections, such as from Blue Cross, and how conservatively it budgets for the governmental reimbursement payments are key elements for distinguishing weak from strong hospital bonds.

Particularly for community-based hospitals (as opposed to teaching hospitals affiliated with medical schools), a unique feature of their financial structure is that their major financial beneficiaries, physicians, have no legal or financial liabilities if the institutions do not remain financially viable over the long term. An example of the problems that can be caused by this lack of liability is found in the story of the Sarpy County, Nebraska, Midlands Community Hospital Revenue Bonds. These bonds were issued to finance the construction of a hospital three miles south of Omaha, Nebraska, that was to replace an older one located in the downtown area. Physician questionnaires prepared for the feasibility study prior to the construction of the hospital indicated strong support for the replacement facility. Many doctors had used the older hospital in downtown Omaha as a backup facility for a larger nearby hospital. Unfortunately, once the new Sarpy hospital opened in 1976, many physicians found that the new hospital could not serve as a backup because it was 12 miles farther away from the major hospital than the old hospital had been. With these physicians not referring their patients to the new Sarpy hospital, it was soon unable to make bond principal payments and was put under the jurisdiction of a court receiver.

The above two factors raise long-term uncertainties about many community-based hospitals, but certain key areas of analysis and trends reveal the relative economic health of hospitals that already have revenue bonds outstanding. The first area is the liquidity of the hospital as measured by the ratio of dollars held in current assets to current liabilities. In general, a five-year trend of high values for the ratio is desirable because it implies an ability by the hospital to pay short-term obligations and thereby avoid budgetary problems. The second indicator is the ratio of long-term debt to equity, as measured in the unrestricted end-of-year fund balance. In general, the lower the long-term debt to equity ratio, the stronger the finances of the hospital. The third indicator is the actual debt-service coverage of the previous five years as well as the projected coverage. The fourth indicator is the annual bed-occupancy rates for the previous five years.

The fifth is the percentage of physicians at the hospital who are professionally approved (board certified), their respective ages, and how many of them use the hospital as their primary institution.

For new or expanded hospitals, much of the above data is provided to the investor in the feasibility study. One item in particular that should be covered for a new hospital is whether or not the physicians who plan to use the hospital actually live in the area to be served by the hospital. Because of its importance in providing answers to these questions, the national reputation and experience of the people who prepare the feasibility study is of critical concern to the investor.

Housing Revenue Bonds. For housing revenue bonds the economic and financial questions vary according to the type of bond security involved. There are two basic types of housing revenue bonds—each with a different type of security structure. One is the housing revenue bond secured by *single-family* mortgage repayments, and the other is the housing revenue bond secured by mortgage repayments on *multifamily* housing projects.

Concerning single-family housing revenue bonds, the strongly secured bonds usually have four characteristics.

1. The single-family home loans are insured by the Federal Housing Administration (FHA), Federal Veterans Administration (VA), or an acceptable private mortgage insurer. If the individual home loans are not insured, then they should have a loan-to-value ratio of 80 percent or less.

2. All conventional home loans are covered by no less than a 10 percent mortgage-pool insurance policy.

3. In addition to a debt reserve that has an amount of monies equal at least to six months interest on the single-family housing revenue bonds, there is a mortgage reserve fund that has an amount equal at least to 1 percent of the bond issue outstanding.

4. The issuer of the single-family housing revenue bonds is in a region of the country that has either stable or strong economic growth as indicated by increased real estate valuations, personal income, and retail sales, as well as low unemployment rates and relatively low state and local government overall tax burdens.

In addition to looking for the four characteristics mentioned above, the investors should review the retirement schedule for the single-family mortgage revenue bonds to determine whether or not the issuer has assumed large, lump-sum mortgage prepayments in the early year cash flow projections. And if so, how conservative are the prepayment assumptions, and how dependent is the issuer on the prepayments to meet the annual debt-service requirements?

It should be noted that single-family housing revenue bonds issued by local governments, such as cities and counties, usually have conservative bond-retirement schedules that do not include any home-mortgage prepayment assumptions. Single-family housing revenue bonds issued by states do use prepayment assumptions. This positive feature of local government-issued bonds is balanced somewhat by the fact that the state-issued bonds usually are secured by home mortgages covering wider geographic areas. Additionally, the state issuing agencies usually have professional in-house staffs that closely monitor the home-mortgage portfolios, whereas the local issuers do not.

For multifamily housing revenue bonds, there are three specific, though overlapping, security structures. The first type of multifamily housing revenue bond is one in which the bonds are secured by mortgages that are federally insured. Usually the federal insurance covers all but the difference between the outstanding bond principal and collectible mortgage amount (usually 1 percent), and all but the non-asset bonds (i.e., bonds issued to cover issuance costs and capitalized interest). The attractiveness of the federal insurance is that it protects the investor against bond default within the limitations outlined. The insurance protects the bondholders regardless of whether or not the projects are fully occupied and generating rental payments.

The second type of multifamily housing revenue bond is one in which the federal government subsidizes under the federal Section 8 program all annual costs, including debt service, of the project not covered by tenant rental payments. Under Section 8 the eligible low-income and elderly tenants pay only 15 to 30 percent of their incomes for rent. Since the ultimate security comes from the Section 8 subsidies, which escalate annually with the increased cost of living in that particular geographic region, the bondholder's primary risks concern the developer's ability to complete the project, find tenants eligible under the federal guidelines to live in the project, and then maintain high occupancy rates for the life of the bonds. The investor should carefully review the location and construction standards used in building the project, as well as the competency of the project manager in selecting tenants who will take care of the building and pay their rents. In this regard, state agencies that issue Section 8 bonds usually have stronger in-house management experience and resources for dealing with problems than do the local development corporations that have issued Section 8 bonds.

The third type of multifamily housing revenue bond is one in which the ultimate security for the bondholder is the ability of the project to generate sufficient monthly rental payments from the tenants themselves to meet the operating and debt-service expenses. Many of these projects receive governmental subsidies (such as interest cost reductions under the federal Section 236 program and property tax abatements from local governments), but the ultimate security is the economic viability of the project. Key information includes the location of the project, its occupancy rate, whether large families or the elderly will primarily live in the project, whether or not the rents necessary to keep the project financially sound are competitive with others in the surrounding community, and whether or not the project manager has proven records of maintaining good services and of establishing careful tenant selection standards.

Other financial features desirable in all multifamily housing bonds include a debt-service reserve fund, which should contain an amount of money equal to the maximum annual debt service on the bonds, a mortgage reserve fund, and a capital repair and maintenance fund.

Still another feature of many multifamily housing revenue bonds, and particularly of those issued by state housing agencies, is the state moral obligation pledge. Several state agencies have issued housing revenue bonds that carry a potential state liability for making up deficiencies in their one-year debt-service reserve funds, should any occur. In most cases if a drawdown of the debt reserve occurs, the state agency must report the amount used to its governor and state budget director. The state legislature, in turn, may appropriate the requested amount, though there is no legally enforceable obligation to do so. Bonds with this makeup provision are the so-called moral obligation bonds.

In 1975, because the New York State Urban Development Corporation's General Purpose Bonds (UDC) were on the brink of default and in fact UDC was in default on its notes for several months, the state and its local units of government experienced severe difficulties in selling their own general obligation bonds and notes. Responding to these market pressures, the state legislature and the governor provided an appropriation of several hundred million dollars to keep UDC's housing bonds solvent. This experience in New York State has been cited by many on Wall Street who argue now that every state legislature would honor the moral obligation pledge to its respective state housing agencies out of fear of losing market access for its own bonds. For the investor, it is far from certain that this would always be the response. The moral obligation only provides a state legislature with permissive authority—*not mandatory authority*—to make an appropriation to the troubled state housing agency. Therefore the analysis should determine (1) whether the state has the budgetary surpluses for subsidizing the housing agency's revenue bonds and (2) whether or not there is a consensus within the executive and legislative branches of that particular state's government to use state general fund revenues for subsidizing multifamily housing projects.

Industrial Revenue Bonds. Generally, industrial revenue bonds are issued by state and local governments on behalf of individual corporations and businesses. The security for the bonds usually depends on the economic soundness of the particular corporation or business involved. If the bond issue is for a subsidiary of a larger corporation, one question to ask is whether or not the parent guarantees the bonds. Is it only obligated through a lease, or does it not have any obligation whatsoever for paying the bondholders? If the answer is that the parent corporation has no responsibility for the bonds, then the investor must look very closely at the operations of the subsidiary in addition to those of the parent corporation. Here the investor must determine also whether the bond is guaranteed by the company or is a lease obligation.

For companies that have issued common stock that is publicly traded, economic data is readily available either in the annual reports, or in the 10-K reports that must be filed annually with the Securities and Exchange Commission. For privately held companies, financial data is more difficult to obtain. However, such credit information services as Dun & Bradstreet have financial information available for many smaller companies and businesses.

In assessing the economic risk of investing in an industrial revenue bond, another question to ask is whether the bondholder or the trustee holds the mortgage on the property. Although holding the mortgage is not an important economic factor in assessing either hospital or low-income, multifamily housing bonds where the properties have very limited commercial value, it can be an important strength for the holder of industrial development revenue bonds. If the bond is secured by a mortgage on a property of either a fast-food retailer, such as MacDonalds, or an industrial facility, such as a warehouse, the property location and resale value of the real estate may provide some protection to the bondholder, regardless of what happens to the company that issued the bonds. Of course, the investor should always avoid possible bankruptcy situations regardless of the economic attractiveness of the particular piece of real estate involved. This is because the bankruptcy process usually involves years of litigation and numerous court hearings, which no investor should want to be concerned about.

Lease-Rental Bonds. Lease-rental bonds are usually structured as revenue bonds, and annual rent payments, paid by a state or local government, cover all costs including operations, maintenance, and debt service. The public purposes financed by these bond issues include the construction of public office buildings, fire houses, police stations, university buildings, mental health facilities, and highways, as well as the purchase of office equipment and computers. In some instances the rental payments may only come from student tuition, patient fees, and earmarked tax revenues, and the state or local government is not legally obligated to make lease-rental payments beyond the amount of available earmarked revenues. However, for many lease-rental bonds the underlying lessee state, county, or city is required to make annual appropriations from its general fund. For example, the Albany County, New York, Lease Rental South Mall Bonds were issued to finance the construction of state office buildings. Although the bonds are technically general obligations of Albany County, the real security comes from the annual lease payments made by the state of New York. These payments are annually appropriated. For such bonds, the basic economic and financial analysis should follow the same guidelines as for general obligation bonds.

Public Power Revenue Bonds. Public power revenue bonds are issued to finance the construction of electrical generating plants. An issuer of the bonds may construct and operate one power plant, buy electrical power from a "wholesaler" and sell it "retail," construct and operate several power plants, or join with other public and private utilities in jointly financing the construction of one or more power plants. This last arrangement is known as a joint-power financing structure. Although there are revenue bonds that can claim the revenues of a federal agency (for example, the Washington Public Power Supply System's Nuclear Project No. 2 Revenue Bonds, which if necessary can claim the revenues of the Bonneville Power Administration) and many others that can require the participating underlying municipal electric systems to pay the bondholders whether or not the plants are completed and operating (for example, the Massachusetts Municipal Wholesale Electric Company's Power Supply System Revenue Bonds), the focus here is how the investor determines which power projects will be financially self-supporting without these backup security features.

There are at least five major questions to ask when evaluating the investment soundness of a public power revenue bond.

1. Does the bond issuer have the authority to raise its electric rates in a timely fashion without going to any regulatory agencies? This is particularly important if substantial rate increases are necessary to pay for either new construction or plant improvements.
2. How diversified is the customer base among residential, commercial, and industrial users?
3. Is the service area growing in terms of population, personal income, and commercial/industrial activity so as to warrant the electrical power generated by the existing or new facilities?
4. What are the projected and actual costs of power generated by the system, and how competitive are they with other regions of

the country? Power rates are particularly important for determining the long-term economic attractiveness of the region for those industries that are large energy users.
5. How diversified is the fuel mix? Is the issuer dependent on one energy such as hydro dams, oil, natural gas, coal, or nuclear fuel?

Concerning electrical generating plants fueled by nuclear power, the aftermath of the Three Mile Island nuclear accident in 1979 has resulted in greater construction and maintenance reviews and costly safety requirements prompted by the Federal Nuclear Regulatory Commission (NRC). The NRC oversees this industry. In the past, although nuclear power plants were expected to cost far more to build than other types of power plants, it was also believed that, once the generating plants became operational, the relatively low fuel and maintenance costs would more than offset the initial capital outlays. However, with the increased concern about public safety brought about by the Three Mile Island accident, repairs and design modifications are now expected to be made even after plants begin to operate. This of course increases the ongoing costs of generating electricity and reduces the attractiveness of nuclear power as an alternative to the oil, gas, and coal fuels. For ongoing nuclear plant construction projects, the investor should review the feasibility study to see that it was prepared by experienced and recognized consulting engineers and that it has realistic construction, design schedule, and cost estimates.

Resource Recovery Revenue Bonds. A resource recovery facility converts refuse (solid waste) into commercially salable energy, recoverable products, and a residue to be landfilled. The major revenues for a resource recovery bond usually are the "tipping fees" per ton paid monthly by those who deliver the garbage to the facility for disposal; revenues from steam, electricity, or refuse-derived fuel sold to either an electric power company or another energy user; and revenues from the sale of recoverable materials, such as aluminum and steel scrap.

Resource recovery bonds are secured in one of two ways or a combination thereof. The first security structure is one in which the cost of running the resource recovery plant and paying the bondholders comes from the sale of the energy produced (steam, electricity, or refuse-derived fuel) as well as from fees paid by the haulers, both municipal and private, who bring the garbage to the facility. In this financing structure the resource recovery plant usually has to be operational and self-supporting for the bondholders to be paid. The second security structure involves an agreement with a state or local government, such as a county or municipality, which contractually obligates the government to haul or to have hauled a certain amount of garbage to the facility each year for the life of the facility and to pay a tipping fee (service fee) sufficient to operate the facility. The tipping fee must include amounts sufficient to pay bondholders regardless of whether or not the resource recovery plant has become fully operational.

When deciding to invest in a resource recovery revenue bond, one should ask the following questions. First, how proven is the system technology to be used in the plant? *Mass burning* is the simplest method, and it has years of proven experience, primarily in Europe. In mass burning the refuse is burned with very little processing. Prepared fuels and shredding, the next most proven method, requires the refuse to be prepared by separation or shredding so as to produce a higher quality fuel for burning. More innovative and eclectic approaches require the most detailed engineering evaluations by qualified specialists. Second, how experienced and reliable are the construction contractors and facility operators (vendors)? Third, are there adequate safeguards and financial incentives for the contractor/vendor to complete and then maintain the facility? Fourth, what are the estimated tipping fees that will have to be charged, and how do they compare with those at any available nearby landfills? One way for a state resource recovery revenue bond issuer to deal with the latter concern occurred with the Delaware Solid Waste Authority's Resource Recovery Revenue Bonds, Series 1979. The state of Delaware enacted a law requiring that all residential garbage within a specified geographic region be hauled to its plant. Fifth, is the bondholder protected during the construction stage by reserves and by fixed-price construction contracts? Sixth, are the prices charged for the generated energy fixed, or instead are they tied to the changing costs of the fuel sources such as oil and gas in that particular market place?

Because of the uniqueness of the resource recovery technology, there are additional questions that should be asked. First, even if the plant-system technology is a proven one, is the plant either the same size as others already in operation, or is it a larger-scale model that would require careful investor review? Second, if the system technology used is innovative and eclectic, is there sufficient redundancy, or low-utilization assumptions, in the plant design to absorb any unforeseen problems once the plant begins production? Last, in addition to the more routine reserves and covenants such as debt, maintenance, and special capital improvement reserves along with covenants that commercial insurance be placed on the facility and that the contractor (or vendor) pledge to maintain the plant for the life of the bonds—there should also be required yearly plant reviews by independent consulting engineers. The vendor should be required to make the necessary repairs so that the facility will be operational for the life of the bonds.

For resource recovery revenue bonds that have a security structure involving an agreement with a local government, additional questions for the investor to ask are the following. Is the contractual obligation at a fixed rate, or is the tipping fee elastic enough to cover all the increasing costs of operations, maintenance, and debt service? Would strikes or other *force majeure* events prevent the contract either from being enforceable or preclude the availability of an adequate supply of garbage? Last, the investor should determine the soundness of the budgetary operations and general fund reserves of the local government that is to pay the tipping or service fee. For these bonds, the basic economic analysis should follow the same guidelines as for general obligation bonds.

Student Loan Revenue Bonds. Student loan revenue bonds are usually issued by statewide agencies and are used for purchasing either new guaranteed student loans for higher education, or existing guaranteed student loans from local banks.

The student loans are 100 percent guaranteed. They are either guaranteed directly by the federal government—under the Federal Insured Student Loan (FISL) program for 100 percent of principal and interest—or by a state guaranty agency—under a more recent federal insurance program, the Federal Guaranteed Student Loan (GSL) program. This latter program provides federal reimbursement for a state guaranty agency on an annual basis for 100 percent of the payment on defaulted loans up to approximately 5 percent of the amount of loans being repaid, 90 percent for claims in excess of 5 percent but less than 9 percent, and 80 percent for claims exceeding 9 percent. The federal commitments are not dependent on future congressional approvals. Loans made under the FISL and GSL programs are contractual obligations of the federal government.

Although most student loans have federal government support, the financial soundness of the bond program that issues the student loan revenue bonds and monitors the loan portfolio is of critical importance to the investor. This is because of the unique financial structure of a student loan portfolio. Although loan repayments from the student or, in the event of student default, repayments from the guaranty agency are contractually assured, it is difficult to precisely project the actual loan repayment cash flows. This is because the student does not begin repaying the loan until he or she leaves college or graduate school and all other deferments, such as military service, have ended. Before the student begins the loan repayments, the federal government pays the interest on the loans under prescribed formulas. Therefore the first general concern of the investor should be to determine the strength of the cash flow protection.

The second general concern is the adequacy of the loan guaranty. Under all economic scenarios short of a depression, in which the student loan default rate could be 20 percent or greater, the GSL sliding federal reinsurance scale of 100-90-80 should provide adequate cash flow and bond default protection as long as the student loan revenue bond issuer effectively services the student loan repayments, has established and adequately funded loan-guaranty and debt-reserve funds, employs conservative loan-repayment assumptions in the original bond-maturity schedule, and is required to call the bonds at par if the student loan repayments are accelerated. This latter factor prevents a reinvestment risk for the bondholder.

There are eight specific questions for the investor to ask. (1) What percentage of the student loans are FISL and GSL backed, respectively? (2) Has a loan-guarantee fund been established and funded? Usually a fund that is required to have an amount at least equal to 2 percent of the loan principal outstanding is desirable. (3) Is the issuer required to maintain a debt-reserve fund? Usually, for notes a fund with at least six-months interest, and for bonds a fund with a one-year maximum annual debt-service are desirable. (4) If the bond issuer has purchased portfolios of student loans from local banks, are the local lenders required to repurchase any loans if there are either defaults or improperly originated loans? (5) What in-house capability does the issuer have for monitoring and servicing the loan repayments? (6) What is the historic loan-default rate? (7) How are the operating expenses of the agency met? If federal operating subsidies are received under the "Special Allowance Payment Rate" program, what are the rate assumptions used? In this program the issuer receives a supplemental subsidy, which fluctuates with the 91-day U.S. Treasury bill rate. (8) If a state agency is the issuer, is it dependent on appropriations for covering operating expenses and reserve requirements?

Water and Sewer Revenue Bonds. Water and sewer revenue bonds are issued to provide for a local community's basic needs and as such are not usually subject to general economic changes. Because of the vital utility services performed, their respective financial structures are usually designed to have the lowest possible user charges and still remain financially viable. Generally, rate covenants requiring that user charges cover operations, maintenance, and approximately 1.2 times annual debt-service and reserve requirements are most desirable. On the one hand, a lower rate covenant provides a smaller margin for either unanticipated slow collections or increased operating and plant maintenance costs caused by inflation. On the other hand, rates that generate revenues in excess of 1.2 times could cause unnecessary financial burdens on the users of the water and sewer systems. A useful indication of the soundness of an issuer's operations is to compare the water or sewer utility's average quarterly customer billings to those of other water or sewer systems. Assuming that good customer service is given, the water or sewer system that has a relatively low customer billing charge generally indicates an efficient operation, and therefore strong bond-payment prospects.

Key questions for the investor to ask include the following. (1) Has the bond issuer through local ordinances required mandatory water or sewer connections? Also, local board of health directives against well water contaminations and septic tank usage can often accomplish the same objective as the mandatory hookups. (2) In regard to sewer revenue bonds in particular, how dependent is the issuer on federal grants either to complete ongoing construction projects or to supplement the cost of future expansions of the sewer system? The level of dependence is particularly important in light of President Reagan's efforts in Congress to reduce the multibillion dollar federal sewage treatment grant program for states and local governments. (3) What is the physical condition of the facilities in terms of plant, lines, and meters, and what capital improvements are necessary for maintaining the utilities as well as for providing for anticipated community growth? (4) For water systems in particular, it is important to determine whether the system has water supplies in excess of current peak and projected demands. An operating system at less than full utilization is able to serve future customers and bring in revenues without having to issue additional bonds to enlarge its facilities. (5) What is the operating record of the water or sewer utility for the previous five years? (6) If the bond issuer does not have its own distribution system, but instead charges other participating local governments that do, are the charges or fees either based upon the actual water flow drawn (for water revenue bonds) and sewage treated (for sewer revenue bonds), or upon gallonage entitlements? (7) For water revenue bonds issued for agricultural regions, what kind of produce is grown? An acre of oranges or cherries in California will provide the grower with more income than will an acre of corn or wheat in Iowa. (8) For expanding water and sewer systems, does the issuer have a record over the previous two years of achieving net income equal to or exceeding the rate covenants, and will the facilities to be constructed add to the issuer's net revenues? (9) Has the issuer established and funded debt and maintenance reserves to deal with either unexpected cash flow problems or system repairs? (10) Does the bond issuer have the power to place tax liens against the real estate of those who have not paid their water or sewer bills? Although the investor would not want to own a bond for which court actions of this nature would be necessary before the investor could be paid, the legal existence of this power usually provides an economic incentive for water and sewer bills to be paid promptly by the users.

Additional bonds should only be issued if the need, cost, and construction schedule of the facility have been certified by an independent consulting engineer and if the past and projected revenues are sufficient to pay operating expenses and debt service. Of course, for a new system that does not have an operating history, the quality of the consulting engineer's report is of the uppermost importance.

RED FLAGS FOR THE INVESTOR

In addition to the areas of analysis described above, certain red flags, or negative trends, suggest increased credit risks.

General Obligation Bonds

For general obligation bonds, the signals that indicate a decline in the ability of a state, county, town, city, or school district to function within fiscally sound parameters include the following:

1. Declining property values and increasing delinquent taxpayers.
2. An annually increasing tax burden relative to other regions.
3. An increasing property tax rate in conjunction with a declining population.
4. Declines in the number and value of issued permits for new building construction.
5. Actual general fund revenues consistently falling below budgeted amounts.
6. Increasing end-of-year general fund deficits.
7. Budget expenditures increasing annually in excess of the inflation rate.
8. The unfunded pension liabilities are increasing.
9. General obligation debt increasing while property values are stagnant.
10. Declining economy as measured by increased unemployment and declining personal income.

For Revenue Bonds

For revenue bonds, the general signals that indicate a decline in credit quality include the following:

1. Annually decreasing coverage of debt service by net revenues.
2. Regular use of debt reserve and other reserves by the issuer.
3. Growing financial dependence of the issuer on unpredictable federal and state-aid appropriations for meeting operating budget expenses.
4. Chronic lateness in supplying investors with annual audited financials.

5. Unanticipated cost overruns and schedule delays on capital construction projects.
6. Frequent or significant rate increases.
7. Deferring capital plant maintenance and improvements.
8. Excessive management turnovers.
9. Shrinking customer base.
10. New and unanticipated competition.

Early Redemption (Put) Options on Fixed Income Securities*

5 ROBERT W. KOPPRASCH, Ph.D., C.F.A.
Vice President
Salomon Brothers Inc

An early redemption option on a fixed income security can remove much of the risk associated with investment in such securities. The purpose of this chapter is to discuss the factors and variables involved in analyzing and valuing early redemption options. These options are frequently referred to as puts, although they may not be puts in the traditional sense because they cannot be detached and traded separately. Nevertheless, the term *put* is descriptive and has become accepted Street usage; therefore, we will also use the term *put*.

EARLY PUT ISSUES

Although a number of recent issues have included puts, they are not an entirely new development. In 1974 Citicorp sold a floating-rate issue that included a put provision, and recently the company

---

*The author would like to express his appreciation to Martin L. Leibowitz for assisting in the development of this chapter.

Although the information in this chapter has been obtained from sources that the author believes to be reliable, Salomon Brothers Inc cannot guarantee its accuracy, and such information may be incomplete or condensed. All opinions and estimates included in this chapter constitute judgment as of this date and are subject to change without notice.

sold another. Beneficial Corporation now has several fixed coupon issues outstanding that give the holders early redemption options.

In Canada, bonds known as extendables and retractables have long been common. A 30-year bond "retractable" to a 10-year maturity has, in essence, a put attached with an effective exercise date 10 years after issue. An extendable technically incorporates a call option, but a 10-year bond extendable to 30 years is, practically speaking, indistinguishable from a 30-year bond retractable to 10 years. Either can be redeemed after 10 years, or after 30 years. Thus both extendables and retractables may be included under the broad category of puts.

Recent interest-rate volatility has increased investor awareness of the vulnerability of bond portfolios to increases in rates. Because of the early redemption feature, issues with puts will generally experience less downside fluctuation, thus making them attractive to investors. If the recent level of interest-rate volatility continues, one would not be surprised to see a resurgence of interest in issues with various types of put provisions.

BASICS OF A PUT

A number of factors must be known to assess the attractiveness, or risk-reducing ability, of a put. These factors, each of which will be considered later in detail, are the following:

1. The early redemption price, known as the *strike price.* (This assumes that the redemption is for cash, although there are other possibilities.) The strike price may be defined in terms of dollar price or yield.
2. How often the early redemption privilege is "active" (e.g., every coupon date).
3. The first date when the put may be exercised (first exercise date).
4. The last date the put may be exercised (expiration date).

Two factors, external to the put itself, will also have some impact: the maturity of the bond and, especially, the shape of the yield curve. In fact, the yield curve has a major impact on putable bond pricing.

The consideration of the yield curve will be deferred until a later section and will be ignored in the early examples. We will assume here that yield curve effects are not significant, thus implicitly assuming a flat curve.

The primary value of an early redemption option is the privilege of selling the bond back to the issuer at the strike price. This privilege should tether the price of the bond to a level close to the strike price near "active" dates, thus reducing downside price risk.

AN EXAMPLE

Assume that straight debt with a 30-year maturity and 12 percent coupon could be issued at par. If a bond with identical terms but incorporating a one-year put at par could be sold to yield 11.5 percent (price = 104.20) the put premium would be 4.20. (Most issues are not structured in this way but rather have a reduced coupon and are sold at par. However, as considerations of an "in the money" strike price and coupon differential would complicate the example and charts, this technique allows us to concentrate on the explicit cost of the put alone, without either implied costs due to lower coupons or exercise prices that differ from the original issue price. We will alter the example to "real world" specifications in a later section.)

The price yield curve for the bond one year later when the put can be exercised is shown in Exhibit 1. Obviously the bond that includes a put with a strike price at par will sell for par at all market yields above 12 percent because of the put. Straight bonds will sell below par as shown in the figure. If we compute the profit or loss for the two types of bonds, we will see that the put-bond holder can lose a maximum of 4.2—the premium paid for the put—but the straight-bond holder's loss will depend upon how much yields move above 12 percent. If yields decline, both straight and putable bonds will be priced along the price yield curve on the put's expiration date, with the profit depending upon whether the investor paid 100 (straight debt) or 104.2 (putable) for the bond. Profits and losses for various yields are shown in Exhibit 2.

Two points in Exhibit 2 are likely to be of interest to the investor. If yields decline to 11.5, the bond will sell for 104.20, and the inves-

Exhibit 1
Price-Yield Curve for 30-Year 12 Percent Coupon Bond

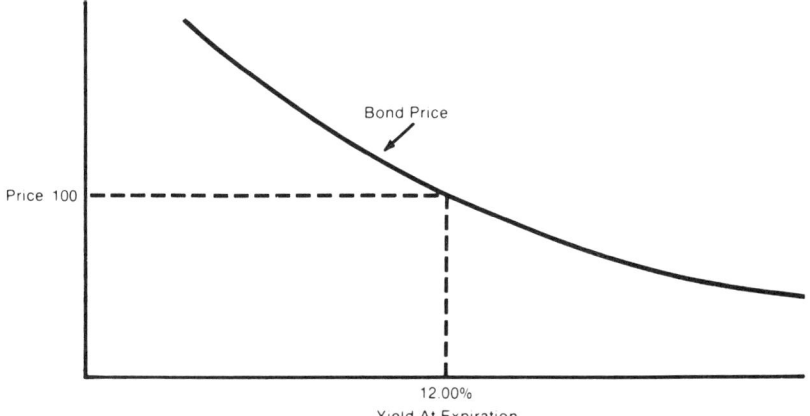

Exhibit 2
Price-Yield Curve for 30-Year 12 Percent Coupon Bond

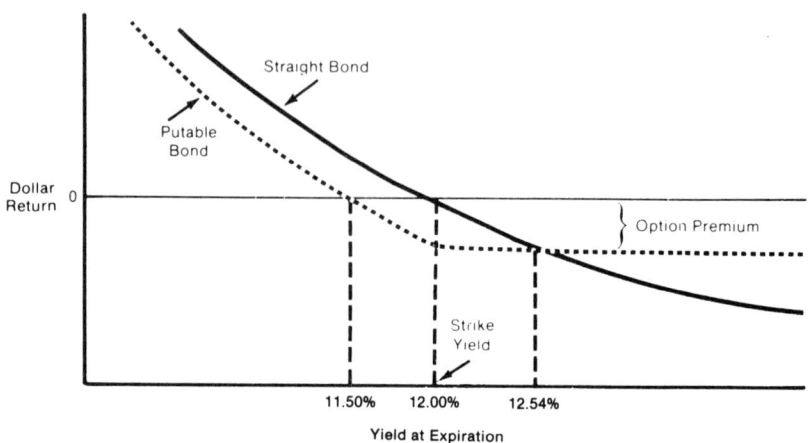

Note: Chart assumes investment in one bond and one option, as opposed to equal dollar investments. Coupon income is ignored.

tor who bought a putable bond will break even. If yields increase instead to 12.54, both the straight-bond holder and the putable-bond holder will show a loss of 4.2, thus establishing an indifference point. At any higher yield, the straight-bond holder will have a greater loss. At any lower yield, he or she will have a smaller loss or greater profit. (The problem of different initial investments will be remedied when the example is changed.)

The profit patterns in Exhibit 2 make clear the risk and return trade-off of the buyer of the putable bond. The maximum possible loss—the premium paid—is limited and known in advance, but the potential profits are reduced only by the amount of the premium.

THE VALUE OF THE PUT

Although most puts cannot be detached from the underlying bonds, we can strip the put from the bond for analytical purposes and look only at the value of the put. At market yields below 12 percent, the put clearly has no intrinsic value because the bond can be sold for more than the strike price in the open market. At yields above 12 percent, the put (if exercisable immediately) has an intrinsic value equal to the strike price less the normal (nonputable) price for that yield. The intrinsic value, derived from the price yield curve shown in Exhibit 1, is shown in Exhibit 3.

Before buying a put issue, an investor will probably consider the value likely to be realized at expiration. One method of valuation for

5: Early Redemption (Put) Options on Fixed Income Securities

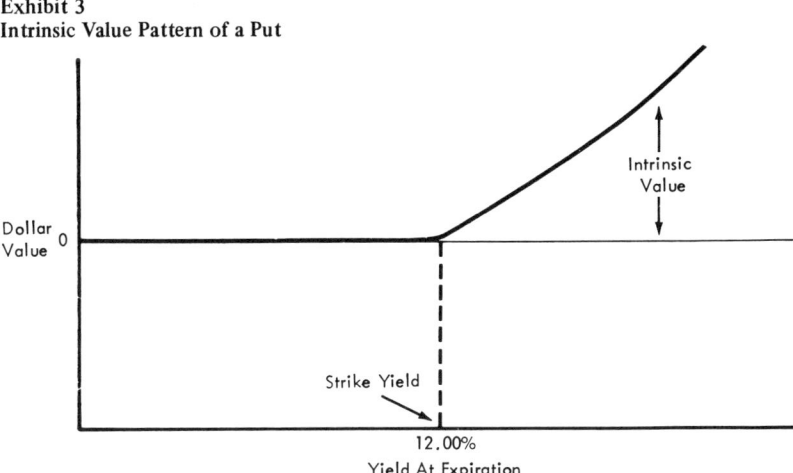

Exhibit 3
Intrinsic Value Pattern of a Put

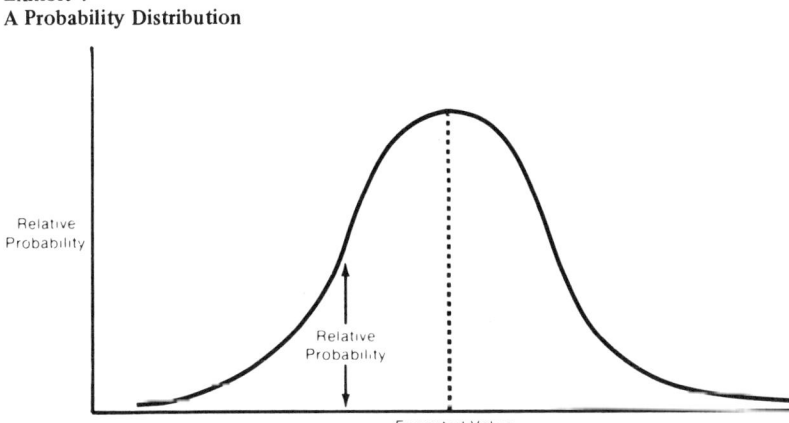

Exhibit 4
A Probability Distribution

a put would be to consider the range of likely yields at expiration and to assign some subjective probabilities to these yields. A symmetrical probability distribution, such as the one shown in Exhibit 4, provides a good starting example.[1]

The center (highest point) of the distribution is placed over the investor's expected yield at the put date. The width of the distribu-

---

[1] For a more detailed description of fixed income option valuation, see Robert W. Kopprasch, "Contingent Take-Down Options on Fixed Income Securities," chapter 23 in *The Handbook of Fixed Income Securities,* eds. Frank J. Fabozzi and Irving M. Pollack (Homewood, Ill.: Dow Jones-Irwin, 1982).

tion recognizes that there is some potential error in the predicted yield. Statistically, the measure of dispersion (a width measure) usually used is the standard deviation. If the standard deviation of the prediction is large, the investor perceives that there is a possibility that the put may be very valuable (toward the right in Exhibit 4). Without going any deeper into option valuation theory the following observations will be made.

1. Higher expected yields lead to higher put values.
2. Higher standard deviations lead to higher put values.
3. Longer maturity of the bond itself leads to higher put values because of increased sensitivity to yield changes.

IN-THE-MONEY PUTS

The basic example used earlier assumed that the put premium was paid in addition to the par amount for the purchase of the bond. In the more likely case, the issue will carry a lower coupon than the market yield for that type of instrument, but will nevertheless sell at par to reflect the inclusion of the put. This presents some pricing problems that need to be discussed.

When a *call* option is included with a bond issued at par, the par price includes both the value of the option and the value of the bond. Thus the bond's value, based on its coupon, maturity, and other features, is less than par, and the option to buy another *at par* is "out of the money"; that is, the bond must move in a favorable direction just to reach the exercise price. This option is worth less than an "at the money" option because the option holder does not participate in the initial price appreciation of the bond.

Similarly, when a putable bond sells at par, the put value is the difference between the bond's straight price and par. In contrast to the call option, however, the put option is "in the money" because the bond can be sold (redeemed) at par, although its straight value is less than par. In fact, it would be difficult to correctly price such an issue if the put were exercisable immediately because the price being paid for the put is simply its intrinsic value, with no value attached to its potential for a large payoff in the future. Obviously this type of put cannot be struck at par at the outset if the bond-put unit is issued at par.

ALTERING THE EXAMPLE FOR AN ISSUE AT PAR

Let us consider the earlier example, amended as follows: the putable 30-year bond will be issued at par in a 12 percent market but will carry an 11.5 percent coupon. Thus the bond's value is 95.96, and the put premium is 4.04 (100 − 95.96). The strike price, as before, is 100.

Notice that the premium paid for the put is equal to its immediate exercise value of 4.04. That is, the bond that is worth 95.96 can be sold (to the issuer) immediately for 100, for a gross gain of 4.04. Thus the buyer is paying no time-value premium, and the advantage to the issuer is minimized.

There are several ways to rectify the pricing problem. One method would be to lower the strike price to the actual bond value (without put) at issue. In the example above, then, the strike would be 95.96. This approach is very similar to the earlier example except on a scaled-down basis. Although theoretically clean, it is not the approach taken in most of the putable bonds available today.

Another method is to defer activation of the put for several years. In this case, the 4.04 value would not be available immediately, but perhaps five years later. Thus today's value of the 4.04 is its discounted present value, and the buyer is paying up for the option.

The example above will be used in later sections as a reference point. For the next section, however, we will again assume a near-term exercise possibility for the purpose of illustrating another pricing dilemma: the yield curve.

THE IMPORTANCE OF THE YIELD CURVE

An early redemption option on a bond makes it more difficult to place the issue on the yield curve because of the possibility of early "maturity." This section will address pricing considerations for short-term puts and deferred puts in light of the shape of the yield curve.

Let us assume that the yield curve is positively sloped, rising from about 10 percent in the 1-year maturity area to 12 percent for 30 years. If the putable bond were given a coupon of 11.5 percent as in the earlier example, it would clearly dominate all other one-year securities that yielded 10 percent. It would be quickly purchased by one-year investors as a superior investment, and they would intend to put the bond in one year. The bond would quickly trade to a premium to yield a return competitive with other 1-year investments, but this would leave it uncompetitive with other 30-year instruments. Although adjustments to the strike price could potentially solve this problem, the example illustrates the basic dual maturity nature of putable bonds with a single put date.

Market forces will cause the putable bond to trade to the maturity point at which it is most competitive. Thus the yield levels at both the early redemption and normal maturity must be considered as important in the pricing of putable bonds. Additionally, because the bondholder has the option of electing the other maturity if it becomes more advantageous to do so (i.e., the option still has value), the bond should trade at a slightly higher price/lower yield than a bond at the selected maturity without this option.

For example, consider the 11.5 percent, 30-year bond with an early redemption option (exercisable after one year) that is trading at 101.39 so as to have a 10 percent yield that is competitive with 1-year instruments. If the yields in the 30-year area dropped, the bond would be worth more as a 30-year bond and would perhaps trade to 110. Similarly, if restrictive monetary policy caused short rates to rise sharply, the bond might simply be priced at the 30-year point because that became the higher price. This option to change maturities will command a premium in price and result in some reduction in yield. The magnitude of the premium will probably reflect market participants' aggregate sense not only of the probability that a switch in optimum maturity will occur, but also whether that switch would produce extra profit or soften a loss.

THE YIELD CURVE AND MULTIMATURITY BONDS (MULTIPLE EXERCISE DATES)

If a putable bond has several exercise dates for early redemption, the yield at each potential maturity becomes important in pricing the bond. The bond's price should be the maximum price obtained by pricing it to the yield at each relevant redemption date. As with dual-maturity bonds, if the bond's price does not reflect its maximum value, arbitrage or normal bond swapping would force it to the maximum price, *plus* the premium to reflect the multimaturity option.

Although it is theoretically possible to construct a probabilistic model for valuing the maturity switch option, practical considera-

Exhibit 5
Terms of Putable Corporate Bonds*

Name	S & P Rating	Coupon	Issued Amount	Maturity	Put Date, Terms
Avco Financial Services	A	9.75%	$125	8/1/99	12/1/87
Beneficial Corporation	AA-	8.00	150	6/15/01	every 6/15, from 1982-2001
Beneficial Corporation	AA-	8.40	150	5/15/08	every 12/15, from 1986-2008
Beneficial Corporation	AA-	11.50	250	1/15/05	1/15/84, then coupon drops to 9%
Ford Motor Credit	A	16.25	250	1/15/87	1/15/85
Transamerica Financial	A+	8.50	50	7/1/01	every 7/1, from 1984-2001
ITT Financial	A	8.875	125	6/15/03	6/15/87, 6/15/92, 6/15/97

*Excludes floating rate issues. There are also some municipal bonds with puts.

tions, involving conditional probabilities at dates long into the future, make this approach unwieldy. In order to provide some market evidence regarding putable bond pricing, let us consider the seven putable bonds described in Exhibit 5.

Exhibit 6 provides prices as of May 29, 1981, with corresponding yields to maturity and yields to first redemption.

In order to place these yields in a more meaningful perspective, they are plotted in Exhibit 7 against the Treasury yield curve for the same date. It can be seen that the yields to maturity all lie below the Treasury curve, indicating that these bonds are certainly not priced on a yield-to-maturity basis. When viewed as intermediate-term

Exhibit 6
Putable Corporate Bonds: Yield to First Put versus Yield to Maturity

Name	Coupon	Price	Maturity	Yield to Maturity	First Put Date	Yield to First Put
Avco Financial Services	9.75%	79⅜	8/1/99	12.67	12/1/87	14.805
Beneficial Corporation	8.00	88⅛	6/15/01	9.32	6/15/83	15.116
Beneficial Corporation	8.40	76	5/15/08	11.25	12/15/86	14.931
Beneficial Corporation	11.50	92⅝	1/15/05	10.49	1/15/84	15.007
Transamerica Financial	8.50	84½	7/1/01	10.35	7/1/84	14.980
ITT Financial	8.875	77½	6/15/03	11.75	6/15/87	14.619

Note: Ford Motor Credit 16¼ was issued after the pricing date of this table. Its yield to put would probably not differ significantly from yield to maturity because the put date is only two years prior to maturity.

Exhibit 7
U.S. Treasury Yield Curve versus Putable Bond Yield Curves (as of the close of Friday, May 29, 1981)

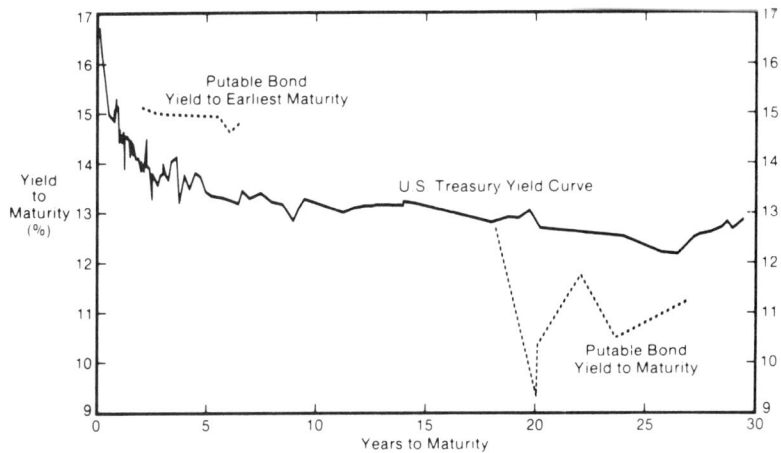

bonds, however, their yield levels are more appropriate. It is obvious that the early redemption option has not gone unnoticed by investors.

MULTIMATURITY BONDS AS INVESTOR CALL OPTIONS

The maturity switch option that gives a putable bond its multimaturity nature can also be thought of as a call option. Consider the 11.5 percent, 30-year bond mentioned earlier that is putable in one year and is now trading as if it were a 1-year bond. This bond can be thought of as a bond with a 1-year maturity, with a call on a 29-year bond exercisable at the end of 1 year. That is, at the redemption of the "1-year" bond, the investor can, at his or her option, reinvest the funds in a 29-year, 12 percent bond. The bond's current price should reflect the value of this call option. If, at the 1-year date, the 29-year bond is worth more than the redemption price, the investor can "exercise" the call option by *not* redeeming the bond early. The investor has in effect rolled the redemption proceeds into the long maturity bond (purchased the bond at the strike price). If, on the other hand, the 29-year bond were trading below the redemption price, the option could be allowed to "expire" by the act of early redemption. An investor who desires a 29-year, 12 percent bond in his or her portfolio can buy one in the open market for less than the redemption proceeds. In option parlance, we would say that the option was "out of the money" and thus worthless at "expiration."

Consider the Avco 9.75 of '99 listed in Exhibit 5 as having a single put date of 12/1/87. This bond is worth more than others maturing late in 1987 with similar quality and coupon because the Avco includes a "call" on "another" bond maturing 8/1/99. If the call is close to "at the money," the bond should sell at a premium and lower yield.

If a put has many exercise dates, the value of the "call" option is more difficult to determine. Assume that the bond is trading as a one-year instrument. The option allows the investor to "purchase" at the redemption strike price another bond, the value of which depends upon whether it is considered a one-year bond, a five-year bond, and so on. Each of the feasible maturity bonds includes another call option on a bond, or a string of bonds, whose last maturity is 29 years later. Although a precise value is difficult to determine, some value is obviously inherent in such an option. The Beneficial Corporation's 8s and 8.40s provide examples of this variable maturity structure.

The next several sections will deal with variations in the terms of the put, with the modified example being used as the reference point. Before proceeding with the changes, however, it is necessary to establish some benchmark value. Although there are probably a number of ways to measure the value, we have chosen to use the present value of the cash flows over the next 30 years associated with the original investment. The bond's yield at the time of the analysis is used as the discount rate. Thus, if the bond is not redeemed early, the cash flows consist of coupon payments and normal redemption. If the bond is put, the cash flows consist of the early coupons, redemption at the strike, and coupons and redemption of the subsequent investment. The put will be considered active at the five-year point for one time only unless otherwise specified.

One advantage of using the present value approach is that it is equally applicable to the issuer and the bondholder because they are on opposite sides of each cash flow. Thus the present value of future receipts (assuming reinvestment if the bond were put) is the same as the cost to the issuer of future payments (assuming refinancing if the bond were put) if we ignore taxes. In the examples that follow, a 12 percent discount rate will be applied to all future cash flows. Thus a 12 percent, 30-year straight bond would have a present value of 100. This then is the benchmark. A lower figure represents a savings to the issuer and a cost to the investor and vice versa.

Naturally, if the yield for straight debt on the expiration date exceeds the strike yield, the bonds will be put back to the issuer. The investor will receive the strike price and reinvest this amount at the new higher market yield, thus increasing the investor's return. The issuer will have to refinance at the higher market yield, resulting in higher cost thereafter. The present value profile of the putable bond is shown versus straight debt in Exhibit 8.

Notice that we have ignored the possibility of the bond being

Exhibit 8
Present Value Pattern of Putable Bond versus Straight Bond

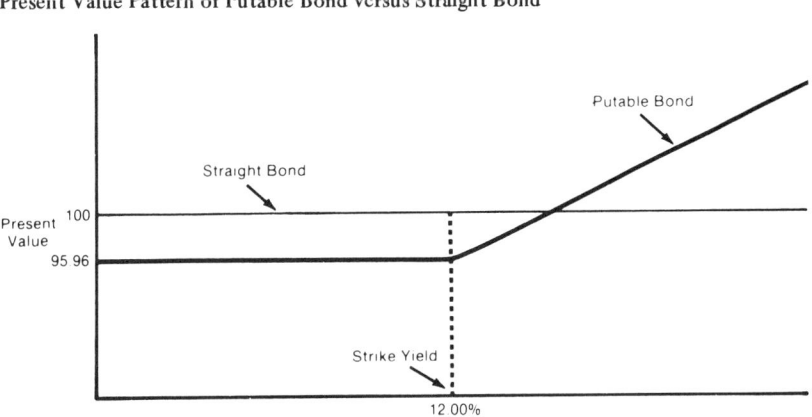

called if yields decline. This would naturally lower the investor's return and issuer's cost if yields declined. A detailed treatment of the effect of the call feature can be found elsewhere.[2]

THE STRIKE YIELD

The strike yield is an important parameter because it effectively sets the early redemption price. If the market yield is above the strike yield (i.e., the market price is below the strike price), it is reasonable to expect that the bond will be put back to the issuer for early redemption. By setting a strike yield above the yield at the time of issue, the put options are effectively out of the money, and the issuer can establish some cushion of downward price movement necessary before the bonds will be put for early redemption. The present value patterns for the benchmark example and several higher strike yields are shown in Exhibit 9.

Exhibit 9
Present Value Patterns for Different Strike Yields

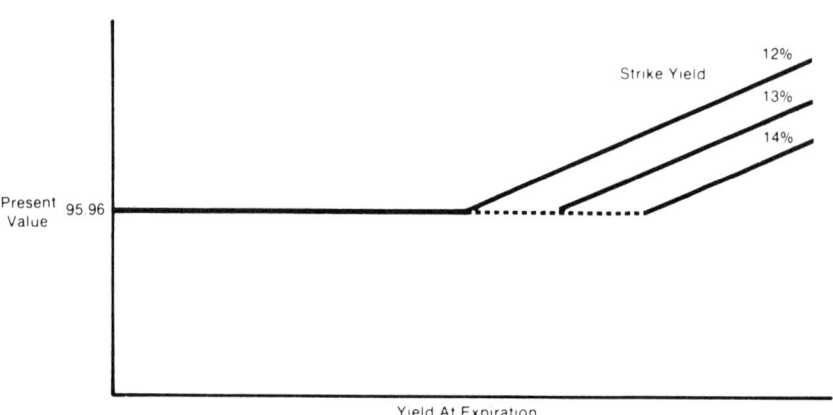

One can see that higher strike yields (lower strike prices) result in lower returns for investors and lower costs for issuers than the benchmark if yields increase and the bonds are put. (Recognizing this, however, investors would probably demand a higher coupon to offset the lower level of price protection. This would have little effect if the bonds were put after a year but would have more significant impact on return if the issue remained outstanding for the entire 30 years.)

---

[2] Martin L. Leibowitz, *The Maturity Decision: The Issuer's Choice between the Intermediate and Long-Term Debt Markets* (New York: Salomon Brothers Inc, 1980).

PUT RATIO

One of the areas of concern to the issuer is the need to have the cash available on exercise dates if it appears that the bonds will be put. Normally this would involve refinancing in a higher yield environment. Because the issuer may want to limit the risk of refinancing the entire issue when yields are high and capital potentially scarce, the entire issue may not be subject to early redemption. The holder may be allowed, for example, to have one half of his or her bonds redeemed early. Thus two puts may be necessary to redeem one bond, much as several "rights" are necessary to purchase new shares in an equity rights offering.

Exhibit 10 compares the present values of issues with different put ratios, the ratio being defined as the number of bonds redeemable per number of bonds in the original issue. It is assumed in Exhibit 10 that the terms of the various issues are identical except for the put ratio. In practice, if a 1:1 ratio resulted in a 50-basis-point concession, a 1:2 ratio issue would presumably have a higher coupon to reflect the diluted put value.

Exhibit 10
Present Value Patterns for Different Put Ratios

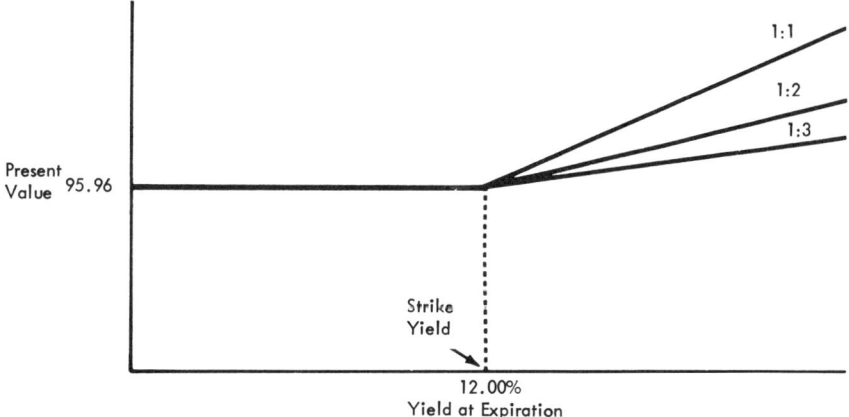

CONCLUSION

The debt market has seen the introduction of a number of new investment vehicles and sweeteners in recent years as issuers have found it necessary to entice buyers into a volatile market. Warrants to buy additional bonds capitalize on upside price volatility, and puts provide protection from downside volatility. The dollar-for-dollar downside protection is not linked with dollar-for-dollar upside losses, and the new pattern of return and risk makes these bonds an excellent hedging vehicle.

If downside volatility is perceived as a continuing threat, we would not be surprised to see additional issues of this form. They provide a special benefit to portfolios that are constrained from taking losses, and when trading as intermediates, they provide "call options" to long-term investors.

Puts should receive strong consideration from both issuers and investors as they search for investments with features that are attractive in the rapidly changing debt market of the 1980s.

section 3

Portfolio Management

INTRODUCTION

Studies of market efficiency support the position that the stock market is efficient in the weak and semistrong forms. That is, market participants cannot consistently outperform the market on a risk-adjusted basis after giving proper consideration to transaction costs and management fees associated with the execution of an active equity portfolio strategy. How, then, should portfolio managers construct an equity portfolio when they face an efficient market? James R. Vertin, in Reading 6, describes passive equity management strategies that can be utilized by portfolio managers.

In Reading 7, Peter L. Bernstein explains how personal portfolios should be managed. He also describes how the management of personal portfolios differs from the management of institutional portfolios.

Dr. Martin L. Leibowitz discusses trends in bond portfolio management in Reading 8. In the first part of this reading, he describes the nature and evolution of the forces that led to active bond portfolio management. In the second part, Dr. Leibowitz presents a general overview of the process of bond portfolio management. In the overview, he suggests that the focus on short-term total returns may be a dangerously narrow approach when dealing with fixed income portfolios that usually have quite discernible long-term goals. In particular, direct comparisons of a portfolio's return against peer portfolios or against a broad market index can be quite misleading. He argues that the real aim of short-term performance analysis should be to evaluate the portfolio's progress toward long-term goals. He proposes the concept of a "baseline" portfolio technique to achieve the more appropriate performance evaluations.

The total return from holding a bond consists of three sources: (1) coupon interest payments, (2) interest earned from reinvesting the coupon interest (commonly called the "interest-on-interest" component), and (3) any capital gain or loss realized when the bond is sold. The traditional yield-to-maturity measure of investment return considers all three components; however, it is assumed that (1) the coupon interest can be reinvested at a rate equal to the yield-to-maturity and (2) the bond is held to maturity and redeemed at full value by the issuer. Consequently, the yield-to-maturity is a promised yield that will only be realized if these two conditions are met. If coupon interest payments are actually reinvested at an average interest rate that is less than the computed yield-to-maturity, the total return realized from the bond will be less than the promised yield.

In the early 1980s, interest rates reached record high levels. Portfolio managers feared a decline of interest rates, making it necessary to reinvest interim interest payments at interest rates less than the prevailing high rates. To cope with this problem, portfolio managers began employing a strategy to lock in existing rates by hedging against a drop in interest rates. A strategy of locking in existing interest rates for a bond portfolio is called bond immunization. In Reading 9, Dr. Sylvan Feldstein, Peter Christensen, and I explain the principles of bond portfolio immunization and illustrate this strategy with a simulated portfolio.

A 1979 survey by Greenwich Research Associates in Greenwich, Connecticut found that 19 percent of the 200 largest U.S. companies invested a portion of their pension funds in foreign securities. Another 15 percent indicated that they intended to do so within the next year or two. However, when the survey was conducted in 1977, none of the respondents indicated that they were investing a portion of their pension funds abroad. In Reading 10, Dr. Gary L. Bergstrom, John K. Koeneman, and Martin J. Siegel discuss the advantages of and the risks associated with international investing.

Passive Equity Management Strategies

6   JAMES R. VERTIN, C.F.A.
Senior Vice President
Wells Fargo Investment Advisors
San Francisco, California

The broadest definition of passive equity management is satisfied when neither the design of the portfolio nor its ongoing operation is based on any attempt to assess whether or not the underlying fundamentals of its holdings are reflected fairly in prices. Index funds designed to track the performance of a defined "market of stocks" such as is represented by the Standard & Poor's 500 Index constitute the only widely accepted current form of passive equity management. Although operational strategies for the accomplishment of the goal of index-matching are a phenomena of the 1970s, the idea of a formalized passive equity strategy was not new when Wells Fargo Investment Advisors created the first equity index portfolio in June 1971, a fund designed to track the performance of the New York Stock Exchange Composite Index on an equal-dollar-weighted basis. The conceptual basis for passive management originated from early-1950s work by Harry M. Markowitz concerning the construction of "optimal" and "efficient" investment portfolios, maximizing expected return at a given level of risk, investor risk preferences considered.[1]

---

[1] Harry M. Markowitz, "Portfolio Selection," *Journal of Finance* 7, no. 1 (March 1952), pp. 77-91.

Extensions in the mid-1960s by Sharpe,[2] Lintner,[3] and Mossin,[4] gave rise to the concept of the market portfolio as offering the highest level of return per unit of risk in an efficient market. This concept of a market portfolio, representing capitalization-weighted shares of all available types of risky assets, is the single most important theoretical notion underlying the use of passive investment management strategies.

Recognition of the economic value of indexing an equity investment portfolio occurred in the late 1960s in certain academic circles and spread to several investment management organizations about that time. Along with developments in portfolio theory, a growing body of analysis documenting stock market efficiency in the U.S. became available, supplemented by an expanding availability of portfolio performance data.[5] Several investment managers, utilizing increasingly more thorough analysis, identified the risk-return implications of passive investment management strategies vis-a-vis conventional portfolio management strategies. The severe decline of stock prices in the 1973-74 bear market, which was particularly injurious to poorly-diversified portfolios, together with a growing awareness on the part of pension plan sponsors of both the absolute and relative performance produced by their portfolio managers over time, led a number of plan sponsors to consider this alternative form of equity market exposure and to direct some of their equity assets into index funds. By 1978, at least $6 billion of institutional monies had been so placed and about 30 organizations were offering equity index fund management, usually based on the S&P 500 Index as their market proxy.

PASSIVE VERSUS ACTIVE MANAGEMENT

Some Issues

In choosing to track a market of stocks through a passive approach an investor either accepts the proposition that the benefits from trading stocks on the basis of forecasted future prices is not likely to consistently cover the higher management fees and transaction costs associated with active management, or the investor has

---

[2] William F. Sharpe, "Capital Asset Prices: A Theory of Market Equilibrium under Conditions of Risk," *Journal of Finance* 19 (September 1964), pp. 425-42.

[3] John Lintner, "Security Prices, Risk and Maximal Gains from Diversification," *Journal of Finance* 20 (December 1965), pp. 587-616.

[4] Jan Mossin, "Equilibrium in a Capital Asset Market," *Econometrica* 34 (October 1966), pp. 768-83.

[5] Eugene Fama, "Efficient Capital Markets: A Review of Theory and Empirical Work," *Journal of Finance* 25 (May 1970), pp. 393-417.

been frustrated in attempting to identify—before the fact—which active managers will benefit from market inefficiencies. Also to be considered are the differences in management fees between passive and active management, the levels of stock selection skills believed to be possessed by active managers, the transaction costs associated with seeking to exploit assumed under- or overpricing through stock trading, and the statistical odds against successfully selecting a set of managers who, individually, will turn out to be superior performers.

In the absence of demonstrated stock selection, market timing or other active management skills, and confidence in their persistence, passive management should be favored by a rational equity investor who prefers more wealth to less and who is normally risk-averse, since higher levels of risk-taking require higher levels of expected return and vice versa. If the skill is not there, active management will simply incur higher costs without producing a compensating return. In addition, the typical actively-managed portfolio is more risky than a passive portfolio because uncompensated risk is being taken which could have been diversified away.

Since investors in the aggregate can not earn more return than the market itself produces, the stock market is said to be a "zero sum game." When one investor wins relative to the market, some other investor must have lost. In this sense, investors in the aggregate cannot have stock selection skill and, therefore, the average active investor should expect to lose relative to the market because the market does not incur management fees or transaction costs. With lower management fees and transaction costs, the passive portfolio should enjoy an advantage over the typical actively managed portfolio. How well the passive portfolio does relative to active management (i.e., what proportion of active managers will underperform the passive portfolio) depends on just how efficient the market is, on the size of the differential management fees and transaction costs, on how aggressively active portfolios are managed and over what time interval one chooses to measure the contest.

The Question of Market Efficiency

If an investor could routinely and consistently identify stocks which were underpriced and/or overpriced, he or she would regularly outperform the average active and passive investor. As long as this active investor maintained the secret of his or her success, he or she could continue to outperform. However, as soon as the secret became known, other investors would begin competing and the advantage would disappear. In a highly-developed, mature market there are few opportunities to identify and exploit insider information or to discover new ways to better evaluate publicly-available information.

The net result of everyone trying to gain a performance advantage is to produce a market where existing prices tend to be fair prices. The stronger the competitive nature of the market, the more efficient the market will be. In the extreme, if the consensus expectation correctly discounts all information, stock prices will fluctuate randomly as they adjust to new information. Moreover, an upward trend in stock prices over time should be observed if earnings and dividends are upward-trending. If stock performance is a random walk about a trend, then actively managed portfolios will also exhibit this upward-trending characteristic over time.

The fact that active portfolios deliberately take on risk that can be diversified away will produce in any given year an outcome where some active portfolios (usually less than half) will outperform the market, even if the market is perfectly efficient. Of course, the winners will claim skill. Even over a succession of years, in an efficient market, some number of active portfolios can be expected to outperform the market every year. But, this would be expected to occur by chance. Tests of market efficiency have included examination of whether the proportion of actively managed portfolios which outperform the market over time is greater than the number one would expect to occur by chance alone. The results of such tests are discouraging for those who believe the U.S. equity market to be inefficient and, therefore, routinely "beatable" through the application of typical active management methods and skills.

Transaction Costs

An active portfolio manager who can identify "mispriced" stocks can only exploit that advantage by trading. Thus, the costs of acting on such information must be taken into account. These costs include not only the commission charged by the stock broker, but also the spread charged by the specialist for making a market in the stock. If a broker charges a $.125 per share commission on a $25 stock and the specialist employs a spread of 1/4 point, the transaction costs amount to a one-way minimum of 1.50 percent. In many cases the costs of trading will be even higher; for example, if the specialist employs a larger spread as in the case of an illiquid issue.

Management Fees

The fees for passive management are lower than for active management. A $20 million portfolio would typically incur an annual passive management fee of about 0.1 percent of market value, while a $20 million active portfolio will typically incur annual fees from 0.3 to 0.5 percent or more, depending primarily on the type of management organization employed. This is not a trivial difference for either the manager or the client to consider.

Risk-Return Considerations

Since active management incurs additional risk, compensating additional return beyond that required to cover higher fees and transaction costs is needed. In addition, since risk-averse investors demand to be compensated at an increasing rate for taking on additional risk, the size of the required gross compensating return level is again adjusted upwards. No such compensatory return requirements exist in the passive case.

We observe that higher management fees and higher transaction costs put the average active manager approximately 1 percentage point per annum behind the passive portfolio, assuming 25 percent sales turnover. In comparison, the additional return required to justify taking on the higher risk of active management is smaller. Given our estimate of the degree of risk aversion for the typical pension plan, for example, additional return in the area of 0.3 percent per annum is required to leave the plan as well off with an active as with a passive portfolio in terms of "utility." (This observation is based on our estimate that the average level of diversifiable risk found in institutionally managed portfolios reflects a residual standard error of 6 percentage points per annum.) In total, then, active management must generate at least 1.25 percentage points of gross additional return to break even with passive management. If turnover and/or risk is higher than found in the typical active portfolio case, then the required differential in return production will be greater than this 1.25 percentage point minimum.

Passive Management Performance

Between 1968 and 1977, according to the Becker Securities Funds Evaluation Service, the S&P 500 Index portfolio ranked on average in the 37th percentile of annual equity portfolio investment returns. In terms of cumulative ranking over the 1968-77 period, the S&P 500 Index portfolio was in the 17th percentile, which means that 83 percent of the managers surveyed failed to outperform the Index over this period. Because the survey permits additions to and deletions from the sample, the actual results of active management on a cumulative basis may be worse than those reported. The very interesting fact is that the S&P 500 Index portfolio improves its position as the time interval lengthens. Active managers are not consistently good or bad, year-to-year, and different portfolios come and go as better performers over time. Every year each manager must compete against the market where, on average, fewer than half will win. In the very long run, only a very few actively managed equity portfolios can hope to outperform the market if the market is reasonably efficient. Hence, the market portfolio will be an increasingly good performer over time.

MANAGING PASSIVE PORTFOLIOS

Choosing an Index

The original market-weighted index fund had as its performance benchmark the Standard & Poor's 500 Composite Stock Price Index. This index was selected because its composition includes almost 70 percent of the market value, on a capitalization-weighted basis, of all outstanding U.S. equity issues and because of the wide recognition accorded its movements as a standard of equity investment performance. Pragmatically, this index provides a practical way to invest in a substantial portion of the capitalization-weighted equity market that is collectively owned by all investors and consists of approximately 5,000 exchange-listed and over-the-counter issues. Thus, the economics of the "zero-sum game" environment are captured in a form in which portfolio investment can be easily effected.

This form is also highly representative of aggregate institutional equity investment. Collectively, institutional market participants invest largely in the liquid sector of the total equity market generally represented by the S&P 500 Index. This can be seen in evidence compiled by the U.S. Comptroller of the Currency regarding domestic national bank trust departments and is illustrated in Figure 1.

Similar evidence involving insurance company equity portfolios is available. Thus, the S&P 500 Index can be considered as a good proxy for the market of stocks utilized in institutional portfolios. Any other index could, however, be used instead, depending on the characteristics desired. The larger the number of issues and the market value included in the index, the more representative of all stocks the sample will be.

Portfolio Construction—Duplication or Sampling?

Assume that the S&P 500 Index is chosen as the passive portfolio's benchmark. The operating objective is to duplicate as closely as possible the performance of the index over any time period at the lowest possible cost to the investor. There are two general forms of portfolio construction employed in operating an index-matching fund: "full capitalization weighting" and "stratified sampling." A choice

Figure 1
Distribution of the Total Market Value of the S&P 500 Issues in the Composite Index versus Their Distribution in the Aggregate Bank Portfolio at Year-End 1976

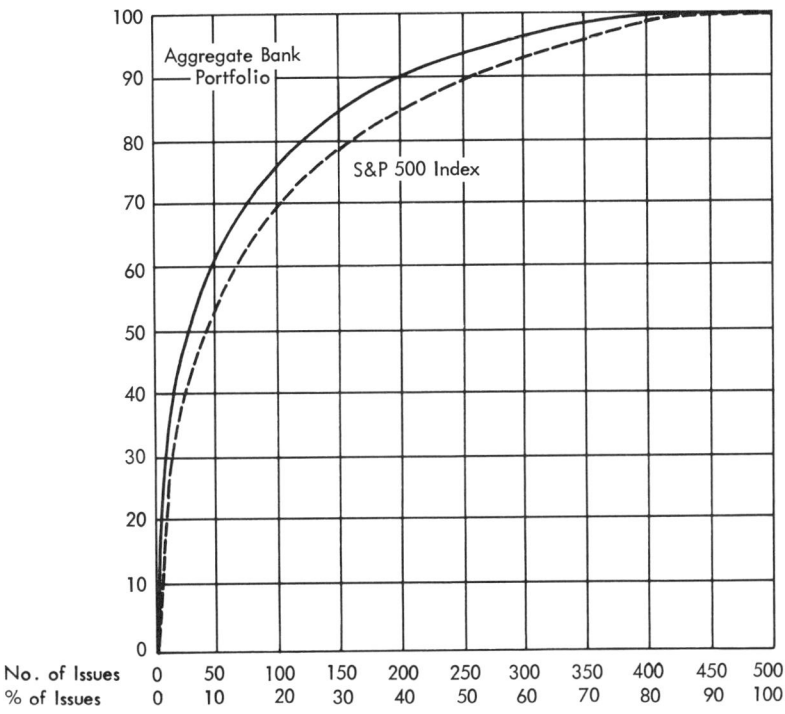

Source: Hans J. Schueren, "Special Market Analysis Comment: Indexing—A Passing Fad or an Evolving Trend?" Merrill Lynch, Pierce, Fenner & Smith, Inc., *Institutional Report,* July 1977.

must be made between them. Figure 2 shows the basic scheme of each approach for using the S&P 500 Index.

The *full capitalization weighting approach* is essentially a duplication of the actual S&P 500 Index construction. All S&P 500 issues, or as many as are deemed acceptable for investment purposes, are included and maintained in their respective market capitalization weightings, typically to the nearest round lot. The *stratified sampling approach* utilizes a smaller number of issues, typically a 200-300 issue sample of S&P issues, to track the performance of the index. The sampling concept is to capture a significant portion of the market capitalization weight of the index in a "core" portion which, in the illustration, comprises the largest 150 issues. These securities are maintained in their respective market weightings and represent perhaps 85 percent of the capitalization weight of the index. The sampled portion of the portfolio will include a varying number of addi-

Figure 2
Full Capitalization Weighting and Stratified Sampling Weighted Index Portfolios

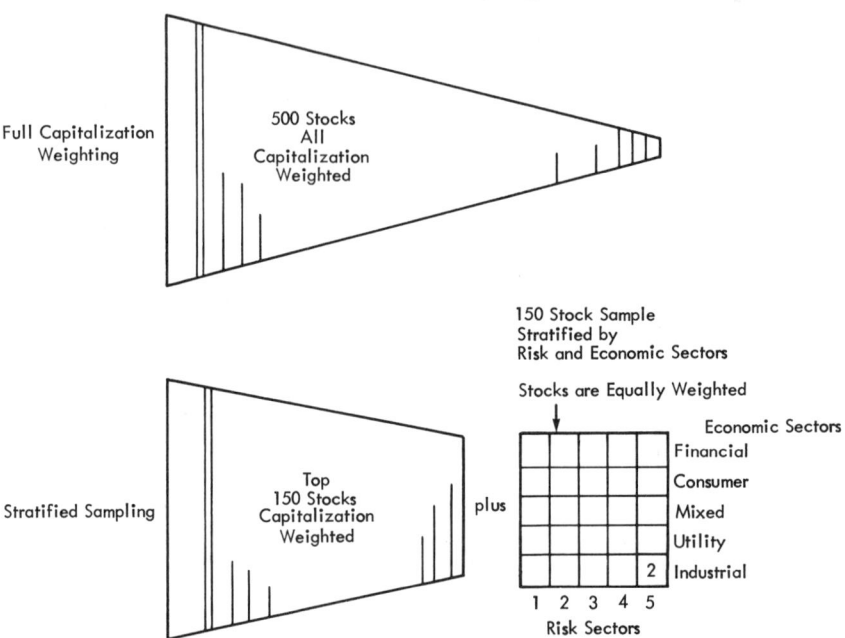

tional issues, depending generally on the asset size of the portfolio. The goal of the sampled portion is to reproduce the performance of those stocks in the index which are not maintained in the core portion. The term *stratified* simply denotes the manner in which the stocks are grouped. The example in Figure 2 involves a 150-stock noncore sample stratified across five risk and economic sectors, which is the simplest way to reproduce that portion of the index not captured in the core. Each stratified grouping, comprising a combination of one risk sector and one economic sector, is given a portfolio weight approximating the market capitalization weighting of that combination in the S&P 500 Index. Selection of issues for each grouping is not a random matter. Rather, after adjusting for the market capitalization weight of those issues held in the core portion, stocks are selected in descending order of capitalization weight to accommodate the capitalization requirement of each grouping and are typically equal-dollar-weighted in the portfolio. The diagram shows that after adjusting for the market capitalization weight of the core issues in the combination of risk sector 5, economic sector "Industrial," this noncore grouping will receive 2 percent of the portfolio's capitalization weight. The issues selected to populate this

6: Passive Equity Management Strategies

grouping will be those with the requisite general characteristics that also have the largest capitalization weights.

There are a number of important differences between these two basic approaches to the construction of passive portfolios. First and foremost, the full capitalization weighting approach tracks the performance of the index with substantially better resolution than does any sampling approach. Since the use of the sampling technique naturally introduces divergence into the construction process, the sampled index portfolio will produce perhaps four times as large a tracking error (i.e., difference from the index rate of return) as the full capitalization weighting approach.

There are at least five sources of tracking error associated with the operation of an index portfolio attempting to match the performance of the S&P 500. Of these, two are unique to the stratified sampling approach: the tracking error produced by the divergence discussed above, and that produced by the need for periodic portfolio rebalancing—both of which are inherent in the approach. The other three affect both approaches. First, the effect of recognizing monthly dividend income on the date each S&P stock goes "ex-dividend" (which, of course, is well before the payment is actually available for reinvestment) creates a cash drag that reduces fund performance relative to index performance to the extent of the proportion of cash accrual to portfolio market value. Second, the brokerage cost of dividend reinvestment also represents a deduction from fund performance. Third, transaction costs associated with adjusting to changes in the composition of the index itself represent another source of performance difference. Finally, if a "prudency screen" is utilized to provide a quality control element for the portfolio, the differences thus engendered in portfolio composition also create tracking error. These various sources of return deviation, index portfolio versus S&P 500, rank in severity in the following order: (1) sampling divergence; (2) cash drag effects; (3) rebalancing costs; (4) dividend reinvestment costs; and (5) prudency screen effects. Recent experience has shown that the magnitude of the tracking error resulting from sampling divergence can be as much as 150 basis points in a given year; the other effects are much less serious.

Table 1 illustrates the difference in tracking error that the two approaches produce. The first section of the table shows the monthly tracking results of the Wells Fargo Bank Index Fund (WFB) over the period January 1974-June 1975. During the period, the fund employed a stratified sampling technique because its asset value was insufficient to attain full capitalization weighting. The second section provides the tracking results for July 1975-August 1978, the time period over which the fund utilized the full capitalization

Table 1
Comparison of Index Fund Management Methods Monthly Tracking Record

I. Period of Stratified Sampling*

Period	WFB Index Fund Return	S&P 500 Total Return	Return Difference
1974			
January	−0.89%	−0.84%	−.05%
February	0.07	0.03	+.04
March	−2.11	−2.00	−.11
April	−3.81	−3.73	−.08
May	−3.20	−2.92	−.28
June	−1.08	−1.10	+.02
July	−7.54	−7.58	+.04
August	−8.30	−8.52	+.22
September	−11.66	−11.70	+.04
October	16.22	16.69	−.47
November	−4.41	−4.45	+.04
December	−1.77	−1.80	+.03
1975			
January	12.60	12.47	+.13
February	6.56	6.70	−.14
March	2.14	2.23	−.09
April	4.67	4.88	−.21
May	4.92	5.07	−.15
June	4.50	4.65	−.15
Cumulative total return	2.80%	3.90%	−1.10%

II. Period of Full Capitalization-Weighting†

Period	WFB Index Fund Return	S&P 500 Total Return	Return Difference
1975			
July	−6.53%	−6.55%	+.02%
August	−1.51	−1.53	+.02
September	−3.24	−3.30	+.06
October	6.55	6.44	+.11
November	3.09	3.07	+.02
December	−0.92	−0.96	+.04
1976			
January	11.86	11.91	−.05
February	−0.59	−0.60	+.01
March	3.26	3.31	−.05
April	−0.94	−0.93	−.01
May	−0.76	−0.76	.00
June	4.30	4.33	−.03
July	−0.84	−0.71	−.13‡
August	0.16	0.14	+.02
September	2.41	2.43	−.02
October	−1.99	−2.02	+.03
November	−0.07	−0.06	−.01
December	5.41	5.44	−.03
1977			
January	−4.91	−4.91	.00
February	−1.49	−1.53	+.04
March	−1.26	−1.23	−.03
April	0.20	0.17	+.03

Table 1 *(concluded)*

II. Period of Full Capitalization-Weighting† *(continued)*

Period	WFB Index Fund Return	S&P 500 Total Return	Return Difference
May	−1.52	−1.50	−.02
June	4.69	4.73	−.04
July	−1.52	−1.52	.00
August	−1.25	−1.26	+.01
September	−0.02	−0.04	+.02
October	−4.16	−4.15	.00
November	3.63	3.64	−.01
December	0.58	0.55	+.03
1978			
January	−5.98	−5.99	+.01
February	−1.58	−1.59	+.01
March	2.67	2.69	−.02
April	8.74	8.76	−.02
May	1.35	1.35	.00
June	−1.62	−1.59	−.03
July	5.67	5.68	−.01
August	3.35	3.36	−.01
Cumulative total return	25.13%	25.17%	−.04%

*Annual standard error (67 percent confidence) for period of stratified sampling: .47 percent.
†Annual standard error (67 percent confidence) for period of full capitalization weighting: .13 percent.
‡In July .11 percent of the shortfall was incurred when the index was revised to include the finance industry.

weighting approach after having attained the size necessary for making the switch.

It is apparent that the fund's monthly tracking errors (shown in the *Return Difference* column) are substantially smaller for the period of full capitalization weighting than for the earlier period of stratified sampling. The superiority of the full capitalization weighting approach is further evidenced through the standard error measurement, which shows the magnitude of the difference in the fund's total return in relation to the return of the S&P 500 Index. The period of stratified sampling produced a one-standard-deviation estimate of 0.47 percent per annum from 18 monthly observations. This estimate indicates that 67 percent of the fund's returns occurred within a range of ±0.47 percent around the actual index return, and that 95 percent of the returns occurred within a range of ±0.94 percent of the index return. The period of full capitalization weighting produced an annual standard error estimate of 0.13 percent from 38 monthly observations. Interestingly, if we remove the June 1976 observation, when S&P restructured the index to include the finance industry, the estimated standard error falls to 0.10 percent per annum.

These results serve to illustrate the superiority of the full capitalization weighting strategy in achieving the operating objective of the fund. The goal of minimizing tracking error is extremely important because the magnitude of the error has a progressively increasing impact on investment results as the investment period lengthens. The following simulation demonstrates the effect of accepting increasing amounts of tracking error. The analysis was performed using return data on NYSE stocks for the period December 31, 1925-December 21, 1976. It illustrates the point that a sampled portfolio having the same average annual return as a fully-weighted portfolio will, because of tracking error, produce an inferior investment result over time. (Returns courtesy of Center for Research in Security Prices, University of Chicago.)

$1,000,000 invested December 31, 1925 proportionally by capitalization in NYSE stocks would have, on December 31, 1976, a value of:

$50,552,000—with perfect tracking.
$50,276,000—with 1 percent additional return in even years.
with 1 percent less return in odd years.
$49,554,000—with 2 percent additional return in even years.
with 2 percent less return in odd years.

Another difference between the two approaches is that stratified sampling will produce greater sales turnover than the full capitalization weighting approach. While the sampled portfolio must be rebalanced from time to time when cash inflows are insufficient to maintain the proper weightings, the full capitalization weighted portfolio remains automatically in proper balance. Considering trading liquidity, it is important to note that the construction of a full capitalization weighted portfolio maps directly into the natural liquidity of the marketplace. Since the contents of full capitalization weighted investment programs mirror the capitalization weighted image of the market, their total trading costs tend to be lower than those incurred in investing an equivalent amount of cash in a sampled portfolio. While a full capitalization weighted portfolio deploys the cash across the entire breadth of the index, the sampled portfolio invests an equivalent amount of cash in a smaller number of issues. Thus, the larger individual trading lots required for a sampled portfolio's investment program exert greater pressure on stock prices. A good example of this occurs when the sampled approach requires purchase of a large block of a thinly-capitalized stock while the full capitalization weighted approach, requiring purchase of only a market-weighted position, perhaps utilizes only 100 or 200 shares of the same issue.

The stratified sampling approach is, however, a less costly mode of operation for the manager than the full capitalization weighting approach. Since, on average, perhaps 200 more issues are involved in each investment program and 200 more dividends are collected quarterly, the internal costs of processing greater volumes of transactions for the full capitalization weighting approach must be absorbed by the managing institution. If the management fees charged to the investor are approximately the same, the manager utilizing the sampling approach will enjoy a wider operating margin even though, from the investor's standpoint, trading costs and tracking error considered, it is a more costly approach.

Trading Strategies

To understand and choose effective trading strategies for an index-matching portfolio it is helpful to review the background of transactions and their associated costs in active as well as passive situations. The trading costs incurred in the normal course of value-added or active management stem from two sources: transaction costs and portfolio turnover. Active portfolio management depends upon the information content of its valuation process to produce portfolio trades. These trades are expected to help the manager "win." Specialists and market makers recognize that the information content of the trades in which they are asked to participate may be high enough to exert negative price pressures on their positions. They, therefore, introduce a spread based on position size and their assessment of the probable information content of the trade.

The cost of information-motivated transactions is divided into two parts. In Figure 3, the part of an individual trade depicted above the "water line" is the visible commission cost. It is typically one-fifth the size of the additional cost that may be incurred through the mar-

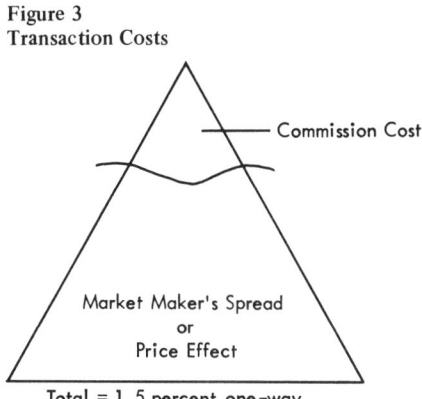

Figure 3
Transaction Costs

ket maker's spread, shown below the "water line." Estimates of typical one-way total transaction costs range from about 0.5 to 3 percent of transaction value. A reasonable single-point estimate derived from available studies would place the typical one-way transaction cost at about 1.5 percent.[6] The actual cost for a particular manager will generally depend upon the liquidity and block size of the stocks being traded and on the way the trades are packaged.

The trading motivation of a passive equity index fund is quite different than in the case of active management. The passive portfolio undertakes trades almost exclusively for "liquidity motivated" reasons. Not only is the specialist or market maker not exposed to information risk, but he usually deals in capitalization-weighted share quantities that reflect the natural liquidity of the marketplace as well. The liquidity motivation of the passive portfolio stems from the desire of the manager to acquire or sell pieces of the market portfolio with no regard for the relative valuation of any individual stock. Since the passive portfolio does not trade on particular information content of any kind, the market maker or specialist is not compelled to seek protection through introduction of a sizable spread. He does, of course, continue to include a smaller spread to bear the risk of general market movements when taking a position with regard to the entire market.

In order to assess the total transaction costs involved in trading a capitalization weighted, S&P Index program of securities, we undertook a six-month analysis following the establishment of negotiated commission rates. The results of this analysis are shown in Figure 4.

Figure 4
Index Fund Trading Costs Using Conventional Trading Methods (period of analysis June to November 1975 – 12 trading programs)

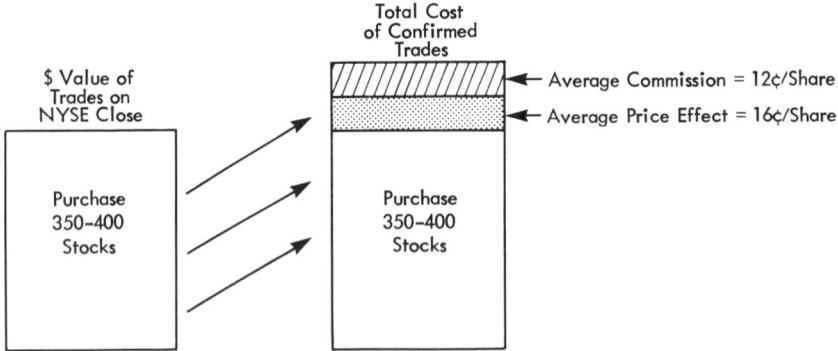

Total trading costs = 28¢ per share or 0.82 percent of contribution value.

---

[6] Larry J. Cuneo and Wayne H. Wagner, "Reducing the Cost of Stock Trading," *Financial Analysts Journal,* November-December 1975, for example.

The test included 12 trading programs executed during the period of June-November 1975. Packages of 350-400 purchase orders were executed at the opening of the business day after being priced at the NYSE close of the prior day. The diagram demonstrates that the total transaction costs incurred in completing these trading programs averaged 28 cents per share or 0.82 percent of the value of the cash invested. Interestingly, the price effect or market maker's spread averaged 16 cents per share, which is quite consistent with the minimum pricing interval used by the brokerage community of $\frac{1}{8}$ point or 12.5 cents for a liquid stock in the marketplace.

A variety of trading techniques are used by index fund managers, ranging from normal market order arrangements to "package" trading programs. The former technique is similar to conventional trading approaches; a package trading program (which may involve as many as 500 issues) is treated as if a single security transaction was being executed. Packaged programs may be executed by a broker on either a nonrisk basis or on an at-risk basis. The latter method involves the transfer of the price effect or market risk to the broker from the manager and, hence, from the investor, eliminating the price effect portion of the total transaction and leaving only the commission cost portion to be absorbed. While the commission cost is higher in such cases, the manager (and the investor) have, in effect, insured themselves against adverse short-term market moves during the period that the program is being executed. Figure 5 illustrates our experience in using the concept of the package program executed on an at-risk basis. Here, the purchase price of the package in each of 100 separate

Figure 5
Index Fund Trading Costs Using Package Trading Procedure
(Period of trading program experience: November 1975 to October 1978–100 trading programs)

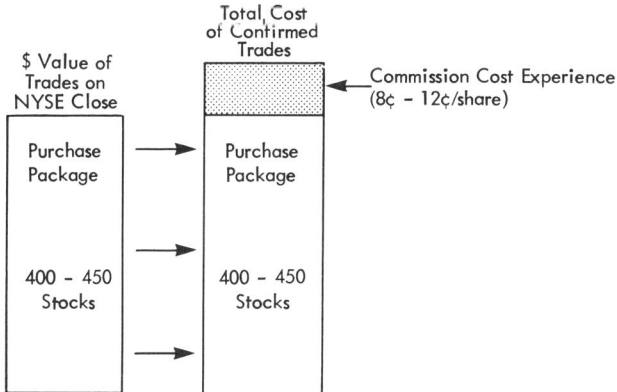

Total trading costs = 8¢-12¢ per share or 0.20-0.30 percent of contribution value.

trading programs (involving 400-450 securities) was struck at the close of business on a designated day. The trades were actually executed on subsequent trading days at the risk of the selected broker. The cost of these package executions ranged from 8 to 12 cents per share and averaged an amount approximating 0.25 percent of the value of the invested cash.

Having established a basis for drawing comparisons between the trading costs of active and passive management strategies, the full effect of trading costs on expected portfolio return can be estimated by taking note of expected portfolio turnover. Conventionally managed portfolio sales turnover averaged more than 30 percent per year in 1975-1976 before declining to 25 percent in 1977. Sales turnover rates for the WFB Index Fund are expected to be less than 1 percent per year. The resulting spread in incurred annual trading costs between these two forms of management is nearly 0.75 percent, assuming a 25 percent sales turnover level for an active account. (See Table 2.)

A reasonable expected return estimate for the equity market at current levels is some 14 percent per year.[7] Given this expected re-

Table 2
Trading Costs Comparison

Conventional equity portfolio sales turnover 1977	25.6%*
Total turnover	
Sales	25%
Repurchases	25%
Two-way	50% × 1.5% = Trading costs = .75%
Wells Fargo Bank Index Fund sales turnover 1977	.07%
Total turnover	
Sales	Less than 1%
Repurchases	Less than 1%
Two-way	Less than 2% × 0.25% = Trading costs = .005%

*Source: Becker Securities, Funds Evaluation Service, 1977. Courtesy of A. G. Becker Incorporated.

[7] *Prospective return from U.S. Equity Market:*

Expected return equals current yield plus nominal growth assume:

Yield on market currently 5.5 percent
Expected inflation rate of 5 percent per year
Expected real growth of economy of 3.5 percent per year
Corporate America's share of GNP is static
Dividends grow proportionally with earnings

Then

Expected return from equities will be 14.0 percent per year

$$(5.5 + 5.0 + 3.5 = 14.0)$$

turn, the effect of the differentially higher trading costs of active management can be evaluated as shown in Table 3.

Table 3
Net Expected Return

	Index Fund (beta 1.0)	Average Active Portfolio (beta 1.0)
Expected return	14.00%	14.00%
Penalty for assuming diversifiable risk	–	–0.30
Trading costs	–0.005	–0.75
Management fee	–0.10	–0.30-0.50
Net expected return	13.89%	1.25-12.45%

After deducting the expected trading costs of each approach and their typical annual management fees, and the cost incurred from assuming (relative to market) diversifiable risk, it is clear that the average active manager must provide at least 1.25 percent per annum of added return to draw even with the passive approach.

The active-passive trade-off is further complicated by the fact that the typical active manager will underperform the average active manager. This means that choosing a manager at random carries with it less than a 50 percent chance that the manager's future results will be average or above. Just as individual stock returns are skewed to the left, so are stock portfolio returns skewed; the median, 50th percentile return will be below the average return. The limit on negative returns is (minus) 100 percent, but positive returns are not limited to (plus) 100 percent. One should expect the median portfolio to underperform the average portfolio by an estimated 20 to 30 basis points per year over time.

In retrospect, the economics of the marketplace as well as the published empirical evidence attest to the difficulty of outperforming the S&P 500 Index by the required amount. Figure 6 provides the range of annualized equity portfolio performance results for approximately 3,000 funds. The measurements were made for one- to ten-year cumulative periods ending December 31, 1977. The range of results is divided into quartile and other groupings, and the diamond-shaped figures denote the position of the S&P 500 Index performance result within that range. The percentile ranking of the S&P 500 within this range is provided in the row labeled "Percent Rank." Over the 1-, 5-, and 10-year periods shown, the annualized rate of total return of the median actively-managed equity portfolio under-

Figure 6
Equities: Annualized Rates of Return for Periods Ending December 31, 1977

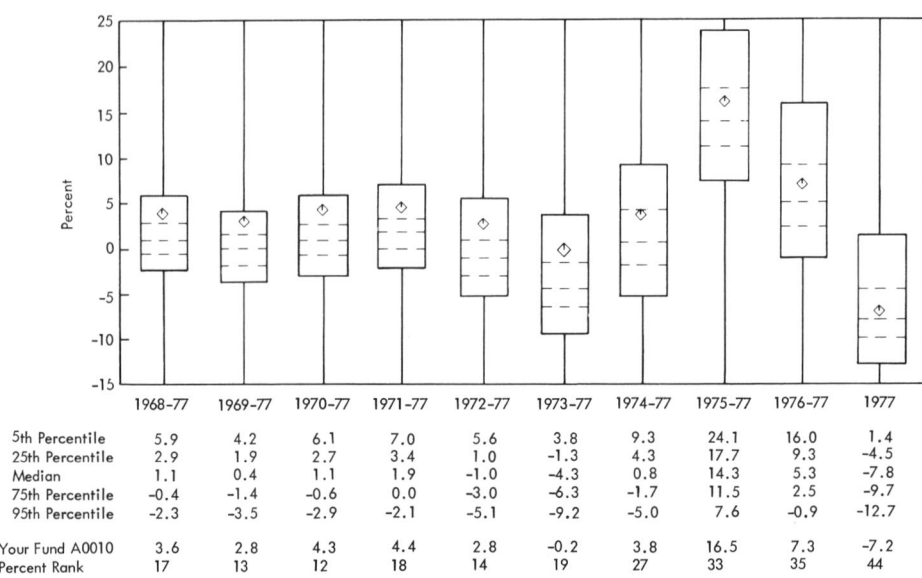

	1968-77	1969-77	1970-77	1971-77	1972-77	1973-77	1974-77	1975-77	1976-77	1977
5th Percentile	5.9	4.2	6.1	7.0	5.6	3.8	9.3	24.1	16.0	1.4
25th Percentile	2.9	1.9	2.7	3.4	1.0	-1.3	4.3	17.7	9.3	-4.5
Median	1.1	0.4	1.1	1.9	-1.0	-4.3	0.8	14.3	5.3	-7.8
75th Percentile	-0.4	-1.4	-0.6	0.0	-3.0	-6.3	-1.7	11.5	2.5	-9.7
95th Percentile	-2.3	-3.5	-2.9	-2.1	-5.1	-9.2	-5.0	7.6	-0.9	-12.7
Your Fund A0010	3.6	2.8	4.3	4.4	2.8	-0.2	3.8	16.5	7.3	-7.2
Percent Rank	17	13	12	18	14	19	27	33	35	44

Source: Becker Securities, Funds Evaluation Service, 1977. Courtesy of A. G. Becker Incorporated.

performed the S&P 500 Index by a minimum of 0.6 percent and a maximum of 4.1 percent; in no year was there a positive difference in favor of the median active portfolio. In both the 5- and 10-year periods, the S&P 500 outperformed more than 80 percent of the sample of some 3,000 portfolios.

Pooled versus Individual Portfolios

Passive equity portfolios are currently managed on either a pooled or an individual basis. The pooled approach provides several economies of scale to the investor that are unavailable on an individually invested basis. First, pooling enables a group of investors who, individually, would be unable to fund a full capitalization weighting portfolio approach, to avail themselves of the economic benefits of that approach at extremely low cost. Second, the combined cashflows of pooled participants create other cost-saving opportunities. As the dollar value of index fund investment programs increases, the transaction costs incurred as a percentage of the cash invested tends to decrease. This occurs generally because of cost economies available to the brokerage community in processing larger, as compared with smaller, share volume. In addition, when individual S&P 500 issues from an existing equity portfolio can be made available to an index fund for direct transfer, a significant portion of a total contribution may be absorbed "in kind" without incurring any transaction costs at all. (An "in-kind" transaction is effected with stock instead of cash, obviating any need to buy the issues involved.) Wells Fargo's experience over the past five years has been that between 35 percent and 70 percent of the dollar value of an existing equity portfolio presented for conversion to index fund participation can be accommodated through the in-kind transfer process. In fact, the pooled fund approach to indexing maximizes the proportion of an existing equity portfolio's value that can be accommodated in-kind, vis-a-vis the "stand-alone" index fund alternative. When the cash flow associated with a pooled index fund is combined with an existing equity portfolio, the larger total amount available for investment increases the purchase requirements for each stock in the index fund over what it would otherwise have been. This means that more shares of the existing equity portfolio can be accepted into the index fund through in-kind transfer. The size of this transfer is substantially greater than would be possible if a new stand-alone index fund was being created from the same existing-portfolio securities, absent the pooled fund's cash flow. In addition, the existence of cash inflows to the pooled portfolio may assist investors in incurring minimal transaction costs in exiting the fund.

In our view, there is no real economic reason to recommend a separate index portfolio versus the pooled alternative. Two noneconomic reasons for individual or stand-alone portfolios may be encountered, however. First, the inventory fund concept requires the creation of an individual portfolio since legal considerations preclude the use of a pooled portfolio with multiple participants for this purpose. In addition, certain investors have a definite aversion to individual companies, types of companies, and even whole industries. If such issues must be dropped from the index being matched, then an individual portfolio excluding them is a necessity.

PASSIVE EQUITY MANAGEMENT STRATEGIES

Core-Noncore (Passive-Active) Portfolios

It is common in the case of large pension plans to hire a number of equity managers. Each manager, within a set of generally broad guidelines, is free to pursue an equity investment strategy. Each manager, usually implicitly, chooses a portfolio beta and a level of diversifiable risk (i.e., the risk associated with stock selection) for her or his individual piece of the whole. In the context of the total pension plan equity commitment, the aggregate portfolio beta is a weighted average of the individual portfolio betas. However, the level of diversification of the total equity portfolio is lower than the average of the individual portfolios because, collectively, the managers cancel out one another's positions to some extent. In many cases, the total portfolios of large multiple-manager pension plans resemble "closet" index funds. Unfortunately, because of higher management fees and trading costs, their performance will very likely fall short of that produced by a real index fund.

In addition, because managers tend to view their individual portfolios on a stand-alone basis, they introduce a conservative bias by overdiversifying their portfolios relative to the investment opportunities they perceive. Limitations on the size of holdings—by issue, industry, or market sector—and other constraints are common. In protecting the portfolio (as well as reducing personal business risk), the manager often fails to take full advantage of stock selection or other value-related judgments. In general, in multiple-manager plans, each manager individually could substantially increase the level of diversifiable risk in a separate portfolio with only a moderate increase in risk for the portfolio as a whole.

In this context, a passive portfolio can be useful not only in managing the risk of the equity portion of the asset base and in reducing overall management and trading costs, but also in providing active managers with a larger opportunity to more fully exploit their management skills. The idea is to establish a "core" passive portfolio as an addition to the manager set. The active portfolios would then represent the "noncore" position. The balance between the core and noncore portions would be specified, and the active managers instructed as to the desirable level of portfolio beta, the range of portfolio beta and the minimum and maximum levels of diversification to be attained. The set of portfolios then work in harmony, anchored by the passive portion, in compliance with the sponsor's plan objectives and goals.

How Much Passive Management?

A decision must be made as to the "optimal" size of the core portfolio. The critical inputs are judgments regarding the ability of the active managers to provide additional net return over the passive rate of return, and judgments regarding the client's risk-aversion and investment-planning horizon.

A typical pattern of core-noncore use which maximizes client satisfaction is presented in Figure 7. The optimal core-noncore balance is reported as "percent active" (rounded to the nearest 10 percent). The determination of the optimal core-noncore split is based on an application of modern portfolio theory, where estimates of return, risk, and client risk-aversion are employed in a Markowitz-type

6: Passive Equity Management Strategies

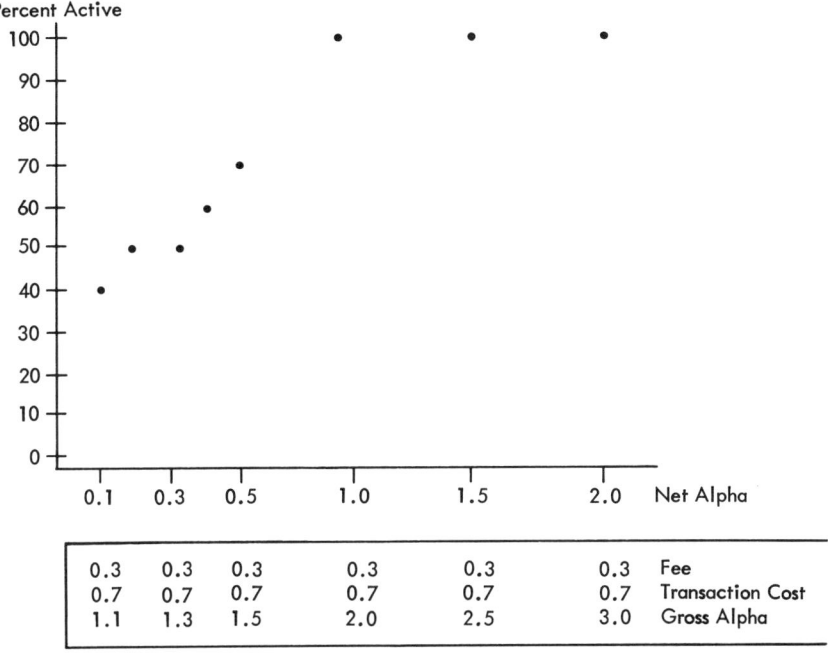

Figure 7
Active-Passive Decision

0.3	0.3	0.3	0.3	0.3	0.3	Fee
0.7	0.7	0.7	0.7	0.7	0.7	Transaction Cost
1.1	1.3	1.5	2.0	2.5	3.0	Gross Alpha

Other assumptions (per annum):
Expected return, stock market .... 14 percent
Risk, stock market (standard deviation) .... 18 percentage points
Diversifiable risk, active manager (standard deviation) ...... 6 percentage points
Investment horizon .... 5 years
Passive management fee .... 0.1 percent
Active management fee .... 0.3 percent
Risk aversion .... Average

mean-variance model. The assumptions used in the analysis are listed. Given a net additional return (net alpha) of 0.5 percent per annum, the optimal size would be 70 percent active and 30 percent passive. Several important conclusions result from our work in this area. First, there is economic justification for mixing active and passive management under realistic sets of assumptions. Second, if a plan sponsor confidently expected to receive an additional net return from active management of more than 1 percentage point per annum, use of the passive alternative would generally not be warranted, assuming typical levels of diversifiable risk. Of course, if the expectation is that active management may not produce an additional net return, the economic conclusion would be that the entire equity portfolio should be managed passively. As noted earlier, the typical active manager can be expected to underperform the market while incurring higher risk. Moreover, if the stock market is reasonably efficient, it will be quite difficult for pension plan sponsors to identify and engage, in advance, that group of active managers who can be expected to consistently outperform by 1 percentage point or more per annum. Neither extreme is probably the right answer. Pragmatically, if the active managers can add as little as 0.1 percent net, then the solution calls for some inclusion of active management.

Asset Allocation Assistance

The single most important decision made in managing an institutional investment portfolio is the mix between alternative asset classes, principally stocks and bonds. Where changes in the mix employ timing procedures, use of a passive equity portfolio as the trading vehicle can significantly enhance performance. Large trading programs can very quickly move into and out of equities at a fraction of conventional trading costs. Importantly, this can be accomplished with no effect whatsoever on the existing actively-managed portfolios. Use of companion short-term and fixed-income funds in the hands of the passive manager can cover both sides of the mix change routinely. Thus, the passive manager can act as a balancing manager for the plan, efficiently adjusting the mix without interfering with any other manager.

To the extent the plan sponsor desires, the existing group of active managers can have a say in the asset mix decision. Or a special advisor can be hired to manage the asset mix decision. The special advisor may or may not be the organization that actually manages the passive portfolio.

Market Inventory Fund

The passive equity index fund is recognized as a significant development in the process of investment management. Both the economic value and the utility of the concept have been proven through operational experience and realized results. Encouraged by this, there has been a recent application of some of the elements of the passive equity index fund concept in a new form: the *market inventory fund*. This application combines some of the diversification and cost effectiveness associated with a standard index fund with the capacity to fulfill a market-making function among a group of affiliated active-equity managers.

The market inventory fund is generally an S&P 500 form of index fund which can, within limits, accommodate the trades of a pension plan's multiple-manager equity portfolio. The purpose of a market inventory fund is to act as an intermediary between active managers in order to eliminate situations where different managers purchase and sell the same stocks through an outside market maker during a quarterly time period. Long and short positions are created in the market inventory fund in relation to the composition of the S&P 500 Index in order that the portfolio can accept the sales of S&P 500 issues or fill the purchasing needs of the active managers in those issues. The importance of this concept is that the trading costs normally incurred when an active manager executes a transaction with an outside market maker can be completely eliminated in these specific situations. The impact of the concept on overall pension plan equity investment operations is twofold. First, operating cost reductions are expected to occur since redundant trades are crossed within the plan's system, thereby eliminating the need to utilize the services of an outside broker or market maker. Second, since the trading costs incurred by the liquidity-motivated index fund are much smaller than those involved in information-motivated active management, the passive vehicle provides a more economically effective approach to clearing and resupplying the multiple manager system, as long as the brokerage community views inventory trading as being passive in nature. The market inventory fund is designed specifically to reduce turnover and trading costs within the system while delivering total return relative to the S&P 500 Index within a desired range of performance limits.

From a technical viewpoint, the market inventory fund concept appears to be a viable approach to reducing the costs of a pension plan's equity management activities. More study should be given to a possible problem, however, regarding the effect of information-motivated trades within the system since these trades may tend to produce results which are the reverse of those desired. Since active managers are engaged for their ability to employ special investment insights in their management activities, the presence of a sale (or purchase) order should generally indicate that the issue is expected to decline (or rise) in value following the transaction. The market inventory fund becomes underdiversified relative to the S&P 500 Index in order to accommodate these trades by taking positions while awaiting possible internal crossing transactions. Since the price impact stemming from the information content of these transactions will tend to force the value of the passive portfolio's long positions down and of its short positions upward, the process may result in negative bias to the tracking error for the portfolio or, more directly, financial losses for the total pension plan that could have been avoided. To the extent that the manager initiating a trade really has valuable information concerning the issue involved, failure to add (or subtract) the issue to (or from) the portfolio negates the value of the information to the fund.

The potential cost savings from a market inventory fund depend primarily upon the frequency with which active trades can be internally crossed through the plan's system. To date, there has been little published verification of the volume of such trades actually experienced by plans employing a market inventory fund. Moreover, the cost saving aspect depends upon the ability of market inventory funds to command the preferential transaction cost treatment normally accorded only to liquidity-motivated index fund trades. To the extent that information-motivated trades overflow the fund's capacity to inventory the issues involved, they may well be seen to be information-motivated trades in selected issues. It would be only logical to expect that at some point the brokerage community may refuse to accord the preferential treatment and, hence, cease to offer the cost savings by introducing trading spreads approximating those normally associated with the information-motivated trades of active management.

Other Passive Possibilities

The use of passive strategies need not be confined to domestic equity investment alone. Indeed, several managers have already extended the concept to the bond market and have also worked out management techniques for passive investment in the major foreign equity markets. Several closed-end real estate funds, passive once they are formed, also exist. In addition, strategies that utilize options written against passive equity portfolios are being discussed. In fact, there is no conceptual reason why any area of portfolio investment strategy should not be considered for application of passive portfolios. Such portfolios could be "yield-tilted" or "growth-tilted," for example, or take any one of a number of alternative forms—the concept is there, it works, and it lends itself to innovative utilization.

Management of Individual Portfolios

7 PETER L. BERNSTEIN
Peter L. Bernstein, Inc.
New York, New York
and Editor, *The Journal of Portfolio Management*

IS THERE A DIFFERENCE BETWEEN PERSONAL AND INSTITUTIONAL PORTFOLIO MANAGEMENT?

When institutional holdings of common stocks were much less than they are today, the professionals who managed the security portfolios of individuals also took on the task of managing institutional accounts. Today, however, the functions are separate in most organizations, with portfolio managers specializing in either one area or the other, but the twain seldom meet.

While this gives one the impression that somehow the investment problems are unrelated and that each requires different types of understanding, experience, and skill, the essential principles of portfolio management are in fact identical. Of course, portfolios differ widely in their requirements, time horizons, risk thresholds, and cash flows. The objective of portfolio management is to reconcile these variables in such a manner as to minimize risk and maximize return, but the goal and the process of reconciling the variables is the same regardless of who happens to own the assets in question.

Admittedly, individual accounts frequently differ from institutional accounts in two areas: (1) many individuals are unable to add fresh cash to their investment portfolio in a systematic and predictable fashion—indeed, some individuals consume capital rather than accumulate it and (2) many institutional portfolios are exempt from income and capital gains taxes. As we shall see, however, these are just two of the many variables that enter into the construction of an investment program, but in all cases the theoretical considerations are the same.

All portfolios share one objective: to provide the largest possible pool of assets from which the owner can finance expenditures now or at some future date. Since the future is uncertain, however, we can never know precisely what the value of the assets will be over time, and we know even less about what their purchasing power will be. The degree of risk that we take should therefore vary in each case, based on the time horizon within which we have to work and the likelihood that the portfolio will enjoy a net cash inflow or will be subject to cash withdrawals. The art of portfolio management consists of nothing more than selecting securities that fit within the time and cash flow constraints of the client: the application of this process to differing portfolios is only a variation on a constant theme.

DEFINING INVESTMENT OBJECTIVES

Conventionally, portfolio managers differentiate among three goals: maximum income, capital appreciation, and preservation of capital. If we look at the matter rationally, however, all investors should want to achieve all three of these goals: obviously, no one wants to lose money, while everyone wants to have as much as possible.

The problem is that most of the time circumstances deny us the opportunity to achieve all three goals simultaneously. The search for capital gain is never assured of success, so it inevitably involves risk of loss of capital; assured income is seldom available with opportunities for capital gain; high income is frequently associated with high risk. Consequently, when the time horizon is short or when the investor has to face cash withdrawals from the portfolio, we lean toward those assets with greatest certainty of income and capital value; while when the time horizon stretches out into the future and when the investor is adding to rather than withdrawing principal, we can live more comfortably with uncertainty.

Nevertheless, leaving tax considerations aside for more detailed discussion later on, the temptation to look at income and principal as separate pools of money can frequently lead to poor decisions. Admittedly, income is more certain than capital appreciation and therefore seems a more appropriate objective for the investor whose risk threshold is low. On the other hand, what he really wants is money, or, perhaps more accurately, purchasing power. If his income is high relative to his expenditure requirements, he will be able either to minimize his capital withdrawals or, in fact, to add to his capital. On the other hand, if his capital grows, he can draw on it to supplement his income or will have more money available to finance outlays at a later date.

As a result, the relatively new concept of *total return* is a refreshing addition to the terminology of portfolio management. It emphasizes that the objective of investment is to have the largest possible pool of money to finance outlays either now or later, that money is money no matter what its source, and that the search for income and for capital gain are only variations on the basic theme of maximizing return and minimizing risk.

Thus, generous income can allow an individual or a pension fund to accumulate assets at a time when the opportunities for capital appreciation seem limited. On the other hand, when the opportunities are right, capital appreciation can also increase the size of the assets or finance a higher level of expenditure. Exclusive focus on one or the other may lead to minimizing returns or maximizing risks (or both) when market considerations as well as the requirements of the portfolio might lead to a different set of decisions. And all of this applies with equal significance to institutional and individual portfolios.

HOW SHOULD RISK BE CONSIDERED?

Risk essentially means the degree of certainty or uncertainty regarding the outcome of a decision. When we buy a U.S. government bond, we know precisely what our income will be and precisely how much money we will have at a specified date in the future; when we drill for oil, no one can tell us precisely how much income or principal we will have at any date in the future. When we buy stock in a company selling consumable products to millions of customers and with a strong proprietary position in its market, the chances of unpleasant surprises are smaller than when we buy stock in an armament manufacturer with only one big customer or in a company operating in a fiercely competitive field. Similarly, projecting future earnings is more certain for a company without debt than for one that is highly leveraged.

Risk varies in degree from the chance of *total* loss of capital—such as drilling for oil or a new and untried venture—to its more benign aspect of *variability* of capital value rather than total loss. The risk considerations involved in most of the assets that go into a conventional investment portfolio usually take the latter form, although even here they can be real enough: the shrinkage in equity values from 1929 to 1932 ran to 90 percent on the average, and the investor who bought in 1929 had to wait about 25 years to break even on capital values. Even in October 1973, U.S. Steel was selling below its level of 1959.

Thus, for most investment decisions, the major uncertainty is the probable volatility in the price of the asset and, in particular, its volatility relative to the prices of all similar types of assets. The term *beta* refers to the degree to which any individual common stock fluctuates relative to the fluctuations in the stock market as a whole.

Assets that are closest to cash—that is, assets like savings accounts or very short-term securities, whose dollar value fluctuates either not at all or only in a negligible range—obviously have a high degree of certainty as to their value in the future. Assets like long-term debt instruments may fluctuate widely between purchase date and maturity but will clearly fluctuate within a narrowing range as their maturity date approaches. Meanwhile, the investor does know precisely what his income will be and what the value of the security will be at a specified date in the future. Equities, on the other hand, have no maturity date and therefore have no limit to their possible price swings between infinity and zero.[1]

Investors will rationally choose assets with less certainty as to their future value only if they expect such assets to provide a higher return than assets with more limited volatility. But what we are really saying here is that the investor who seeks higher returns has a greater probability of losing money than the investor who settles for lower returns. Since everyone obviously wants to make as much money as possible, the determining question in structuring a portfolio is the *consequence of loss*. This is far more important than the *chance* of loss. Even if the chance of loss is small (such as the probability of dying at the age of 35), the consequences can be so serious that the individual must either avoid the risk altogether or must insure against it if he is unable to avoid it.

This is why the widow is conventionally viewed as an investor unable to take much risk. Because she typically has neither the life expectancy nor the earning power outside her portfolio to provide the opportunity to recoup losses, any diminution in her capital or income may immediately impact her standard of living. Her mythological opposite, the aggressive young businessman, on the other hand, has sufficient earning power to sustain his living standard and also has many years in which to recoup his losses. At an even further extreme, the consequences would be virtually minimal for a young man who will inherit millions from aging parents.

---

[1] An interesting corollary of this is that cold arithmetic automatically stacks the cards in the investor's favor: he can lose only 100 percent but can gain an infinite amount.

But is this the end of the matter? If the degree of risk that we are willing to take is a function of the consequences of loss, loss is nevertheless an unpleasant possible outcome to *any* investment decision, no matter how small the consequences. In other words, we should also ask some questions about the consequences of *gain*. To what extent would an increase in capital or income significantly improve the living standard of the investor? A widow with less than $100,000 to invest might lead an entirely different life if it were $200,000, while the multimillionaire (and his heirs) might live precisely the same whether his assets never changed in value or whether they doubled.

Two cases of actual investors serve to emphasize this point. One, whose company had just gone public and put him in the multimillionaire class, stated without qualification, "Just remember you don't have to try to make me rich—I am rich!" The other, a man in his mid-50s, had lost his job two years earlier with only $15,000 to his name. He realized that if he lost the whole $15,000 playing the market, his family would be broke just one year sooner than if he had used the money to cover their living expenses, so he margined the $15,000 to the hilt, bought three of the hottest stocks in the market, and parlayed the $15,000 into $200,000 after paying off the margin debts.

In other words, the apparent *ability* to sustain losses frequently fails to go hand in hand with the *necessity* to take risks to maximize gains. The consequences of gain and the consequences of loss seldom fit in such a way that the risk exposure of the portfolio is easy to determine. In many instances, this is a subjective decision: some people never feel rich enough, while others would rather take the chance of going broke next year than this year, but the more rational approach to this question is illustrated by the two clients I have just described.

The principles involved here illustrate clearly the identity of basic considerations in individual and institutional portfolio management. A pension fund whose contributions will exceed its benefit payments for the indefinite future is surely in an ideal position to take big risks, because both time and net cash inflow provide full opportunity to recoup losses. On the other hand, since actuarial calculations can provide a precise projection of how much it must earn to meet its ultimate objectives, why should it take the risk of falling short of those objectives when low-risk assets such as long-term bonds may readily do the job?[2]

---

[2] Of course, beating the actuarial requirement would permit either higher benefits to beneficiaries or lower cost to the employer.

HEDGING AGAINST RISK

Experience tells us that, *on the average,* the greater the risk, the greater the probable return. Even investors who are risk-averse for one reason or another should want to take advantage of profitable opportunities that fit within the risk constraints of the portfolio.

The implications of this statement are crucial for successful portfolio management. Indeed, the statement highlights what portfolio management is all about. Portfolio management is not stock selection, which is the task of security analysis. Portfolio management is the adjustment of the overall risk exposure of the portfolio to the needs of the client. To put it another way, good portfolio management enables the client to seek the higher returns implicit in higher risk without exceeding the total amount of risk that the client wants to take.

Seen from this viewpoint, much of the common practice of portfolio management falls short of its potential. Traditionally, some types of securities are considered appropriate for widows, and entirely different securities are considered appropriate for the aggressive businessman's account. Some are used in institutional portfolios and others in individual accounts.

But this is irrational. At all times, the process of security analysis and stock selection should designate those securities whose risk/reward ratio is most promising at any particular moment. If the most attractive stock the portfolio manager knows happens to be a highly volatile one, why should his widow clients miss the opportunity to enjoy the rewards he expects from it? If no volatile stocks appear attractive, why should the aggressive businessman take the risk of owning them when his prospective total return might be greater in the tax-exempt bonds the manager is buying for his widow clients?

All securities that appear attractive to the manager are appropriate for all clients; no issues of lesser attractiveness are appropriate for any client. The crucial question is the *proportion of the total portfolio* that he concentrates in securities of one type or another. The overall volatility of a widow's account should in all likelihood be low, which means that the volatile sector should be small and offset by larger holdings of low volatility—but that is different from saying that the manager should never buy volatile stocks for that account. On the other hand, the client mentioned above with $15,000 who decided to shoot the moon would have defeated his purpose if he had concentrated his portfolio in anything other than highly volatile stocks.

Thus, portfolio management turns out to be a process of hedging against the risks that the investor must take if the outcome is to be a successful one. Hedging against risk has nothing to do with avoiding risk. Rather, it is an effort to reduce the probabilities of loss that are implicit in every risk-taking decision. While part of this effort is obviously involved in limiting the overall volatility of the portfolio, as we have just seen, the other crucial aspect of it is to avoid involuntary liquidation of assets at depressed prices.

This is why the conventional wisdom of portfolio management places so much emphasis on the resources the investor owns in addition to his volatile assets. A steady job with good earning power in a sound company, comfortable balances in the savings bank to cover emergency needs, and adequate life insurance all provide *staying power*—the ability to hold depressed securities until they recover in price or until they can be sold and the proceeds used to purchase securities with more promise.

The investor who has no liquid resources to meet the emergencies of life or to cover other needs unrelated to his investment program will always face the unpleasant necessity to dip into his portfolio to raise cash for these external purposes. No one can have any preordained guarantee that the moment for such sales will be precisely the most appropriate one. In fact, loss of a job, appeals for help from other members of the family, or margin calls have the uncomfortable habit of coinciding with depressed security prices.

Any investment program will be disrupted if decisions to sell depend upon anything other than investment considerations. Unless the investor has liquid reserves over and above his security portfolio, in fact, he may have to be selling early to be sure he has cash reserves when, in a properly hedged program, he could hold out longer and take the risk of greater price fluctuations in his portfolio.

Thus, although most people look at the investor's outside resources as a device to protect the investor himself, we should really look at them as a means of protecting his portfolio *from him!*

A CASE STUDY

The following case study is a true story that illustrates most of the principles analyzed above, even though the situation was a most unusual one.

Late in 1959, a young man was referred to us after he had sustained a hideous accident. Although the accident had deprived him of any chance of earning a decent living and, in all probability, of getting married, it left him with a normal life expectancy of 50 years or so. To make matters worse, he had been the sole support of aging and ailing parents. The insurance company had just presented him with a check for $200,000.

Here was a case where invasion of capital was perilous, for the $200,000 was going to have to take care of him for many years. On the other hand, the maximum income available from quality securities at that time—primarily from bonds yielding less than 5 percent—was insufficient to provide for the family's needs, to say nothing of the inflation risk inherent in putting all one's resources into bonds. Here was a case where the investor simply had to take some risks, even though his capability to absorb losses was clearly limited.

We solved the problem by putting about three quarters of the account into bonds and the remainder into what appeared at the time to be pretty aggressive investments, such as IBM, MMM, American Hospital Supply, and a small highly speculative mutual fund. Thus, individual items in the portfolio had high volatility, but the portfolio as a whole had the low volatility that was appropriate to this particular individual. The income we sacrificed by buying these low-yielding stocks would, hopefully, be more than compensated for by capital appreciation, but in any case, the income sacrifice was small relative to the total picture.

While the success of this program speaks for itself, the important point is that this man never would have gone broke even if the stock selections had been less fortunate. Furthermore, since the bonds had less volatility than the stocks, the bonds were available to cover capital withdrawals if the stocks were depressed; this provided the staying power to hold the stocks until they recovered. As it happened, things went the other way, so that the appreciated values of the stocks were used to meet capital withdrawals, which both kept the overall volatility of the account down and also enabled the portfolio manager to avoid liquidating the bonds when they were depressed.

This example is a good illustration of the factors involved in determining overall volatility, in establishing staying power, and in using the concept of total return. Even though this particular individual's circumstances were unusual, they differ hardly at all from the considerations that must be faced by the portfolio manager of a mutual fund who may be faced with a continuous flow of net redemptions. Here, too, he must attempt to preserve and enhance the assets of those stockholders who are holding rather than redeeming, at the same time that he must avoid liquidating assets at depressed prices when redemptions come in. Furthermore, given the necessity to limit the overall volatility of the portfolio and therefore the probabilities of large total capital gains for the portfolio as a whole, he must instead try to increase the stockholder's return by generating a higher level of income.

TAX CONSIDERATIONS

Taxes are just one more external factor that should not interfere with rational investment decision making. When taxes dominate the investment decision, investors frequently end up regretting it. Indeed, taxes frequently lead people to make moves that they would never make under any other circumstances and that are therefore irrational.

In the first place, many individual investors tend to exaggerate the impact of the capital gains tax. The tax on capital gains is taken at 40 percent of the investor's top bracket on regular taxable income, with a maximum of 20 percent. This means that the tax will be equal to 20 percent of the capital gain only when it pushes the investor's top bracket up to the maximum bracket of 50 percent. On single returns, this was $41,500 of taxable income in 1982; on joint returns, it was $85,600 of taxable income. Many investors, particularly those who live only on the income from their securities, have taxable incomes that fall well short of those figures and will therefore pay capital gains taxes of less than 20 percent.

Furthermore, since the tax falls on the gain only, it will have a major impact on the proceeds only when the gain is unusually large. Thus, on a gain equal to 50 percent of the cost price, the tax is at most going to be 20 percent of one third of the proceeds, or less than 6.7 percent of the total amount realized from the sale; many stocks fluctuate much more than that in the course of a year or even a few months. In general, suppose that a stock is purchased at a price P and it appreciates to nP. If T is the capital gains rate, then the capital gains tax as a percentage of the sales price is:

$$T \frac{(n-1)}{n}$$

Since the ultimate outcome of establishing a long-term gain rests as much with the new security that might be purchased as with the action of the security that might be sold, and since no one can guess with any accuracy the double movements involved, reluctance to sell stock A to buy stock B simply because of tax considerations is likely to be the cause for ultimate regret.

In addition, since under present law, the only way to avoid the capital gains tax is to hold a security until it declines to a point where the gain is wiped out, which is obviously irrational, or until one dies. Experience tells us over and over that no company's fortunes are precisely predictable for a period of more than a few years at a time, so the decision to hold something until death is equally irrational unless the investor's life expectancy is shrinking rapidly; even the greatest companies of one era have been known to fade from glory in a later era, for reasons that no one could foresee.

Even then, the investor may tend to exaggerate the impact of the capital gains tax and be unnecessarily reluctant to make portfolio shifts that he would make under any other circumstances. The ultimate impact of the unified transfer tax (gross death tax) should always enter into the calculations of an older investor.

Take the case of a wealthy investor whose capital gains tax bracket will be 20 percent but whose top unified transfer tax bracket will be 40 percent. Let us assume he holds a security worth $30,000 with a cost basis of $10,000. Assuming also that the security remains unchanged in price from the moment when he might have sold it until the moment he dies, his estate will pay no capital gains tax but it will pay a unified transfer tax of 40 percent of $30,000, or $12,000. If he sells it and pays the capital gains tax of 20 percent of $20,000, or $4,000, his estate will be worth $4,000 less but the estate tax will be diminished by 40 percent of $4,000, or $1,600. If we offset the $1,600 estate tax saving against the $4,000 capital gains tax, the true impact of the tax was only $2,400—only 12 percent of the gain and only 8 percent of the proceeds, which are amounts that might well justify a portfolio switch that made sense from a strict investment viewpoint.

But investors become infatuated with taking losses as much as they fear taking gains. Here, too, they frequently fail to do the arithmetic needed to arrive at rational decisions that they would otherwise make if free of tax considerations.

Except on very large transactions, brokerage eats up about 3 percent of the proceeds if the investor sells one stock and buys another. Furthermore, he usually sells on the bid and buys on the offer. If the transaction is large, the sale will depress the price of one stock, while the purchase will push up the price of the other; this spread is likely to more than offset any savings in brokerage. Consequently, the investor should calculate the size of the tax saving in relation to the transaction cost. For example, consider an investor in the 20 percent capital gains tax bracket with a stock that cost $30 and is now selling for $20. He would save $2.00 in taxes by establishing the loss but would incur about $1.50 in brokerage plus the spread between bid and offer. Would a saving of less than 1.7 percent of the price of the stock, justify making the sale on pure investment considerations? If he were in a 15 percent capital gains tax bracket, the transaction cost would substantially wipe out the tax saving.

If a little arithmetic will protect the investor from selling a depressed security that fundamental investment considerations would otherwise induce him to hold, he should be equally rational in selecting a security to substitute for the one on which he has established a loss. Many investors want to replace one security with another at the same price, or equally depressed, or in the same industry, or even all three where possible. They thus often end up buying something they would never have bought under any other circumstances. They should realize that the proceeds of a sale consists of cash and that cash should be used to purchase the most attractive security they can find at that moment, which may only coincidentally be an equally depressed security in the same industry.

One final point is worth remembering. The rule that taxes are paid on capital gains only when the gains are realized in effect means that the investor who avoids paying a capital gains tax has in effect an interest-free loan from the government. But, unless he holds a security until he dies, it is still a loan. If he offsets a gain with a loss and uses the proceeds of the security on which the loss was taken to buy something else that then appreciates, he may well ultimately have to pay the capital gains tax on the new security in any case. Establishment of losses, in other words, may postpone the payment of the tax but seldom avoids it.

PROFESSIONAL CONSIDERATIONS

Professional portfolio managers in recent years have increasingly insisted upon discretionary authority in the management of individual portfolios. While this obviously makes life simpler for the portfolio manager, it also should work out to the benefit of the client.

The client should—and must—participate in the determination of the overall strategy for the account. The consequences of loss or gain in many instances are as much a subjective consideration as an objective one and are properly as much the client's problem as the advisor's. The risk exposure and game plan for the portfolio should be worked out jointly, explicitly set forth in writing, and reviewed on regular occasions.

Within the limitations of the overall strategy, however, the portfolio manager should have full authority for security selection. If the client must approve all moves, then it is ultimately the client who is managing the portfolio. Furthermore, he will be the victim of the manager's salesmanship, which may or may not coincide with the manager's best judgment. The manager will tend to make only those suggestions to which he expects the client to agree and will refrain from making suggestions that will result in argument and disagreement—even if the advisor's better judgment would favor the latter set of moves. This is hardly the basis for rational portfolio management.

The use of discretionary authority, however, should in no way reduce the portfolio manager's responsibility to maintain communication with the client, to keep him informed of the progress of the portfolio, and to advise the client of the advisor's uncertainties as well as his expectations. Full and honest communication, particularly when things are going less well than anticipated, is the surest way to keep the client's confidence and sustain a mutually profitable relationship.

One final matter deserves some comment. Many advisors like to select the broker through whom transactions are placed, either to facilitate good executions or to receive research services. Most clients will agree to this arrangement if the reasons for it are set before them and they understand that it is for their benefit. On the other hand, research generated through one client's brokerage is frequently used to make portfolio changes for another client, so the manager has an explicit responsibility to make certain that some sort of equitable relationship exists between any one client's brokerage costs and the research applied to his security holdings. Conflicts of interest are occasionally less apparent and more complex than many people believe!

Appendix: Capital Gain and Loss Tax Treatment*

FRANK J. FABOZZI, Ph.D., C.F.A., C.P.A.
Fordham University

In this appendix, the current federal tax treatment of capital gains and losses as it pertains to *individuals* is explained.

SOME DEFINITIONS

Gross Income, Adjusted Gross Income, and Taxable Income

Investors often use the term *income* in a very casual way. The Internal Revenue Code (IRC), however, provides a more precise definition of income. The IRC distinguishes between *gross income, adjusted gross income* and *taxable income.*

Gross income is all income that is subject to income tax. For example, interest income and dividends are subject to taxation. However, there is a statutory exemption for interest from certain types of debt obligations, for example, municipal bonds. For such obligations, interest income is not included in gross income.

Adjusted gross income is gross income minus certain business and

---

*For a more detailed discussion, see Frank J. Fabozzi, "Federal Income Tax Treatment of Fixed Income Securities," Chapter 3 in *The Handbook of Fixed Income Securities* edited by Frank J. Fabozzi and Irving M. Pollack (Homewood, Ill.: Dow Jones-Irwin, 1983).

other deductions. For example, for investors an important deduction from gross income to arrive at adjusted gross income is the long-term capital gain deduction. This deduction will be discussed later.

Taxable income is the amount on which the tax liability is determined. It is found by subtracting the personal exemption allowance and other permissible deductions, other than those deductible in arriving at adjusted gross income, from adjusted gross income.

Tax Basis of a Capital Asset, Capital Gain, and Capital Loss

The IRC provides for a special tax treatment on the sale or exchange of a *capital asset,* such as stocks and bonds. In order to understand the tax treatment of a capital asset, the *tax basis* of a capital asset must first be defined. In most instances the *original basis* of a capital asset is the price paid by a taxpayer on the date it is acquired. The *adjusted basis* of a capital asset is its original basis increased by capital additions and decreased by capital recoveries.

The proceeds received from the sale or exchange of a capital asset are compared to the adjusted basis to determine if the transaction produced a capital gain or capital loss. If the proceeds exceed the adjusted basis, the taxpayer realizes a *capital gain;* on the other hand, a *capital loss* is realized when the adjusted basis exceeds the proceeds received by the taxpayer.

TAXATION OF A CAPITAL GAIN OR LOSS

Once a capital gain or loss is determined for each capital transaction during the tax year, there are special rules for determining the impact on adjusted gross income and taxable income. It is first necessary to ascertain whether the sale or exchange has resulted in a capital gain or loss that is *long term* or *short term.* The classification depends upon the length of time the capital asset is held by the taxpayer. The general rule is that if a capital asset is held for one year or less, the gain or loss is a short-term capital gain or loss.[1] A long-term capital gain or loss results when the capital asset is held for one day more than one year, or longer. Usually, the day of acquisition is not counted in determining the holding period but the day of sale is counted.

Second, all short-term capital gains and losses are combined to

---

[1] An exception to this general rule applies to "wash sales." A wash sale occurs when "substantially identical securities" are acquired within 30 days before or after a sale of the securities *at a loss.* In such cases, the loss is not recognized as a capital loss. Instead, the loss is added to the basis of the securities that caused the loss. The holding period for the new securities in connection with the wash sale then includes the period for which the original securities were held.

produce either a *net short-term capital gain* or a *net short-term capital loss*. The same procedure is followed for long-term capital gains and losses. Either a *net long-term capital gain* or a *net long-term capital loss* will result.

Third, an overall *net capital gain* or *net capital loss* is determined by combining the amounts in the previous step. If the result is a net capital gain, the entire amount is added to gross income, However, net long-term capital gains are given preferential tax treatment. A deduction is allowed from gross income in determining adjusted gross income. The permissible deduction is 60 percent of the excess of net long-term capital gains over net short-term capital losses.[2] Table 1 provides six illustrations of the treatment of a net capital gain.

If there is a net capital loss, it is deductible from gross income. The amount that may be deducted, however, is limited to the lesser of (1) $3,000 (but $1,500 for a married taxpayer filing separate returns), (2) taxable income without the personal exemption and without capital gains and losses minus the zero bracket amount, and (3) the total of net short-term capital loss plus one-half the net long-term capital loss. The third limitation is the so-called "$1 for $2" rule and is the basic difference between the tax treatment of net short-term capital losses and net long-term capital losses. While the former is deductible dollar for dollar, the latter requires $2 of long-term capital loss to obtain a $1 deduction.

Because of the difference in the tax treatment of net long-term capital losses and net short-term capital losses, the order in which these losses are deductible in a tax year are specified by the Treasury. First, net short-term capital losses are used to satisfy the limitation. Any balance to satisfy the limitation is then applied from net long-term capital losses using the "$1 for $2" rule. Any unused net short-term or net long-term capital losses are carried over on a dollar-for-dollar basis.[3] When they are carried over, they do not lose their identity but remain either short term or long term. These losses can be carried over indefinitely until they are all utilized in subsequent tax years.

Table 2 provides 10 illustrations of the net capital loss deduction rule. In the illustrations it is assumed that taxable income as defined previously in (2) is greater than $3,000 and the taxpayer, if married, is not filing a separate return.

---

[2] A capital gain deduction taken by an individual could result in a minimum tax liability.

[3] However, in determining the amount of the net capital loss deduction in future tax years, the "$1 for $2" rule applies.

Table 1
Tax Treatment of a Net Capital Gain

	\multicolumn{6}{c}{Illustration}					
	1	2	3	4	5	6
1. Net long-term capital gain (loss)	$ 35,000	$ 35,000	$ 35,000	$ -0-	$(3,000)	$(8,000)
2. Net short-term capital gain (loss)	(15,000)	15,000	-0-	15,000	15,000	15,000
3. Net capital gain: increase in gross income	20,000	50,000	35,000	15,000	12,000	7,000
4. Excess of net long-term capital gain over net short-term capital loss	20,000	35,000	35,000	-0-	-0-	-0-
5. Capital gains deduction (60 percent of line 4)	(12,000)	(21,000)	(21,000)	-0-	-0-	-0-
6. Increase in adjusted gross income (line 3 minus line 5)	8,000	29,000	14,000	15,000	12,000	7,000

Table 2
Tax Treatment of a Net Capital Loss

	Illustration									
	1	2	3	4	5	6	7	8	9	10
1. Net long-term capital gain (loss)	$ -0-	$(7,000)	$(7,000)	$(7,000)	$(3,000)	$(4,000)	$ 6,000	$(4,000)	$(12,000)	$ 4,000
2. Net short-term capital gain (loss)	(5,000)	-0-	(5,000)	(2,000)	(1,000)	-0-	(7,000)	1,000	2,000	(14,000)
3. Net capital loss	5,000	7,000	12,000	9,000	4,000	4,000	1,000	3,000	10,000	10,000
4. Capital loss deduction*	3,000	3,000	3,000	3,000	2,500	2,000	1,000	1,500	3,000	3,000
5. Long-term capital loss carryover	-0-	1,000	7,000	5,000	-0-	-0-	-0-	-0-	4,000	-0-
6. Short-term capital loss carryover	2,000	-0-	2,000	-0-	-0-	-0-	-0-	-0-	-0-	7,000

*Assumes that the taxpayer (1) is not married or, if married, not filing a separate return and (2) has taxable income without the personal exemption and without capital gains and losses minus the zero bracket amount greater than $3,000.

Trends in Bond Portfolio Management

8   MARTIN L. LEIBOWITZ, Ph.D.
Managing Director,
Bond Portfolio Analysis Group
Salomon Brothers Inc
New York, New York

The last decade has witnessed a revolution in the management of bond portfolios. There has been an explosion in the variety of fixed income securities as well as in the range of available trading techniques. Within the ranks of the larger fee-based management organizations, "active bond management" has progressed from the status of a novelty to that of the norm.

The first part of this article will attempt to explore both the nature and the evolution of the forces that led to the remarkable transformation of what was formerly thought to be a bastion of rather staid (if not stuffy) conservatism.

As one comes to understand these new markets and competitive forces, one realizes that they are not an unmixed blessing. The drift away from the older fundamentals has created a potentially dangerous separation between goals and practice. Active bond management does not by itself automatically insure progress in the direction of the portfolio's basic objectives. Indeed, in some instances, the hot pursuit of total return may be inconsistent with the reasons for the original allocation of the funds to the fixed income area.

In the second part of the article, the "baseline" approach is set forth as one practical way to blend modern management techniques with the earlier, more fundamental view of the bond portfolio function. By harnessing the short-term total-return focus of the active manager to the fund's longer-term objectives, the baseline method can provide concrete guidelines for the goal-oriented management of bond portfolios.

THE EVOLUTION OF ACTIVE BOND MANAGEMENT

The Scope of Bond Management Activity

The modern bond portfolio manager has a wide selection of both strategic and tactical options available every day. One can select from coupons ranging from 2½ percent to over 10 percent. One can choose from a spectrum of maturities ranging from one day to distant dates deep into the next century. One can select issuers with names known and respected around the world, or move into obscure situations requiring specialized credit analysis. One can move, in many ways, toward greater protection from the threat of a refunding call, or can be paid for accepting greater call risks. One can reach for the accelerated payback and market strength of a strong sinking fund or a pass-through security, or can elect for a longer "lock up" of an attractive initial yield.

The manager can structure a portfolio to maximize returns over any time horizon from the very short term to very long term. One can split a portfolio into two segments; one segment focused on maximum yields with minimum management, and the other segment kept in highly marketable securities and earmarked for intensive short-term management.

One can manipulate the timing of commitment of new money flows.

One can try to anticipate overall changes in the long interest rates by adjusting the volatility of the portfolio.

One can try to take advantage of changing yield curves.

One can try to take advantage of the changing yield spread relationships between market sectors differentiated by quality, by coupon, by type of issuer, by type of issue, etc.

One can trade one bond for a closely-related issue at an apparently attractive spread. One can monitor the markets for the opportunity to reverse a trade and swap back into an original holding. Or one can make a further spread move into a third bond and begin a whole chain of swaps.

A manager can construct package swaps which combine two or more bond holdings in order to offset the impact of some specific factor, e.g., matching capital losses with capital gains, maintaining a given volatility, keeping a given maturity structure, sustaining existing levels of current yield, etc.

One can consolidate a large number of fragmented holdings by swapping them for a highly marketable set of issues. One must then recognize an obligation to make these marketable securities pay their own way. One pays a certain cost premium for marketability. If the potential value of this marketability is not utilized in some way, then this cost premium is just being wasted.

If the portfolio is subject to taxation, then the portfolio manager can and should thoroughly address the process of tax liability management.

These options are most fully available to the manager of a long-term portfolio. However, the thoughtful manager of a short-term portfolio can take partial advantage of many of these same options, especially where one is free to incorporate long-term instruments into a portfolio on a controlled-risk basis.

These are only a sampling of the many possible courses of action available to today's bond portfolio manager. None of them carries a guarantee. Each course of action entails a certain degree of risk. The level of risk varies widely, from the relative safety of a constant volatility like-for-like swap to the all-out risk of a major maturity restructuring.

One of the problems is that the terms "active bond management" and "bond swapping" have been used indiscriminately to cover a range of very different market activities. To help provide a structure for this bewildering variety of possible market activities, the following broad classification scheme has been proposed [1]:*

1. Pure yield pick-up swaps.
2. Substitution swaps.
3. Sector (or intermarket spread) swaps.
4. Rate anticipation.

In the subsequent sections, these four swap categories will be described in the context of their role in the historical evolution of modern bond portfolio management.

In one sense, active bond management is not a new phenomenon. A certain number of U.S. investment managers have been using the most sophisticated "modern" techniques for many years. However, outside this relatively small circle, bond management activity consisted primarily of allocating the portfolio's new cash flow among new long issues. Figure 1 shows the general pattern of long-term interest rates over recent years. The rise in long corporate yields in the late 1960s provided bonds with a respectable level of return and

---

*Numbers in brackets refer to references at end of chapter.

Figure 1
New AA Utility Yields

YIELD OVER TIME PERIOD

helped to spark a broader interest in bond portfolio management. In these early days, when managers talked about a bond swap, they usually meant a traditional pure yield pick-up swap.

The Pure Yield Pick-Up Swap and Loss-Constrained Portfolios. In a *pure yield pick-up swap,* a portfolio bond is replaced by a higher-yielding bond similar in all characteristics important to the fund (e.g., quality, maturity). The objective is to increase the total contractual return over the bond's life.

In practice, one of the major sources of pure yield pick-up swap opportunities has been the combination of the long-term secular rise in interest rates together with various portfolio constraints against realizing book losses [7]. These constraints forced many portfolios to carry positions of relatively low-yielding bonds long beyond the point where they represented appropriate holdings for the portfolio. As these constraints were then gradually relaxed, the managers of these previously-frozen portfolios found themselves presented with many swap opportunities that improved the overall portfolio structure and, at the same time, achieved significant pick-ups in yield. In order to appreciate how this situation came about, one first must understand the pervasive and corrosive effects of the accounting fiction which might be termed "loss constraint."

Many large bond portfolios are limited, in one way or another, in their ability to sustain book losses. This problem afflicts portfolios of virtually all types—pension funds, insurance companies, casualty companies, commercial banks, mutual savings banks, savings and loan associations, corporations, etc. Loss constraint encumbers both very small portfolios and many multibillion dollar portfolios. The operational and accounting rationale that dictate this policy differ from one institution to the next. But the net effect is the same. All holdings where the current market price is below the book cost, i.e., holdings carried at an unrealized loss, become essentially unsaleable. Such holdings therefore constitute frozen assets no matter how liquid or how marketable the securities themselves may be. The real problem is that these loss-frozen holdings must then be retained even when they have become quite inappropriate to the portfolio's current objectives.

Because of the extraordinary rise in interest rates over the past 20-30 years, any portfolio which has been a regular purchaser of long-term bonds will naturally find many of its holding locked in by losses. It would be very surprising if all these older holdings remained totally suitable to the portfolio's new goals. Inevitably, in any loss-constrained portfolio, one can find a number of glaring examples of loss-locked, inappropriate security holdings. With the passage of time since their purchase, the market role in these securities has somehow changed, so that they are now in dissonance with the fund's basic purpose.

These dissonant securities may be perfectly valid investment vehicles—for some other portfolio! In fact, this may be the source of their problem. When certain securities have a strong special appeal for one class of investors, their market prices will be bid up above normal levels for bonds of similar quality, maturity, etc. These securities will then provide a relatively low market yield, and consequently will not pay their own way in portfolios which cannot make use of their special features. This creates the classic situation for pure yield pick-up swaps.

The so-called "flower bonds" are a prime case in point. These are U.S. Treasury bonds floated in the period 1953-63 and bearing coupons ranging from 3 to 4¼ percent. Their special feature is that when used to pay off estate taxes, their value is assessed at par. Because of this special feature, the market for flower bonds is chronically priced well above normal levels for current coupon Treasury bonds of comparable maturities. This enhanced price level translates into a yield disadvantage. On March 15, 1979, the 3½s of 1998 were priced around 77 for a yield-to-maturity of 5.42 percent. By comparison, current coupon long Treasuries (affording essentially the same degree of call protection) were priced to yield about 9.00 percent, i.e., over 350 basis points more than the flower bond.

Other examples of inappropriate holdings which often underyield the market can be found among short- and intermediate-term discount bonds—both corporates and Treasuries. Because of the large capital gain component in their return, these bonds have a special appeal to certain taxpayers. (The appeal is particularly strong for many taxpayers who have a sufficient supply of potential tax losses to assure an effective capital gains tax rate of 0 percent!) [11]

Discount bonds with strong sinking funds are another example of dissonant holdings in certain loss-constrained portfolios. These bonds have a special appeal both for defensive investors and for professional managers interested in the sinking fund "play." The issuer of these bonds must enter the open market periodically to buy bonds to satisfy its sinking fund requirement. As time progresses, there is a tightening in the available supply of bonds, and the price naturally rises. In addition, some portfolio managers may try to collect these bonds in order to further capitalize on the periodic surges of demand from the issuer. This collection process can lead to an even higher price level being established. As a result, collected sinking fund bonds may provide a market yield-to-maturity that is far below the general level for comparable securities.

The collector's basic hope is that the issuer will at some point find it necessary to pay a particularly good price for their whole collection. Other investors interested in the sinking fund play may hope to pick up capital gain on the collector's coattails, so to speak.

However, for loss-constrained portfolios, where these bonds were originally purchased near par, even a very attractive bid would still entail accepting a sizable book loss. Consequently, the stringently loss-constrained manager is not likely to have the flexibility required to really benefit from the issuer's open market purchases. In fact, many sinking fund players make a point of examining how an issue is distributed among various types of institutions. Those bonds held by institutions thought to be severely loss-constrained—e.g., insurance companies—are then excluded from their estimate of the "floating supply." In other words, these sinking fund players actually count on insurance companies being totally unable to part with their bonds at any price below par. (There may be some surprises here.)

The lowest yielding holding may not always be the best candidate for a pure yield pick-up swap. First of all, it may carry a deep book loss with the attendant low ratio of proceeds-generated-per-loss-taken. Second, a low market yield by itself is not necessarily evidence of a security's dissonance relative to the portfolio's objectives. Deep discount long Telephones often provide a relatively low yield. However, these securities could function as uniquely valuable components of a well balanced portfolio for certain types of funds. For example, suppose a growing pension fund were concerned about the possibility of a secular downtrend in interest rates. A sustained downtrend would indeed reduce the coupon reinvestment rate of the existing portfolio, lower the rollover rate of maturing proceeds, perhaps lead to refunding calls of the higher coupon bonds, force the flow of net new contributions into relatively low-yielding investments, and even reduce the nominal dollar amount of the annuity that could be purchased for each dollar of future asset value [3]. For a fund concerned with this potential deterioration in overall return, deep discount long Telephones (or any deep discount high-grade corporate) might be an excellent counter-balance.

During the late 1960s and early 1970s the prohibitions against realizing book losses were gradually lifted for a number of state and city pension funds. In some cases, the book loss constraint was removed altogether and the portfolio manager was granted the flexibility to make investment decisions based solely upon market considerations. More frequently, the authorization to realize losses was limited by some requirement that sufficient incremental cash flow be gained in the swap to "recover" the book loss. A veritable garden of accounting fictions sprung up reflecting various formulas for determining loss recovery times and/or for amortizing realized losses as a charge against the portfolio's future income stream. Many of the formulas were inconsistent or flawed from a pure investment viewpoint. For example, they often failed to deal correctly with the reinvestment and compounding process in growing portfolios [5]. Nevertheless, virtually all these loss recovery formulas could be satisfied with a sufficiently large improvement in yield-to-maturity. The preceding years of total loss constraint insured that many portfolios contained ample opportunities for sizable yield improvements. This led to increasing levels of pure yield pick-up swapping. Some of the older pension funds spent years moving out of massive holdings of low-yielding Treasury and corporate bonds that they had accumulated over the years.

While many portfolios were by-passed and, in fact, many still remain frozen today, the trend towards greater flexibility advanced further in the early 1970s. A new breed of active managers then came into view. They recognized that most high-grade bond portfolios contained large holdings of highly liquid, marketable bonds. Naturally, this liquidity had an associated cost in the form of generally lower yields. This new breed was determined to make this liquidity pay for itself on an on-going basis.

The Substitution Swap and the Give-Up of Nominal Yield. This determination led to an increasing focus on short-term trading activity in general, and to the rapid development of "substitution swapping" in particular. In a *substitution swap,* the portfolio manager tracks the yield spread relationships among groups of similar "substitutable" bonds. When the spread between any two like bonds reaches some extreme limit, presumably as a result of transient market imbalances, a swap is executed in the hope of obtaining a profitable reversal as the spread later returns to more normal levels.

The rewards from a successful chain of substitution swaps could be very clear and dramatic, especially when it consisted of a significant takeout of dollars combined with a return to the original portfolio holding. Moreover, to the extent that truly substitutable bonds were involved, the incremental risks were very small. For many managers, a cleanly executed string of substitution swaps paved the way towards greater investment flexibility. In particular, it demonstrated the importance of permitting the manager to swap in the direction of giving up yield-to-maturity.

This freedom to *give up* yield is a crucial, and yet sometimes a very difficult, step for many portfolios. To individuals outside the bond community (and this includes many members of the investment committees who set fund policy), to give up yield on a swap seems tantamount to willingly giving up return. Of course, just the opposite is true: such swaps give up long-term nominal yields with the intention of increasing real returns over somewhat shorter time frames. However, unless the manager obtains authorization for yield give-up trades, one's portfolio would be condemned to a one-way street which, at best, would result in a refrozen portfolio at some higher yield level, and at worst, would lead to an ill-structured portfolio vulnerable to call and possibly filled with significant credit risk.

While substitution swapping proved one way to tap the liquidity resources of bond portfolios, it soon became clear that it could not, by itself, constitute a comprehensive approach to bond management. First of all, the initiative for substitution swaps rests more with the marketplace than with the manager. Second, while such swaps could be highly profitable in absolute dollars and in terms of return on the specific holdings involved, they could have only a limited impact on total portfolio returns (except perhaps for smaller funds). Finally, the more intensive substitution swapping had become concentrated on a relatively small number of high-grade, widely-held, marketable issues. As the swap activity increased within this limited field, the extent of the aberrations became less and less, and consequently, there were fewer and fewer dramatic opportunities.

The substitution swap still remained a worthwhile activity, especially for the manager who was organized to carry it out on a low-cost, low-effort basis. But it could no longer justify being the sole focus of the manager's attention.

The Sector Swap and Professional Market Insight. In 1972, the sector swap began to be "rediscovered." In the *sector swap* (or *intermarket spread swap*), the manager tries to take advantage of the changing yield spread relationships between market sectors differentiated by quality, by coupon, by type of issuer (e.g., utility to industrial to finance to Canadian to Treasuries to Agencies), by type of issue (e.g., private versus public, strong sinking fund versus weak sinking fund), etc. As with all these techniques, the sector swap had been continuously and artfully practiced for decades by certain U.S. managers. However, its following among the newer breed of managers seemed to develop after the "squeezing out" of the substitution swap.

The sector swapper's professionalism and flexibility provide a definite edge. One is continually studying yield spread relationships among different sectors in the market. When one detects what appears to be a transient aberration, one can dig deeper into the fundamental sources of this aberration. The swapper's market experience and widespread daily contacts will aid in this effort. One's knowledge and insights into market forces will count here. This can put one in a position to make the key judgment as to whether the existing sector relationship is, in fact, a transient aberration which will revert to more normal levels over time—or whether it is the first signalings of a new trend and a new market structure. This approach to the marketplace does not belong equally to everyone. Here, the truly professional portfolio manager should have an edge.

Another advantage of sector swaps is that they can be initiated across significant portions of the overall portfolio. They can involve major swap programs. They can impact the overall portfolio performance.

While clearly riskier than substitution swaps, sector swaps can, by and large, keep the portfolio within the general confines of the long-term debt market, or more broadly speaking, within the confines of the portfolio's original maturity structure. Consequently, the manager can fairly well control the incremental risk entailed in a sector swap relative to the prior risk level established by the portfolio's basic structure.

In 1972 and 1973, there were a number of unusually clearcut examples of sector swap situations. One of the classic situations occurred in the fall of 1973 when the yield of GNMA pass-throughs rose to unprecedented levels relative to both corporate and other Agency issues. Delving behind the statistics, the underlying cause could easily be traced to a drying up of new investable funds among thrift institutions. These had been the primary buyers of the then relatively new pass-through instrument. Because of their apparent complexity relative to straight bonds, the pass-throughs had not yet established a wide following among pension fund managers. (Actually, the evaluation of the probable true yields of the pass-throughs is far more complex—and more important—than is generally recognized even today.) However, at the extraordinarily attractive nominal yields that then prevailed (and the even more attractive probable cash flow yields), it was fairly likely that some major pension fund managers would soon overcome their initial problems with GNMA pass-through analysis and accounting. In fact, this is precisely what occurred. The bond manager who moved quickly and massively into pass-throughs reaped considerable rewards as the spread relative to corporates narrowed by over 75 basis points in the course of the next six months.

The GNMA example also illustrates the "new vehicle" type of sector swap. A portfolio manager who recognizes the value in a newly introduced sector may then reap sizable rewards as the sector becomes increasingly accepted by the marketplace at large. (A particularly clear example of this new vehicle sector swap was the introduction of "Yankee" bonds in 1976.)

Another classic example of a sector swap opportunity presented itself both in 1972 and early 1973. By giving up as little as 15 basis points, one could have swapped out of A Utilities into the very highest grade AAA Telephone issues. Even without the benefit of hindsight, this would have seemed like a very narrow give-up at the time. Once again, by delving behind the historical yield spreads, the manager could have determined that this narrow spread arose in part from an unusually forceful "reaching for yield" by many major market participants. It was not too difficult to expect that this special condition would abate at some point in the future, and that quality differentials would consequently widen. During this time, a number of portfolio managers actually implemented very sizable swap programs into the higher quality corporates. (In certain cases, these managers found themselves having to continually defend the resulting give-ups in yield.) Such sector swaps proved *enormously* profitable over the ensuing months, probably far more so than could have reasonably been expected.

The sector swap has many appealing aspects, and it is thought by many to be one of the most professional forms of the bond manager's art.

At times in 1973, the field of bond portfolio management seemed ready to embark upon a grand new era of sector swapping.

Then performance measurement came to the bond market.

The Rise of Performance Measurement. From the end of 1972 through the fall of 1974, interest rates on new AA long Utility issues rose by over 300 basis points. A typical portfolio of long corporates had its market value eroded by 6 percent over calendar 1973, and by a further 16 percent in the first nine months of 1974. The resulting effect upon the asset value of bond portfolios is well known. The enduring effects of these markets upon bond portfolio management may not be quite so evident.

These market problems came at a time when bond portfolio management was becoming increasingly competitive. Bond portfolios were beginning to be subjected to the same type of short-term performance measurement as had been applied to equity portfolios. The performance results of successful bond managers were being rapidly incorporated into the process for marketing their services.

Since calendar years constitute regrettably important time frames in the world of investment performance, the results of calendar 1973 loomed particularly large. Unquestionably, the 1973 markets gave a great boost to the use of performance measurement in the bond world. In 1973 and most of 1974, anyone who believed that long rates would rise could move into the short-term markets and get an incentive yield to do so, because of the higher short rates relative to long rates. A number of major fund managers did believe this and acted accordingly. Large reserve positions were accumulated. Conversely, there were others who for various reasons, ranging from an uncertainty to a conscious philosophy, kept investing their cash flows into the long-term markets. This sequence of events led to a great gulf between the short-term performances obtained by managers who followed one point of view versus those who followed the other. The magnitude of this gulf led to a trumpeting and comparison of performance results that may have significantly accelerated the incursion of the performance concept into the bond market.

It also led to very difficult times for those bond managers who remained in the long market. No matter how meticulously and profitably they may have executed pure yield pick-up swaps, substitution swaps, or sector swaps, their performance results were disastrous when compared with the managers who stayed in the short term market.

These effects are clearly shown by the Salomon Brothers Total Return Index for the high-grade long-term corporate bond market. This index was developed in 1973 (with results backdated to 1969) [4]. Figure 2 shows how a $100 investment in the index on January 1, 1969 would have grown, assuming full reinvestment of coupon income, to a cumulative value of $180 by the beginning of 1979.

Figure 3 provides a somewhat more sobering picture, at least for the bond portfolio manager. The year-by-year index returns are compared with the assured annual returns available in one-year Treasury bills.

While volatile bond markets did not originate with the 1973-74 debacle, this was the first time that such horrendous results were

Figure 2
Salomon Brothers High-Grade Long-Term Corporate Rate-of-Return Index—Cumulative Change in Market Value of Rate-of-Return Index (including reinvestment)

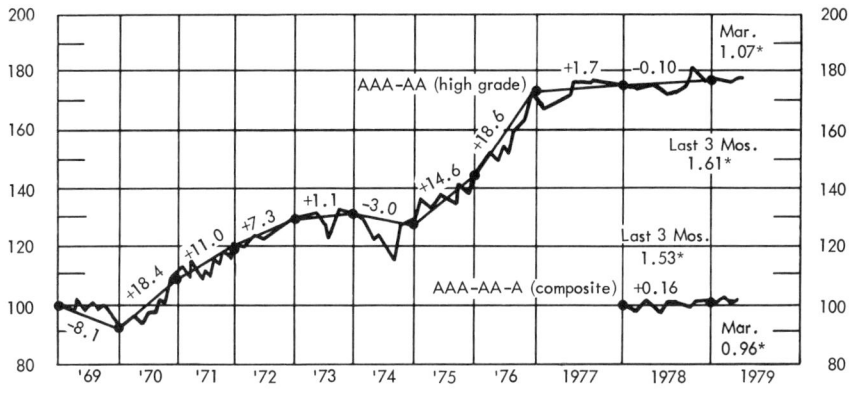

Note: Numbers indicate percent total return for calendar years.
*Nonannualized.
Source: Copyright © Salomon Brothers Inc., 1979.

Figure 3
Annual Total Returns: Long Corporates versus One-Year Treasury Bills

Year	One-Year Treasury Bills	Salomon Brothers High-Grade Long-Term Corporate Rate-of-Return Index	Incremental Return from High-Grade Long-Term Corporates
1969	6.55%	−8.10%	−14.65%
1970	8.09	18.38	+10.29
1971	4.89	11.02	+6.13
1972	4.13	7.26	+3.13
1973	5.68	1.14	−4.54
1974	7.21	−3.04	−10.25
1975	7.07	14.64	+7.57
1976	6.31	18.64	+12.33
1977	4.82	1.70	−3.12
1978	6.93	−.10	−7.03
Ten-year period	6.16%	5.79%	−.37%

accompanied by widespread tracking of portfolio performance. The sorry returns of 1974 (or perhaps "nonreturns" would be a more apt expression) led to several important changes in the perception and practice of bond portfolio management.

One immediate effect was to put to rest the myth that the corporate bond market could be viewed as an essentially low-volatility haven for balanced portfolios. Over the years, many fund sponsors had come to view their portfolio allocation in terms of two components: (1) a risky, volatile equity portion and (2) a safe, reliable (and usually dull) bond portion. In essence, this meant that the key decision was to determine the equity fraction, with the remainder being tacitly assigned to the "nonequity" asset—bonds. As Figure 3 shows all too clearly, while bonds may not be able to match the historical return volatility of common stocks, today's bond market has a significant wild streak all its own. For sponsors seeking reductions in their fund's overall level of volatility risk, this clearly implied a greater focus on the intermediate and shorter maturity areas of the fixed income markets. This may have led to a shortening in the average maturity of many bond portfolios whose purpose was to provide this "nonequity" alternative.

A different effect was felt among the more fully managed bond portfolios. With these funds, the primary objective was to achieve the maximum rate-of-return within the fixed income market. Given this objective, the most successful managers were those who had foreseen the 1973-74 surge in interest rates and had acted to restructure their portfolios into the shorter maturities. These were the managers who had successfully engaged in the first step of the fourth form of swap activity—the rate anticipation swap. The overt and well-advertised success of these managers who had "gone to cash" in the 1973-74 period forced many other portfolio managers to give more serious consideration to the benefits of rate anticipation. In particular, it led to a more open view regarding opportunistic departures from the long term maturity area that many managers had previously considered to be the "natural" arena for their fixed income assets.

In fact, at times in 1974, the short-term market looked almost too good to many investors. Some managers began to question whether long-term bonds were ever worth the extra risk relative to the assured return available in the then higher yield short-term market. There was a tendency to forget that the short-term market had its own type of risk. This particular overswing of the pendulum was dramatically corrected by the events of 1975 and 1976.

In 1975 and 1976, interest rates turned lower. As Figure 2 shows, the long-term corporate bond market provided outstanding levels of total return in 1975 (14.6 percent) and again in 1976 (18.6 percent). This turnaround confirmed the total return viability of the long-term market. Moreover, as seen in Figure 3, this was accompanied by reductions in the returns available in the short-term market.

Over this four-year period from 1973 to 1976, the best performance was achieved not by constant adherence to the long-term market nor by continually rolling over short maturities. Rather the managers with outstanding performance were those few who had "gone to cash" during the 1973-74 period and then had been able to reinvest themselves into the long market in time to participate in the 1975-76 rally. This underscored the "round trip" character of successful rate anticipation. One good timing decision is not enough. To be effective, the rate anticipator must not only "go to cash" at the right time, but must then subsequently choose the right time to "go long" again.

In 1977 and 1978, the bond market turned sour once again. The High-Grade Index provided returns of +1.7 percent and −.1 percent, respectively, in each of these years. The year 1978 ended with an inverted yield curve that was reminiscent of the 1974 era. These combined events demonstrated in practice what had been obvious in theory: when interest rates exhibit a strong cyclic pattern that dominates any secular trend, then consistently superior portfolio returns can only be found through successful "riding of the cycle," i.e., through rate anticipation.

Rate Anticipation and the Yield Illusion. The rate anticipation swap can be the most productive bond portfolio action; it is also the riskiest.

The key to successful rate anticipation is correct timing judgment.

With effective timing being such a critical element, it is most important that the portfolio manager avoid having one's judgment distracted or biased by secondary or tertiary factors. Unfortunately, the traditional instinct toward yield improvement can often exercise just such a distractive influence on the rate anticipation swapper. For example, high levels of interest rates are often accompanied by inverted yield curves. Under such conditions money market rates exceed the yields of long-term bonds and it is very natural for a bond portfolio manager to feel comfortable having a large reserve portion of funds "parked" in the short-term market. Even if one expects long-term rates to peak out at some point during the next several months, the higher yields earned on the reserve funds can be quite enticing. Indeed, with the yields favoring the short-term market, it would only be human for one to feel somewhat more at ease with one's present portfolio structure, to be somewhat less anxious in tracking of the long-term market, and, therefore, to be somewhat less eager to initiate any extension process on an anticipation basis.

On the other hand, if short-term rates were to fall, especially if they were to decline rather precipitously, then this same portfolio manager might well shift one's orientation and begin to focus on the relative yield loss entailed in remaining short. This apparent opportunity cost might then make the manager more eager to invest one's reserve into the now higher-yielding long market. This sense of an opportunity cost might consequently influence one's timing judgments regarding the bottoming out of the long market.

In the first case, the portfolio manager feels secure with the reserve portion because of its high relative yield rate. In the second case, the manager is becoming more anxious because the reserve now represents a yield loss. In both cases, the portfolio manager could be making the very big mistake of being beguiled by the "yield illusion."

The nature of this mistake can be seen from the simple mathematics of total return. Over a period of months, the incremental return accumulated by being short under even a sharply inverted yield curve can be wiped out by a very minor movement in the long-term market. Figure 4 shows the yield moves in the long market required to wipe out the accumulated return from having funds "parked" in the higher yielding market for a prescribed period of time. For example, with short rates at 10 percent and long rates at 8.5 percent, the accumulated yield advantage of being short for three months would be wiped out if long rates suddenly moved downward by as little as 4 basis points.

The key point here is that the portfolio manager should not allow timing judgments to be unduly influenced by the level of return available in the short-term "parking lot." This is not to say that the short-term market should be ignored. The action of short rates will, of course, influence the long market and might even provide clues regarding a turn in the long market. However, this role of the short-

Figure 4
Basis Point Move in Long Rates (30-year 8.5 percent par bond) Required to Offset Accumulated Yield Gain or Loss in Short Market

Short Rates	Time Invested at Short Rate			
	3 Months	6 Months	9 Months	12 Months
11.00%	−6	−12	−17	−23
10.50	−5	− 9	−14	−18
10.00	−4	− 7	−11	−14
9.50	−3	− 5	− 7	− 9
9.00	−1	− 2	− 4	− 5
8.50	+0	+ 0	+ 0	+ 0
8.00	+1	+ 2	+ 3	+ 5
7.50	+2	+ 5	+ 7	+ 9
7.00	+3	+ 7	+10	+14

Note: Short rates are quoted on simple annualized returns and no reinvestment is assumed for the long bond.

term market as a possible signal should be distinguished from consideration of the short-term market as a relatively attractive or unattractive haven for waiting funds. This conclusion depends on the waiting period being measured in months, not years. For the portfolio manager who believes that the long bond market is in for a sustained slide and that any turnaround will be years in coming, then the level of available short (and intermediate) rates must, of course, enter more significantly into the manager's risk-reward equation.

For the portfolio manager engaged in rate anticipation, the crucial focus must be on effective round trip timing of entries into and exits from the long market. The manager cannot become distracted by the changing level of short rates. The relative yield advantage or yield loss on the reserves temporarily placed in the short market will have a miniscule impact on performance compared with even a modest movement in the long market. If the market situation follows the manager's scenario, then the superior performance will be accorded to the manager who correctly anticipates the turning point—not just verbally—but in terms of a well-timed and well-implemented restructuring of a significant portion of "parked" reserve funds.

Yield Curve Anticipation: Snap-Ups and Snap-Downs. The preceding discussion placed the primary emphasis on effective timing. This is particularly true for a long-term fund. However, it tacitly implied that there is only one method of reentering the long market— direct investment in long-maturity instruments. In light of how the 1974-75 market evolved, there are a number of alternative "reentry" techniques that are worthy of serious consideration. For example, Figure 5 shows the Treasury yield curves on September 1, 1974 and March 1, 1975. Over this six-month period, rates not only declined, but the yield curve "snapped down" from an inverted shape to a mildly positive shape. This "snap down" effect resulted in intermediate maturities undergoing a much greater downward movement in yield than the longs. For example, the five-year maturity declined by 170 basis points, almost 2½ times greater than the 68 basis point improvement at 30 years. Moreover, an investment in the five-year maturity on September 1, 1974, would have "aged" to a 4½-year maturity over the six-month holding period, thus adding some further yield improvement. The combination of these factors is shown in Figure 6. Here, the vertical axis depicts the annualized total return obtained from a continuously held investment at the indicated maturity point. From Figure 6, one can see that the performance of the five-year investment came very close to that of the long end over this particular period.

This should not be interpreted as a general endorsement of the intermediate maturity. It merely indicates that the "snap down" from a peaking inverted curve can lead to surprisingly attractive

Figure 5
Historical Yield Curves

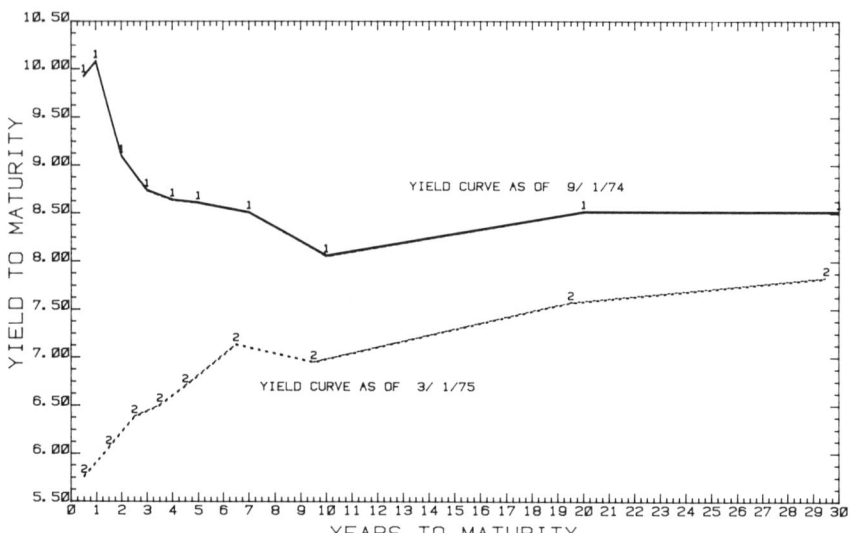

Figure 6
Annualized Historical Returns from September 1, 1974 to March 1, 1975

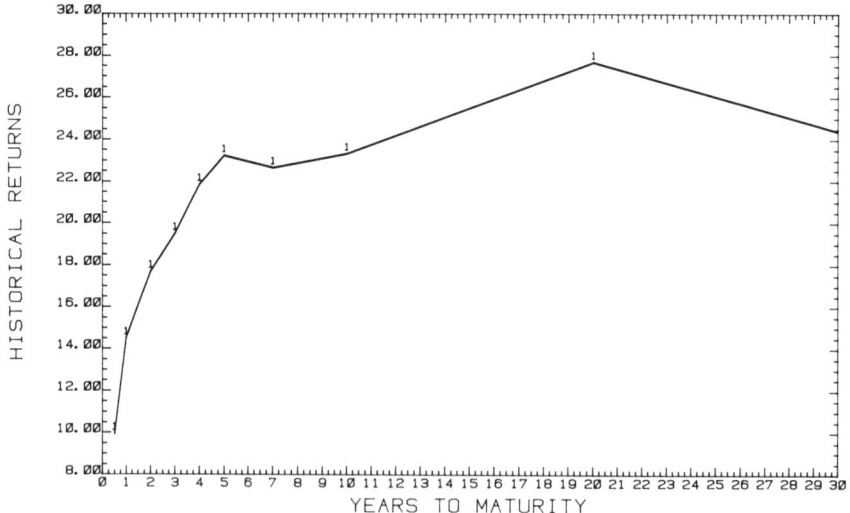

intermediate returns. It should also be pointed out that in deteriorating markets, there can also be a "snap up" effect with the result that intermediates perform worse than longs. This snap up has burned numerous investors who believed that intermediates offered reduced price volatility relative to longs. (On average, the intermediates probably do have less price volatility than longs. However, strongly inverted or strongly positive yield curve shapes are not reflective of average conditions.)

A good example of the snap up occurred in the course of calendar 1978, when the Treasury yield curve changed significantly in both level and shape. As depicted in Figure 7, the change in the level of rates over 1978 ranged from approximately +100 basis points in 30-year maturities to over +350 basis points at the one-year point. These yield changes reshaped the yield curve. The moderately positive shape at the beginning of 1978 turned into a strongly inverted shape at the end of the year. One measure of this shape change is the spread of 30-year over one-year rates. This spread began the year at about +100 basis points and ended at over −150 basis points.

This was not a good year for reaping returns from the bond market. Figure 8 shows the total returns achieved over 1978 by investments along the yield curve. An investment in a 30-year Treasury security at the beginning of 1978 would have led to a market loss of some 9 points. The price loss would have more than offset the coupon income resulting in a negative total return over the one-year period. There is little surprise in the result that with such movements

Figure 7
Yield Curves at Beginning and End of 1978

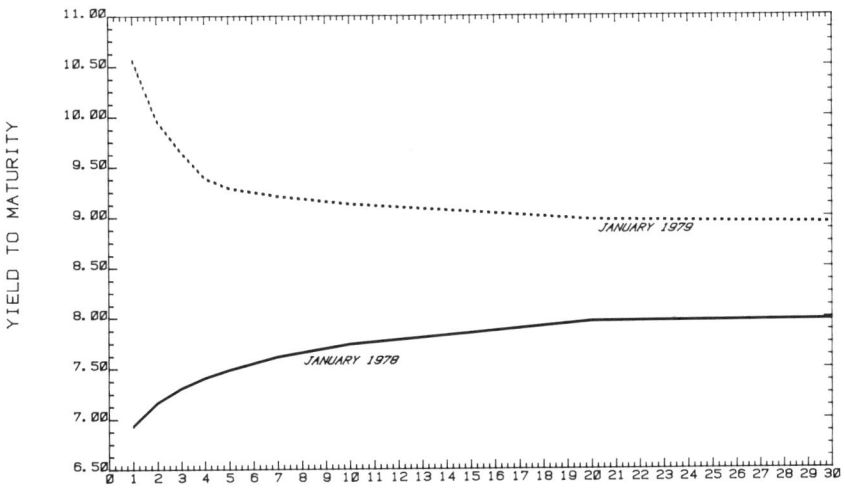

Figure 8
Historical Returns (January 1, 1978-January 1, 1979)

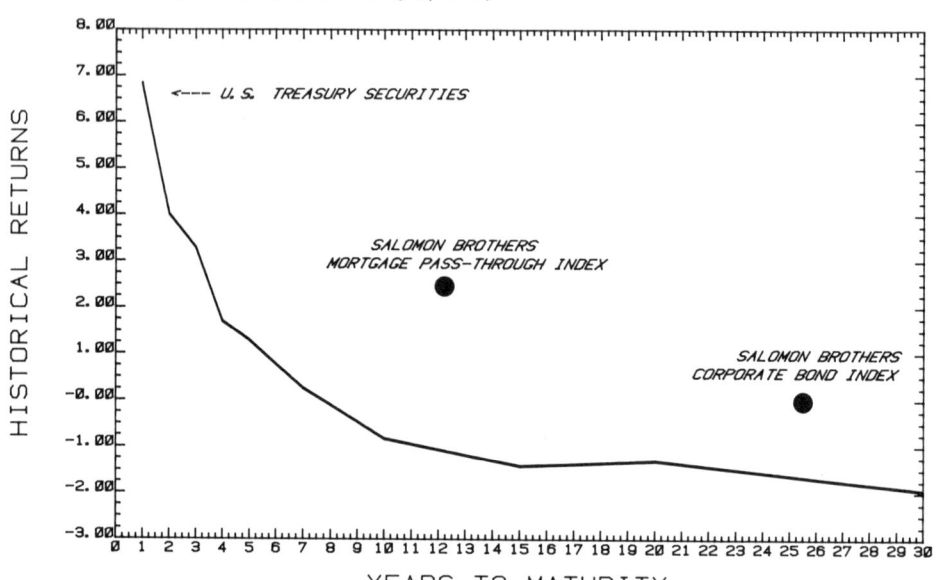

in rate levels, long-term bonds provided negative total return. However, many investors might be surprised to learn that any investment along the yield curve with a maturity of seven years or longer resulted in an essentially zero or negative return. In fact, for investments between 7 and 30 years, the investment returns all fell within the narrow range of −2.0 percent to +.2 percent.

As a point of comparison with the corporate bond market, the Salomon Brothers Long-Term Bond Index provided a 1978 return of −.1 percent. In Figure 8, the index return is plotted to correspond with its average maturity of 24 years. As a second point of comparison, Figure 8 also shows the 1978 performance figure of 2.39 percent from the Salomon Brothers Total Return Index for Mortgage Pass-Through Securities [12].

Figure 8 clearly shows that, to have avoided the adverse effects of 1978, the bond portfolio manager with good hindsight would have needed to have been fully invested in maturities under three years (or even better yet, under one year!).

This pattern of returns of 1978, including the sorry behavior of the intermediate area, reflects the snap up in the shape of the yield curve that is evident from Figure 7. This provides an interesting contrast to the snap down effect over the six-month period following the peaking of rates in September, 1974.

In both periods, even though the market moved in opposite directions, the total return behavior of intermediates came significantly close to that of the longs. There were two reasons for this close comparability. First of all, the 1978 snap up and the 1974 snap down both resulted in intermediate yields changing considerably more than long rates. The second reason is that maturity is only a crude guide to price volatility. For example, even given the same movement in yield, a 30-year bond would only have a 50 percent greater price movement than a 12-year bond. The intermediates' much higher yield volatility compensated for their reduced price volatility to produce returns that were comparable with longs—over these two particular periods.

The prospects of yield curve reshaping can add an important refinement and balance to the rate anticipation process. For example, suppose a manager with a defensive short-term posture anticipates that the long market rates are approaching a peak. The manager must then determine the correct time to begin deploying at least a portion of short-term reserves. This action may be based either on the manager's definite belief that the peak level of rates is actually at hand or simply as a counterbalance to one's uncertainty as to when and how that peak will occur. In any case, once the decision has been made to commit some reserves, then the second decision must be to select the most appropriate maturity sector. If the manager believes that there is a good prospect for lower rates to be accompanied by a snap down in the yield curve, then intermediate maturities should be explored as an interesting reentry vehicle on a risk-reward basis. On the one hand, if rates improve and the yield curve does snap down to a more positive shape, then the right intermediate maturities can provide returns that are comparable to the long market. On the other hand, should long rates continue to rise (without a significant increase in the degree of inversion) then the shorter maturity of the intermediates will provide a certain protection against the full deterioration that would be experienced in the long market.

Finding the best distribution of maturities to take advantage of yield curve reshaping is no simple matter. In many instances, the proper balance of return may be available only with a rather narrow range of maturities. A number of analytic techniques have been developed to assist portfolio managers who wish to incorporate yield curve anticipation into their strategic process [6].

Productive use of yield curve judgments has a long history with commercial bank portfolios and other institutions with sizable short-term portfolios. However, until recently, this approach has not found widespread use among managers of long-term pension funds. This appears to be changing, as pension fund managers become more aware of the important edge that yield curve anticipation can offer at certain points in the interest rate and yield curve cycle.

Prospective Problems in Rate Anticipation

In 1973, and even in 1974, there were relatively few bond portfolio managers who were significant rate anticipators.

However, over the subsequent four years, long-term interest rates followed a cyclic pattern (Figure 1) that was roughly similar to the 1970-74 experience. The resulting cyclic pattern of total returns (shown in Figure 2) underscored the potential of rate anticipation for bond managers who found themselves coming under increasing competitive pressure based upon performance comparisons. This proved to be an almost irresistible attraction, and more and more managers became partially or even totally committed to rate anticipation.

The tidal wave markets of 1973-78 seemed to sweep aside all the minutiae of what used to be called professional bond management. The incremental returns from yield pick-up, substitution, and sector swapping all appeared inconsequential in comparison with the massive effects of overall rate movements in the long market. The only question of import seems to be: whither long rates? Rate guessing, rate talking, rate anticipation have become the major and sometimes the sole preoccupation of many bond market participants.

This trend, if continued, would mean that only one form of active bond management would appear worthwhile—the rate anticipation swap.

This creates a number of basic problems for the practice of bond portfolio management.

First of all, many portfolio managers judge rates to be high or low based largely upon their experience with past rate cycles. For these managers, rate anticipation shares the danger in any cycle-related mode of investment that the manager's judgment may be biased by the belief (either explicit or implicit) that historical patterns will continue into the future.

Cycles do get broken. Aberrant events do occur. Debacles do take place. Secular trends do fade out and are sometimes reversed. Unforeseen problems do arise—in fact, frequently. Yet the world manages to muddle through and even find new ways of coping with adverse trends and overcoming seemingly overwhelming obstacles.

For example, in 1973-74, the financial markets appeared to be discounting a variety of "horror scenarios." By and large, these disasters failed to materialize (at least right away), and there followed enormous rallies in both the bond and stock markets. On the one hand, one could read this lesson as a cyclic event supporting maximum market commitment at the point of deepest gloom and doom. On the other hand one could argue that the markets were basically correct in their assessment of the possibility of dire events—but that these horrors just didn't happen that particular time. (From this latter viewpoint, the lesson is that the financial markets attempt to reflect the full range of possible economic and political scenarios. Since only one of these possible scenarios can actually take place, the market's judgment can hardly be faulted in its perceptions just because all the other scenarios failed to occur. In other words, the market may not have been wrong in its grim judgment—the world may have been simply lucky!)

All of this suggests that a superficial reading of the history of past cyclic events may prove a shaky guide for future action.

A second danger, related to the first, is that the very proliferation of rate anticipators could make rate anticipation much more difficult. During 1973-78, the force of economic events and market fundamentals overshadowed the role of bond portfolio managers. During this period, rate anticipators did not have to worry about other anticipators getting in their way and perhaps even preempting changes in the market's direction. However, as the rate anticipators crowd the market, this will in itself create a sizable new element of uncertainty.

When there is widespread accumulation of anticipatory reserves, the problem of correct timing becomes much more difficult than usual. Once the market is perceived to be reaching a major peak, one can envision a torrent of funds being injected into the market within a concentrated period of time. Under such conditions correct timing must be interpreted as "anticipating the anticipators," and getting one's own funds largely invested before the market moves to new rate levels. In an environment where huge amounts of funds are poised to anticipate the next change in long-term rates, it is hard to see every money manager outperforming colleagues on a sustained round-trip basis by correctly calling (and implementing) each topping- and bottoming-out of the rate cycle.

Theoretically, one could envision so many funds engaged in rate anticipation that their activity could itself largely determine the level of the long-term bond market. The longer maturity area of the bond market would then tend to become delinked from the underlying economic cycle. Since any fundamental cyclic pattern could be fully anticipated and then discounted, one could ultimately see the disappearance of interest rate cycles as we know them today. Naturally, the closer the market approaches this theoretical point of full anticipation, the harder it will become to be a consistently successful rate anticipator.

A third general problem is that rate anticipation tends to overwhelm the incremental returns from any other form of bond management, even those that could prove more reliable on a year-after-year basis.

This third problem of rate anticipation is not a simple question of whether the portfolio manager should or should not try to forecast changes in long interest rates and act accordingly. In fact, it may be impossible for a manager not to be influenced by his or her own general market expectations. Moreover, one can legitimately argue that every form of swap activity is affected, to some degree, by overall movements in long rates. There is no relationship between two issues or two sectors which is totally free from the effects of a major market move. (As a result of the subsequent general deterioration in the long market after the fall of 1973, even the classic sector swap involving GNMA pass-throughs proved more successful than could have been anticipated on the basis of spread relationships alone.)

The question is not one of trying to stonily ignore one's market expectations, but rather a question of degree and intent. Ideally speaking, in substitution and sector swaps, the intention is to render a primary judgment on spread relationships and to factor out, to the extent possible, the impact of overall market movements.

Nor is the question one of trying to rule out rate anticipation swaps. This has proven enormously profitable for some portfolios, and no one should try to deny that success. A high degree of rate anticipation is embedded in the style of many very successful managers. Many managers devote great efforts, both individually and organizationally, to staying attuned to the latest public and private economic thinking. Rate anticipation is a perfectly legitimate form of swap activity, but it is characterized by a high potential payoff and an especially high risk.

By their nature, fixed income portfolios tend to be very risk-sensitive. The avoidance of risk often constituted the primary reason for the funds having been directed into the fixed-income markets in the first place. Consequently, any effort to obtain incremental return should be viewed through a prism reflecting the specific risk structure of the given portfolio.

The danger comes from lumping together all forms of bond management activity into one basket, without differentiation as to risk and intent. This danger is compounded when one crude performance yardstick is used to measure and compare portfolios and management efforts which differ widely in purpose and character. Without risk differentiation, the impact of rate movements would overwhelm all other forms of management activity. Without risk differentiation, the professional manager whose style runs more to substitution and sector swaps would, no matter how competent or successful, be deprived of both due credit and credibility. And all bond managers would be forced by these circumstances into concentrating solely on a continuing day-to-day frenzy of trying to anticipate an ever more anticipatory market, under a growing specter of serious performance and principal losses. This would be a most unfortunate state of affairs and one which would ultimately prove to be a no-win situation for professional bond management as a whole.

THE BASELINE METHOD FOR RELATING SHORT-TERM PERFORMANCE TO LONG-TERM GOALS

The Yardstick of Total Return

Many of the problems confronting today's bond portfolio manager can be traced to the sole reliance upon total return comparisons over short-term periods. Total return measurements do provide a useful yardstick of the extent to which the portfolio manager took advantage of general market opportunities during the measurement period. But this is only one factor in the complex process of portfolio management. A fundamental problem seems to arise when a single yardstick—total return measurement over short-term periods—is taken as the sole yardstick for all management activity.

This concentration on the single yardstick of total return can force dangerously simplistic comparisons among portfolios that may actually differ widely in function and purpose. In fact, the same level of achieved return may represent a very satisfactory result for one portfolio while having quite dismal implications for another portfolio with a different set of goals.

Moreover, even within a given portfolio, an overemphasis on short-term return can lead to conflicts with the long-term goals of the fund. For example, it could lead the portfolio manager into concentrating activity on catching short-term swings in interest rates. In turn, this excessive rate anticipation could lead to a frequent series of major portfolio shifts, thereby introducing considerable timing risk into the overall management process. The resulting volatility risk might be in direct contradiction to the original purpose of placing the funds into a fixed-income portfolio in the first place. This is just one instance of how an exclusive focus on maximization of total return over short periods can violate a fund's policy constraints and cause deviations from the fund's true long-term objectives.

These problems are particularly acute for fixed-income portfolios because of certain distinctive characteristics of the bond market. Much of the institutional investment in bonds is motivated by long-term, risk-avoidance purposes. These long-term purposes typically overshadow any specific requirement for total return over short-term periods.

Thus, the ideal solution would be to find some concrete way of relating the returns achieved over short-term measurement periods to the fund's long-term goals.

We believe that such goal-oriented management is indeed possible through application of a technique which we call "the baseline portfolio." This technique combines the modern total return approach with a back-to-the-fundamentals concept reminiscent of the pre-1970s style of bond portfolio management [2].

The Baseline Portfolio

In theory, the portfolio management process can be viewed as consisting of the four major steps shown in Figure 9. The first step is to

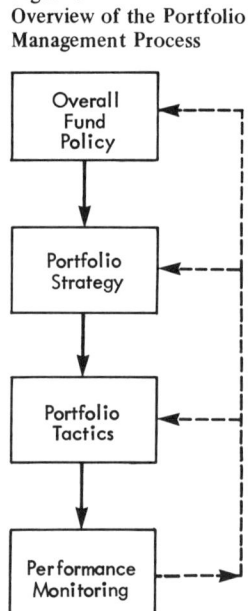

Figure 9
Overview of the Portfolio Management Process

identify the long-term objectives of the fund. The second step commences with the manager's judgments regarding market prospects. At this point, the manager must make the broad decisions that relate to portfolio strategy, i.e., to determine the portfolio's maturity structure. The rate and yield curve anticipation efforts would fall into this category of strategy decisions. Once this has been done, the third step consists of deciding upon the detailed portfolio tactics to be employed. These consist of selecting specific sectors to take advantage of perceived market opportunities. Sector and substitution swap activity would lie in this area of tactical decisions. The fourth step then consists of a continuing performance monitoring (in the most general sense) to ensure that the portfolio objectives are being fulfilled.

The first step is far more difficult than generally believed. It is no simple matter to identify a full set of portfolio objectives and then to define these objectives in a useful way. Such efforts tend to lead to either a frustratingly vague description of the objectives or an impossibly long collection of goals which mix the minor considerations in with the major ones.

For example, Figure 10 illustrates a partial list of the many objectives that could be ascribed to fixed-income portfolios. Moreover,

Figure 10
Portfolio Objectives

Maximum long-term nominal return	Tax liability management
Maximum long-term real return	liquidity warehouse
Match prescribed liability schedule	stability of principal
Reserve against uncertain liabilities	Stability of income over time
earnings contribution	Facilitate corporate flexibility
Earnings management	corporate compliance
Aura of balance and prudence	

any set of objectives are closely intertwined with an associated set of risk factors. (In this connection, risk is being defined in a far broader sense than the single volatility measure which has become traditional in many modern analyses. In the sense used here, risk entails all those potential events that could interfere with the portfolio being able to fulfill its long-term objectives.) When there are a large number of potential objectives and associated risk factors, it is no easy task to generate concrete guidelines for portfolio managers.

The purpose of the baseline portfolio is to provide a practical procedure for articulating the fund's long-term objectives in a concrete and useful fashion. The underlying idea is to take advantage of the relatively well-defined sector structure of the fixed income market.

An important characteristic of the bond market is the structural clarity of its asset classes. This clarity enables the return-risk relationships among the different market sectors to be relatively well-defined, especially over longer term horizons. The longer term motivation of investors and the market's structural clarity obviously fit hand-in-glove, allowing for the identification of market sectors that are particularly well suited for serving the specific goals of a given fund. By selecting market sectors to match the fund's objectives and associated risk factors, one should be able to develop a portfolio structure which best suits the fund's long-term goals (see Figure 11). This is called the fund's baseline portfolio [10].

Since the baseline portfolio structure should be determined primarily by the long-range considerations, it should be relatively independent of the active manager's day-to-day market judgments. Thus,

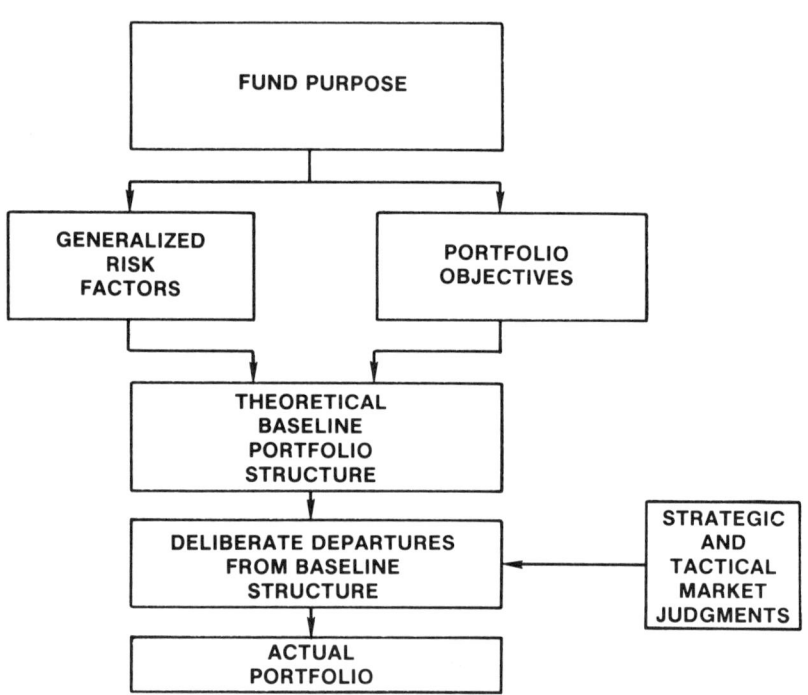

Figure 11
The Theoretical Baseline Portfolio

the baseline portfolio could be defined as the most balanced possible fulfillment of all of the fund's complex objectives and goals in the absence of an active market-related management activity. In other words, the baseline is that passive portfolio which carries the least risk relative to the fund's long-term goals.

Management Activity Relative to the Baseline Portfolio

From the vantage point of the baseline portfolio, one purpose of investment management is to take advantage of market opportunities. Active management can then be viewed as a series of strategic and tactical judgments such as those shown in Figure 12. These judgments would lead to market-motivated departures from the baseline portfolio in an effort to achieve improved portfolio results. The resulting portfolio improvements—as well as the incremental risks incurred in achieving them—should theoretically be measured against the yardstick of the baseline portfolio itself.

The portfolio manager, in selecting the actual portfolio, clearly incurs an incremental risk in departing from the baseline portfolio.

Figure 12
Active Bond Portfolio Management

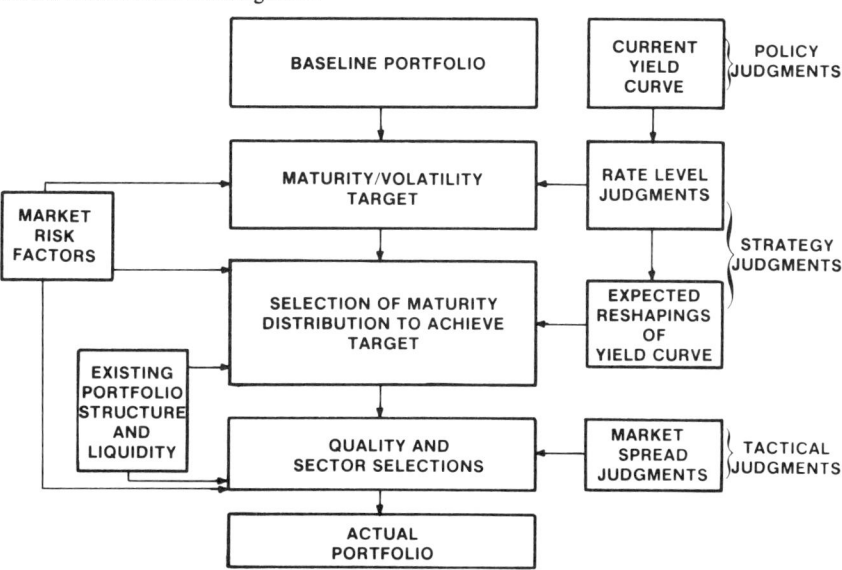

By so doing, one seeks an incremental return above and beyond what could be achieved with the baseline portfolio. Therefore, the benchmark for measuring the portfolio's return is the return that could have been achieved by simply holding the baseline portfolio. In essence, the baseline constitutes a sort of total return index customized to the fund's individual goals. To the extent that the achieved return exceeds the baseline return, the portfolio manager has added to the achievement of the portfolio goals as denominated in the currency of the baseline portfolio itself.

Evaluating Proposed Departures from the Baseline

The baseline portfolio can serve prospective as well as retrospective functions. At the beginning of each investment period, the baseline can help the portfolio manager to gauge—in a quantitative, objective fashion—the incremental risk incurred relative to these same goals. This prospective application of the baseline portfolio may be the most important one of all.

Figure 13 illustrates how a manager can compare one's actual portfolio's return profile to that of the baseline. Here the projected returns from the two portfolios are plotted across a range of potential movements in the overall level of interest rates. These "return vectors" [6] clearly show the nature of the tradeoffs involved in the de-

Figure 13
Dependence of Incremental Returns upon Direction of Market Movement

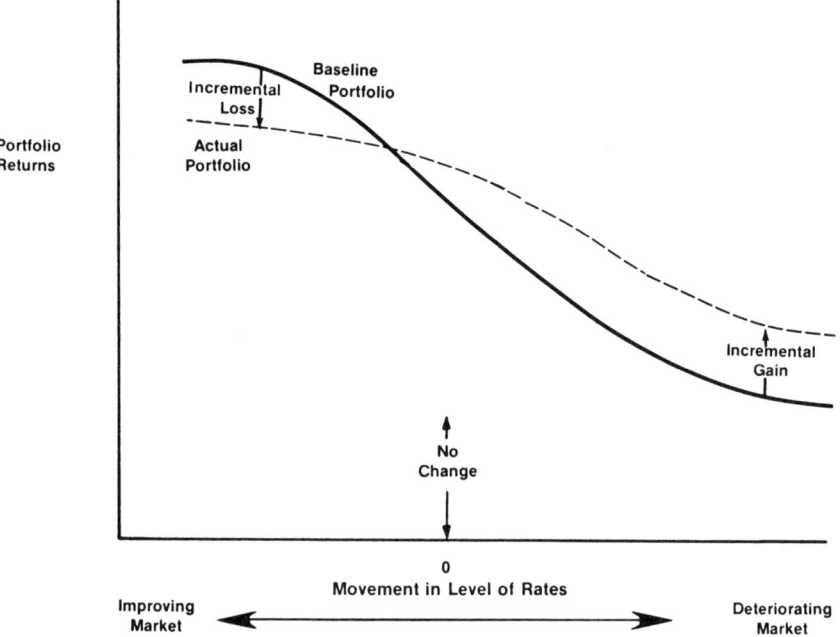

parture from the baseline. The actual portfolio is considerably more defensive than the baseline; as long as the market stays at the same level or deteriorates (i.e., rises in yield level), the actual portfolio will outperform the baseline. There will be a loss relative to the baseline only under improving market conditions (i.e., declining yields). The choice of the actual portfolio suggests that the manager has a rather pessimistic outlook on the market, or feels that incremental performance is more important in dreary markets.

Another way of exploring this risk-return trade-off is for the manager to assign probabilities to the different rate movements. The expected returns (i.e., the probability-weighted average returns) can then be plotted as shown in Figure 14. The horizontal axis in Figure 14 represents some measure of portfolio aggressiveness—i.e., interest rate risk.

As noted earlier, the maturity structure is the most important decision made by an active portfolio manager. By varying the maturity structure, one can control the amount of interest rate risk contained in the portfolio. Various proxies for the interest rate risk of a portfolio have been proposed—average maturity, historical variability, percentage price volatility, Macaulay's duration, horizon volatility, pro-

Figure 14
Market-Motivated Departures from the Baseline Portfolio

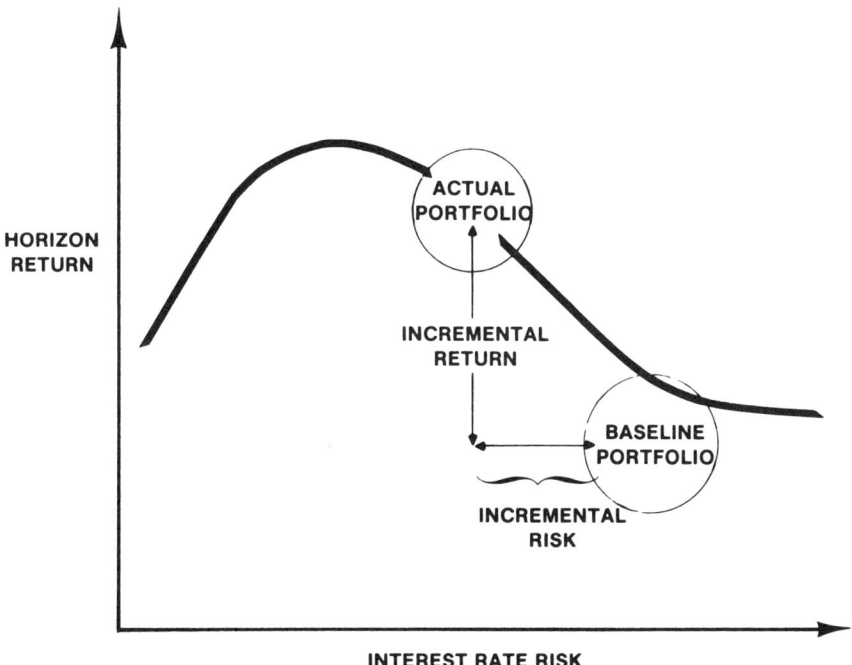

portional volatility [8]. However, for any of these measures, the baseline can be viewed as the reference point. To the extent that the active manager departs from this baseline level of interest rate risk, one risks falling below the baseline's performance.

This holds true for departures in both directions.

In the case of Figure 14, the manager is making a "defensive departure" from the baseline's risk level. By choosing a portfolio with less interest rate sensitivity than the baseline, the manager hopes to obtain a sizable improvement in incremental returns, given a basically pessimistic outlook. However, the manager is exposing the portfolio to a considerable shortfall in return relative to the baseline in the event that this pessimistic outcome fails to materialize.

One should take note of the apparent paradox in the situation portrayed in Figure 14. The greatest risk here is the prospect of a stronger-than-expected downward move in interest rates. This action would normally be viewed as an improving market. However, in this case, such a market improvement would lead to underperformance relative to the baseline portfolio, and hence would constitute the gravest threat to the fund's progress towards its long-term goals.

Figure 14 thus shows how a manager can gauge incremental interest rate risk relative to the baseline and, by implication, measure more generalized risk relative to long-term goals. There may be some controversy regarding what constitutes a satisfactory measure of interest rate risk. However, there is no disagreement that a greater level of risk consciousness needs to be introduced into the management process. Once any such volatility measure has been selected, the procedure implied in Figures 13 or 14 can be quantified, thereby providing the manager (and the sponsor) with a concrete, numerical indication of the incremental risk associated with a prospective portfolio strategy.

Sources of Return

This approach can be further refined by combining it with an analysis of the component sources of prospective return. In the first part of this article, we described four main categories of bond portfolio activity—pure yield pick-up, substitution swap, sector spread swaps, and rate anticipation. A given portfolio structure will typically contain (intentionally or not) some degree of each activity. By identifying the components of bond return, one can associate each category of management activity with its corresponding contribution to the return-risk characteristics of the overall portfolio. One such technique identifies eight component sources of return:

1. Yield curve accumulation.
2. Sector spread accumulation.
3. Rolling yield effect.
4. Revaluation in sector spread.
5. Market shifts.
6. Yield curve reshaping.
7. Sector response to yield curve changes.
8. Specific issue spread action beyond that of the associated sector.

Another way of analyzing these return components is in terms of the kind of risks they represent. Thus, the combination of the first three components is simply the sector's rolling yield [9]. This rolling yield return is fairly well assured for sectors whose quality is not in doubt. In contrast, the revaluation return reflects a spread judgment that the sector is undervalued. There may be considerable risk surrounding any such projected revaluation.

The next three components of return, the resulting yield curve reshaping, and the sector spread response, all depend on the magnitude of the overall market movement. It is useful to combine these three volatility factors into a measure of the sector's total market volatility.

Figure 15 provides a graphic representation of the relationships

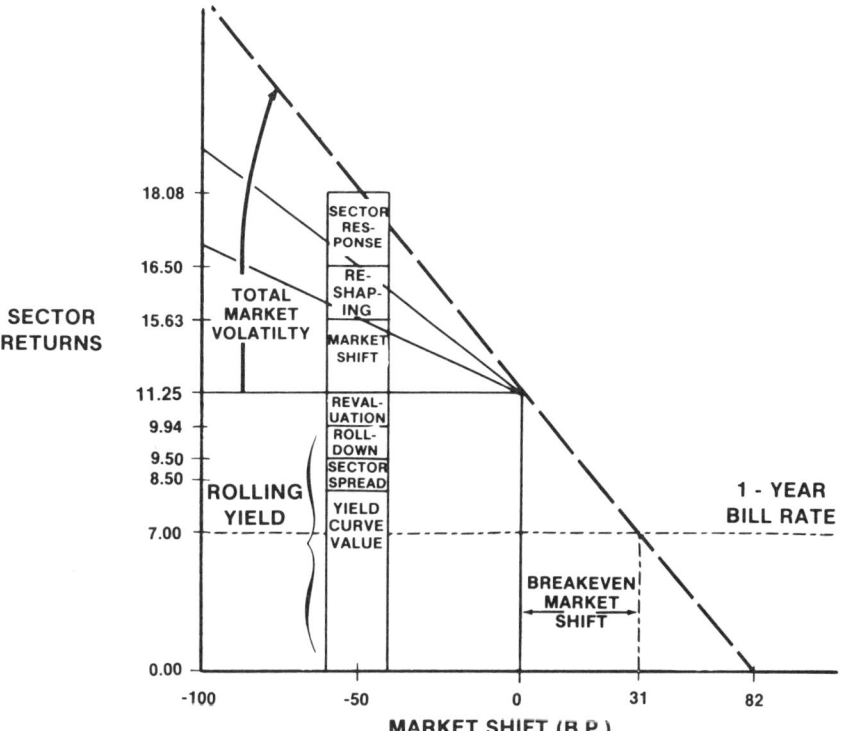

Figure 15
Sector Returns for a Range of Market Shifts

among these different return components and risk categories. A detailed explanation of this approach is contained in the author's study *Sources of Return in Corporate Bond Portfolios* [10].

These classification techniques have been developed to assist the investment manager in organizing and quantifying the many market judgments that are embedded in one's portfolio structure. The classification process also highlights the nature of the different risks incurred, as well as the differences in their portfolio impact over varying investment horizons. By analyzing the marketplace in terms of this same classification system, the manager may be better able to construct a portfolio having a desired set of characteristics. This classification procedure could also prove helpful in more precisely identifying the manager's motivation behind an intended departure from a goal-oriented baseline portfolio.

Communication between Sponsor and Manager

The baseline portfolio approach can facilitate the communication process between sponsor and manager.

At the outset, the baseline portfolio should itself be the result of discussions between the fund's sponsor and the manager. In these initial discussions, the sponsor must try to convey her sense of the fund's purpose, to define her overall objectives and their relative priorities, and to identify, and delimit, the risk factors that concern her. On the other hand, the manager contributes knowledge of the behavioral characteristics of the various asset classes, along with beliefs as to how they will function in the context of different portfolio structures. (At this point, the manager should try to put aside personal perceptions of immediate market value, and concentrate on the general long-term characteristics of the various market sectors.)

In all too many instances, this interchange tends to remain at a rather fuzzy level of generality, with both parties espousing the obviously desirable "Nirvana points," e.g., maximum return with minimum risk, highest yield without sacrifice of quality, minimum volatility with greatest stability of income, etc. If the discussion of goals ends at this point, then neither party has communicated a sense of the appropriate trade-offs. In a rather fundamental sense, no real understanding has been achieved.

However, a joint determination to specify a baseline portfolio can drive these discussions down to the concrete level. It will force the difficult choices to be made—and made jointly by both sponsor and manager. The sponsor must articulate the subtle priorities that can organize many objectives, and must develop a clear-cut structure by relating these priorities—with the manager's help—to choices between specific market sectors. The manager must rise above his or her active orientation to define the most balanced, passive portfolio structure matching the client's needs. In this fashion, both parties are able to merge and consolidate their different points of view. In essence, by specifying a baseline portfolio, they have come to agree on a practical, passive alternative to active management.

As with any real process of communication, these interactions may prove painful and arduous at the outset. However, once defined, the baseline can prove a mutual vantage point for interpreting the actual returns achieved over time. The all-too-common ongoing confusion between conflicting short-term results and long-term goals will be reduced. Because of the sponsor's role in defining the baseline, the manager will no longer be quite so vulnerable to criticism for the many portfolio effects that are (in reality) mandated by the nature of the fund. In particular, having the baseline may considerably reduce artificial pressures on a manager with regard to high volatility, yield give-ups, particularly high- or low-quality postures, having the portfolio balanced away from the general market structure, or for deviations from the performance returns achieved by general market indices or theoretical peer groups.

Moreover, by concentrating the objective-setting in an initial phase shared with the sponsor, the baseline approach should allow the investment manager to focus more clearly on day-by-day market activities in the fund's behalf. At the same time, the fund sponsor will achieve the security of knowing that long-term risk-return objectives are not being inadvertently compromised in the pursuit of short-term performance.

REFERENCES

1. Homer, Sidney, and Martin L. Leibowitz. *Inside the Yield Book.* Englewood Cliffs, N.J.: Prentice-Hall, and New York Institute of Finance, 1972.
2. Leibowitz, Martin L. "Goal-Oriented Bond Portfolio Management: The 'Baseline' Method for Relating Short-Term Performance to Long-Term Goals." New York: Salomon Brothers, May 15, 1978. (Now chapter 1, in *Total Return Management.* New York: Salomon Brothers, 1979.)
3. Leibowitz, Martin L. "The Horizon Annuity: An Investment Measure for Linking the Growth and Payout Phases of Long-Term Bond Portfolio." New York: Salomon Brothers, 1976.
4. Leibowitz, Martin L., and Richard I. Johannesen, Jr. "Introducing the Salomon Brothers Total Performance Index for the High-Grade Long-Term Corporate Bond Market." New York: Salomon Brothers, November 2, 1973.
5. Leibowitz, Martin L. "New Tools in Bond Portfolio Management." *Trusts and Estates,* January 1973.
6. Leibowitz, Martin L. "Portfolio Returns and Scenario Analysis." New York: Salomon Brothers, March 20, 1978. (Now chapter 5, in *Total Return Management.* New York: Salomon Brothers, 1979.)
7. Leibowitz, Martin L. "Profits, Losses, and Portfolio Objectives." New York: Salomon Brothers, June 15, 1976.
8. Leibowitz, Martin L. "The Risk Dimension." New York: Salomon Brothers, October 5, 1977. (Now chapter 4, in *Total Return Management.* New York: Salomon Brothers, 1979.)
9. Leibowitz, Martin L. "The Rolling Yield." New York: Salomon Brothers, April 21, 1977. (Now chapter 2, in *Total Return Management.* New York: Salomon Brothers, 1979.)
10. Leibowitz, Martin L. "Sources of Return in Corporate Bond Portfolios." Salomon Brothers, August 3, 1978. (Now chapter 6, in *Total Return Management.* New York: Salomon Brothers, 1979.)

11. Leibowitz, Martin L. "Total After-Tax Bond Performance and Yield Measures." New York: Salomon Brothers, June 1, 1974.
12. Waldman, Michael. "Introducing the Salomon Brothers Total Rate-of-Return Index for Mortgage Pass-Through Securities." Salomon Brothers, March 15, 1979.

Bond Portfolio Immunization*

9

SYLVAN G. FELDSTEIN, Ph.D.
Vice President and Bond Analyst,
Moody's Investors Service

PETER E. CHRISTENSEN
Vice President, The First Boston Corporation

FRANK J. FABOZZI, Ph.D., C.F.A., C.P.A.
Professor of Economics, Fordham University

The volatility of interest rates since 1978 has created unprecedented risks for bond portfolio managers. Those who tried to time the cyclical downturn in interest rates by committing money to the intermediate and long ends of the bond market have seen heavy erosion at various times in their asset values. In this chapter we illustrate a bond portfolio strategy that can be employed to minimize the risk of interest-rate volatility over a predetermined horizon. The strategy, known as *immunization,* has been used by bank trust departments and pension funds for bond portfolios and by life insurance companies as a funding vehicle for their "guaranteed" annuity products.[1]

---

*The authors wish to acknowledge the assistance of Calvin C. Cooper and Jan Lehrman in the preparation of the simulated illustration presented in this chapter.
 In this presentation the simulated illustration of an immunized portfolio is for a portfolio of municipal bonds. For a simulated illustration of immunization applied to a portfolio of federal government bonds, see: P. Christensen, S. Feldstein and F. Fabozzi, "Bond Portfolio Immunization," Chapter 36 in *The Handbook of Fixed Income Securities,* ed. Frank J. Fabozzi and Irving M. Pollack (Homewood, Ill.: Dow Jones-Irwin, 1983).

[1] For a discussion of immunization applied to specific institutions, see the following: R. M. Redington, "Review of the Principle of Life-Office Valuations," *Journal of the Institute of Actuaries* 78 (1952), pp. 286-340; Irwin T. Vanderhood, "The Interest-Rate Assumption and the Maturity Structure of the Assets of a Life Insurance Company," *Trans-*

Although bond immunization may not be appropriate for all bond portfolio managers, and particularly not for trust departments and individual investors with more active portfolio strategies, it is attractive for those who either need to reduce their funding risks by matching at least a portion of their bond assets to anticipated liabilities or for those who just want to lock in prevailing rates over a predetermined time horizon.

THE NEED FOR STABLE RETURNS IN A VOLATILE INTEREST-RATE ENVIRONMENT

Is there a way to hedge against the uncertainty surrounding the volatility in interest rates? Is there a way to minimize or control interest-rate risk? Is there a way to protect at least a portion of your assets from the unpredictable or uncontrollable? The British were the first to respond to these portfolio management problems through the development of immunization theory. The British naturally found it easier to develop these concepts, since they had related experience in reducing risk by matching assets and liabilities in varying currencies.

In the same manner that currency risk can be controlled, an immunized bond strategy can also minimize or control interest-rate risk. As such, immunization is a strategy suitable for investors who require safety for at least a portion of their assets. It is a strategy also well suited for those who wish to avoid committing themselves 100 percent to an "active position" in the bond market.

The risk an investor assumes with the purchase of a bond portfolio is related not just to security and other portfolio characteristics, but also to the investor's time horizon and the interest-rate fluctuations that occur over that horizon. Interest-rate risk, including reinvestment risk, can be effectively eliminated, however, by implementing a portfolio strategy based upon the concept of *duration,* which is the building block of immunization. Duration very simply is a mathe-

---

actions of the Society of Actuaries, May-June 1972; G. O. Bierwag, George G. Kaufman, and Alden Toevs, "Management Strategies for Savings and Loan Associations to Reduce Interest-Rate Risk," *Proceedings of the Conference on New Sources of Capital for the Savings and Loan Industry* (Federal Home Loan Bank of San Francisco, 1979); Richard Keintz and Clyde Stickney, "Immunization of Pension Funds From Interest-Rate Changes," Dartmouth College working paper, 1977; D. Don Ezra, "Immunization: A New Look for Actuarial Liabilities," *Journal of Portfolio Management,* Winter 1976, pp. 50-53.

For a discussion of immunization theory, see the following: Lawrence Fisher and Roman Weil, "Coping with the Risk of Interest-Rate Fluctuations: Returns to Bondholders from Naive and Optimal Strategies," *Journal of Business,* October 1971, pp. 408-31; G. O. Bierwag and George G. Kaufman, "Coping with the Risk of Interest-Rate Fluctuations: A Note," *Journal of Business,* July 1977, pp. 364-70; Seymour Smidt, "Investment Horizons and Performance Measures," *Journal of Portfolio Management,* Winter 1978, pp. 18-22.

matical measure of the *term* of a bond, taking into account all coupon and principal payments as well as the time value of money (reflecting prevailing yields).[2] The price sensitivity of a bond to changes in interest rates is related to its duration. (See the appendix for the computation of a bond's duration, its properties and the relationship between a bond's duration and price sensitivity.)

By matching the duration (or term) of a portfolio to a specific time horizon over which they would like to lock in rates, portfolio managers can hedge their portfolios, minimize the risk of repeated and unexpected changes in interest rates, and lock in prevailing yields. With immunization, managers find that assets and liabilities are equally affected by changes in interest rates. They are therefore able to achieve a highly predictable rate of return over the planning horizon, independent of the future fluctuations in interest rates that always occur in the bond market.

Knowledge of the immunized position is also of crucial value to active portfolio managers. Based on their perceptions of changes in the direction of interest rates, they must purposefully aim the duration of their portfolios away from the neutral or immunized position according to their forecast of interest rates in order to incrementally increase their holding period return.

In this instance, "active" or "contingent" immunization may be used by active managers to provide a "floor" or baseline return to a portfolio (say, 8 or 9 percent) that is a level below the immunized rate (say, 11 percent), yet allow them wide discretion in actively managing their bond portfolio. If performance is so short of target that total compounded return over the planning horizon approaches the floor or baseline, then the portfolio is immunized for the remaining time in the planning period.

Immunization and duration may also be used by active managers to assess their risk position relative to the neutral or immunized state. For instance, if we assume a planning horizon on September 15, 1981, of seven years and a set of performance standards for this period, active managers cannot position themselves long with the purchase of State of Connecticut General Obligation 9.10s of 1994. In spite of the 13 years to maturity, the Connecticut 9.10s represent an immunized position relative to the portfolio planning period. This is because the duration of the Connecticut 9.10s is precisely equal to the planning horizon. That is, the duration is also seven years. To position themselves long, managers must instead purchase lower

---

[2] Frederick R. Macaulay, *Some Theoretical Problems Suggested by the Movements of Interest Rates, Bond Yields, and Stock Prices in the United States since 1856* (New York: National Bureau of Economic Research, 1938).

coupon or longer maturity bonds with longer durations. *The key point to remember for active or neutral managers is that bonds must be purchased for their durations, not their maturities.*

In contrast to the measured assumption of risk, the immunization strategy offers the opportunity to *control* or minimize interest-rate risk over a specific planning horizon by reducing the standard deviation of return. Clearly this is not necessarily an optimal strategy. It is however an efficient strategy and therefore one that may suit the preferences of many types of investors. It does not replace active bond management. Rather it is a strategy designed for those investors who may have a fixed sum liability due at specific periods in the future. It is also a strategy designed for those investors who wish to have a "core" of their portfolio appreciate at a fixed, assured rate over a finite period and thereby lock in prevailing rates.

WHAT IS AN IMMUNIZED BOND PORTFOLIO?

Immunization, as it is presently conceived, is a duration-matching strategy. In 1952 F. M. Redington defined immunization as "the investment of the assets in such a way that the existing business is immune to a general change in the rate of interest."[3] He also stated that the average duration of assets, when set equal to the average duration of liabilities, will immunize a portfolio from the effects of a change in interest rates. By matching durations on both sides of the ledger, we ensure that assets and liabilities are equally affected by changes in interest rates. For any change in yield, both sides of the ledger are equally affected, and therefore the relative values of assets and liabilities are not changed.

Interest-rate risk appears then as a result of assets having a longer or shorter duration than liabilities. The greater the disparity between durations, the greater the risk. However, the greater the quality of average durations, the better the immunity, and the better the probability we could fully fund any fixed liabilities or meet interest-rate goals regardless of market interest-rate fluctuations. It is important to repeat at this juncture that immunization is not necessarily an optimal strategy. It is, however, an efficient strategy and therefore one that may suit the preferences of many types of investors. It is well suited for those investors who have fixed-sum liabilities due at specific points in the future. It is also well suited for those who wish to have a "core" of their bond portfolio appreciate at a fixed, assured rate over a finite period (i.e., lock in prevailing rates). Immu-

---

[3] Redington, "Life-Office Valuations."

nization maximizes the likelihood that a high fixed rate of return will be achieved over a fixed time horizon. It tends to minimize the degree of risk that is assumed in the portfolio over that horizon. At that same time it must be noted that it also restricts opportunities to position a portfolio to benefit from a series of unexpected, or even expected but favorable, interest-rate changes as well.

THE NONIMMUNIZED PORTFOLIO

Alternatively, a nonimmunized portfolio must bear the risk of fluctuating bond values as well as the consequent risk that the portfolio will not have earned sufficient return to fully fund its liabilities. This condition may result from quarter-to-quarter positioning of the portfolio to take maximum advantage of anticipated changes in interest rates. If rates do not shift according to the anticipated plan, the long-term health of the bond portfolio may be thwarted by efforts to maximize short-term performance.

For this reason, a longer term framework can serve as a better guide when managing bonds that will eventually either be matched against long-term liabilities or be used for achieving predetermined interest-rate goals. Knowing the immunized or neutral position for a portfolio will give managers a better understanding of the degree of risk they have assumed. The portfolio manager who has firm expectations about the future direction of interest rates can also use the immunized position as the reference from which to base an active position. In this way, the manager is able to gauge the degree of risk he or she is assuming and plan the returns to be expected from the directional change in interest rates.

CONSTRUCTION OF AN IMMUNIZED PORTFOLIO

Lawrence Fisher and Roman Weil have defined an immunized portfolio as follows:[4]

> A portfolio of investments in bonds is *immunized* for a holding period if its value at the end of the holding period, regardless of the course of interest rates during the holding period, must be at least as large as it would have been had the interest-rate function been constant throughout the holding period.
>
> If the realized return on an investment in bonds is sure to be at least as large as the appropriately computed yield to the horizon, then that investment is immunized.

---

[4] Fisher and Weil, "Coping with the Risk of Interest-Rate Fluctuations."

Fisher and Weil have demonstrated that to achieve the immunized result, the average duration of a portfolio of bonds must be set equal to the remaining time in the planning horizon.

As time passes however, the bond portfolio must be rebalanced so that the duration of the bond portfolio is set equal to the remaining life in the planning period. This requires that coupon income, interest on coupon income, matured principal, and proceeds from possible liquidation of longer bonds be reinvested in order to continually maintain the duration equal to the remaining life in the planning period. Because of these multiple rebalancings, the bond portfolio is maintained in an immunized state throughout the planning period and should achieve its interest-rate target return in spite of periodic shifts in rates.

An immunized bond portfolio, therefore, can be constructed once a time horizon has been established. Since duration is inversely related to both the prevailing yields and the coupon rate, it may not be possible to immunize a portfolio beyond a certain number of years. For example, when yields in the bond market reached a historic high in 1981, it was not possible to immunize a portfolio of taxable bonds beyond 8 years or a portfolio of municipal bonds beyond 10 years.

Of course, the actual targeted return on an immunized portfolio will depend on the level of interest rates at the time the program is initiated. An immunized portfolio hedges interest-rate risk irrespective of rate changes. Though bond values may for example decline as interest rates rise, the future value of the portfolio (or security) based on the new (higher) reinvestment rate and lower principal value will still correspond to the original targeted yield. As we demonstrate later, duration is the key control of reinvestment rates and asset values as interest rates fluctuate.

The important point to remember is: The standard deviation of return on an immunized portfolio will be much lower over a given horizon than that on a nonimmunized portfolio—whether measured around the sample mean or promised yield. With interest-rate risk minimized (when held over an assumed time horizon), the performance of the immunized portfolio is virtually assured, regardless of reinvestment rates. For example, if we wanted to achieve a target return over five years, we could purchase, say, five-year bonds and hold them to maturity. By so doing, we can be certain (assuming no defaults occur) of receiving the specified coupon payments over the five-year period as well as the principal repayment at redemption. These two sources of income are fixed in dollar amounts. The third and final source of income is the interest earned on the semiannual coupon payments. "Interest on coupon" is not fixed in dollar amounts; rather it depends upon the interest-rate environments at the various times of payment. Thus to secure a targeted level of return five years hence, one must reduce or eliminate this "reinvestment risk" associated with the interest-on-coupon source of income.

Immunization seeks to do just that. By targeting the duration of the *portfolio* rather than specific maturities to the prespecified investment period of five years, we again see the offsets of capital gain and reinvestment return occurring in equal measure. Moreover, by varying the maturity pattern around the time horizon while still maintaining the same duration on the portfolio (i.e., barbell, even-ladder, or bullet maturity patterns[5] — we find different risk-return characteristics. The barbell and even-ladder strategies incorporate greater reinvestment risk, since matured principal must be reinvested in future unknown yield environments.

Ideally, the exact maturity pattern to an immunized portfolio should not be of significance to the fixed result. However, there are two simplifying assumptions used in the theoretical literature on immunization, the harmful effects of which can be neutralized or minimized if we employ the bullet (or clustered) maturity pattern. The Macaulay duration measure assumes (1) a flat yield curve and (2) parallel shifts of a flat yield curve.[6]

Since both assumptions are wholly unrealistic, we minimize their otherwise harmful effects by compressing the maturity pattern into a bullet, thereby creating a relatively flat yield curve over the restricted range of maturities. In any conceivable yield environment therefore, we minimize our violation of these two harsh assumptions with a bullet maturity pattern. As such, we are able to lock in prevailing rates for a fixed number of years regardless of future fluctuations in interest rates.

MATURITY MATCHING: THE REINVESTMENT PROBLEM WHEN IMMUNIZATION IS NOT USED

Suppose an investor wishes to lock in prevailing interest rates for a 10-year period. Then why not buy a 10-year bond?

An investor, however, will *not* be protected from changes in interest rates with the purchase of a 10-year bond. A reinvestment problem arises as the reinvestment of coupon income occurs at rates below the original target yield. Note from Exhibit 1 that as interest rates shift and remain at new levels for a 10-year period, the total

---

[5] For a discussion of these strategies, see H. Russell Fogler, William A. Groves, and James G. Richardson, "Managing Bonds: Are 'Dumbbells' Smart?" *Journal of Portfolio Management,* Winter 1976, pp. 54-60.

[6] For a further discussion, see G. O. Bierwag, George G. Kaufman, Robert Schweitzer, and Alden Toevs, "The Art of Risk Management in Bond Portfolios," *Journal of Portfolio Management,* Spring 1981, pp. 27-36.

"holding period" return on a 9 percent par bond due in 10 years will vary considerably. The initial effect will appear in the value of the asset. A capital gain (or loss) will appear immediately.

As the holding period increases after a change in rates, the interest-on-coupon component of total return begins to exert a stronger

Exhibit 1
Total Return on a 9 Percent, $1,000 Bond Due in 10 Years and Held through Various Holding Periods

Interest Rate at Time of Reinvestment	Income Source	Holding Period in Years					
		1	3	5	6.79*	9	10
5%	Coupon income	$ 90	$270	$450	$611	$ 810	$ 900
	Capital gain or loss	287	234	175	100	39	-0-
	Interest on interest	1	17	54	105	191	241
	Total return	$378	$521	$679	$816	$1,040	$1,141
	(and yield)	(37.0%)	(15.0%)	(11.0%)	(9.0%)	(8.5%)	(8.2%)
7%	Coupon income	$ 90	$270	$450	$611	$ 810	$ 900
	Capital gain or loss	132	109	83	56	19	-0-
	Interest on interest	2	25	78	149	279	355
	Total return	$224	$404	$611	$816	$1,108	$1,255
	(and yield)	(22.0%)	(12.0%)	(10.0%)	(9.0%)	(8.6%)	(8.5%)
9%	Coupon income	$ 90	$270	$450	$611	$ 810	$ 900
	Capital gain or loss	-0-	-0-	-0-	-0-	-0-	-0-
	Interest on interest	2	32	103	205	387	495
	Total return	$ 92	$302	$553	$816	$1,197	$1,395
	(and yield)	(9.0%)	(9.0%)	(9.0%)	(9.0%)	(9.0%)	(9.0%)
11%	Coupon income	$ 90	$270	$450	$611	$ 810	$ 900
	Capital gain or loss	−112	−95	−75	−56	−18	-0-
	Interest on interest	2	40	129	261	502	647
	Total return	$−20	$215	$504	$816	$1,294	$1,547
	(and yield)	(2.0%)	(6.7%)	(8.5%)	(9.0%)	(9.7%)	(9.8%)

*Duration of a 9 percent bond bought at par and due in 10 years.

influence. At 10 years, we note that the interest on coupon exerts a dominance over capital gain (or loss) in the determination of holding period returns.

Intuitively we know that these relationships make sense. Capital gains appear instantly, whereas changes in reinvestment rates take time to exert their effect on the total holding period return on a bond.

Understanding the forces operating on the total return of a bond, we may now ask at what point do the forces of capital gain and reinvestment rate *equally* offset one another in a manner similar to a break-even? If rates jump from 9 percent to 11 percent and a capital loss occurs today, at what point will that capital loss be made up because we are reinvesting those coupon income payments in a higher (11 percent) rate environment? The two offsetting forces of capital value and reinvestment return equally offset at the duration of the bond—in this case at 6.79 years. In order to earn the original 9 percent target return (the original yield to maturity at the time of purchase) in this example, it is necessary to hold that bond for the period of its duration—6.79 years. If we wanted to lock in a market rate of 9 percent for a 10-year period, we would select a bond with a duration of 10 years (not a maturity of 10 years). The maturity for such a par bond in this yield environment is roughly 23 years.

From Exhibit 1 we note that regardless of the interest-rate fluctuations (in Exhibit 1 they fluctuate from 5 to 11 percent), we are still able to earn the 9 percent total return if our holding period is 6.79 years—the duration of the bond.

Similarly, in order to control the interest-rate risk of a portfolio of bonds, we must monitor the duration of the portfolio so that the direction of the portfolio always stays on that point of break-even. Regardless of how rates fluctuate, we are able to lock in rates and effectively eliminate the reinvestment risk that is associated with the maturity matching strategy.

Finally, the duration of a portfolio will not move in lock step with the passage of time. Therefore we must monitor and adjust the "duration wandering" that takes place by rebalancing the portfolio on an annual or as-needed basis. To illustrate, suppose the remaining life in the planning period has declined by a year—from 10 years to 9 years. The duration of that bond may have declined by less than a year—to, say, 9.2 years. In order to neutralize the harmful effects of this tendency, we should rebalance the portfolio in order to match the duration of the portfolio with the remaining time in the planning period. Left unchecked, duration wandering will effect the performance of a portfolio. By monitoring and adjusting the portfolio's duration, we remain immunized in the face of multiple shifts in interest rates and eliminate in the process the so-called reinvestment problem.

A SIMULATED ILLUSTRATION OF AN IMMUNIZED BOND PORTFOLIO

Active immunization strategy will be illustrated for a municipal bond portfolio. The following assumptions are made:

1. We begin our investment initially with $5 million on September 15, 1981.
2. The investment horizon is five years.
3. The portfolio will consist of state general obligation bonds.

4. Our beginning yield established on September 15, 1981, was 11.258 percent.
5. The specific state general obligation bonds used in the simulation are shown in Exhibit 2.
6. The yield curve assumptions used in this simulation for Aa/AA-rated state general obligation bonds are presented in Exhibit 3.

Exhibit 2
State General Obligation Bonds Used in Simulation

Issuer	Security	Coupon	Maturity
State of Florida	General obligation	5.25%	2/1/86
State of Florida	General obligation	6.10	5/1/85
State of Florida	General obligation	9.60	4/1/89
State of Oregon	General obligation	4.80	1/15/87
State of Oregon	General obligation	5.00	2/15/87
State of Oregon	General obligation	5.10	8/15/87

Exhibit 3
Assumed Yield Curves: 1981-86*

Maturity of Bonds	Year 0 1981	Year 1 1982	Year 2 1983	Year 3 1984	Year 4 1985	Year 5 1986
1 year	10.00%	8.75%	7.25%	8.75%	10.00%	10.25%
2 years	10.20	9.00	7.25	9.00	10.20	10.50
3 years	10.45	9.20	7.25	9.20	10.45	10.75
5 years	11.00	9.60	7.25	9.60	11.00	11.25
7 years	11.30	10.00	7.50	10.00	11.30	11.75
10 years	11.75	10.60	7.75	10.60	11.75	12.60
20 years	13.00	11.50	9.00	11.50	13.00	13.50
30 years	13.25	11.75	9.40	11.75	13.25	13.95

*For Aa/AA-rated general obligation bonds.

These are *not* interest-rate projections. They are used here in order to subject an immunized portfolio to a wide variety of interest rates over the five-year horizon.

7. The initial municipal bond portfolio as of September 15, 1981, is shown in Exhibit 4. It should be noted that if the bonds in this portfolio are held to maturity, a capital gains tax of $212,000 would have to be paid. This amount is derived by a 20 percent tax rate on the capital gains portion. Although we note this cost factor in the simulation, we do not factor it into our target or actual yields.
8. We assumed a transaction cost of $5 per bond per trade.

9: Bond Portfolio Immunization

9. The capital gains taxes to be paid is at the 20 percent tax rate and is the tax on the net capital gains after transaction costs are subtracted.

Exhibit 4 presents the following information for the portfolio at the beginning of each year: issues in the portfolio, market value of each issue in the portfolio, total market value, duration, average

Exhibit 4
Portfolio Status at the Beginning of Each Year

Initial Portfolio Status: September 15, 1981

Percent	Par*	Issue	Coupon	Maturity	Yield	Price	Market Value
21.30	1,400	Oregon	4.80	1/15/87	11.20	74.798	$1,058,377
18.30	1,200	Oregon	5.00	2/15/87	11.21	75.277	908,327
22.00	1,460	Oregon	5.10	8/15/87	11.14	74.321	1,091,284
38.40	2,000	Florida	9.60	4/1/89	11.38	91.135	1,910,167

Total market value: $4,968,155   Transaction fees: $30,300
Duration: 5.04 years   Overspent: -0-
Average maturity: 6.33 years   Cash remaining: $1,545
Average coupon: 6.748%
Average yield: 11.258%
Target yield: 11.258%

Portfolio Status: Year One, September 15, 1982

Percent	Par	Issue	Coupon	Maturity	Yield	Price	Market Value
62.00	4,295	Oregon	4.80	1/15/87	9.47	83.699	$3,629,222
17.30	1,200	Oregon	5.00	2/15/87	9.48	84.126	1,014,512
20.70	1,460	Oregon	5.10	8/15/87	9.58	82.747	1,214,309

Total market value: $5,858,043   Transaction fees: $24,475
Duration: 4.02 years   Overspent: $337
Average maturity: 4.47 years   Cash remaining: -0-
Average coupon: 4.897%
Average yield: 9.495%
Target yield: 11.258%

Portfolio Status: Year Two, September 15, 1983

Percent	Par	Issue	Coupon	Maturity	Yield	Price	Market Value
69.30	5,065	Oregon	4.80	1/15/87	7.85	91.195	$4,659,525
16.40	1,200	Oregon	5.00	2/15/87	7.86	91.567	1,103,806
14.20	1,000	Florida	5.25	2/1/86	7.61	94.951	956,069

Total market value: $6,719,400   Transaction fees: $16,150
Duration: 3.00 years   Overspent: -0-
Average maturity: 3.21 years   Cash remaining: $1,346
Average coupon: 4.897%
Average yield: 7.818%
Target yield: 11.258%

Exhibit 4 *(concluded)*

Portfolio Status: Year Three, September 15, 1984

Percent	Par	Issue	Coupon	Maturity	Yield	Price	Market Value
72.80	5,605	Oregon	4.80	1/15/87	9.27	90.798	$5,134,085
27.20	2,000	Florida	5.25	2/1/86	9.08	95.142	1,915,957

Total Market Value: $7,050,042
Duration: 1.99 years
Average maturity: 2.07 years
Average coupon: 4.922%
Average yield: 9.218%
Target yield: 11.258%

Transaction fees: $13,700
Overspent: -0-
Cash remaining: $2,174

Portfolio Status: Year Four, September 15, 1985

Percent	Par	Issue	Coupon	Maturity	Yield	Price	Market Value
69.10	5,605	Oregon	4.80	1/15/87	10.06	93.57	$5,289,613
30.90	2,395	Florida	5.25	2/1/86	9.95	98.30	2,369,997

Total market value: $7,659,610
Duration: 1.02 years
Average maturity: 1.04 years
Average coupon: 4.939%
Average yield: 10.026%
Target yield: 11.258%

Transaction fees: $1,975
Overspent: -0-
Cash remaining: $2,065

*Par value in thousands of dollars.

maturity, average coupon, average yield, and transaction fees. Notice that the duration of the portfolio is adjusted each year so as to approximately match the remaining period in the time horizon. Exhibits 5 through 9 summarize the actual portfolio transactions each year.

Since the target yield is 11.258 percent, the target value after five years is $8,469,375.[7] The total market value of the portfolio at the end of the fifth year is $8,353,539. Thus the actual yield is approximately 10.95 percent. We should add that our actual yield is quite conservative. We did not revise the target yield calibration to account for rolling down the yield curve. If we had, the *actual* result should have compared more favorably to our *target* yield because of the positive slope in the municipal market. The reasons for the further discrepancy between the target yield and the actual yield are discussed below.

---

[7] Since the initial investment is $4,968,155 and the target yield is 11.258 percent, the target value is:

$$(1.11258)^5 \times \$4,968,155 = \$8,269,375$$

We started with an investment of $5 million but reduced this amount after transaction costs were deducted. We should note that transaction costs in the municipal bond market tend to be substantially higher than those in the taxable markets.

Exhibit 5
Municipal Bond Immunization Year-End Transactions (year one, September 15, 1982)

	Coupon Income	+	Interest on Coupon	Matured Principal		
1. Income received during year:	$393,660	+	$17,223	$0	=	$ 410,883
				Plus carryover cash:		$ 1,545
						$ 412,428

	Par	Issue	Coupon	Maturity	Yield	Price	Market Value
2. Sell:	2,000	Florida	9.60	4/1/89	9.91	98.524	$2,057,950
					Less transaction fee:		$ 10,000
							$2,047,950

3. Available to reinvest: $2,460,378

	Par	Issue	Coupon	Maturity	Yield	Price	Market Value
4. Buy:	2,895	Oregon	4.30	1/15/87	9.47	83.699	$2,446,240
					Plus transaction fee:		$ 14,475
							$2,460,715

5. Remaining cash: −$337 $ −337

6. Capital gains taxes to be paid: $25,557

Exhibit 6
Municipal Bond Immunization Year-End Transactions (year two, September 15, 1983)

	Coupon Income	+	Interest on Coupon	+	Matured Principal		
1. Income received during year:	$340,620	+	$12,347	+	$0	=	$ 352,967
					Plus carryover cash:		$ −337
							$ 352,630

	Par	Issue	Coupon	Maturity	Yield	Price	Market Value
2. Sell:	1,460	Oregon	5.10	8/15/87	7.93	90.623	$1,329,293
						Less transaction fee:	$ 7,300
							$1,321,993

3. Available to reinvest: $1,674,623

	Par	Issue	Coupon	Maturity	Yield	Price	Market Value
4. Buy:	1,000	Florida	5.25	2/1/86	7.61	94.951	$ 956,069
	770	Oregon	4.80	1/15/87	7.85	91.195	$ 708,358
						Plus transaction fee:	$ 8,850
							$1,673,277

5. Remaining cash: $1,346 $ 1,346

6. Capital gains taxes to be paid: $44,682

Exhibit 7
Municipal Bond Immunization Year-End Transactions (year three, September 15, 1984)

1. Income received during year:

Coupon Income		Interest on Coupon		Matured Principal		
$355,620	+	$15,558	+	$0	=	$ 371,178

Plus carryover cash: $ 1,346

$ 372,524

2. Sell:

Par	Issue	Coupon	Maturity	Yield	Price	Market Value
1,200	Oregon	5.00	2/15/87	9.28	90.913	$1,095,959

Less transaction fee: $ 6,000

3. Available to reinvest: $1,462,483 $1,089,959

4. Buy:

Par	Issue	Coupon	Maturity	Yield	Price	Market Value
1,000	Florida	5.25	2/1/86	9.08	95.142	$ 957,978
540	Oregon	4.80	1/15/87	9.27	90.708	$ 494,631

Plus transaction fee: $ 7,700

$1,460,309

5. Remaining cash: $2,174 $ 2,174

6. Capital gains taxes to be paid: $35,126

Exhibit 8
Municipal Bond Immunization Year-End Transactions (year four, September 15, 1985)

	Coupon Income		Interest on Coupon		Matured Principal			
1. Income received during year:	$374,040	+	$18,702	+	$0	=	$	392,742
					Plus carryover cash:		$	2,174
							$	394,916

	Par	Issue	Coupon	Maturity	Yield	Price	Market Value
2. Sell:	—	—	—	—	—	—	—
					Less transaction fee:		—

3. Available to reinvest: $394,916

	Par	Issue	Coupon	Maturity	Yield	Price	Market Value
4. Buy:	395	Florida	5.25	2/1/86	9.95	98.30	$ 390,876
					Plus transaction fee:		$ 1,975
							$ 392,851

5. Remaining cash: $2,065 — $ 2,065

6. Capital gains taxes to be paid: $0

Exhibit 9
Municipal Bond Immunization Year-End Transactions (year five, September 15, 1986)

	Coupon Income		Interest on Coupon		Matured Principal			
1. Income received during year:	$394,778	+	$38,293	+	$2,395,000	=	$2,828,071	
					Plus carryover cash:		$ 2,065	$2,830,136

	Par	Issue	Coupon	Maturity	Yield	Price	Market Value	
2. Sell:	565	Oregon	4.80	1/15/87	10.25	98.244	$5,551,428	
						Less transaction fee:	$ 28,025	$5,523,403

3. Available to reinvest: $8,353,539 $8,353,539

	Par	Issue	Coupon	Maturity	Yield	Price	Market Value
4. Buy:	—	—	—	—	—	—	—
						Plus transaction fee:	—

5. Remaining cash: $0

6. Capital gains taxes to be paid: $157,554

GENERAL CONCERNS WHEN IMMUNIZATION IS USED

There are four concerns that have to be considered when applying the concept of immunization to a bond portfolio.

1. Although an immunized portfolio is a hedge against changes in interest rates, it is not a hedge against credit risk. All bonds used in the portfolio would have to be reviewed in terms of creditworthiness.

2. Taxes must be considered when income from the portfolio to be immunized is taxed. Consequently, not all of the coupon interest payments can be reinvested except in the case of tax-exempt obligations. Moreover, if discount bonds are used and later are sold at higher prices or mature at par, the taxes to be paid on the capital gains would have to be factored into the overall yield expectations. As an example, in the simulation the total long-term capital gains taxes to be paid over the life of the five-year planning horizon is $279,289, versus $212,000 if the bonds in the original portfolio had just been held to maturity. This $67,289 difference represents an approximate 18-basis-point reduction in yield.

3. The credit quality of the portfolio must be kept constant throughout its life. If the initial portfolio is composed of A-rated bonds, and a target yield is initially determined on that basis, swapping into Aa/AA or better bonds would adversely impact the performance in relation to the target yield.

4. When bonds are sold at their durations and new bonds purchased (i.e., when swaps are made), the spreads must be as narrow as possible. For example, unlike the U.S. government market wherein the spreads are consistently narrow, spreads in the municipal market regardless of credit quality, maturity, or dollar price, can range over a very short period of time from a "lock" position to one of several points. Therefore, careful market timing must be utilized so as to obtain the most economical swaps. Otherwise, the expected immunized yields could be adversely impacted. In the simulated illustration we found that the transaction costs and yield curve roll reduced the immunized yield by approximately 31 basis points (i.e., a target yield of 11.258 percent versus an actual yield of 10.95 percent). In our model simulation we assumed transaction costs of $5 per bond per transaction. Higher costs could increase the difference between the target and actual yields substantially.

Appendix: Bond Duration

FRANK J. FABOZZI, Ph.D., C.F.A., C.P.A.
Professor of Economics
Fordham University

Duration is a weighted average term to maturity where the cash flows are in terms of their present value. Mathematically, duration is measured as follows:

$$\text{Duration} = \frac{PVCF_1(1)}{PVTCF} + \frac{PVCF_2(2)}{PVTCF} + \frac{PVCF_3(3)}{PVTCF} + \ldots + \frac{PVCF_n(n)}{PVTCF}$$

where

$PVCF_t$ = The present value of the cash flow in period t discounted at the prevailing yield-to-maturity

t = The period when the cash flow is received

n = Remaining number of periods until maturity

$PVTCF$ = Total present value of the cash flow from the bond where the present value is determined using the prevailing yield to maturity

For a bond in which there are no sinking fund or call effects and in which interest is paid semiannually, the cash flow for periods 1 to $n-1$ is just one half of the annual coupon interest.[1] The cash flow in

---

[1] The computation of a bond's duration when a sinking fund or call must be considered is illustrated by Frank K. Reilly and Rupinder S. Sidhu, "Duration and Its Properties,"

period n is the semiannual coupon interest plus the redemption value. The discount rate is one half the prevailing yield-to-maturity. The resulting value is in half-years when semiannual interest payments are used in the computation. To obtain duration in terms of years, duration in half-years is divided by two.[2] Since the price of a bond is equal to its cash flow discounted at the prevailing yield to maturity, *PVTCF* is nothing more than the current market price, including accrued interest.

Table 1 shows how the duration of a 7 percent coupon bond with eight years to maturity and selling for $887.70 to yield 9 percent is computed; assuming coupon interest is paid semiannually. The duration for this bond is 6.1335 years.

Three properties of a bond's duration should be noted. First, except for zero coupon bonds, the duration of a bond is less than its maturity. Second, the duration of a bond decreases the greater the

Table 1
Worksheet for Computation of the Duration of a 7 Percent Coupon Bond with Eight Years to Maturity, Selling at $887.70 to Yield 9 Percent (semiannual interest payments assumed)

Period	Cash Flow	PV at 4.5%	PVCF	PVCF × Period
1	$ 35	.9569	$ 33.4915	$ 33.4915
2	35	.9157	32.0495	64.0990
3	35	.8763	30.6705	92.0115
4	35	.8386	29.3510	117.4040
5	35	.8025	28.0875	140.4375
6	35	.7679	26.8765	161.2590
7	35	.7348	25.7180	180.0260
8	35	.7032	24.6120	196.8960
9	35	.6729	23.5515	211.9635
10	35	.6439	22.5365	225.3650
11	35	.6162	21.5670	237.2370
12	35	.5897	20.6395	247.6740
13	35	.5643	19.7505	256.7565
14	35	.5400	18.9000	264.6000
15	35	.5167	18.0845	271.2675
16	1,035	.4945	511.8075	8,188.9200
Total			$887.6935	$10,889.4080

Duration in half-years = 10,889.4080/887.6935
= 12.2671

Duration in years = 12.2671/2
= 6.1335

Chapter 35 in *The Handbook of Fixed Income Securities*, ed. Frank J. Fabozzi and Irving M. Pollack (Homewood, Ill.: Dow Jones-Irwin, 1983).

[2] In general, if there are m coupon payments per year then duration in years is computed by dividing the duration based upon m payments per year by m.

Appendix: Bond Duration

coupon rate. Finally, as market yields increase, the duration of a bond decreases.

The specific link between a bond's duration and its bond price volatility for small changes in interest rates was demonstrated by Professors Michael Hopewell and George Kaufman.[3] They show that:

$$\text{Percentage change in bond's price} = -(\text{Modified duration}) \left(\frac{\text{Change in market yield in basis points}}{100} \right)$$

where modified duration is duration divided by (1 + Market yield/Number of coupon payments per year).

For example, the duration of the 7 percent coupon bond with eight years to maturity and selling to yield 9 percent is 6.1335. Hence, modified duration is 6.1335/(1 + .09/2) or 5.8694. The percentage decline in the bond's price if market yields rise by 50 basis points is 2.93 percent, as shown in the formula:

$$\text{Percentage change in bond's price} = -(5.8694)\left(\frac{50}{100}\right)$$
$$= -2.93\%$$

---

[3] Michael H. Hopewell and George C. Kaufman, "Bond Price Volatility and Term to Maturity: A Generalized Respecification," *American Economic Review*, September 1973, pp. 749-53.

International Securities Market

10
GARY L. BERGSTROM, Ph.D.
President
Acadian Financial Research, Inc.
Boston, Mass.

JOHN K. KOENEMAN
Vice President
State Street Bank & Trust Co.

MARTIN J. SIEGEL*
Vice President
Salomon Brothers Inc

INTRODUCTION

As of year-end 1979, the aggregate market value of the common stocks of major companies domiciled outside the United States was approximately equal to the total value of the shares of U.S. companies. Table 1 provides a detailed breakdown of the market value of major publicly traded equity securities in Europe, Canada, Australia, South Africa, and the Far East. A number of smaller countries with stock markets—such as Mexico, Brazil, South Korea, and the Philippines—have not been included because of lack of comparable data. Nevertheless, Table 1 gives at least a rough approximation of the composition of a world equity market portfolio. There are also substantial markets for debt securities in many of these same countries, as well as in the Euro markets and other offshore marketplaces. Owing primarily to the lack of comprehensive data on fixed-income instruments, we shall concentrate here on the opportunities for investing in equity securities outside of the United States.

---

*The authors would like to give special thanks to Jon L. Hagler, Vice President and Treasurer, the Ford Foundation; Professor Jay O. Light of Harvard University; and Professor Donald R. Lessard of the Massachusetts Institute of Technology for their many contributions.

10: International Securities Markets

Table 1
The 10 Largest Market Capitalizations and Their Share of National Stock Markets

USA total market capitalization: $870 billion	$ million	% of total
I B M	44 727	5.1
AMERICAN TEL & TEL	38 666	4.4
EXXON CORP	22 761	2.6
GENERAL MOTORS	16 960	1.9
GENERAL ELECTRIC	11 316	1.3
STANDARD OIL INDIANA	9 471	1.1
EASTMAN KODAK	9 251	1.1
SCHLUMBERGER	9 201	1.1
STANDARD OIL CALIFORNIA	8 003	0.9
MOBIL OIL	7 870	0.9
TOTAL TOP TEN	**178 226**	**20.4**

JAPAN total market capitalization: $299 billion	$ million	% of total
TOYOTA MOTOR	6 455	2.2
NISSAN MOTOR	4 885	1.6
TOKYO ELECTRIC POWER	4 212	1.4
NIPPON OIL	4 011	1.3
NIPPON STEEL	3 981	1.3
MATSUSHITA ELECTR IND	3 869	1.3
HITACHI LTD	3 042	1.0
DAIICHI KANGYO BANK	2 922	1.0
NOMURA SECURITIES	2 878	1.0
SANWA BANK	2 760	0.9
TOTAL TOP TEN	**39 022**	**13.0**

UNITED KINGDOM total market capitalization: $142 billion	$ million	% of total
BRITISH PETROLEUM	8 718	6.2
SHELL T & T	8 475	6.0
GENERAL ELECTRIC	4 557	3.2
IMPERIAL CHEMICAL	4 280	3.0
MARKS & SPENCER	3 011	2.1
UNILEVER	2 320	1.6
BARCLAYS BANK	2 156	1.5
GREAT UNIVERSAL STORES	2 070	1.5
B A T INDUSTRIES	2 037	1.4
BEECHAM GROUP	2 007	1.4
TOTAL TOP TEN	**39 651**	**27.9**

GERMANY total market capitalization: $73.3 billion	$ million	% of total
SIEMENS	4 464	6.1
DAIMLER-BENZ	4 057	5.5
R W E	3 163	4.3
BAYER	3 026	4.1
VOLKSWAGENWERK	2 833	3.9
DEUTSCHE BANK	2 825	3.9
BASF	2 761	3.8
HOECHST	2 574	3.5
BHF - BANK	2 326	3.2
VEBA B	2 175	3.0
TOTAL TOP TEN	**30 204**	**41.3**

FRANCE total market capitalization: $43.0 billion	$ million	% of total
ELF AQUITAINE SNEA	2 564	6.0
DASSAULT-BREGUET	1 084	2.5
SAINT-GOBAIN-P-A-M	1 032	2.4
AIR LIQUIDE	1 031	2.4
FRANCAISE PETROLES	987	2.3
MICHELIN B	881	2.1
PEUGEOT-CITROEN PSA	818	1.9
CARREFOUR	706	1.6
PARIS PAYS-BAS	655	1.5
THOMSON-CSF	646	1.5
TOTAL TOP TEN	**10 404**	**24.2**

SWITZERLAND total market capitalization: $40.1 billion	$ million	% of total
NESTLE	4 554	11.3
SCHWEIZ BANKGESELL UBS	3 762	9.4
SCHWEIZ BANKVEREIN SBS	3 331	8.3
HOFFMANN-LA ROCHE	3 225	8.0
CIBA-GEIGY	2 662	6.6
SCHWEIZ KREDITANSTALT	2 486	6.2
OERLIKON-BUHRLE	1 989	4.9
SANDOZ	1 474	3.7
ZURICH VERSICHERUNG	1 103	2.8
SCHWEIZ RUCKVERS	872	2.2
TOTAL TOP TEN	**25 438**	**63.4**

AUSTRALIA total market capitalization: $28.0 billion	$ million	% of total
BROKEN HILL PROP	2 700	9.7
CONZINC RIOTINTO	1 368	4.9
M I M HOLDINGS	1 003	3.6
HAMERSLEY HOLDINGS	722	2.6
BOUGAINVILLE COPPER	584	2.1
COMALCO	541	1.9
WESTERN MINING	540	1.9
BANK NEW SOUTH WALES	533	1.9
CSR	532	1.9
ANZ GROUP HOLDINGS	503	1.8
TOTAL TOP TEN	**9 026**	**32.3**

NETHERLANDS total market capitalization: $22.2 billion	$ million	% of total
ROYAL DUTCH PETROLEUM	8 860	39.8
PHILIPS	1 979	8.9
UNILEVER	1 879	8.5
ALGEMENE BANK	963	4.3
AMRO BANK	799	3.6
NATIONALE-NEDERLANDEN	730	3.3
HEINEKEN	470	2.1
NED MIDDENSTANDSBANK	465	2.1
AKZO	418	1.9
AMEV	273	1.2
TOTAL TOP TEN	**16 836**	**75.7**

SPAIN total market capitalization: $16.3 billion	$ million	% of total
TELEFONICA NACIONAL	2 035	12.5
BANCO CENTRAL	1 304	8.0
HIDROELECTRICA	1 025	6.3
BANCO HISPANO AMER	873	5.4
BANCO ESPANOL CREDITO	856	5.2
IBERDUERO	823	5.1
BANCO BILBAO	823	5.1
BANCO SANTANDER	732	4.5
FECSA	478	2.9
UNION ELECTRICA	336	2.1
TOTAL TOP TEN	**9 285**	**57.1**

BELGIUM total market capitalization: $12.3 billion	$ million	% of total
PETROFINA	1 853	15.0
INTERCOM	1 339	10.9
EBES	901	7.3
SOLVAY	622	5.0
STE GENERALE DE BANQUE	554	4.5
UNERG	468	3.8
KREDIETBANK	451	3.7
STE GENERALE DE BELGIQUE	377	3.1
BANQUE BRUXELLES LAM	302	2.4
TRACTION ELECTRICITE	280	2.3
TOTAL TOP TEN	**7 147**	**58.0**

ITALY total market capitalization: $11.6 billion	$ million	% of total
FIAT	1 006	8.7
ASSICURAZIONI GENERALI	1 004	8.7
SIP	607	5.2
ITALSIDER	579	5.0
STET	461	4.0
MONTEDISON	448	3.9
ALITALIA	400	3.5
LEPETIT	296	2.6
MEDIOBANCA	281	2.4
CREDITO ITALIANO	260	2.2
TOTAL TOP TEN	**5 342**	**46.2**

SWEDEN total market capitalization: $9.0 billion	$ million	% of total
L M ERICSSON B	675	7.5
SKANDINAVISKA ENSKILDA	443	5.0
ELECTROLUX B	453	5.0
SANDVIK	407	4.5
SVENSKA HANDELSBANK	395	4.4
VOLVO	352	3.9
SVENSKA CELLULOSA	347	3.9
ASEA	296	3.3
SKANSKA CEMENTGJUTER	291	3.2
ATLAS COPCO	290	3.2
TOTAL TOP TEN	**3 963**	**44.0**

Market capitalization is defined as the total number of shares outstanding times per share price (at 25 May 1979). The 10 largest companies for all countries are selected from the 1600 companies included in *Capital International Perspective*. The total market capitalization for each country is an estimate of the aggregate market value of all listed shares, excluding foreign securities and investment trusts. The total market capitalization of the U.S.A. refers to the New York Stock Exchange only, that of Japan to first section only. For industry classification of the above companies, see quarterly issues of *Capital International Perspective*.

Source: *Capital International Perspective* (Geneva, Switzerland, June 1979).

Table 2
Companies outside North American with Market Capitalization over $1,500 Million

RANK	COMPANY NAME	COUNTRY	29 October 1979 US$ million	in % of country total	1 January 1979 US$ million	in % of country total	INDUSTRY GROUP	RANK
1	BRITISH PETROLEUM	United Kingdom	12 244	9	4 624	6	Energy	1
2	ROYAL DUTCH PETROLEUM	Netherlands	10 169	43	5 318	47	Energy	2
3	SHELL T & T	United Kingdom	8 006	6	4 856	6	Energy	3
4	TOYOTA MOTOR	Japan	5 626	2	805	2	Automobiles	4
5	NIPPON OIL	Japan	5 095	2	78	n	Energy	5
6	ELF AQUITAINE, SNEA	France	4 921	10	641	3	Energy	6
7	SIEMENS	Germany	4 909	7	1 386	4	Electrical & Electronics	7
8	NESTLE	Switzerland	4 581	11	1 101	7	Food & Household Products	8
9	SCHWEIZ BANKGESELL UBS	Switzerland	4 336	10	662	5	Banking	9
10	IMPERIAL CHEMICAL ICI	United Kingdom	4 198	3	3 038	3	Chemicals	10
11	NISSAN MOTOR	Japan	4 141	2	400	1	Automobiles	11
12	GENERAL ELECTRIC	United Kingdom	3 826	3	1 565	2	Electrical & Electronics	12
13	MATSUSHITA ELECTRIC INDUSTRIAL	Japan	3 683	1	1 673	4	Radio, TV & Appliances	13
14	DAIMLER BENZ	Germany	3 665	5	1 759	5	Automobiles	14
15	SCHWEIZ BANKVEREIN SBS	Switzerland	3 641	9	611	5	Banking	15
16	R W E	Germany	3 564	5	1 481	4	Utilities	16
17	TOKYO ELECTRIC POWER	Japan	3 514	1	674	1	Utilities	17
18	MITSUBISHI CORP	Japan	3 297	1	207	n	Other Services	18
19	BROKEN HILL PROP	Australia	3 116	9	2 635	8	Steel	19
20	DEUTSCHE BANK	Germany	3 107	4	1 094	1	Banking	20
21	HOFFMANN-LA ROCHE	Switzerland	3 031	7	2 617	21	Health & Personal Care	21
22	NIPPON STEEL	Japan	2 998	1	726	2	Steel	22
23	BASF	Germany	2 956	4	1 616	4	Chemicals	23
24	BAYER	Germany	2 955	4	1 636	4	Chemicals	24
25	DAIICHI KANGYO BANK	Japan	2 855	1	383	1	Banking	25
26	HITACHI	Japan	2 792	1	987	2	Electrical & Electronics	26
27	SUMITOMO BANK	Japan	2 741	1	670	1	Banking	27
28	SANWA BANK	Japan	2 741	1	480	1	Banking	28
29	DE BEERS	South Africa	2 729	n.a.	2 911	n.a.	Other Consumer Durables	29
30	SCHWEIZ KREDITANSTALT	Switzerland	2 707	6	476	4	Banking	30
31	CIBA - GEIGY	Switzerland	2 698	6	1 717	14	Chemicals	31
32	MITSUBISHI BANK	Japan	2 695	1	576	1	Banking	32
33	FUJI BANK	Japan	2 680	1	576	1	Banking	33
34	HOECHST	Germany	2 524	3	1 879	5	Chemicals	34
35	MARKS & SPENCER	United Kingdom	2 496	2	1 477	2	Merchandising	35
36	VOLKSWAGENWERK	Germany	2 492	3	797	3	Automobiles	36
37	KANSAI ELECTRIC POWER	Japan	2 471	1	511	1	Utilities	37
38	NOMURA SECURITIES	Japan	2 407	1	210	n	Financial Services	38
39	PETROFINA	Belgium	2 364	18	375	6	Energy	39
40	TOKIO MARINE & FIRE	Japan	2 360	1	213	n	Insurance	40
41	BHF - BANK	Germany	2 327	3			Banking	41
42	OERLIKON BUHRLE	Switzerland	2 167	5	n.q.	n.a.	Machinery & Engineering	42
43	HONGKONG & SHANGHAI BANK	Hong Kong	2 086	12	311	14	Banking	43
44	CHUBU ELECTRIC POWER	Japan	2 049	1	415	1	Utilities	44
45	BARCLAYS BANK	United Kingdom	1 981	1	758	1	Banking	45
46	TELEFONICA NACIONAL	Spain	1 952	14	1 575	10	Telecommunications	46
47	INDUSTRIAL BANK OF JAPAN	Japan	1 946	1	240	1	Banking	47
48	UNILEVER NV	Netherlands	1 922	8	1 013	8	Food & Household Products	48
49	PHILIPS	Netherlands	1 911	8	1 983	16	Radio, TV & Appliances	49
50	VEBA	Germany	1 897	3	810	2	Utilities	50
51	UNILEVER LTD	United Kingdom	1 890	1	1 393	2	Food & Household Products	51
52	GREAT UNIVERSAL STORES	United Kingdom	1 886	1	1 161	1	Merchandising	52
53	BEECHAM GROUP	United Kingdom	1 873	1	712	1	Health & Personal Care	53
54	B A T INDUSTRIES	United Kingdom	1 848	1	1 943	2	Other Consumer Non-Durables	54
55	DRESDNER BANK	Germany	1 823	2	702	2	Banking	55
56	KUBOTA	Japan	1 811	1	411	1	Machinery & Engineering	56
57	TOA NENRYO KOGYO	Japan	1 737	1	174	n	Energy	57
58	MITSUBISHI ESTATE	Japan	1 726	1	402	1	Energy	58
59	DISTILLERS	United Kingdom	1 714	1	1 084	1	Beverages	59
60	MITSUI & CO	Japan	1 670	1	181	n	Other Services	60
61	FRANCAISE DES PETROLES	France	1 653	3	633	3	Energy	61
62	NATIONAL WESTMINSTER	United Kingdom	1 643	1	660	1	Banking	62
63	LONG TERM CREDIT BANK	Japan	1 608	1	n.q.	n.a.	Banking	63
64	SONY	Japan	1 594	1	804	2	Radio, TV & Appliances	64
65	RIO TINTO-ZINC	United Kingdom	1 568	1	1 148	2	Non Ferrous Metals	65
66	GRAND METROPOLITAN	United Kingdom	1 560	1	243	n	Leisure & Tourism	66
67	MITSUBISHI HEAVY	Japan	1 544	1	452	1	Machinery & Engineering	67
68	TOKAI BANK	Japan	1 529	1	275	n	Banking	68
69	MANNESMANN	Germany	1 518	2	226	1	Steel	69
70	SANDOZ	Switzerland	1 517	4	618	6	Health & Personal Care	70

The above title is based on the non-American companies listed in the quarterly issues of Capital International Perspective. A similar analysis of North American markets would show 25 U.S. companies and 8 Canadian companies with market capitalization over U.S. $1,500 million. Market capitalization is defined as shares outstanding times share prices; prices and exchange rates are those applicable at date indicated. The columns "in % of country total" relate each company's market capitalization for its country as estimated by Capital International S.A.

n: negligible
n.a.: not available
n.q.: not quoted

Source: *Capital International Perspective* (Geneva, Switzerland, November 1979).

These foreign markets trade the equities of substantial and in some cases unique companies (Table 2). Although the U.S. equity market is the largest in the world, it represents, as noted above, only about 50 percent of the aggregate international equity market. Moreover, owing to more rapid economic growth in most foreign nations, the relative importance of the U.S. market has been declining. The same phenomenon can be observed in annual share turnover, with the U.S. market now representing less than half the value of world equity trading volume (Table 3).

Despite the substantial size of foreign equity markets, U.S. investors have generally held very modest positions abroad in recent years. In 1975 it was estimated, for example, that U.S. institutional investors had invested less than 2 percent of their equity assets outside of North America.[1] This is particularly surprising since, over the past decade, a number of articles and research studies have been published that conclude there are significant benefits for U.S. investors who diversify some of their equity holdings into foreign markets.

BENEFITS OF INTERNATIONAL INVESTING

The essence of the most common argument for international investing is straightforward. Not all world equity markets have moved together in a highly synchronized fashion. In varying degrees each national stock market has had its own performance cycle because different national economies are typically subject to varying socioeconomic and political forces. Since the returns on common stocks in different markets have not moved in lockstep, the opportunity has existed with equity portfolios to significantly reduce risks for a given return or to increase the return with a given level of risk by diversifying across stock markets as well as within them.[2]

For example, during 1977, when the U.S. stock market index lost 12.2 percent (excluding dividend income), the French market declined 1.2 percent (in U.S. dollars). During this same year, the Tokyo market rose 13.2 percent, the German market increased 21 percent and the London market was up 50.2 percent. In the language of the statistician, the correlation or degree of comovement between some world stock markets has been relatively low. More specifically, Table 4 shows a number of estimates of the correlations between the U.S.

---

[1] Gary L. Bergstrom, "A New Route to Higher Returns and Lower Risks," *Journal of Portfolio Management,* Fall 1975, pp. 30-38.

[2] By *risk* we mean the uncertainty of portfolio returns. We also assume in accordance with historical evidence that over the long term, risk and return will be positively related so that investors in more risky securities on average receive higher rates of return.

Table 3
A. Turnover on Major Stock Exchanges

Nation	Exchange	Total Value of Share Turnover in U.S. $ Billion*						Percent of Total	
		1978	1977	1976	1975	1974	1973	1978	1973
United States	New York S.E.	199.9	154.8	164.5	133.7	99.2	146.4	47.1	54.0
Japan	Tokyo 1st Section	148.4	77.4	76.4	51.2	41.6	52.9	35.0	19.5
United Kingdom	London	18.6	17.6	12.9	19.6	14.8	21.0	4.4	7.8
Germany	All exchanges	17.3	12.0	9.9	11.1	5.1	7.1	4.1	2.6
Canada	All exchanges	11.2	6.9	6.7	5.4	6.2	8.9	2.6	3.3
France	Paris	10.6	4.5	5.6	7.3	5.3	10.0	2.5	3.7
Hong Kong	All exchanges	5.8	1.3	2.7	2.1	2.2	9.2	1.4	3.4
Netherlands	Amsterdam	4.5	3.6	2.7	2.5	1.8	3.2	1.0	1.2
Italy	All exchanges	2.3 (est.)	1.0	1.7	2.1	3.3	4.7	0.5	1.7
Singapore	Singapore	1.5	0.5	0.8	0.8	0.5	1.0	0.4	0.4
Spain	All exchanges	1.4 (est.)	1.5	2.9	3.0	3.7	3.3	0.3	1.2
Belgium	Brussels	1.2	1.1	1.4	1.3	1.2	1.7	0.3	0.6
Australia	Sydney	1.2	0.7	0.8	0.7	0.8	1.0	0.3	0.4
Sweden	Stockholm	0.4	0.4	0.5	0.5	0.5	0.5	0.1	0.2
Denmark	Copenhagen	0.1 (est.)	0.1	0.1	0.1	0.1	0.2	Negligible	
Austria	Vienna	0.1	0.1	0.1	0.1	0.1	0.1	Negligible	
Total of major stock markets		424.5	283.5	289.7	241.5	186.4	271.2	100	100

*The annual figures for turnover values in U.S. dollars are calculated by converting monthly values at month-end exchange rates.

Table 3 *(concluded)*
B. Annual Turnover in Percent of Total Market Capitalization

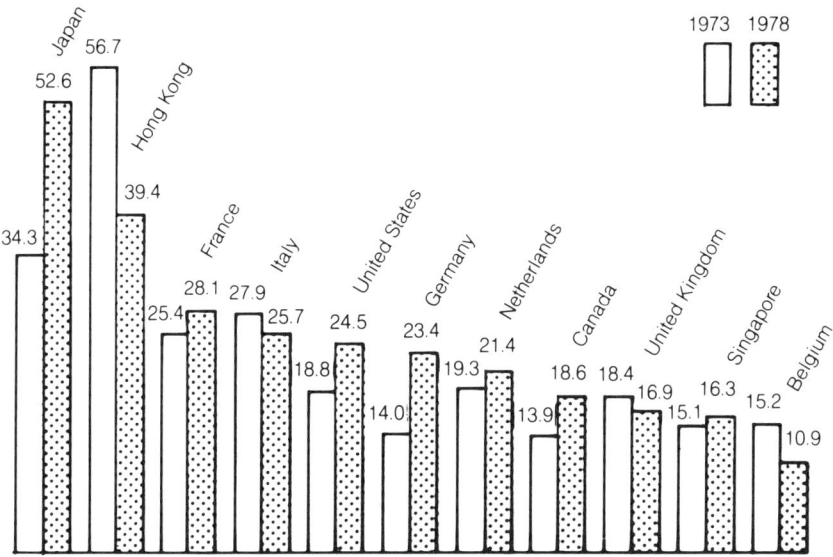

Note: Turnover data refers to common stocks only. It includes foreign shares listed, except in Germany and the Netherlands.
Source: *Capital International Perspective* (Geneva, Switzerland, March 1979).

stock market and other major stock exchanges for varying time periods.[3]

Using monthly data from 1959 through 1966, Herbert Grubel estimated the correlation coefficients between the United States and other major stock markets.[4] He found the Canadian and U.S. markets had the closest relationship from 1959 through 1966 with a correlation coefficient of +0.7, indicating that on average one could have explained about half of the price change in Toronto only by knowing what happened to quotations in New York during the same month.[5] Most of the major European markets and the Japanese market fall in the range of +0.1 to +0.3 over this interval, indicating that less than 10 percent of the price change in these markets was related to changes in the U.S. market during the same month.

---

[3] Two markets that have a correlation of +1.0 would move in perfectly synchronized fashion, while markets with a correlation of −1.0 would move in exactly contracyclical fashion.

[4] Herbert G. Grubel, "Internationally Diversified Portfolios: Welfare Gains and Capital Flows," *American Economic Review,* December 1968, pp. 1299-1314.

[5] The correlation coefficient squared (the R-squared) is a statistical measure of the degree to which one variable "explains" another. In this case, (0.7) (0.7) equals 49 percent.

Table 4
Correlations versus U.S. Market Index

Stock Market	Grubel (published: 1968) (data: 1959-1966)	Solnik (published: 1973) (data: 3/66-4/71)	Lessard (published: 1975) (data: 1/59-10/73)	Koeneman and Bergstrom (unpublished) (data: 1/69-12/78)
Australia	0.06	—	0.23	0.51
Austria	—	—	0.12	0.11
Belgium	0.11	0.47	0.46	0.42
Canada	0.70	—	0.80	0.74
Denmark	—	—	0.04	0.24
France	0.19	0.06	0.25	0.37
Germany	0.30	0.22	0.38	0.32
Italy	0.15	0.07	0.21	0.16
Japan	0.11	0.19	0.13	0.32
Netherlands	0.21	0.51	0.61	0.53
Norway	—	—	0.17	0.41
South African gold mines	0.16	—	—	—
Spain	—	—	0.04	0.14
Sweden	—	0.29	0.33	0.35
Switzerland	—	0.44	0.49	0.49
United Kingdom	0.24	0.20	0.29	0.44

Bruno Solnik has also computed similar estimates of the correlations between many of these same stock markets using monthly data for the period March 1966 through April 1971.[6] Solnik's results are found in the second column of Table 4. A comprehensive set of estimates of the correlation structure between world stock markets is found in a paper by Professor Donald Lessard of the Sloan School of Management at MIT.[7] He used monthly market indices prepared by Capital International Perspective of Geneva, Switzerland, as his primary source of stock market data. Finally, using Capital International data, Bergstrom and Koeneman estimated the correlations between 15 major markets for the period 1969 through 1978.[8]

While these four sets of correlation numbers are not in perfect agreement, they certainly suggest a considerable degree of independence between markets over time. Therefore, diversification across stock markets, as well as within markets, could have provided significantly lower portfolio uncertainty or *risk* than keeping all investments in the U.S. stock market.

OTHER EVIDENCE OF RISK REDUCTION FROM INTERNATIONAL INVESTING

A number of careful empirical studies have directly estimated the extent to which the uncertainty or risk in an equity portfolio could have been reduced through international diversification. Using data on the U.S. and seven European stock markets for the period 1966-1971, Solnik found that, in terms of variability of return, a well-diversified international equity portfolio would have in excess of a 30 percent reduction in risk versus a well-diversified portfolio of U.S. stocks with the same number of holdings.[9] In this study, Solnik utilized data on over 300 common stocks traded in major European stock markets in addition to data for New York Stock Exchange (NYSE) issues. Sets of portfolios holding varying numbers of different stocks were randomly selected. Some of these sets of portfolios consisted of issues traded in only one national market, while others were selected from the entire data sample without restriction as to national origin. The average volatility or risk in each set of identically

---

[6] Bruno H. Solnik, *European Capital Markets: Towards a General Theory of International Investment* (Lexington, Mass.: D. C. Heath & Company, 1973).

[7] Donald Lessard, "World, Country, and Industry Relationships in Equity Returns," *Financial Analysts Journal,* January-February 1976.

[8] John K. Koeneman and Gary L. Bergstrom, State Street Bank & Trust Co., unpublished memorandum, Boston, Mass., 1979.

[9] Bruno H. Solnik, "Why Not Diversify Internationally Rather than Domestically," *Financial Analysts Journal,* July-August 1974.

selected portfolios was computed and plotted for sets of portfolios holding from one to over 50 securities.

Figure 1 illustrates that, even with a very large U.S. stock portfolio, it is not possible to reduce risk below about 52 percent of the risk of a typical individual security. This minimum risk level exists, of

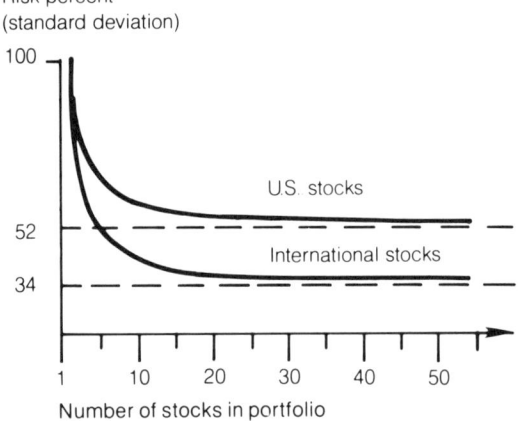

Figure 1
The Riskiness of U.S. versus International Equity Portfolios

Source: Bruno H. Solnik, "Why Not Diversify Internationally Rather than Domestically?" *Financial Analysis Journal,* July-August 1974.

course, because of the common economic, political, and social influences on all stocks in the U.S. market. The international portfolios, selected with an equal chance of holding securities in each country had significantly lower risk, on the order of 34 percent of the risk of a typical individual security in the sample. This was true even after adjusting for currency changes. These results, to be sure, reflect the currency experience before floating rates, when currency fluctuations were usually modest and major changes infrequent. On the other hand, this study did not consider common stocks from Japan, Australia, and other equity markets that offer further possibilities for diversification.

A number of other research studies encompassing additional stock markets and other time periods generally support Solnik's findings. Considering all of this evidence, it is likely that the potential benefits to a U.S. investor of a carefully designed international investment strategy are substantial—perhaps a 20 percent to 40 percent reduction in portfolio variability or risk without sacrificing expected return or commensurately enhanced performance without increased portfolio risk.

The State Street Bank has presented some direct evidence on the risk reduction which has been actually obtained by professionally managed equity portfolios, primarily mutual funds, which have invested internationally (Figure 2).[10] From 1971 through 1977, all four U.S.-managed international funds in their sample displayed significantly less risk, as measured by standard deviation of return, than the Standard & Poor's 500 index of the U.S. market.

Moreover, it is likely that these benefits of international diversification will continue in the future. Different nations' economies will continue to be dependent upon somewhat different economic forces, and the financial results of their private sectors will continue to be affected by different sociopolitical factors. As in the past, there will

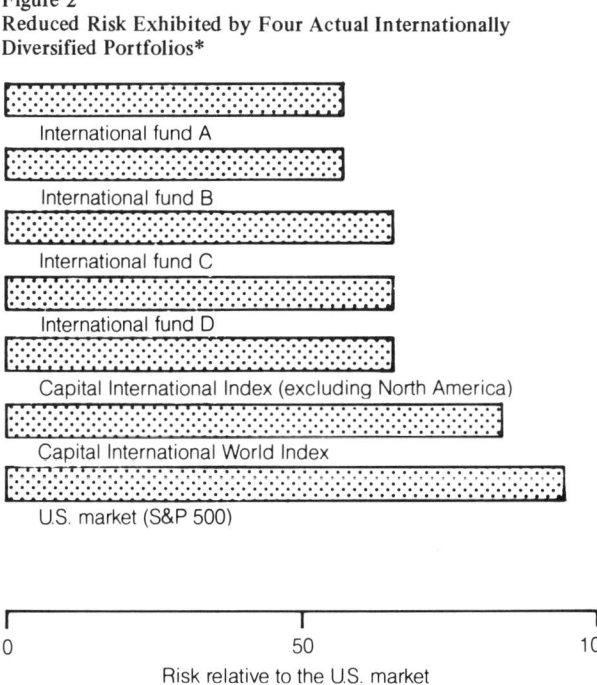

Figure 2
Reduced Risk Exhibited by Four Actual Internationally Diversified Portfolios*

*Since 1971. Includes exchange rate fluctuations.
Source: John K. Koeneman, State Street Bank & Trust Co., unpublished manuscript, Boston, Mass., 1979.

---

[10] John K. Koeneman, State Street Bank & Trust Co., unpublished manuscript, Boston, Mass., 1979.

FUTURE INVESTMENT RETURNS

The merits of international investment depend not just upon the potential for risk reduction, but also upon the rates of return that can be expected in foreign equity markets. While the projection of future stock market returns is naturally fraught with difficulty, one can begin to grapple with this problem with several alternative hypotheses about the process by which stock market returns are generated. The essential question is whether foreign markets are likely to have such a low expected rate of long-term return *relative* to the United States that the previously described benefits of risk reduction would be completely eroded. Both history and logic support the conclusion that, for countries of practical investment interest, future rates of return will be at least generally competitive with the U.S. equity market. As a corollary, it seems unlikely that a diversified portfolio selected from major foreign equity markets will, over long periods, underperform the U.S. market to a degree that the substantial benefits of risk reduction would disappear. Indeed, to the contrary, it may very well experience higher returns, if history is at all suggestive of the future.

First, consider the historical evidence on economic and stock market performance. Looking at economic growth during the decade from 1967 through 1977, for example, the real gross national product (GNP) grew at an average of 2.9 percent per year in the United States, while the GNP of an average of seven major countries in the Organization for Economic Cooperation and Development (OECD) increased 4.3 percent. Real growth of all other OECD countries over this period averaged 4.5 percent per annum. Looking at important economies abroad, Germany grew at 3.8 percent, Canada at 4.4 percent and Japan at 7.4 percent. Among major OECD countries, only the United Kingdom, at 1.9 percent per year, experienced slower growth in real GNP than did the U.S. economy (see Table 5).

The reasons some countries achieve more rapid economic growth than others are obviously complex and range far beyond the scope of this chapter. Furthermore, fast growth in an economy has carried with it no assurances that the holders of equity securities would be commensurately rewarded. Nevertheless, the evidence seems to suggest that countries with equity markets that have achieved high returns, at least in recent years, have most often been those also experiencing rapid real economic growth.

More specifically, the historical record shows that the U.S. market (as measured by the NYSE index) ranked 18th of 20 world equity

Table 5
Average Annual Real GNP Growth Rate,
1967-1977

Japan	7.4%
Spain	5.1
Austria	4.6
France	4.5
Norway	4.5
Canada	4.4
Netherlands	4.3
Australia	4.0
Belgium	4.0
Germany	3.8
Italy	3.6
United States	2.9
Denmark	2.9
Sweden	2.5
Switzerland	2.0
United Kingdom	1.9

Source: U.S. Department of State, Bureau of Intelligence and Research.

markets in total investment return for the 21-year period from 1959 through 1979 (see Table 6). Over the 10-year period from 1970 through 1979, the U.S. market again maintained the unenviable position of 16th of 20 world markets (see Table 7).

The key question, of course, is whether this pattern of more rapid growth in foreign stock markets is likely to persist in the future.

Several alternative theories and methodologies may be helpful in attempting to assess *future relative* stock market returns in an international context. While none of them individually is likely to provide totally satisfactory insights, in the aggregate they can provide a useful perspective.

One theory of economic growth holds that a country's future economic potential, and eventually, presumably, its security market returns, are heavily influenced by the productivity improvements generated from new capital investment. The comparison in Table 8 of the major industrialized economies (taking the latest available fiscal years as representative) shows that the United States is clearly the lowest in both categories, with its capital formation rate being only about half the average level of the other six countries. These statistics illuminate the low recent rates of capital formation in the U.S. economy. According to this economic theory, such rates are not encouraging for future relative growth prospects in the domestic economy.

Most fundamentally, however, the value of a stock market should be related to aggregate corporate earning power and the risks inherent in future earnings. All else being equal, higher long-term eco-

Table 6
Stock Market Returns, 1970-1979

Stock Market	Estimated Total Return (10 years to December 31, 1979) (percentage change in U.S. dollars)	Mean Return (percent per year, compound)
Hong Kong*	851.23	25.26
South Africa (Gold Shares)	798.16	24.55
Norway	411.69	17.73
Singapore†	396.70	17.38
Japan	376.23	16.89
Austria	266.07	13.86
Switzerland	220.47	12.35
Belgium	199.11	11.58
Denmark	166.53	10.30
Netherlands	153.30	9.74
Germany	148.70	9.54
Canada	125.84	8.49
United Kingdom	117.97	8.10
France	106.81	7.54
Sweden	77.64	5.91
United States	59.10	4.75
Australia	38.68	3.32
Spain	−9.55	−1.00
Brazil ‡	−15.28	−1.64
Italy	−46.27	−6.02

With certain noted exceptions, index data are from *Capital International Perspective,* Geneva, Switzerland. All returns include reinvestment of estimated dividends and are adjusted to U.S. dollars at current exchange rates. Source withholding taxes on dividends for a U.S.-domiciled investor have been deducted. For most markets, this tax rate is about 15 percent.

*Hang Seng Index—base 1964 = 100
†Straits Time Industrial Index—base 1966 = 100
‡From Walter L. Ness, Jr. "The Rate of Return to Investors in Brazilian Shares, 1955-1971," New York University. IBV Index is a total value index for Brazilian shares.

Source: Putnam Management Company.

Table 7
Stock Market Returns, 1959-1979

Stock Market	Estimated Total Return (21 years to December 31, 1979) (percentage change in U.S. dollars)	Mean Return (percent per year, compound)
Hong Kong (15 yrs., 5 mos.)*	2,099.35	22.20
Singapore (13½ years)†	758.79	17.27
South Africa (Gold Shares)	2,603.34	17.00
Japan	1,923.34	15.40
Norway	1,279.16	13.31
Switzerland	1,054.39	12.35
Austria	873.90	11.45
Germany	744.72	10.70
Brazil ‡	655.15	10.11
United Kingdom	615.40	9.82
Australia	595.94	9.68
Sweden	516.68	9.05

Table 7 (concluded)

Stock Market	Estimated Total Return (21 years to December 31, 1979) (percentage change in U.S. dollars)	Mean Return (percent per year, compound)
Netherlands	497.62	8.89
Belgium	458.48	8.54
Canada	428.68	8.25
Denmark	382.24	7.78
Spain	364.31	7.59
United States	305.10	6.89
France	288.49	6.68
Italy	12.61	0.57

With certain noted exceptions, index data are from *Capital International Perspective*, Geneva, Switzerland. All returns include reinvestment of estimated dividends and are adjusted to U.S. dollars at current exchange rates. Source withholding taxes on dividends for a U.S.-domiciled investor have been deducted. For most markets, this tax rate is about 15 percent.

* Hang Seng Index — base 1964 = 100

† Straits Time Industrial Index — base 1966 = 100

‡ From Walter L. Ness, Jr. "The Rate of Return to Investors in Brazilian Shares, 1955-1971," New York University. IBV Index is a total value index.

Source: Putnam Management Company.

Table 8
Capital Formation in Major Industrialized Countries

	Savings Ratio (as percent of personal disposable income)	Gross Fixed Capital Formation (excluding residential construction) as percent of GNP
Australia	18.2%	20.0%
Canada	10.8	19.0
France	15.7	21.0
Germany	14.3	16.0
Japan	24.4	23.6
United Kingdom	14.7	15.8
United States	5.8	9.9

Source: *OECD Economic Outlook*, December 1977, p. 116.

nomic growth eventually translates into faster corporate profits growth and, eventually, correspondingly higher stock prices. While it is difficult to evaluate the accuracy of such projections, the consensus forecast of many economists again seems to call for higher relative long-term growth rates in many foreign economies, especially the higher-income developing economies. Some economies, particularly in continental Europe, will have to contend with the continuing problems of high energy costs and possible negative developments in the political environment. The stock markets of some of these countries, however, are already at relatively low levels as market participants have reacted and discounted these problems. And, of course, the United States is not immune to these same problems.

POTENTIAL OBSTACLES[11]

There are, of course, a number of obstacles and risks to international equity investing that must be overcome. One must explore whether the cumulative effects of currency and political risks, possible capital flow restrictions, taxes, and relatively thin markets in some countries abroad are likely to be so large as to offset many or all of the advantages.

The Effects of Currency Fluctuations on International Equity Portfolios

Some empirical analyses of international equity investing have directly examined the impact of currency changes on portfolio riskiness. During the 1966-1971 period, currency factors were of very minor importance as they only slightly increased the risk of international equity portfolios. This period, characterized by "pegged" exchange rates among most major currencies, is, of course, not at all representative of the current era of floating rates (see Figure 3).

In a floating currency environment, like the present, there are a number of important points about exchange rates which must be addressed. The first of these simply relates to the size of exchange rate fluctuations. If they were small enough, then little consideration of their effects upon international portfolios would be necessary. Empirical examinations of data from the floating exchange-rate period (post-1971) indicate that, while the magnitude and, therefore, the importance to investors of exchange rate fluctuations has increased considerably in recent years, they are still, in general, smaller than stock market fluctuations. They are, however, large enough to be a significant consideration in designing international investment strategies. During the April 1973-March 1975 period, for example, the world economy was buffeted by the worst recession since World War II, sharply increased inflation rates, an enormous escalation in energy costs, and rapid shifts of financial reserves among countries. While extraordinary stresses were placed on foreign exchange markets, the variability (measured by annual standard deviations) of the U.S. dollar versus the Canadian dollar, the British pound, and the German mark was 2.4 percent, 6.6 percent, and 13.9 percent, respectively. During this same unusually volatile interval, the compara-

---

[11] This section follows Donald Lessard, "International Diversification," in *Investment Manager's Handbook*, ed. S. Levine (Homewood, Ill.: Dow Jones-Irwin, 1980), pp. 359-88.

Figure 3
Risk Levels of Hedged and Unhedged International Portfolios, 1966-1971*

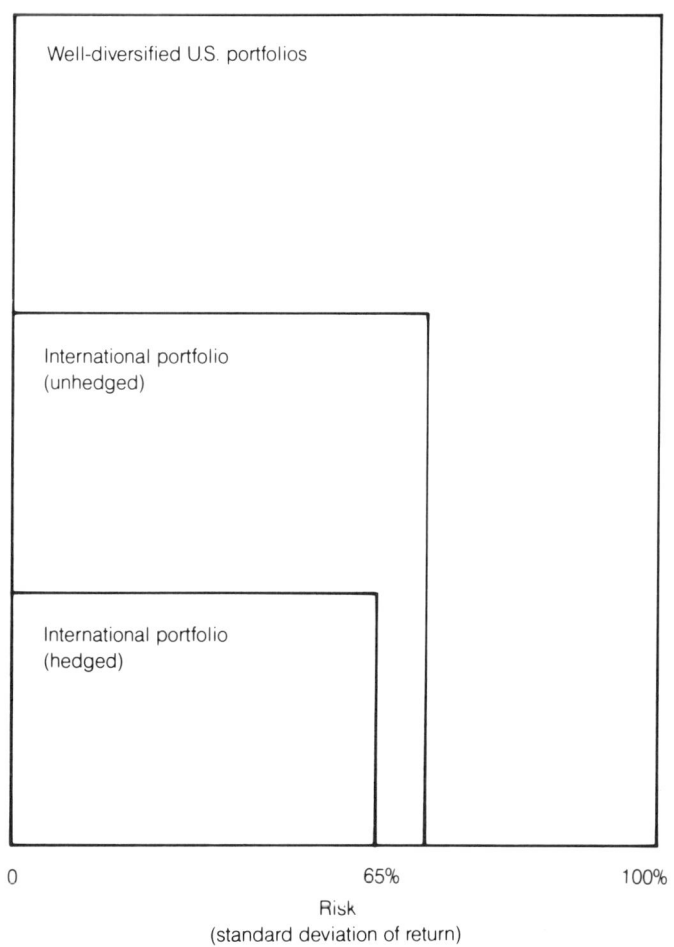

*International unhedged indicates the risk level of portfolios that are fully exposed to currency fluctuations. *International hedged* describes portfolios against which currency risk has been "insured" by the purchase of forward currency contracts to offset exchange rate shifts.

Source: Bruno H. Solnik, "Why Not Diversify Internationally Rather than Domestically?" *Financial Analysis Journal,* July-August, 1974.

ble variability of U.S. equities was 30.1 percent and the variability of U.S. Treasury bill returns was 3.1 percent. Thus, currency fluctuations were about half the magnitude or less of fluctuations in the U.S. stock market, suggesting that, while they are of significance, they are not nearly as important as fluctuations in the underlying equity markets.[12]

A second critical concern about currency markets relates to their degree of *efficiency,* and therefore, practically speaking, the possibility of realizing abnormal rewards through astute trading strategies. Generally, the notion of efficiency in these markets is analogous to the concept of stock market efficiency. Careful observation suggests that major currency markets, like equity markets, are highly competitive with many well-informed participants, substantial trading volumes, and low transaction costs. This would suggest that exchange rates are likely to quickly and fully reflect most relevant information and, therefore, be quite efficient. The major counterargument which has been raised against high levels of efficiency is the instances of periodic intervention by central banks—a clear practical reality in the present environment. Even such intervention, however, might be quickly discounted by market participants.

In the end, of course, currency market efficiency is an empirical question. Considerable evidence is accumulating that generally suggests that floating-currency markets are efficient enough so that few participants are likely to earn large, systematic trading profits. Obviously, a careful assessment of these studies should preface the design of international investing strategies.

Efficient foreign exchange markets do not necessarily mean stable or trendless markets, however. If the long-term expected inflation rate in Switzerland is, say, 3 percent per annum, while foreign exchange markets expect the rate in the United States to be 7 percent, well-ordered exchange markets will take this into account and exhibit a downward trend for the dollar versus the Swiss franc. The difference in interest rates between currencies, however, will prevent anyone from systematically exploiting these trends to earn extraordinary returns. Continuing the above example, high-quality Swiss franc bonds might reasonably be expected to yield about 4 percent (3 percent expected inflation plus an assumed 1 percent real return), while comparable quality dollar denominated issues return 8 percent (7 percent expected inflation plus 1 percent real return). On average then, the dollar would be expected to depreciate about 4 percent per annum versus the Swiss franc leaving a bondholder with the same real return in each case. Viewed the other way, interest rate differentials

---

[12] In comparison, long-term variability of the U.S. equity market has averaged about 20 percent per annum.

will account for most, but not all of the observed differentials in "strength" of currencies in foreign exchange markets.

In a floating exchange-rate environment, significant long-term exchange-rate shifts are likely to continue to occur, primarily due to differential inflation rates and other structural factors like productivity differences between countries (see Figure 4). Many of these differences are caused by sociopolitical factors, which in turn influence domestic economic policies. In recent years, West Germany, Switzerland, and Japan, for example, have shown less tolerance for inflation than have Great Britain and the United States. Over time, the existence of such differential inflation rates becomes embedded

Figure 4
The Relationship between Exchange Rate Movements and Difference in Inflation Rates, 1975-1978*

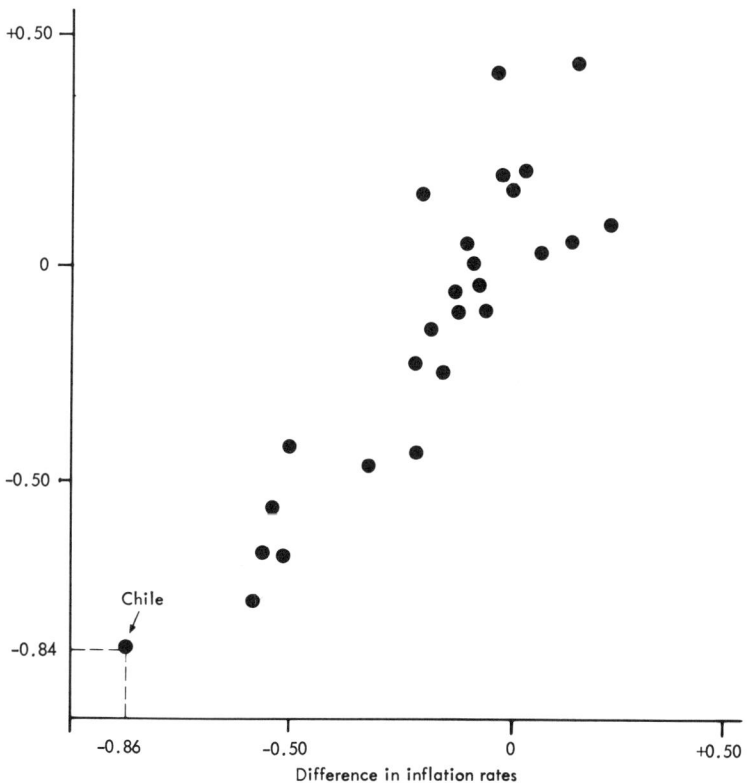

*The vertical axis shows the relative appreciation of foreign currency (1978 spot rate minus 1975 spot rate, expressed as a percentage of the latter). The horizontal axis shows the difference in inflation rates (domestic rate minus foreign rate, expressed as a percentage of one plus the foreign rate).

Source: Richard Brealey and Stewart Myers, *Principles of Corporate Finance* (New York: McGraw-Hill, 1980), chap. 31, Fig. 31-1. Used with the permission of McGraw-Hill Book Company.

not only in foreign exchange rates, but in domestic debt and equity markets as well. The practical import of this is that when viewed from a U.S. dollar perspective, part of the return to a U.S. holder of Swiss equities will come "labeled" as currency appreciation.

To illustrate, consider the earlier example of Switzerland and the United States. Swiss bonds yielded 4 percent, while similar quality U.S. bonds returned 8 percent. Long-term U.S. financial history suggests the U.S. equity market has provided a return of about 5 percent per annum *on average* about the return on long bonds. Therefore, one might reasonably anticipate earning about 13 percent per annum on U.S. equities in such an environment. Under similar assumptions, the Swiss equity market might return about 9 percent per annum (4 percent on long bonds plus a 5 percent risk premium for owning equities), but expressed in Swiss francs. Over time, however, one would expect the dollar to erode, *on average* about 4 percent per annum versus the Swiss franc because of a higher U.S. inflation rate. When viewed from a U.S. dollar perspective, therefore, the Swiss market would also provide a likely annual return of about 13 percent (9 percent Swiss equity market return plus an expected 4 percent currency appreciation of the franc versus the dollar).

Finally, even if exchange rates in generally efficient foreign currency markets properly reflect long-term trends in differential inflation rates, international investors still must contend with what are often substantial short-term fluctuations. Recent empirical results suggest however, that such fluctuations can be quite effectively diversified away in an international equity portfolio invested in a number of currencies. Jacquillat and Solnik studied the relationship between U.S. stock market returns and short-term exchange-rate fluctuations in major foreign currencies.[13] These correlations range from +0.24 from the British pound to −0.07 for the Dutch guilder with correlations clustered near zero. These results indicate that, in general, there have been no systematic relationships between price changes in the U.S. equity market and fluctuations in foreign currency values. This evidence is important because it suggests that most short-term exchange-rate fluctuations have, in fact, tended to "cancel out" in a well-diversified global portfolio.

Political Risks

Political or *sovereign* risks including the possibility of capital withdrawal restrictions, expropriation, or punitive taxation, do have a

---

[13] Bertrand Jacquillat and Bruno H. Solnik, "Multi-Nationals Are Poor Tools for Diversification," *Journal of Portfolio Management,* Winter 1978, p. 8.

major influence on securities prices. Particular questions about their effects on capital markets include:

1. Are equity prices in specific national markets likely to properly reflect the political uncertainties in that country?
2. Is it operationally feasible to predict significant political events in a foreign country more accurately and more quickly than the leading edge of all investors, so as to correctly "time" participation in different markets?

Recent evidence suggests that most major world markets are generally efficient in rapidly reflecting new information. To the extent this is true, when political risks increase, local and foreign investors alike will sell securities, and prices will adjust to a new lower equilibrium level where other investors are satisfied to hold them. Thus, individual markets generally can be presumed to be reflecting most political uncertainties at any given time, and foreign investors, therefore, are unlikely to pay too high an entry price because of political risks which only the locals can understand. Indeed, the domestic investor may be more likely to engage in "overkill" selling in reaction to potential political risks because he typically has more of his assets at stake and he may more easily be influenced by local emotion.

Even with political risks, however, the historical record suggests that a well-diversified international portfolio can incur difficulties in particular equity markets and still provide productive results in the aggregate. Also, to the extent that markets are reasonably efficient, one is likely to be rewarded by higher returns on average in those countries where political risks are greater. Finally, it should be noted that the vast majority of a typical U.S. individual's or institution's assets will continue to be exposed to various domestic political risks. These include explicit or implicit tax increases, unanticipated inflation, and various domestic government initiatives, which, even if well intended, may have a detrimental effect on shareholders of U.S. corporations. Equity investors cannot avoid political risks, but with an international strategy, it is at least possible to diversify away some of them.

TAX FACTORS

Most foreign governments levy a source-withholding tax against the dividends and interest paid to nonresident holders of equity or debt securities domiciled within their borders. Rates, conditions, and possible exemptions vary significantly from country to country. As a generalization, however, most major countries assess such taxes on U.S. residents holding their securities at rates ranging from 7.5 to 15 percent of the amount of dividends or interest paid (see Table 9). However, it is sometimes possible for a U.S.-based investor who is tax-exempt domestically to secure an exemption or a rebate in certain foreign markets on some or all of these withholding taxes. Also, taxable U.S. investors can usually claim the amount of foreign taxes withheld as a credit against their U.S. income-tax liability.

At a minimum the existence of these withholding taxes complicates the implementation of international investing strategies because

Table 9
Dividend Taxation

DIVIDEND TAXATION
Imposition des dividendes
Dividendenbesteuerung

Company's domicile / Shareholder's domicile		Australia	Austria	Belgium[1]	Canada[2]	Denmark	France[3]	Germany[12]	Hong-Kong	Italy[4]	Japan	Luxemburg[5]	Netherlands	Norway	Singapore[6]	Spain	Sweden	Switzerland	UK[8]	US
Australia	I		20	15	15	30	15[3]	15	0	30	15	15	15	25	0	15[14]	30	35	0	15
	II		C	C	C	C	C	C	–	C	C	C	C	C	–	C	C	C	–	C
Austria	I	30		15	25	10	15[3]	25	0	30	20	15	15	15	0	15	10	5	15[11]	15
	II	D		C	D	C	C	C	–	D	C	C	C	C	–	C	C	C	C	C
Belgium[9]	I	15	15		15	15	15[3]	15	0	15	15	15	15	15	0	15	15	35	0	15
	II	D.C	D.C		D.C	D.C	D.C	D.C	–	D.C	D.C	D.C	D.C	D.C	–	D.C	D.C	D.C	–	D.C
Canada	I	15	20	15		15	15	25	0	30	15	15	15	15	0	15[14]	15	15	0	15
	II	C	C	C		C	C	C	–	C	C	C	C	C	–	C	C	C	–	C
Denmark	I	30	10	15	15		0	15	0	15	15	15	15	15	0	15	15	0	15[11]	15
	II	C	C	C	C		–	C	0	C	C	C	C	C	–	C	C	–	C	C
France	I	15	15	15	15	0		15	0	15	15	15	15	10	0	15	0	5	15[11]	15
	II	C	C	C	C	–		C	–	C	C	C	C	C for 5'	–	C	–	C	C	C
Germany	I	15	20	15	25	15	0[3]		0	30	15	15	15	15	0	15	15	15	0	15
	II	C	C	C	C	C	–		–	C	C	C	C	C	–	C	C	C	–	C
Hong-Kong[10]	I	30	20	20	25	30	25	25		30	20	15	25	25	0	15[14]	30	35	0	30
	II	–	–	–	–	–	–	–		–	–	–	–	–	–	–	–	–	–	–
Italy	I	30	20	15	25	15	15	25	0		15	15	0	25	0	15[14]	15	15	0	15
	II	C[13]	C[13]	C[13]	C[13]	C[13]	C[13]	C[13]	–		C	C[13]	–	C	–	C[13]	C[13]	C[13]	–	C for I
Japan	I	15	20	15	15	15	15	15	0	15		15	15	15	0	15	15	15	0	15
	II	C	C	C	C	C	C	C	–	C		C	C	C	–	C	C	C	–	C
Luxemburg	I	30	15	15	25	30	15[3]	15	0	30	20		15	25	0	15[14]	30	35	0	15
	II	C	C	C	C	C	C	C	–	C	C		C	C	–	C	C	C	–	C
Netherlands	I	15	15	15	15	15	15[3]	15	0	30	15	15		15	0	15	15	15	15[11]	15
	II	C	C	C	C	C	C	D,	–	D	C	C		C	–	C	C	C	C	C
Norway	I	30	15	15	15	15	15	10	15	0	30	15	15		0	15	15	5	15[11]	15
	II	D	C	C	C	C	Qfor5'	C	–	C	C	C	D		–	C	C	D	C	C
Singapore	I	15	20	15	15	15	15[3]	15	0	10	15	15	15	0		15[14]	15	15	15[11]	30
	II	C	D	C	C	C	C	C	–	C	C	D	C	–		D	C	C	C	D
Spain	I	30	15	15	25	15	15[3]	15	0	30	15	15	15	15	0		15	15	15[11]	30
	II	C	C	C	C	C	C	C	–	C	C	C	C	C	–		C	C	C	C
Sweden	I	30	10	15	15	15	15[3]	15	0	15	15	15	15	15	0	15		5	15[11]	15
	II	C*	C	C	C	C	C	C	–	C	C	C*	C	C	–	C		C	C	C
Switzerland	I	30	5	20	15	0	15[3]	15	0	15	15	15	15	5	0	15	5		15[11]	15
	II	D	C	D	C	–	C	C	–	C	C	D	C	D	–	C	C		C	D
UK	I	15	15	15	15	15	15[3]	15	0	15	15	15	15	15	0	15	10	15		15
	II	C	C	C	C	C	C	C	–	C	C	C	C	C	–	C	C	C		C
US	I	15	10	15	15	15	15[3]	15	0	15	15	7.5	15	15	0	15[14]	15	15	15[11]	
	II	C	C	C	C	C	C	C	–	C	C	C	C	C	–	C	C	C	C	

Table 9 *(continued)*

Note: Dividend taxation is computed on the basis of information pro.*i*-ded by the Amsterdam Bureau of Fiscal Documentation.

I. Indicates the effective rate of dividend withholding tax.

II. Describes the treatment of the foreign withholding tax in the share's country of residence.

D = Deduction for foreign tax paid; i.e. the shareholder's country of residence imposes its tax on net foreign dividends.

C = Credit for foreign tax paid; i.e. the shareholder's country of residence imposes its tax on gross foreign dividends but the amount of this tax is reduced by the amount of the foreign dividend withholding tax.

[1] Dividends of Belgian companies (as reported on pages 34 to 433) include the *crédit d'impôt*, which is applicable exclusively to Belgian residents. To calculate the net dividend received by nonresident shareholders 31.5% should first be deducted from these reported dividends before applying the withholding tax indicated in this column.

[2] The rates of Canadian withholding tax stated in the table (15% or 25%) are reduced by 5% to 10%, and 20%, respectively, if the distributing company has "a degree of Canadian ownership" as defined in Sec. 257 of the Canadian Income Tax Act.

[3] Dividends of French companies (as reported on pages 34 to 433) include the *avoir fiscal* which is applicable to residents of Australia, Austria, Belgium, France, Germany, Luxemburg, Netherlands, Singapore, Spain, Sweden, Switzerland, the United Kingdom, and the United States. In the case of German shareholders, the avoir fiscal may be credited against German income tax. If a French company distributes a dividend to an Australian, Austrian, Belgian, Dutch, Luxemburg, Singapore, Spanish, Swedish, Swiss, United Kingdom, or United States resident, the avoir fiscal is paid directly by the French government. To calculate the net dividend received by other shareholders, $1/3$ or 33.3% should first be deducted from these reported dividends before applying the withholding tax indicated in this column.

[4] The Italian withholding tax (normally 30%) may be reduced by the amount of foreign income tax imposed on the dividends in the shareholder's country of residence. However, the Italian withholding tax cannot be reduced below a minimum of 10%.

[5] Dividends distributed by Luxemburg holding companies are exempt from Luxemburg withholding tax. The rates indicated apply to nonholding companies only.

[6] Dividends payable by Singapore companies are not subject to dividend withholding tax. However, the companies may deduct for their own benefit the income tax due by them on their distributed profits.

[7] The foreign withholding tax is only partially creditable in the shareholder's country of residence. The remaining foreign tax is deductible.

[8] Unless otherwise provided for by treaty, foreign withholding tax is deductible in Sweden. In addition, a credit may be granted towards Swedish national income taxes.

[9] In Belgium, *net* foreign dividends are included in taxable income. In addition, a credit equal to 15% of the net dividend is granted, irrespective of the rate of the foreign withholding tax on gross dividends.

[10] Due to the territorial basis of the Hong Kong income tax, foreign dividends received are normally exempt from tax in Hong Kong.

[11] In the United Kingdom, resident shareholders are entitled to a special tax credit (30/70 of the dividend received) credited against their income tax liability on the dividend plus the credit. Upon renegotiations of treaties, this credit may also apply to nonresidents in the form of an additional payment, but in that case a 15% withholding tax will normally be imposed. This currently applies to residents of Austria, Denmark, France, Netherlands, Norway, Singapore, Spain, Sweden, Switzerland, and the United States.

[12] Dividends of German companies declared after January 1, 1977 (as reported on pages 34 to 433) include the *Steuerguthaben* which is applicable exclusively to German residents. To calculate the net dividend received by nonresident shareholders 36 percent should first be deducted from these reported dividends before applying the withholding tax indicated in this column.

[13] A limited credit for foreign dividend tax is available for shareholders domiciled in

Table 9 *(concluded)*
Italy: if the country of source does not grant credit relief in the converse situation (Austria, Luxemburg), the credit may not exceed 25% of the Italian tax attributable to the dividend. For other countries, the credit will be between 25% and $66\frac{2}{3}$% of the Italian tax.

[14] Nonresident shareholders receiving dividends from Spanish companies are subject to individual income tax at progressive rates ranging from 15% to 65.51%, unless a treaty provides otherwise. Tax is withheld by the company at the rate applicable to an amount of income equal to the dividend payment.

Source: *Capital International Perspective* (Geneva, Switzerland, July 1980).

of the added administrative burden required to properly cope with them. More importantly, those foreign markets with high dividend yields and substantial withholding-tax rates will appear relatively less attractive to tax-exempt U.S. institutions that have not secured tax concessions in those countries. Therefore, the existence of these foreign source-withholding taxes clearly merits consideration in the design of international investment strategies, especially for investors who are already tax-exempt in the United States.

IMPLEMENTING INTERNATIONAL INVESTMENT STRATEGIES

For a U.S.-based individual or institution, effective implementation of an international equity strategy is generally more complex and demanding than execution of domestically oriented programs. The most effective approach in any situation is particularly dependent upon the size of the assets to be invested abroad. Other important factors which must be addressed include: which countries and securities are permissible for investment; how trading, custody, and administration will be performed; and whether an active or passive investment approach, or both, will be pursued. Naturally, the availability, quality, and timeliness of information on foreign markets and companies is especially critical if an active strategy on country and/or security selection is to be pursued.

AVAILABILITY OF INFORMATION ON FOREIGN EQUITIES

It is widely recognized that the quantity, quality, and timeliness of accounting and other corporate information available abroad is seldom equivalent to U.S. standards. This does not imply that a U.S. investor should avoid foreign equities, but one must tailor an international investing strategy to existing realities. Indeed, the imperfect dissemination of information in some foreign markets should be viewed as providing possible opportunities rather than difficulties.

Obviously, problems can arise when international investors domiciled halfway around the world from a particular stock market attempt to actively trade securities in direct competition with local investors in that market. But, it is possible to avoid these and other potential difficulties by carefully structuring an international strategy. One possibility is to include two quite divergent management styles. The extremes of these styles are as follows:

1. An active approach to international investing, which is undertaken when it is possible to develop some relative information or analysis advantage in a particular market or markets.
2. A carefully executed passive approach that invests in a well-diversified list of major companies in important markets abroad, permitting one to at least do as well, on average, as local market indices, while capturing the diversification benefits of international investing.

INSTITUTIONAL INVESTING

Most U.S. institutions that have invested substantial sums abroad have selected banks or investment counselors with specialized expertise in foreign equity markets to supervise these investments. Leading U.S.-based managers with substantial investments in foreign equities include Morgan Guaranty Trust Co., State Street Bank and Trust Co., the Putnam Management Co., Batterymarch Financial Management, and Fidelity Management and Research. In addition, a number of European-based investment managers have been selected by U.S. institutions in recent years. All of these managers offer individual account management to substantial investors and Morgan Guaranty and State Street also offer commingled foreign securities funds to U.S. pension fund investors. These managers are also equipped to handle or arrange proper custody, administration, and reporting of foreign securities holdings.

The most important differentiating factor amongst these managers is whether they pursue primarily an active or a passive management style. Amongst the major managers mentioned above, at this time State Street and Batterymarch offer primarily passive international management, whereas the others offer active management. There is, of course, no such thing as a purely passive international equity strategy in the same sense that a Standard & Poor's 500 matching fund is passive. Rather, some judgments must always be made as to which countries to invest in and the number of companies in each country to be held. Nevertheless, the important distinction remains that active international managers attempt to select undervalued markets and/or sectors, industries, and companies, and thereby add value to a portfolio versus an appropriate international benchmark index, such as the Capital International Index of Europe, the Far East, and Asia. The evidence, in the form of actual performance results, suggests, at best, that active managers have had mixed results in these attempts. An unbiased interpretation of the available performance studies on international-asset managers suggests that the average active international manager has done somewhat less well than appropriate benchmark indexes after adjusting for risk and deducting expenses.[14] Some active international managers, however, have outperformed benchmark indexes. For this reason, major U.S. institutions investing in international equities have often selected both active and passive investment managers.

INDIVIDUAL INVESTING

The individual or institution desiring to invest a modest sum abroad typically faces a number of problems that the major institutional investor using a specialized adviser is less likely to encounter. Difficulties including a lack of comprehensive and timely data on foreign markets and securities, generally higher transaction costs abroad, and tax and administrative constraints, are often encountered.

These factors usually combine to make it extremely difficult to obtain satisfactory investment results with an individually managed international equity portfolio, unless it has at least several hundred thousand dollars in assets and considerable informed effort is devoted to careful supervision of all aspects of the investment program. For these reasons, it is often most effective for modest-sized investors seeking international exposure in their equity portfolios to purchase shares in one or more mutual funds specializing in foreign investing. A representative list of some of the larger mutual funds specializing in international investments is found in Table 10. As can be seen, some of these funds invest in foreign markets on a diversified basis, while others specialize in particular countries or gold-related holdings.

INTERNATIONAL TRADING

A number of major U.S. brokerage firms have capabilities for executing purchase and sale orders in equities traded abroad. Salomon Brothers, Merrill Lynch, Drexel Burnham Lambert and Arnold, and S. Bleichroeder are particularly well-known for their capabilities in

---

[14] See, for example, Andre L. Farber, "Performance of Internationally Diversified Mutual Funds," in *International Capital Markets,* ed. E. Elton and M. Gruber (New York: Elsevier-North Holland Publishing, 1975); and James R. F. Guy, "An Examination of the Effects of International Diversification from the British Viewpoint on Both Hypothetical and Real Portfolios," *Journal of Finance,* December 1978, p. 1425.

Table 10
International Mutual Funds

12/31/79 Approximate Total Assets ($ millions)	Fund Name	Total Returns Performance	
		Five Years 12/74-12/79	One Year 12/78-12/79
	Broadly Diversified International Funds		
$ 38.6	Putnam International Equities Fund (Adviser: Putnam Management Co., Boston, Mass.)	+143.58%	+19.61%
25.9*	Scudder International Fund (Adviser: Scudder, Stevens & Clark, Boston, Mass.)	+97.93	+19.34
340.5	Templeton Growth Fund (Adviser: Templeton Investment Counsel Ltd., Toronto, Ont.)	+267.42†	+26.83
175.7	Templeton World Fund (Adviser: Templeton Investment Counsel Ltd., Toronto, Ont.)	†	+28.14
	Gold-Oriented Funds		
$190.7	International Investors (Adviser: Van Eck Management Corp., New York, N.Y.)	+117.44	+176.96
43.7	Research Capital Fund (Adviser: Franklin Research, Inc., San Mateo, Calif.)	+88.99	+145.29
53.3*	United Services Fund (Adviser: Growth Research & Management, Inc., Universal City, Tex.)	+58.99	+187.19
	Country Specialist International Funds		
$ 23.4	Canadian Fund (Adviser: Calvin Bullock Ltd., New York, N.Y.)	+68.26	+30.67
168.6	Japan Fund (a closed-end fund traded on the New York Stock Exchange) (Adviser: Asia Management Corp., New York, N.Y.)	+96.13	−22.38

*No load funds.
†Fund not in existence for full period.
Source: Lipper Analytical Services.

foreign securities. In addition, a substantial number of foreign equities are traded by market-makers in the United States, mostly in the form of American depository receipts (ADRs). Some ADRs are listed on the New York Stock Exchange, while many others trade in the over-the-counter market. Most domestic brokerage firms can therefore execute orders in ADRs without difficulty.

Trading in international markets, however, adds a new dimension for the U.S. investor. Settlement dates vary from country to country and are as diverse as the markets themselves. The Hong Kong, Swiss, and Mexican stock markets have one-day settlement periods; London works on a fortnightly basis; two different dates apply in France, depending on whether you deal in the cash market (next day) or forward market (end of the month); in Italy any trades done after the 15th of the month settle on the 30th of the following month. The Japanese market is the most unique. The Tokyo Stock Exchange averages about 450 million shares a day in turnover (reaching one billion shares a day in peak periods). Trades settle in three days, and there are no "fails."

Commission rates abroad are generally higher than those charged on the New York Stock Exchange (see Figure 5). It should be noted, however, that it is sometimes possible to negotiate commission reductions when dealing in certain foreign markets, especially with substantial orders.

Figure 5
Average Commission Rates for Typical Institutional Trades

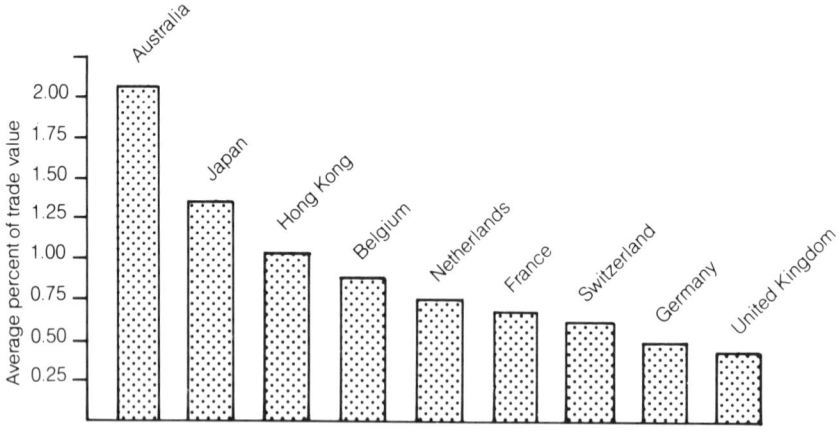

Source: State Street Bank, Boston, Mass.

section 4

Options and Financial Futures

INTRODUCTION

Options are contracts granting the holder of the contract the right to buy or sell a specified number of shares (usually 100) of a specified stock at a predetermined price within a stated period of time. Prior to 1973, options traded only in the over-the-counter market. Testimony before Congress in the early 1970s helped convince policymakers that options might serve a legitimate investment purpose. Congress gave the Securities Exchange Commission (SEC) the task of "experimenting" with exchange listed options. In 1973, the SEC authorized the establishment of "pilot" programs for listed options. Since that time, listed option trading has flourished.

Although money managers of institutions developed an active interest in exchange listed options, institutions were subject to a myriad of complex state and/or federal regulations that limited the ability of money managers to utilize options in managing their portfolios. The initial reluctance of Congress to permit the trading of exchange listed options and regulators of institutions to permit the use of exchange listed options was due to the lack of understanding as to how options can be employed to improve the risk-reward opportunities for market participants. Options were regarded as purely "speculative" investments.

In Reading 11, Gary L. Gastineau explains how the intelligent use of options can be used to control portfolio risk and thereby improve risk-reward opportunities. The advantages of exchange listed options over nonlisted (conventional) options and the tax treatment of options are also discussed. In Reading 12, Professor Richard M. Bookstaber gives an explanation of option pricing models and explains the well-received Black-Scholes option pricing formula. He also demonstrates how to exploit profit opportunities when the market price of an option differs from the value determined from an option pricing formula.

A futures contract is an agreement between a buyer (or seller) and an established exchange or its clearing house in which the party agrees to deliver or accept during a designated period a specified amount of a certain product that adheres to the particular quality and delivery conditions prescribed by the exchange. When the product is a fixed income instrument, the futures contract is called a financial, or interest rate, futures contract. The prudent utilization of financial futures allows a portfolio manager to transfer some or all of the interest-rate risk associated with holding a portfolio of fixed income securities. Portfolio managers have welcomed the opportunity to transfer this risk because of the violent fluctuations in interest rates in recent years. In Reading 13, Allan M. Loosigian explains how financial futures can be used to hedge against adverse interest-rate movements.

After considerable fighting between the SEC and the Commodity Futures Trading Commission over regulatory domain, futures contracts in which the underlying "product" is a designated stock market index began trading in February of 1982. In Reading 14, Dr. Victor Niederhoffer and Professor Richard Zeckhauser demonstrate how such contracts serve useful economic functions as both hedging and speculative instruments. The early experience of market index futures contracts is described by Zeckhauser and Niederhoffer in Reading 15.

Options: Risks and Rewards[*]

11   GARY L. GASTINEAU
Manager, Options Portfolio Service
Kidder, Peabody & Co., Incorporated

INVESTMENT CHARACTERISTICS OF BASIC OPTION CONTRACTS

Definitions

Before we examine the investment characteristics of puts and calls, it will be helpful to define a few terms:

Option: A negotiable contract in which the writer, for a certain sum of money called the option premium, gives the buyer the right to demand, within a specified time, the purchase or sale by the writer of a specified number of shares of stock at a fixed price called the striking price. Unless otherwise stated, options are written for units of 100 shares. They are ordinarily issued for periods of less than one year.

Call option: An option to buy stock from the writer.

Put option: An option to sell stock to the writer.

---

[*]From Gary L. Gastineau, *The Stock Options Manual*, 2d ed. Copyright © 1979 by McGraw-Hill Book Company. Reproduced by permission.

Combination option: An option consisting of at least one put and one call. The individual option contracts which make up the combination are originally sold as a unit, but they may be exercised or resold separately.

Straddle: A combination option consisting of one put and one call with a common striking price and a common expiration date.

Striking price or exercise price: The price at which an option is exercisable, i.e., the price per share that the buyer of a call option must pay the writer for the stock or the price that the writer must pay the holder of a put option.

Option premium: The price of an option contract. In this section the convention of stating the option premium in terms of dollars per share under option is adopted. If the total premium for a 100-share option is $1,000, the option premium is given as $10.

Expiration date: The date after which an option is void.

Option buyer: The individual or, less frequently, the institutional investor who buys options.

Option writer: The individual or institutional investor who sells or writes options.

Spread: (1) For listed options: The purchase of one option and the sale of another option on the same stock. The investor setting up the spread hopes to profit from a change in the difference between the prices of the two options. (2) In the conventional option market: A straddle in which the put side and the call side are written at different striking prices. Typically, the put striking price is below, and the call striking price is above, the market price of the stock at the time the spread is established. In the listed option market this position is usually called a *spraddle*. (3) The put and call dealer's margin between the option premium paid by the buyer and the premium paid to the writer is also called a *spread*.

Risk Modification

No matter how intricate an option investment strategy the investor may adopt, *the principal result of any option purchase or sale is to modify the risk characteristics of an investor's position.* This feature of options can have an important impact on portfolio structure and on the investor's overall risk exposure.

Stock options provide the investor with a unique way to modify exposure to market risk. In particular, listed options traded on securities exchanges around the world are extremely versatile instruments for the modification of risk. This statement appears at odds with the popular view of call options as speculative tools which permit the small investor to obtain superior leverage on a small amount of capital. Options can fulfill much more important functions in an investment portfolio than this popular view suggests. Options can be of substantial aid to investors, large or small, who wish to modify the exposure of their portfolios to market fluctuations and improve their risk-adjusted return on investment.

Risk-Reward Characteristics of Put and Call Contracts

The graph in Figure 1 illustrates the basic investment characteristics of a call option from the respective viewpoints of the buyer and the writer. As most investors who have any familiarity with options

Figure 1
Profit-Loss Positions of the Buyer and Writer of a Call

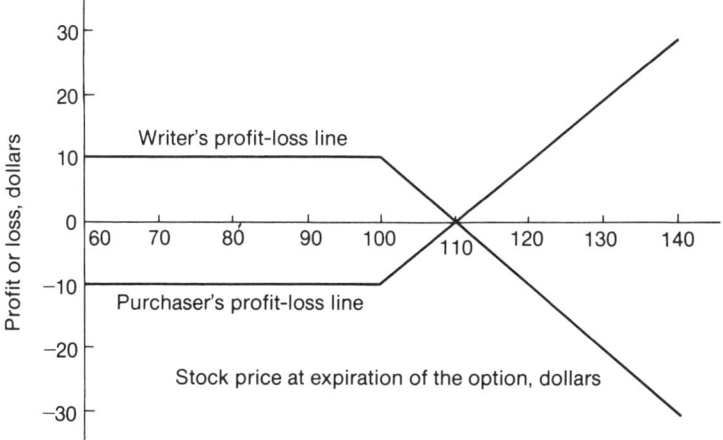

are aware, an option buyer can never lose more than the premium paid for the option contract. On the other hand, if the price of the stock rises substantially over the life of the call option, the buyer's potential reward is theoretically unlimited. This position is illustrated by the line which begins in the lower left-hand corner of Figure 1.

The uncovered or "naked" call writer's position is, in many respects, the exact opposite of the call buyer's position. As the line which begins in the upper left-hand corner of Figure 1 illustrates, the call writer keeps the entire premium unless the stock price rises above the exercise price at the time the option expires or is exercised. In return for the option premium received, the writer of the call agrees to sell the stock at the striking price, no matter how high the stock may go. If the writer does not own the shares covered by the option, the writer's position deteriorates by $1 per share for every point by which the price of the stock exceeds the exercise price.

The essence of the uncovered call writer's position is that he or she can earn no more than the amount of the option premium and can lose a large amount if the price of the underlying stock runs up. In contrast to the call buyer who is fixing the risk at the amount of the premium and accepting the possibility of a widely varying reward, the uncovered writer is fixing the reward at the amount of the premium and accepting a highly variable risk. Figure 2 illustrates the

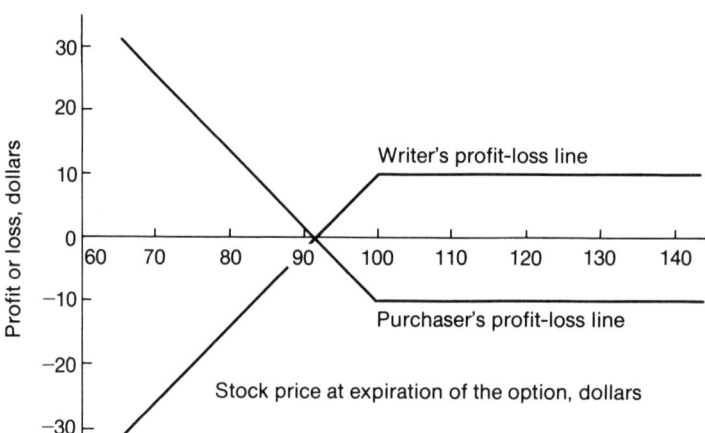

Figure 2
Profit-Loss Positions of the Buyer and Writer of a Put

profit and loss positions of the buyer and writer of an uncovered put. In return for a fixed premium, the buyer of a put obtains the right to receive a reward that increases as the price of the underlying stock declines. As in the case of the call, both the buyer and the writer of a put option fix one side of the risk-reward equation and permit the other side to vary.

The offsetting risk-reward features of the buying and writing positions are clarified by these graphs. Any profit to the option buyer is exactly offset by a loss to the writer, and vice versa. Neglecting transaction costs, *the net effect of an option transaction is simply a reallocation of risk and reward between buyer and writer.*

It is no accident that the word *premium* is used in both the insurance business and the option business. Option contracts, like insurance policies, are used to protect the investor, whether writer or buyer, from unacceptable risk. In these graphs, the option buyer appears to be in a position analogous to that of the owner of an insurance policy. The option writer is like the insurance underwriter who accepts risk in return for premium income. When options are incorporated in an overall portfolio plan, however, the risks and rewards can change remarkably. For example, the call writer who has a position in the underlying stock will actually be *reducing* the overall volatility or market risk of his portfolio by writing the option because the premium he receives protects his assets in the event of a price decline, while his writer's obligation limits his gain on the up side. Although options do not increase or decrease the total level of risk in the financial system, *both parties to a particular option transaction can reduce their portfolio risk simultaneously through a combination of stock, option, and short-term debt positions.*

THE SIGNIFICANCE OF EXCHANGE LISTED OPTIONS

While options in one form or another have been around since the days of ancient Greece (some would argue since the days of the Old Testament), both the modern theory and widespread use of option contracts awaited development of the *listed option,* initiated by the Chicago Board Options Exchange (CBOE) in 1973.

Important Changes Initiated by the CBOE

Prior to 1973 the market in options on securities was one of the less significant segments of the securities business. In that year the Chicago Board Options Exchange, a division of the Chicago Board of Trade, introduced standardized listed option contracts. Neither the stock market nor the option market will ever be the same. Innovations introduced by the CBOE have been adopted by virtually every other securities options market in the world.

Standardization of Terms. The importance of standardized option terms in the development of a secondary market in option contracts cannot be overemphasized. Standardization facilitates secondary trading because the number of distinct contracts a buyer or seller must evaluate is reduced. In contrast to the conventional option market where it is possible to buy or write an option with practically any striking price or expiration date, the terms of contracts available on the exchanges are more limited. The striking price of a listed option always ends in $5, $2.50, or $0 unless a stock dividend or other capital change occurs after trading in the option begins. If American Telephone & Telgraph is selling at $51 a share at the time options for a new expiration month are being listed for trading, the new AT&T option will have a striking price of $50 per share. If the stock price closes above $52.50, the exchange will add $55 contracts for each expiration date beyond 60 days. Barring stock dividends, splits, or other capital changes, it will be impossible to buy or write an AT&T

option on the exchange with a striking price between $50 and $55 per share.

In addition to standardization of striking prices, the exchanges have standardized expiration dates. The expiration date is the Saturday after the third Friday in the month. While most options expire in January, April, July, and October, some underlying stocks have options expiring in February, May, August, and November cycles, and a few use March, June, September, and December cycles.

Fungibility. Fungibility, or interchangeability, is a second important characteristic of listed options necessary for the development of an active secondary market. Fungibility means substitutability or equivalence. Each listed option with a common expiration date and striking price is interchangeable with any similar listed option.

Either party to a listed option can usually close out a position that no longer meets his needs without undue sacrifice. The buyer and writer in a listed option transaction have no direct connection. Each has a contract only with *The Options Clearing Corporation* which is the issuer of listed options. The option buyer relies on the Clearing Corporation to make good on the contract. The writer's obligation is an obligation to the Clearing Corporation, not to the buyer his broker happens to meet on the exchange floor. Either the option buyer or the writer can close out his position by simply reversing the initial transaction. For a more complete explanation of the relationship between the Clearing Corporation and the other parties to an option contract, the reader should examine the relevant sections of *The Options Clearing Corporation Prospectus.*

Lower Transaction Costs. A third important characteristic of listed options is their relatively low transaction cost. The total transaction cost of any listed option trade is substantially lower than the transaction cost of a similar conventional option trade. Lower transaction costs have an important effect on trading volume and market liquidity. As the spread between the premium paid by the buyer and the premium received by the writer grows smaller, the number of transactions will tend to grow larger. If the option premium paid by the buyer is $500 and the amount received by the writer, net of transaction costs, is only $400, a writer who was willing to accept a net premium of $425 and a buyer who was willing to pay a premium of $475 would be excluded from the market. On the other hand, if the spread were narrower, both the buyer and the writer could be accommodated and the total volume of option transactions would increase. Relatively low transaction costs have been an important factor in the high trading volume of listed options.

Organized Secondary Market. In contrast to the conventional options market where both buyer and writer are literally locked into a transaction until the expiration date unless they can reach agreement for an earlier liquidation of their positions, depth of the market in listed options often exceeds the depth and liquidity of the market in the underlying stock.

Because both writer and buyer can close out positions relatively quickly, trading and investment strategies which require the use of options for only a short period of time are feasible. Strategies which depend on an investor's ability to buy or sell additional options as time passes are facilitated by a secondary market.

Published Transaction Prices. The prices at which listed option transactions actually take place are published daily. Published prices and known commission rates assure both buyer and writer of a fair market. While we are not aware of any widespread abuse of the relative obscurity of conventional option dealer spreads, the mere fact that daily trading summaries are published in the newspapers removes some of the mystery and, quite frankly, some of the suspicion from the option market.

Certificateless Clearing. In some respects, one of the most important innovations pioneered by the CBOE is the introduction of certificateless clearing. Except in unusual cases where an option trader insists on evidence of the transaction in addition to a brokerage firm confirmation slip, The Options Clearing Corporation does not issue an actual option contract or certificate. This feature of listed option trading reduces the amount of paperwork and eliminates the physical movement of securities, in this case option contracts, between brokerage firms. The Options Clearing Corporation has sharply reduced the time required to clear a transaction and, as the brokerage community gains additional experience with certificateless trading, the cost of clearing a transaction should decline. The CBOE was a pilot project not only for organized trading of option contracts but also for the introduction of certificateless trading to the securities markets. On the basis of results to date, we can say that both features of the pilot project are unqualified successes.

Comparison of Conventional and Listed Options and Markets

Table 1 compares conventional and listed options and markets.

Comparison of Transaction Costs

Probably the single most significant contribution of listed option trading to the expansion of the option market is that it sharply reduces the cost of a transaction. Both the writer and the buyer of a call can fare better on an exchange than with a conventional call. If commission and other transaction costs are too large, they act as a deterrent to trading. Commissions on the exchange are low enough

Table 1
Comparison of Conventional and Listed Options and Markets

	Conventional	Listed
Type of options traded.	Calls, puts, combination options.	Calls, puts, combination orders permitted.
Striking price.	Any price buyer and writer negotiate.	Standardized price ending in $5, $2.50, or $0.
Expiration date.	Any date buyer and writer negotiate.	Saturday after the third Friday in the designated expiration month.
Expiration time.	3:15 p.m. eastern time.	5 p.m. eastern time.
Last date and time option can be sold.	Same as expiration date and time.	2 p.m. central time. 3 p.m. eastern time on the business day immediately prior to the expiration date.
Adjustment for cash dividend.	Striking price reduced on ex-dividend date.	No change in striking price.
Adjustment for stock dividends, stock splits, and reverse splits.	Both striking price and number of shares covered by options are adjusted to reflect the capital change.	
Adjustment for rights or warrants issued to common shareholders.	Striking price reduced by the value of the rights or warrants.	
Limitation on purchase or sale of options on one stock.	None, but limits have been proposed.	1,000 contracts on the same side of the market (e.g., long calls *and* short puts); limit applies to all expiration dates.
Unit of trading.	One contract is an option on 100 shares of the underlying stock before any adjustments.	
Method of option price determination.	Buyer and writer negotiate through put and call broker.	Central auction market.
Secondary market.	Limited; special options advertised in newspaper.	Very active secondary market.
Buyer's recourse to obtain performance on option contract.	Primary responsibility for performance belongs to the endorsing broker who may be any member of the NYSE.	The Options Clearing Corporation is the primary obligor guaranteeing the writer's performance.
Evidence of ownership.	Bearer certificate.	Broker's confirmation slip.
Method of closing out transaction when stock sells above striking price.	Option may be exercised by buyer or sold to put and call broker who exercises the option and sells the stock.	Exercise is rare; contract is usually closed out in a closing purchase-sale transaction.
Transaction costs.	High.	Moderate.
Commission structure.	Basic charge is negotiated by put and call broker as a spread between premium	Negotiated commission rates since May 1, 1975.

Table 1 *(concluded)*

	Conventional	Listed
	paid by buyer and premium paid to writer.	
Stocks on which options are available.	Almost any stock.	About 300 selected stocks in the United States and a growing list of stocks elsewhere in the world.
Pricing information.	Brokers publish indicated premiums to buyers or writers.	Actual transaction prices published daily.
Procedure for exercise.	Buyer exercises by notifying endorsing broker.	Buyer's broker notifies The Options Clearing Corporation, which selects writers essentially at random.
Extensions.	Available if writer agrees.	Not available.
Tax treatment.	Identical.	
Margin requirement: call buyer.	100% of the option premium.	
Margin requirement: covered writer.	No margin required beyond that needed to carry stock position.	
Margin requirement: uncovered writer.	Minimum requirement is related to price of stock with adjustment for amount of premium received and amount by which option is in or out of the money. Margin requirements should be checked in detail with each brokerage firm.	

that the buyer can consider purchasing options for a relatively small expected move in the stock. The writer has reasonable assurance that the commission cost to close out the transaction will not consume most of the premium. The lower transaction cost leads to more active trading and, consequently, to more liquid markets. The example chosen for Table 2 illustrates a typical difference between transaction costs for a listed option and those for a conventional option. The actual difference in a particular case always depends on what happens to the price of the stock and what the parties do to close out their respective sides of the contract.

Nonetheless, examination of the table reveals that the costs of the conventional option transaction are, in this case, more than 2½ times as high as for the comparable listed option transaction. In fact, commissions and other charges paid by the two parties to the conventional option trade are equal to about two thirds of the total option premium paid by the buyer. If one assumed that the transaction involved *one* call rather than 10, the costs would consume an amount nearly equal to the entire premium. With transaction costs of this

Table 2
Comparison of Transaction Costs: Conventional versus Listed Option Markets

Assumptions:
Buyer buys 10 calls at $500 each with a $50 striking price. Stock rises to $60 where buyer sells or exercises calls, receiving $1,000 per contract before costs. Writer initially buys 500 shares of stock or enough to cover one half of his obligation. All figures are expressed on a per contract basis with commissions calculated on the assumption that the transaction consists of 10 contracts.

	Listed Conventional	Listed
Buyer's position:		
Premium paid by buyer	$ 500.00	$ 500.00
Commission to buyer's broker	12.50	12.70
Cost to buyer to establish position	512.50	512.70
Gross proceeds from selling call ($60 − $50) × 100 shares	1,000.00	1,000.00
Listed option commission		(17.20)
Round-trip stock commission on sale of options	(107.06)	
Transfer taxes	(5.00)	
Subtract: Cost to establish position	(512.50)	(512.70)
Net profit to buyer	$ 375.44	$ 470.10
Writer's position:		
Premium paid by buyer	$ 500.00	$ 500.00
Option commission paid by writer to his broker	(12.50)	(12.70)
Put and call broker's spread (estimated)	(75.00)	
Net premium to writer	412.50	487.30
Cost of repurchasing call from buyer	1,000.00	1,000.00
Add: Listed option commission		17.20
Purchase commissions initial stock position	30.13	30.13
Sale commission initial stock position		33.58
Purchase commission additional stock called	33.58	
Sale commission on stock called	50.83	
Transfer taxes	5.00	2.50
Subtract: Net premium received	(412.50)	(487.30)
Profit on stock owned	(500.00)	(500.00)
Net loss to writer	$ 207.04	$ 96.11
Net profit to buyer	$ 375.44	$ 470.10
Subtract: Net loss to writer	(207.04)	(96.11)
Net profit to investors	$ 168.40	$ 373.99
Total transaction costs	$ 331.60	$ 126.01
Less:	(126.01)	
Difference in transaction costs: Conventional versus listed calls	$ 205.59 per contract	

Notes:
1. If the writer had written conventional straddles instead of two calls against each round lot owned, he would have fared better but the *total* transaction cost would have been even higher.
2. If the stock declines, total transaction costs may drop slightly faster for the conventional option but they are always substantially higher than listed option costs.
3. Transfer taxes are based on New York residence.
4. Commissions are calculated on the basis of an initial position of 10 calls and a stock position of 500 shares bought by the writer. Stock and option commission rates are those in effect prior to May 1, 1975, on the NYSE and CBOE, respectively. These commission charges are then stated on a per call basis. The total charges are 10 times the figures listed.

magnitude, neither buyer nor writer can realistically expect superior performance unless premiums are grossly out of line with any measure of fair value.

THE ROLE OF OPTIONS IN INTELLIGENT PORTFOLIO MANAGEMENT

Background

One reason options are avoided by many investors is that the successful use of options requires more attention and analysis than most people devote to their portfolios. Much of the aura of complexity which surrounds options is due to a tendency to view them as unique or unusual investments. It is far more useful to relate the risk-reward characteristics of options to those of stocks and bonds than to emphasize the differences between options and other investment vehicles. The idea that "highly leveraged" options fit into the same risk-reward hierarchy as corporate bonds or common stocks can be difficult for many investors, including some experienced option traders, to accept at first. Nonetheless, most investors find options easier to understand when they examine them in terms of their impact on total portfolio risk.

The purpose of this section is to demonstrate that the intelligent use of options requires evaluation of option contracts combined with measurement and control of portfolio risk. This discussion is directed at the investor who attempts to analyze investment positions in terms of *risk* and *reward*. Such an investor is sensitive to the trade-off between opportunities to obtain high rates of return and the increased risk of loss which usually comes with such opportunities. Those who view investments in this framework can improve their decision-making process, and perhaps their results, by understanding the risk reward characteristics of stock options.

Risk-Reward Characteristics of Options

To illustrate the risk-reward characteristics of options, we have chosen covered writing of a call option for more intensive analysis. In Figure 3 the ownership of shares of common stock is designated by the solid line (A-A'). The ownership of common stock, combined with the sale of a call option on that underlying stock, is designated by the broken line (B-B'). The vertical axis represents the profit or loss from each of these positions at a particular stock price on the day the option expires. The horizontal axis represents the price of the stock on that day.

In this example the stock is purchased at $95 per share. The shareholder who does not sell the call option participates point-for-point in every increase or decrease in the price of the stock. His profit is theoretically unlimited on the up side and his loss is limited only by a stock price of zero on the down side.

The alternative strategy of covered call writing, illustrated by the broken line, is based on the sale of a call option against the stock

Figure 3
Comparison of Profit/Loss: Long Stock Position versus Covered Writer Position

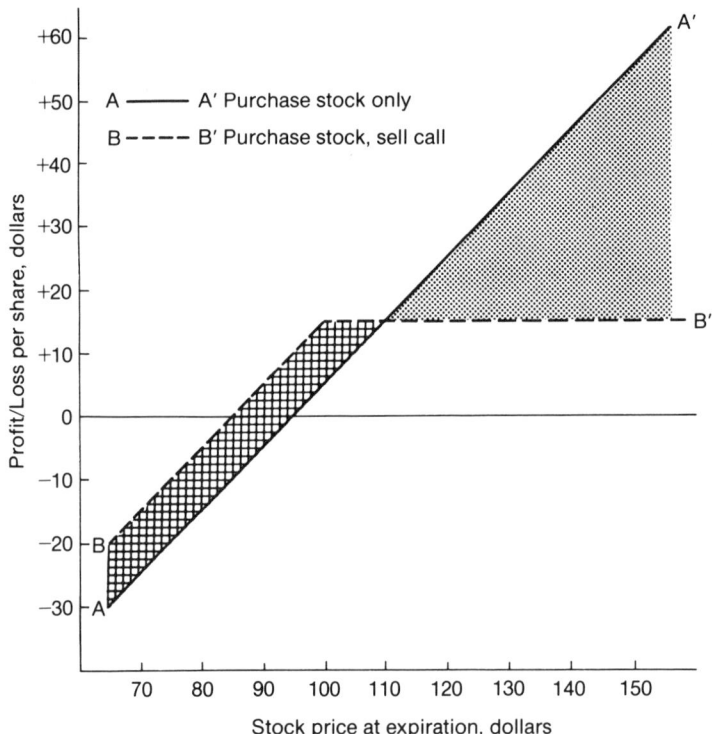

position. The hypothetical call option used in the diagram has a $100 striking price and a life of about six months from the time it is sold. The writer obtains a $10-per-share premium. Any loss on the long stock position will be reduced by the $10 per share obtained from the option.

The covered call writer's position does have some disadvantages. If the price of the stock rises above $110 per share (the striking price plus the call premium), the investor would have been better off not selling the call. In return for a degree of downside protection, he has given up the opportunity to participate in any rise in the price of the underlying stock above $110 per share.

In the diagram, the downside protection provided by the option premium received is designated by the cross-hatched trapezoidal area to the left of the intersection of the two profit-loss lines. The upside opportunity given up by the covered call writer is represented by the shaded triangular area to the right of the intersection of the two lines.

Covered Call Writing

Figure 3 highlights several features of covered call writing. Note that the seller of the covered call option *reduces the variability of his return on investment.* If the stock rises sharply, the return on the stock position will be reduced by the amount of any loss on repurchase of the option. If the stock is called away at a price of $100 per share when the market price at the time of exercise is much higher, the investor may experience a sizable opportunity loss. If the stock declines, the loss will be reduced by the amount of the premium col-

Figure 4
Comparison of Profit/Loss: Long Stock Position versus Covered Writer Position with Low Option Premium

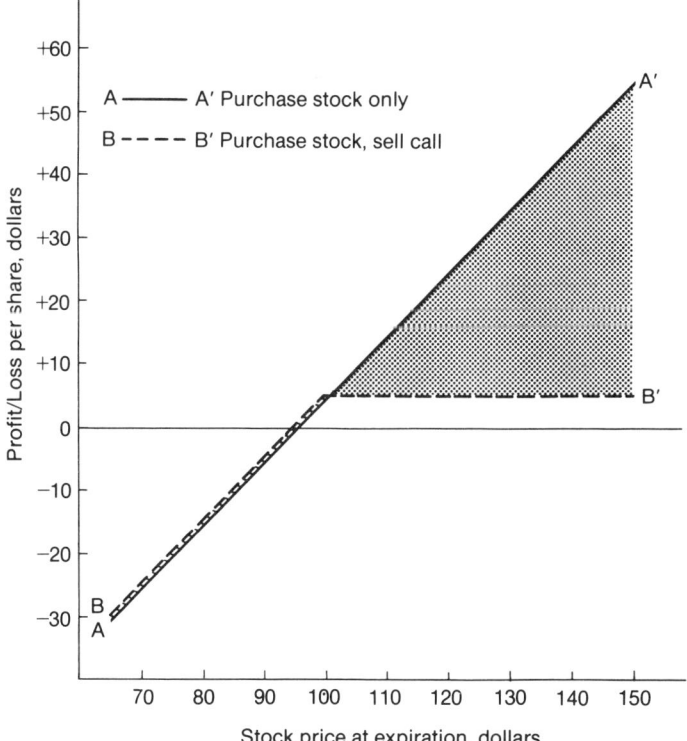

lected. Regardless of the direction in which the stock price moves or how far it moves, *covered call option writing reduces the variability of the return from a portfolio of equity securities.* The importance of this point is hard to overemphasize.

If the value of the premium received is too small relative to the value of the opportunity for appreciation given up, the covered writer will obtain a substandard return on investment over a period of time. When the value of the premium received equals the value of the opportunity forgone, after adjustment for risk, the option is said to be *fairly priced.* When the value of the protection is inadequate, the option is *underpriced.* When the premium is more than adequate to compensate for the capital appreciation opportunity given up, the option is *overpriced.*

To appreciate the importance of the size of the option premiums in determining investment results, the reader should compare Figures 3 and 4. In Figure 4 the option premium received by the covered call writer is only $1, not the $10 assumed in the earlier diagram. With this very low premium for a six-month option, the cross-hatched area representing the downside protection afforded by the premium is much smaller, and the shaded area depicting the upside opportunity loss is considerably larger. A change in the size of the option premium affects the size of *both* areas, with obvious implications for investment results. If any reader needs a demonstration that covered call writing is not a simple technique that almost magically "adds to the income" of a portfolio, Figure 4 should provide that demonstration. Actually, as we will see momentarily, *covered call writing is more likely to reduce portfolio returns than it is to increase them.*

The Risk-Return Trade-Off

Perhaps the significance of overpriced and underpriced options and their effect on investment results can be brought into perspective best by an examination of Figure 5. This diagram represents the expected risk-return trade-off characteristics of a variety of investment opportunities. The vertical axis (Y) measures the investor's expected annual return on investment for different investment opportunities. The horizontal axis (X) measures the degree of risk associated with a particular investment. Risk is expressed as the *standard deviation* (or variability) of the rate of return.

Treasury bills show essentially no variability of return relative to the yield anticipated at the time the bills are purchased. Though the interest rate structure as a whole can move up or down, the Treasury bill rate is fixed for the life of each bill at the level the investor accepts when he buys the bill. If an investor wishes to increase his expected return, he can purchase long-term corporate bonds. Because of changes in the market value of bonds due to interest rate fluctuations and the risk of default by some borrowers, the return from an investment in bonds for a particular time period may be greater or less than the risk-free rate of return on Treasury bills. Most investors will not be willing to hold long-term bonds unless they have the *expecta-*

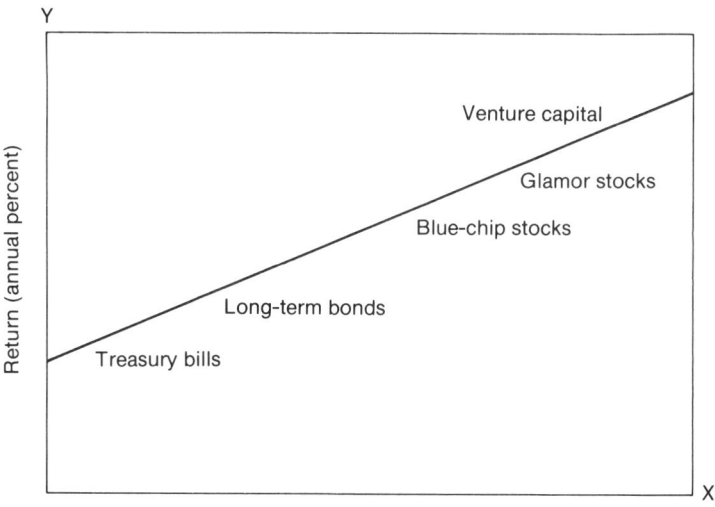

Figure 5
The Risk-Return Trade-Off

tion of a higher rate of return than they would be able to obtain from Treasury bills. The same argument holds for any other investment. If an investor buys common stocks, he will generally require a higher expected total rate of return than he would be willing to accept from long-term bonds or Treasury bills. To compensate for the risk to principal and the consequent variability in the return on investment, the investor in venture capital projects will require an even higher expected rate of return.

Covered Calls and Modern Portfolio Theory

Like any other investment vehicle, options fit into this risk-reward structure. As we saw in Figure 3, selling a call option against a stock position reduces the variability of the rate of return on investment. Thus, selling a call will have the effect of reducing portfolio risk levels. If the call option an investor sells is neither overpriced nor underpriced, sale of the option will also have the *effect of reducing the expected return on investment* because the overall risk of the portfolio will be reduced. By definition, *sale of a fairly priced option will simply move the risk-return position of a portfolio downward and to the left along* the risk-return tradeoff line of Figure 5. On the other hand, purchase of an option will increase the variability of the expected return from a portfolio. An investor who buys a fairly priced call option demonstrates willingness to accept greater variability of return in exchange for the expectation of a higher average rate of return.

If the prospective option investor remembers nothing else from this section, he should keep in mind that selling call options will tend to move the expected risk-reward position of a portfolio down and to the left along the risk-reward tradeoff line of Figure 5, whereas the purchase of call options will tend to move the expected return up and to the right. Theoretically, it is possible to reduce the risk level of a portfolio of glamor stocks to the risk level of a portfolio of Treasury bills through the sale of an appropriate number of call options. In practice, commissions and other trading costs make it difficult to maintain such a low risk level with options. Within reasonable limits, however, it is possible to use options to adjust the risk posture of a portfolio rather closely to an individual's risk preferences.

Improving Risk-Adjusted Returns

The opportunities for risk modification which options provide are extremely important, but they are not the principal reason for using options. It is possible, if option premiums are too high or too low relative to their fair value, to structure a portfolio which provides a *higher expected return per unit of risk* than any portfolio of conventional securities lying along the risk-return trade-off line. If a call option is *overpriced* and an investor sells that option, the risk-reward structure of the portfolio will move not only to the left along the risk-return line but also *above* the line. If the investor starts with Treasury bills or other short-term debt instruments and *buys underpriced* call options with a portion of his assets, it is possible to achieve an expected rate of return *above* the line while obtaining a degree of risk equivalent to the risk associated with owning a portfolio of long-term bonds or common stocks.

In contrast to the seller of overpriced call options, the investor selling underpriced calls will be reducing his return *more than proportionately to the reduction in risk*. This investor would generally be better off reducing the risk exposure of a portfolio by selling a portion of the stock and investing the proceeds in bonds or some other lower-risk investment rather than accepting inadequate option premiums. The risk-return position of a portfolio will fall below the risk-reward trade-off line in Figure 5 if underpriced options are sold against stock positions or if overpriced options are bought.

Selling a call option in a diversified equity portfolio will *always* reduce risk, as measured by the variability of the expected total return on the portfolio. Selling the option will *not* always (or even usually) enhance the overall rate of return. *By consistently selling overpriced options and/or buying underpriced options as part of a program of risk management, an investor can break away from the risk-reward trade-off line.* Few serious investors will use options for any reason other than to enhance the rate of return per unit of risk.

THE INVESTMENT SIGNIFICANCE OF LISTED PUT OPTIONS

Background

Most of the previous examples have been based on call option strategies. This focus on calls reflects the interest of most option users and the fact that an option to buy seems to be easier to comprehend than an option to sell. While many investors will never use puts, an investor will never fully understand calls without some knowledge of the relationship between calls and puts.

Basic Risk-Reward Characteristics of the Put Contract

Examining a possible transaction with the aid of a pair of diagrams should help clarify the risk-reward features of the put contract. Someone who *buys* an option to *sell* (a put) will not exercise that option unless the actual market price falls below the striking price. Consequently, the buyer of a put who holds the option until the expiration date will lose the entire premium paid for the put option unless the stock falls below the striking price. As the stock drops further below the striking price, the put buyer will begin to recover the premium paid and eventually earn a profit. The *writer* of a put will not be required to buy stock unless the market price of the stock falls below the striking price. The writer retains the entire premium if the stock price remains above the striking price.

Figure 6 shows the risk-reward positions for investors on both sides of a put contract with a $40 striking price and a $4 option premium. In Figure 6a the put buyer's profit-loss position is shown as of the date of exercise or expiration. The buyer loses the entire $4 premium if the stock price stays above $40 per share because the right to sell at $40 is worthless if a higher price is available on the stock exchange. The put buyer begins to recover premium as the stock drops below $40 and fully recovers the premium at the break-even price of $36 per share.

If the put buyer can buy stock on the market at $36 and deliver it to the writer of the put contract at a price of $40, the difference of

Figure 6
Comparison of Profit/Loss: Buyer of Put (*a*) versus Writer of Put (*b*)

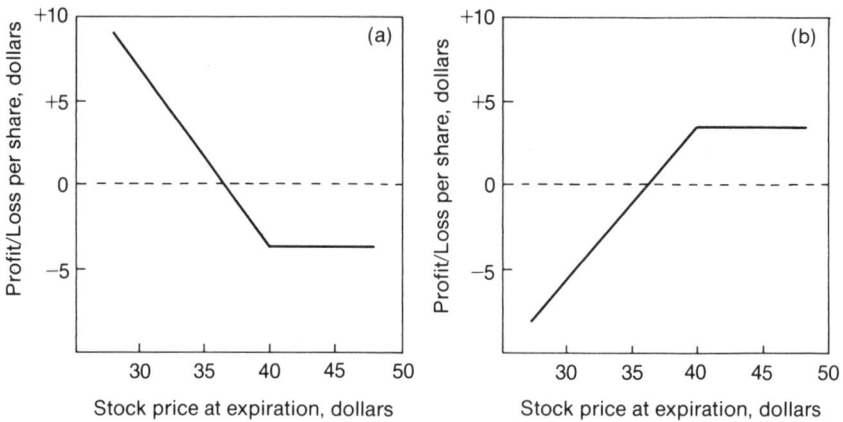

$4 exactly equals the put premium before commissions. Below $36, the put buyer profits point-for-point as the stock continues to decline because the stock can be purchased at the lower price and sold to the writer of the put at $40. The put buyer's profit per share is equal to the $40 striking price less the sum of the $4 premium and the price at which the stock is ultimately purchased.

Figure 6*b*, the put writer's profit-loss line, contrasts with Figure 6*a*. The put writer's profit is the put buyer's loss, and vice versa. If the stock sells above $40, the put writer keeps the entire premium. As the stock drops, the put writer will still be required to buy stock at $40. The put writer's loss per share, like the put buyer's profit, is equal to the $40 striking price less the sum of the $4 premium and the price at which the stock can be sold after the put is exercised.

Anyone who has examined Figure 3 will recognize in Figure 6*b* the same general shape that characterizes the covered call option writer's profit-loss position. The covered call writer, like the put writer, has a fixed profit if the stock is above the striking price on the date the option expires. The covered call writer also has a measure of downside protection, represented by the option premium. The profit-loss diagrams for the put writer and the covered call writer look the same because, *in most important respects, they are the same.*

Conversion: The Key to Analyzing Puts

A thorough understanding of puts requires an understanding of the conversion process. Through conversion, calls can be transformed into puts, and puts transformed into calls. Most of the confusion surrounding puts will be eliminated if the investor keeps in mind that the sale of a put option, margined by a Treasury bill or similar short-term debt instrument, should be the approximate risk-reward equivalent of a covered call writing position using the corresponding listed call option (i.e., the call with the same striking price and expiration date as the put).

The conversion formula expressed in terms of the present value of a put is:

$$Pp = Pc - Ps + D + \frac{S}{1 + nr}$$

where

Pp = Price of a put
Pc = Price of a corresponding call with identical striking price and expiration date
S = Striking price of the options
Ps = Price of the underlying stock
n = Life of the options expressed as fraction of a year
r = Intermediate-term interest rate on Treasury bills or high-grade commercial paper[1]
D = Present value of all dividends expected to be paid before expiration of the options[2]

Apart from tax and commission considerations (which will occasionally lead to material differences) and *neglecting for the moment the possibility of early exercise of the put,* the investor who deposits interest-earning collateral and sells a put at conversion parity with the corresponding call will have an identical profit-loss position to that of the investor who buys 100 shares of the underlying stock and sells the corresponding call option.

This formula is called the conversion equation because some in-

---

[1] For some investors the appropriate rate may be the interest rate a broker charges on debit balances. Learned papers can be written (and undoubtedly will be) on the selection of an appropriate interest rate.

[2] Note that the *present value* of the anticipated dividends will be slightly less than the actual dividend payment.

vestment firms, popularly known as "converters," have used it to convert puts into calls and calls into puts when writers prefer to sell one type of option and buyers want the other type. Once listed puts are trading on all option stocks, the equation will be used primarily *to determine the most efficient way to take a position.* Because the risk characteristics of the covered call writer's position are nearly identical to those of the put writer's position, an investor's return may be improved by taking one of these positions in preference to the other and earning a small arbitrage profit if the prices of the two options differ from the appropriate relationship. While the importance of early exercise of a put will be examined in a moment, arbitrage opportunities based on conversion relationships between puts and calls may be consistently available to certain investors. Understanding these possible arbitrage opportunities will be easier if the reader first understands the calculation of stock risk equivalents for simple stock and option positions.

Conversion and the Calculation of Risk Equivalents

It is possible to translate any listed call option position into a risk equivalent position in the underlying stock by calculating the fraction of a point by which the price of the option will change if a one-point move occurs in the underlying stock (the neutral hedge ratio).

Keeping in mind that an option is ordinarily on 100 shares of the underlying stock, *if the price of an option changes by one half point when the price of the underlying stock changes by a full point, then that option, over a reasonable period of time and a range of stock prices, will behave in essentially the same manner as 50 shares of the underlying stock.* If a call changes in price by one-quarter point for each one-point move in the stock, the option will behave like 25 shares of stock.

The same concept holds for translating put options into stock equivalents. Because the put writer's position is the risk equivalent of covered call writing, *the number of equivalent shares represented by a put is equal to 100 minus the number of equivalent shares represented by the corresponding call.* If a call behaves like the equivalent of 25 shares of the stock, by moving one-quarter point for each one-point move in the stock, then a position in the analogous put contract will be the equivalent of 75 shares (100 shares minus 25 shares). The buyer of the put is "buying" the risk equivalent of a 75-share short position in the stock because, through the conversion mechanism, buying a put is the risk equivalent of buying the analogous call (plus 25 shares) and selling the underlying stock short (minus 100 shares).

Complex option positions are usually less attractive than relatively simple ones because transaction costs rise as the complexity of the position increases. The risk-reward characteristics of complex positions can also be difficult to evaluate. An investor may find that a position he meant to be bearish was, in fact, bullish. A position that is bullish at current stock prices may *become* bearish if the stock advances sharply. *The best way to keep track of a complex position is to translate each component into its common stock equivalent and total these equivalents to get the stock equivalent risk exposure of the entire position.*

Table 3 shows the risk equivalents of a number of simple and complex stock and option positions. The security or combination de-

Table 3
Risk Comparability of Investment Positions

1.	Buy 100 shares	Buy a call Sell a put	
2.	Buy a call	Buy 100 shares Buy a put	
3.	Buy 200 shares Sell two calls	Sell two puts	Buy 100 shares Sell a put Sell a call
4.	Sell a call	Sell 100 shares short* Sell a put	
5.	Buy a put	Sell 100 shares short* Buy a call	
6.	Sell a put Sell a call	Buy 100 shares Sell two calls	Sell 100 shares short* Sell two puts
7.	Buy a put Sell a call	Sell 100 shares short*	
8.	Buy a put Buy a call	Sell 100 shares short* Buy two calls	

Note: The security or combination in the left-hand column is usually the most common of several possible ways of establishing an investment position. If all puts and calls are assumed to have the same striking price and expiration date, the positions in each row have equivalent risk characteristics.

*Positions marked with an asterisk involve a short sale of the underlying common stock and are unattractive for most investors.

scribed in the left-hand column is usually the most common way to establish a position. The other securities or combinations in the same row are risk equivalents of the left-hand column. *Unusual combinations may be the most efficient way to establish a position if they can provide the expectation of an arbitrage-type profit. The opportunity for arbitrage will arise if the market mechanism does not force put and call prices into conversion parity adjusted for the possibility of early exercise of the put.*

Early Exercise of Puts

Sellers of calls are familiar, sometimes distressingly so, with the phenomenon of early exercise. Though other factors occasionally lead to early exercise of calls, the most common cause is the call buyer's desire to obtain a dividend paid on the underlying stock. Consequently, early exercise is most common when the call is in the money and there is a relatively short time period between an ex-dividend date and expiration of the option.

Sellers of puts must be prepared for early exercise under a different set of circumstances. Specifically, the seller of a put that is in the money (i.e., the stock is selling significantly *below* the striking price) will frequently experience early exercise *after* the stock goes ex-dividend if the option has a relatively short remaining life. Whereas sellers of calls find early exercise a problem when the dividend is sizable and the call is in the money, sellers of puts will find early exercise a problem when future dividends will be small or nonexistent and the put is in the money. Early exercise of in-the-money puts will be a particular problem in less volatile stocks. A moment's reflection will suggest that early exercise of puts may become quite common in bear markets and during any period when interest rates are high.

The reasons behind the early exercise of a put are related to the economics of short selling. The total investment return to the holder of *any* security consists of the algebraic sum of any periodic dividend or interest payment and any capital gain or loss. Frequently, there will be no dividend due on the underlying stock during the remaining life of a put. Consequently, the holder of a deep-in-the-money put will not benefit from a stock price reduction on an ex-dividend date. The holder of this put will be carrying the equivalent of a short position in the stock. Only if the put is bought *below* intrinsic value will the buyer of the put get credit for the proceeds of the implicit short sale. On the other hand, if the put is selling below its intrinsic value, an arbitrageur can profit by exercising it and reinvesting the cash received in a security with a higher expected total return. A deep-in-the-money put is an unstable position.

Call writers have learned that the buyer of a call has absolute control over who will receive a particular dividend on the underlying stock. The call buyer may exercise this control to deprive a call writer of the dividend. The owner of a put exercises similar control over who will receive a dividend. Ordinarily, the holder of a put will choose to "receive" dividends or get "credit" for them in the form of a probable decline in the stock price on the ex-dividend date. If there will be no dividends during the remaining life of an in-the-money put option, it can sell at or slightly below intrinsic value. There will probably be a greater tendency to exercise in-the-money puts than in-the-money calls because, in effect, *the carrying cost of a long position can be eliminated by exercising the put.* The effect of early exercise on the value of a put can be significant. Because of the potential for early exercise, the value of a put will always be greater than the value given by the conversion equation.

TAX TREATMENT OF OPTION TRANSACTIONS[3]

Tax Treatment from the Viewpoint of the Options Buyer

Table 4 summarizes the tax treatment of the options buyer if the buyer is an *individual* or some other entity which treats options as capital assets. Tax treatment for broker-dealers and certain other options holders will be materially different.

Tax Treatment from the Viewpoint of the Option Writer

Table 5 shows tax treatment from the viewpoint of an *individual* who is writing put and call options. As in the case of the option buyer, the tax treatment may be somewhat different for other entities.

---

[3] A more comprehensive discussion of tax considerations can be found on pp. 127-71 of Gastineau, *The Stock Options Manual.*

Table 4
Tax Treatment from Option Buyer's Viewpoint

		Tax Treatment of Option Premiums			
Description of Transaction	Holding Period of Option	Nature of Gain or Loss	Timing of Recognition of Gain or Loss	Effect on Common Stock Holding If Any	Comments (also see text)
1. Buy put:					
a. Having owned underlying stock less than 12 months and 1 day.					
(1) Sell put.	Short-term.	Short-term capital gain or loss.	Date of sale of option.	Holding period of stock is eliminated for purposes of long-term gains by purchase of put. Any gain on stock is long term 12 months and 1 day after put is sold. Any loss on stock is long term 12 months and 1 day after stock was purchased.	This is a change from an earlier IRS position that if a put was sold (as opposed to exercise or expiration), the short sale rule did not apply.
	Long-term.	Long-term capital gain or loss.			
(2) Exercise put.	Immaterial.	Cost of put is deducted from proceeds of sale of stock.	Date of exercise.	Any gain on common stock will be short term. Any loss will be long term if the date of exercise is more than 12 months and 1 day after purchase of the stock.	
(3) Let put expire.	Short-term. Long-term.	Short-term capital loss. Long-term capital loss.	Date of expiration.	Holding period of stock for purposes of determining long-term gain begins on date of expiration of put. For purposes of determining loss, holding period begins on day stock was purchased.	

b. Then buy underlying stock one or more days later.			
(1) Sell put.	Short-term.	Short-term capital gain or loss.	Date of sale of option.	If stock is sold for a gain, holding period starts on day option is sold. If stock sold at loss, holding period starts on day stock was purchased.
	Long-term.	Long-term capital gain or loss.		
(2) Exercise put.	Immaterial.	Cost of put is deducted from proceeds of sale of stock.	Date of exercise.	Gain on common stock is short term after deducting cost of put from proceeds. Loss will be long term if stock held more than 12 months and 1 day.
(3) Let put expire.	Short-term.	Short-term capital loss.	Date of expiration.	For purposes of determining taxation of gain, holding period of stock begins on day put expires. If a loss, holding period begins on day stock was purchased.
	Long-term.	Long-term capital loss.		
c. Buy underlying stock on same day and identified put as intended to be used with this stock position.				
(1) Sell put.	Short-term.	Short-term capital gain or loss.	Date of sale of option.	If stock is sold for a gain, holding period starts on day option is sold. If stock sold at loss, holding period starts on day stock was purchased.
	Long-term.	Long-term capital gain or loss.		

Table 4 *(concluded)*

Tax Treatment of Option Premiums

Description of Transaction	Holding Period of Option	Nature of Gain or Loss	Timing of Recognition of Gain or Loss	Effect on Common Stock Holding If Any	Comments (also see text)
(2) Exercise put.	Same as stock.	Cost of put is deducted from proceeds of sale of stock.	Date of exercise.	Loss is short or long term depending on holding period from date of purchase.	
(3) Let put expire.	Same as stock.	Add cost of put to basis of stock.	Date of sale of stock.	Gain or loss on sale of stock is short or long term depending on holding period.	Holding period of stock starts on day stock and put are purchased. Note recognition of put loss is deferred until stock is sold.
d. Do not own related stock during life of put.					
(1) Sell put.	Short-term.	Short-term capital gain or loss.	Date of sale of option.		
	Long-term.	Long-term capital gain or loss.			
(2) Let put expire.	Short-term.	Short-term capital gain or loss.	Date of expiration.		
	Long-term.	Long-term capital gain or loss.			
2. Buy call:					
a. Sell call.	Short-term.	Short-term capital gain or loss.	Date of sale of option.	Purchase of call can cause wash sale.	Short sale of stock does not affect holding period of call. Long-term loss on call can be avoided by exercising call and selling stock even if call has been owned more than 12 months and 1 day.

b. Exercise call.	Immaterial.	Cost of call added to purchase cost to determine basis of stock.	Date of sale of stock.	Purchase of call can cause wash sale. Holding period of stock starts on day call is exercised.
c. Let call expire.	Short-term. Long-term.	Short-term capital loss. Long-term capital loss.	Date of expiration.	Purchase of call can cause wash sale.
3. Buy straddle or other combination option.		Same as separate put and call.		Same as separate put and call. On conventional options cost of straddle is allocated 55% to call and 45% to put unless there is a substantial reason to allocate in another way.
4. Adjustment of striking price or number of shares for dividends or other capital changes.				No effect on income, gain or loss, or tax basis.

Note that recognition of gain or loss on call is deferred until stock is sold.

Table 5
Tax Treatment from Option Writer's Viewpoint

Description of Transaction	Holding Period of Option	Nature of Gain or Loss	Timing of Recognition of Gain or Loss	Effect on Common Stock Holding If Any	Comments (also see text)
1. Write put:					
a. Put expires.	Immaterial.	Short-term capital gain.	Date of expiration.	No effect.	
b. Put exercised.	Immaterial.	Proceeds from sale of put reduce basis of stock purchased.	Date stock acquired through exercise is sold.	Reduces basis.	Holding period of stock starts on day put is exercised. Note that recognition of tax effect of premium is deferred until stock is sold.
c. Put repurchased.	Immaterial.	Short-term capital gain or loss.	Date of repurchase.	No effect.	
2. Write call:					
a. Call expires.	Immaterial.	Short-term capital gain.	Date of expiration.	No effect if shareholder is an individual.	
b. Call exercised.	Immaterial.	Call premiums added to proceeds of sale of stock, character of gain or loss on stock determines nature of total gain.	Date of exercise if stock delivered long, date of covering purchase if stock delivered short.	No effect except on lot of stock delivered against exercise.	Holding period of stock extends from purchase date to exercise date if stock is delivered long.
c. Call repurchased.	Immaterial.	Short-term capital gain or loss.	Date of repurchase.	Might create wash sale in rare instances.	
3. Write straddle or other combination.		Same as separate put and call.		Same as separate put and call.	Special treatment of straddles was eliminated by the Tax Reform Act of 1976.
4. Adjustment of striking price or number of shares for dividends, splits, or other capital changes.					No effect on income, gain or loss, or tax basis.

The Option Pricing Formula

12 RICHARD M. BOOKSTABER, Ph.D.
Associate Professor of Economics and Finance
Graduate School of Business
Brigham Young University

The most important breakthrough in option analysis has been the development of the option pricing formula. The formula gives the price of an option as a function of observable variables, such as the stock price, the exercise price, the time-to-maturity of the option, the riskless interest rate, and the volatility of the stock. The option formula is one of the most powerful tools in finance. The analytical method used in deriving the formula can be applied to virtually any financial security. It has thus opened up a new era in understanding and pricing corporate financial instruments.

Since the variables used in the formula are easily observable, the use of the option pricing formula has extended past the academic sphere to the investment profession at large. There are several option pricing services that provide clients with the theoretical option price. Indeed, most traders on the floor of the CBOE subscribe to option pricing services. Also, several investment firms use the option pricing formula in advising their clients.

However, the number who use the formula exceeds the number who understand it. The formula was originally derived using advanced mathematical methods that obscured the intuition behind

---

*This reading is adapted from chapter 4 of Richard M. Bookstaber, *Option Pricing and Strategies in Investing*, published by Addison-Wesley Publishing Company, 1981.

the formula. The practical implications of the formula for profiting from mispriced options and for deriving hedges in more complex strategies has remained unexplored until recently.

In this chapter we will give an explanation of the pricing formula, and show how to exploit profit opportunities if the market price of the option differs from the option formula price.[1]

A ONE-PERIOD EXAMPLE

Suppose a stock is currently priced at $100 a share, and in one period it will be worth either $95 or $110. There is a call option available on the stock with an exercise price of $100 and one period to expiration. The current price of the option is $800. See Figure 1. The riskless interest rate for both borrowing and lending is 5 percent over the one time period.

Figure 1*

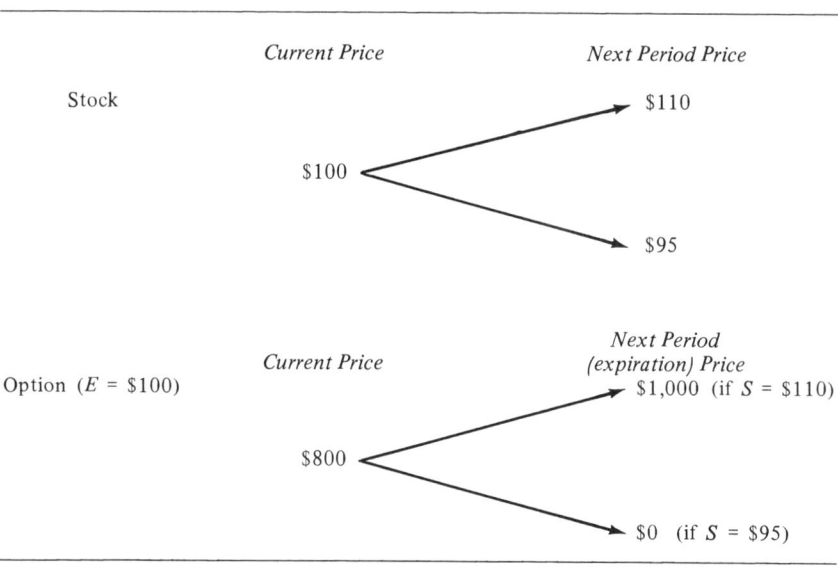

*E = exercise price; S = stock price

Consider the following portfolio strategy. The investor writes three call options, receiving an income of $2,400, and buys 200 shares of the stock at $100 per share. The net initial position is then $17,600. Assume the investor can then borrow at the 5 percent rate to cover

---

[1] The appendix to chapter 4 of Bookstaber, *Option Pricing and Strategies in Investing*, presents an intuitive derivation of the option pricing formula that uses only elementary algebra, progressing from the simple one-period formula to a many-period formula, and then to the more popular continuous-time formula.

the position, so that the net initial investment is zero (the stock is being purchased entirely from the proceeds of the option sale and the borrowed funds). What will the investor's return be at the end of the period?

If the stock drops to $95 by next period, the option will expire worthless. The investor will need to repay $18,480 (the $17,600 plus 5 percent interest to the bank), and will hold $19,000 worth of stock. The net position will be $19,000 − $18,480 = $520. Since the initial investment was zero, the investor will make a profit if the stock drops.

If the stock increases in value to $110, $3,000 will be needed to cover the option position, and the stock will be worth $22,000. With the cost of the borrowed funds, the investor's net position will be $22,000 − $3,000 − $18,480 = $520. Once again the strategy will net a profit. This strategy is illustrated in Table 1.

This transaction is remarkable because not only is a profit made in either case, but the profit is riskless—it is exactly the same no matter

Table 1
Trading Strategy When the Option Price Is $800

	Current Position	End-of-Period Position	
		$S = 95$	$S = 110$
Write 3 call options	$ 2,400	$ 0	$ (3,000)
Buy 200 shares	(20,000)	19,000	22,000
Borrow at 5 percent	17,600	(18,480)	(18,480)
Net profit	$ 0	$ 520	$ 520

which way the stock moves. Also, the profit is made for no net investment. A profit that is obtained at no risk and for no initial investment is called an *arbitrage profit*. If any amount of arbitrage profit is possible, then an investor can make unlimited profits. Given a chance to make a certain profit of $520 with no investment, the investor's position needs only to increase by x times and make x times as great a profit risklessly and with no initial investment.

There is only one price for the option that will eliminate this profit opportunity. As Table 2 shows, if this strategy is followed when the option is priced at $635, there will be no arbitrage profit. If the price is below $635, the reverse strategy of buying three options, selling short 200 shares of stock, and placing the proceeds of the transaction into the riskless asset will yield an arbitrage profit. The results of this strategy are illustrated in Table 3 for an option price of $500.

Table 2
Trading Strategy When the Option Price Is $635

	Current Position	End-of-Period Position	
		$S = 95$	$S = 110$
Write 3 call options	$ 1,905	$ 0	$ (3,000)
Buy 200 shares	(20,000)	19,000	22,000
Borrow at 5 percent	18,095	(19,000)	(19,000)
Net profit	$ 0	$ 0	$ 0

In this simple example the option price of $635 is the correct option price. If the option is at that price in the market, then there is no arbitrage opportunity. If it is mispriced, then there is the possibility of obtaining large profits for no risk. The option pricing formula that we will discuss in the next section gives this correct option

Table 3
Trading Strategy When the Option Price Is $500

	Current Position	End-of-Period Position	
		$S = 95$	$S = 110$
Buy 3 call options	$ (1,500)	$ 0	$ 3,000
Sell short 200 shares	20,000	(19,000)	(22,000)
Lend at 5 percent	(18,500)	19,425	19,425
Net profit	$ 0	$ 425	$ 425

price under far more realistic assumptions than those used in this example. There is no law that requires the market price to equal this correct option price. But if it does not, then the knowledgeable investor can make large profits for little or no risk by taking the appropriate position in the mispriced option and the underlying stock.

The existence of an arbitrage profit puts a mechanism into action that will drive the option price to the value that eliminates the profit opportunity. For example, if the option is initially priced at $800, and more and more investors follow the arbitrage strategy by selling options, the option price will need to drop in order to entice others to buy the increased supply of options. If the option price is below the correct value, the option price will be driven up as investors try to buy more options. The pressure on the option price will continue in either case until the option is priced at $635.

Note that any of the three values—the stock, the option, or the interest rate—can adjust to eliminate the profit opportunity. Just as the arbitrage strategy puts pressure on the option price, it also will tend to move the other values in the direction that eliminates the arbitrage profit. As investors follow the arbitrage strategy, they will buy stock, raising the price of the stock, and they will borrow more funds, putting upward pressure on the riskless rate of interest. Thus, the option price is set by relative, and not absolute, prices.

If an arbitrage profit is possible, the option is no more mispriced than the stock or the interest rate. Given any values for two of the three, there is a unique price for the third that will eliminate the profit opportunity. Since the options market is usually thinner and more elastic than the other markets, it will adjust to a relative price discrepancy before the stock or the riskless asset will. So, for convenience, we generally speak of the option as being mispriced.

Making $1.5 Million at the State Fair

To see what is happening with this strategy, let us take a more down-to-earth example. Assume you are running a refreshment stand at the state fair. You find that there are three other stands there, one selling hot dogs for 50 cents each, one selling nine-ounce cups of cola for 30 cents, and another selling hot dogs with a six-ounce cup of cola for 75 cents.

It is apparent that you can package the hot dogs and six-ounce cola for less than the going price of 75 cents. You purchase hot dogs from the one stand and cola from the other in the proportions of two colas for every three hot dogs, and repackage the two to match the product of the third stand.

If the market is competitive, you can sell all the servings of hot dogs and six-ounce colas you please at 75 cents. The cost of the package is only 70 cents, so by buying the parts and packaging them as the whole, you make a sure profit. If the pricing went the other way, so that the hot dog-cola combination cost only 60 cents, you would buy the package and resell them separately. Refer to Table 4.

The fact that two items can replicate the third indicates that the two must be priced in a certain proportion relative to the third. In particular, to eliminate this profit opportunity, it must be that three hot dogs and two of the nine-ounce colas must sell for the same price as it costs for two of the hot dog-cola combinations.

The pricing of the options relative to the stock and the riskless asset is determined in the same way. The combination of the short position in the call option and the long position in the stock will replicate the riskless asset, in that the return from the position will be riskless. Since the option and stock can be packaged in a particular proportion that replicates the riskless asset, it must be that the portfolio of the two sells for the same amount as the riskless asset. If it does not, then one can construct a "home-made" riskless asset by taking the appropriate position in the option and the stock, with the home-made riskless asset costing less to produce than the going market price for the riskless asset.

Or, one can combine the stock and the riskless asset in a proportion that will yield the same payoff as the option at the time of expi-

Table 4
How to Make $1.5 Million at the State Fair

1. Buy:	Going price
3 hot dogs	$.50 each = $1.50
2 nine-ounce colas	.30 each = .60
Total	$2.10
2. Repackage and sell:	
3 hot dog-six-ounce cola combos	$.75 each = $2.25
Less: Cost	$2.10
Profit	$ .15
3. Repeat 10 million times	

ration. Or, one can combine the option with the riskless asset to assure a return that will be the same as the return to the stock at the end of the period.

For example, if the investor combines a long position in three options with $18,100 in the riskless asset, the return will be the same as if 200 shares of the stock are held. If the stock drops to $95 a share, the investor will receive $18,100 (1.05) = $19,000, and if the stock goes up to $110 a share, the investor will receive $19,000 from the riskless asset and $3,000 from the option, for a return of $22,000. Since the portfolio of the options and the riskless asset exactly replicates the payoff of the stock at the end of the period, it must be that the portfolio of the two is priced so that it equals the stock price at the start of the period. Otherwise, profit opportunities will be possible by taking a long or a short position in the portfolio.

The fact that any two of the assets can be combined to produce a portfolio with the same payoff as the third is the key to the arbitrage opportunities that we demonstrated. If the relative price of the three is such that the replicating portfolio for any of the assets has a different price than the price of the asset itself, then an arbitrage opportunity will exist.

The example shown here is obviously simplified. We are dealing with one time period to expiration, and with stock price movements that are ·unrealistic. Although the extension of this example to a more realistic setting is not presented here,[2] this example does provide the basis for option pricing in the more realistic setting. The formation of the riskless hedge and the possibility for arbitrage profits are the motivating principles for option pricing in the more complex setting.

THE BLACK-SCHOLES OPTION PRICING FORMULA

The option example used in the previous section is unrealistic. The stock can take on any number of values, not just one of two values as assumed. Nor is trading done on a period-by-period basis. The stock market operates continuously during trading hours.

However, a more realistic approach can be developed by extending the example. If we extend the example to many periods rather than one period, and let the length of each time period become small (so that, for example, we have 180 periods of one-day duration rather than using two periods of three-month duration each), then we approach more realistic trading conditions. If we further assume that the stock price can take on any number of values in a given period of time, then we remove the objection of the two-state stock price movement of our example as well.

These assumptions are far less restrictive, and it is possible to fashion an example, such as the one we used in the previous section, with these assumptions. There will still be a correct option price, and it will still be the case that an arbitrage profit is possible if the option price differs from that correct price.

The correct option price in this more realistic case is given by the Black-Scholes formula. The formula determines the option price that is necessary to eliminate the possibility of profit opportunities. As in our one-period example, if the option price does not conform to this price, then there is the opportunity to make large profits by using the correct hedging strategy with the option and the stock. Unlike our example, the Black-Scholes formula finds the correct price under assumptions that more closely resemble the actual trading place.

The Black-Scholes formula is:

$$C = SN(d_1) - Ee^{-rT}N(d_2)$$

where

$$d_1 = (\ln(S/E) + (r + \tfrac{1}{2}\sigma^2)T)/\sigma\sqrt{T}$$
$$d_2 = d_1 - \sigma\sqrt{T}$$

---

[2] The extension appears in the appendix to chapter 4 of Bookstaber, *Option Pricing,* and may be found on a more mathematical level in Richard J. Rendleman and Brit J. Bartter, "Two-State Option Pricing," *Journal of Finance,* December 1979, pp. 1093-1110; and in John C. Cox, Stephen A. Ross, and Mark M. Rubinstein, "Option Pricing: A Simplified Approach," *Journal of Financial Economics,* September 1979, pp. 229-63.

In this formula, C is the option price, E is the exercise price, S is the stock price, T is the time to expiration, r is the interest rate, ln is the natural logrithm, e is the exponential (e = 2.7183), and σ^2 is the instantaneous variance of the stock price, which is the measure of stock price volatility. $N(\cdot)$ is the cumulative normal distribution function.

What Does the Formula Mean?

There is no way around the fact that this formula is complicated. Here we just present some ideas to relate the formula as more than a mass of algebra.

Consider the simple case where the underlying stock has a return that is certain. This means that the variance of the stock price, σ^2, is equal to zero. As σ^2 approaches zero, both d_1 and d_2 will become very large, and the value of the normal distribution function in both parts of the formula, $N(d_1)$ and $N(d_2)$, will equal one. The Black-Scholes formula in that case will simply be equal to $C = S - Ee^{-rT}$.

In other words, in the extreme case when the stock price movement is known for certain, and hence when the stock volatility is equal to zero, the Black-Scholes formula reduces to the current stock price minus the present discounted value of the exercise price. It is well known that this is the fair option price in the riskless case. To illustrate this, consider the following hypothetical strategy: Suppose an investor buys 100 shares of stock worth $5,400 on margin. However, instead of securing the typical margin loan, the investor makes an initial payment, C, and promises a future payment of $5,000 in six months. The future payment is promised on a no-recourse basis, with the stock used as collateral. If the investor fails to make the payment on the maturity date of the loan, the lender gains ownership of the stock and has no further recourse or claim on the investor. If the investor makes the final payment, the stock is received free and clear.

What will be the investor's best course of action once the loan comes due? Clearly, if the stock is worth more than the promised payment of $5,000, the investor will pay off the loan to gain clear ownership to the stock. The net profit will be the value of the stock at the maturity of the loan, S^*, less the loan payment, or $S^* - 5,000$. If the stock is worth less than the promised payment, the investor will be better off just walking away from the loan and letting the lender get claim to the stock, since the payment of $5,000 to reclaim the stock will net a loss.

The position of an investor under this loan arrangement is the same as an investor who has purchased a European option on the stock with an exercise price, E, of $50 and time to expiration, T, of six months. (A European option is an option that can only be exercised at the time of maturity.) With this loan and for an initial payment of C, the investor has obtained the right to purchase the stock for a payment of E dollars per share on the maturity date T.

Concluding the hypothetical strategy, since the investor promises to pay the lender E dollars at the maturity of the loan, the present value of the payment (assuming it were riskless) is Ee^{-rT}. If the loan were riskless, the initial payment would be the difference between the stock that is being delivered, S, and the present value of the promised future payment, or $S - Ee^{-rT}$.

When the stock price movement is uncertain, things get more difficult. If σ^2 is greater than zero, $N(d_1)$ and $N(d_2)$ will be between zero and one. The Black-Scholes formula will then involve some weighting of S and Ee^{-rT}, with the weights being between zero and one. That is, rather than having the simple case of $C = S - Ee^{-rT}$, the formula will have the form $C = pS - qEe^{-rT}$, where $p = N(d_1)$ and $q = N(d_2)$. These weights are actually probabilities drawn from the normal distribution function.

Computing the Correct Option Price with the Black-Scholes Formula

The use of the formula requires the input of five variables: the stock price, the exercise price, the time of maturity, the interest rate, and the volatility of the stock. To illustrate the use of the formula, we will specify particular values for these variables to calculate the value of a Honeywell October 60 option that has 88 days to expiration:

$S = 68$
$E = 60$
$T = 88/365 = .241$ years
$r = 6$ percent per annum
$\sigma = .4$

The first three variables are easily observable from the option quotation. The time-to-maturity is obtained by counting the number of calendar days until the time of maturity, and then dividing it by 365 to get the time-to-maturity in annual terms.[3] T, r, and σ are all ex-

---

[3] The method for estimating the interest rate and the volatility is discussed in chapter 5 of Bookstaber, *Option Pricing*, as well as in the following references: M. Parkinson, "The Extreme Value Method for Estimating the Variance of the Rate of Return," *Journal of Business*, January 1980, pp. 61-65; M. Garman and M. Klass, "On the Estimation of Security Price Volatilities from Historical Data," *Journal of Business*, January 1980, pp. 67-78; and H. Latane and R. Rendleman, "Standard Deviations of Stock Price Ratios Implied in Option Prices," *Journal of Finance*, May 1976, pp. 369-81.

pressed in annual terms. Recalling the formula and substituting the appropriate variables, we have the option price as:

$$C = 68 N(d_1) - 60 e^{-.06\,(.241)} N(d_2)$$

where

$$d_1 = \frac{\ln\left(\frac{68}{60}\right) + (.06 + \tfrac{1}{2}\,.16)\,.241}{.4 \times .491} = \frac{(.125 + .034)}{.196} = .808$$

$$d_2 = .808 - .196 = .612$$

From normal distribution tables, we find:

$$N(d_1) = N(.808) = .790$$
$$N(d_2) = N(.612) = .729$$

The values for $N(.808)$ and $N(.612)$ are tabulated in most elementary probability and statistics texts, and are also in mathematical handbooks. Using these values, we obtain the call option price:

$$C = 68(.790) - 60 e^{-.01446}(.729) = 10.60$$

This option formula gives the correct option price in the sense that if the option price differs substantially from this price, there will be significant profit opportunities. The strategies to use in reaping those profits will be discussed later.

This option formula conforms with the well-known properties of options.[4] The correct option price as given by the formula will depend on the stock price, the exercise price, the time to expiration, the riskless interest rate, and the volatility of the stock. With this formula we can determine just what the option price must be to eliminate profit opportunities.

In terms of practical usefulness, what the formula *does not* depend on is almost as important as what it does depend on. In particular, the formula does not depend on any assessment of the future or expected stock price. Also, it does not depend on investors' attitudes toward risk. Since these are not observable, any formula that required them as inputs would be useless. The fact that the option formula is independent of expectations and other subjective measures bodes well for its applicability.

---

[4] These properties are discussed in chapter 3 of Bookstaber, *Option Pricing,* and in Robert C. Merton, "Theory of Rational Option Pricing," *Bell Journal of Economics and Management Science,* Spring 1973, pp. 141-83.

THE HEDGE RATIO

Going back to our initial example, the detection of the mispriced option was just the start of the arbitrage strategy. A position was not only taken in the option, a position was taken in the stock as well. This position gave the investor a hedge against unfavorable stock price movements—no matter which way the stock price moved, the value of the investor's position and the profit were unchanged.

As this suggests, a successful option strategy not only involves taking the appropriate position in a mispriced option, it also involves the second step of taking the appropriate hedge position in the underlying stock. The option position allows the investor to profit from the mispriced option, and the hedge position in the stock allows the profit to be obtained risklessly, unaffected by shifts in the stock price.

The hedge ratio is of critical importance in formulating option strategies. It is not enough for the investor to find a mispriced option; a profit can only be assured if the mispriced option is properly hedged. Without the proper hedge, an adverse stock price movement can wipe away the profit from a slight mispricing in the option position. Because the calculation of the proper hedge is related to the Black-Scholes formula, it will be explained in the balance of this chapter.

Suppose an investor feels that a particular option currently selling at 7 is overpriced in the market. If it is overpriced, the investor will get a premium for writing it that is above the fair premium. But once the option is written, the investor will be subject to the risks of later changes in the stock price. The option may be overpriced now, but if the underlying stock increases a few points, the option will rise in price. If the investor's position in the option is not covered, a substantial amount could be lost because of the stock price changing, even if the investor was initially correct about the mispricing. Suppose the option price changes by half as much as any change in the stock price. If the stock rises by one point, the option will rise by half a point. A one-point rise in the stock will mean the value of the investor's position in the option will drop. To cover the position after the stock rise, the option that the investor originally sold for only $700 will need to be bought back for $750. The .5 point rise in the option will mean a loss of $50.

The investor can guard against this possible loss by taking a hedge position in the stock. If 50 shares of stock are bought, the investor will be hedged against a shift in the stock price—if the stock rises (or drops), the total position will be unaffected.

If the stock rises by one point, the option position will drop by

$50, but the stock position will increase in value by $50—the $1 increase in the stock price multiplied by the 50 shares of stock held long.

If the stock drops a point, then the option position will increase in value by $50, since the option sold for $700 can now be bought back for $650. However, the stock position will drop by $50 from the one-point decline in the stock price. In either case, the net position is unchanged—the investor has been insulated from movements in the stock price.

If the investor had bought the option rather than writing it, the position in the option would be hedged by selling the stock short rather than by buying the stock. The hedge position in the stock is always the opposite of the position in the call option. If long in the option, the investor is short in the stock. If short in the option (that is, if the investor writes the option), then a long position should be taken in the stock to hedge. The position is always opposite because the call option moves in the same direction as the stock price, while in a hedge the option and stock position must move in opposite directions. The option may move up half a point with a one-point move in the stock, but since the investor has opposite positions in the option and the stock, one position will move up and the other will move down. And if the stock and the option are held in the right proportions, the movements will exactly counterbalance each other, so that the investor's total position will be unchanged.

The ratio of the number of shares of stock that must be held per option held in order to fully hedge against movements in the stock price is called the *hedge ratio*.

In this example, the hedge ratio was $-.5$. The minus sign is used to remind us that the stock and option are held in opposite positions. If the option is held long (a positive position), then the stock must be held short (a negative position). Since one position is always negative and the other positive, the ratio of the two positions will be negative. By convention, a long position in a security is denoted by a plus and a short position by a minus. A -100 share position in the stock means 100 shares are held short. Similarly, a -5 option position means the investor has written (is short) 5 options.

The ideal hedge ratio from the standpoint of eliminating the investor's exposure to the risk of the stock is denoted by h, and is given by setting the hedge ratio according to the formula $h = -N(d_1)$, where $N(\cdot)$ is the cumulative normal distribution function, and where d_1 is defined as in the Black-Scholes formula. The term $N(d_1)$ is part of the first term in the Black-Scholes option formula. This term gives the change in the option price caused by a change in the stock price; that is, $N(d_1) = \Delta C/\Delta S$ where Δ means "change in." Thus, if the hedge ratio is set equal to $N(d_1)$, so that h times as much stock is held in a position opposite to the position of the option (that is, with the stock held long if the option is written, and with the stock sold short if the option is bought), then the movement in the option position will exactly counteract any movement induced by shifts in the stock price, and the value of the investor's position will be unchanged on net.

Using the Honeywell 60 option from the example in the last section, we can compute the hedge ratio for that option as $h = -N(.808) = -0.790$. This hedge ratio means that if the Honeywell stock changes in value by one point, the value of the call option will change by just under 0.8 points. If the stock goes from 68 to 69, the option will go from 10.60 to 11.39. Thus, if 79 shares of stock are used to hedge each call, the change in the stock price will counterbalance any change in the option price, and the investor's position will be unaffected by the movement in the stock price. See Table 5.

Once a mispriced option is discovered, the investor can form a riskless hedge by buying $N(d_1)$ shares of stock for each option written (if the option is above its correct price), or by selling short $N(d_1)$ shares of stock for each option bought (if the option is below the correct price).

Table 5
Effect of Stock Price Change on Hedge Position

Current price:	
Honeywell stock	$68
Honeywell October 60 call	$10.60
New price:	
Honeywell stock	$69
Honeywell October 60 call	$11.39
Initial position ($h = -.790$):	
Buy one Honeywell October 60 call	
Sell short 79 shares of Honeywell stock	
Effect of price change on position:	
Profit on option position	1,139 − 1,060 = $79
Profit on stock position	−79 × (69 − 68) = −$79
Net change in position	$ 0

The hedge position for the option will change as the stock price changes. It will also change as the time-to-expiration changes. Thus, the hedging strategy involves a dynamic hedge. The ratio must be reevaluated frequently and the riskless hedge adjusted whenever the stock price changes significantly, and as the time-to-expiration declines. Also, the hedge ratio is a local measure. That is, it represents a riskless hedge only if the stock price moves by small amounts. If the stock price suddenly jumps 5 or 10 points, the ratio will not assure the riskless hedge will be maintained. This means that the possibility of jumps in the stock price that cannot be covered by adjusting the hedge will affect the riskiness of the hedging strategy.

OVERVIEW OF THE OPTION PRICING LITERATURE

The seminal paper in the option pricing literature is the 1973 article by Fischer Black and Myron Scholes.[5] This is the first paper to derive the option pricing formula by using the arbitrage argument.

Other attempts to derive an option pricing formula preceded the work of Black and Scholes, and many bear a strong similarity to the Black-Scholes formula. However, none of the previous formulas were developed in a general equilibrium framework, and none could be computed solely on the basis of observable variables. Clifford W. Smith provides a review of these other pricing formulas and a general survey of the option pricing literature.[6]

Robert Merton derives the continuous-time time option formula under a set of less restrictive assumptions.[7] Both the Black-Scholes and the Merton papers are very technical. Later authors have presented less difficult derivations of the formula. John C. Cox, Stephen A. Ross, and Mark Rubinstein[8] and Richard J. Rendleman and Brit J. Bartter[9] present a binomial approach to the formula that was initially suggested by William F. Sharpe.[10] The method of derivation used in this chapter closely follows their approach, and a formal demonstration of the relationship between the discrete and the continuous-time formulas is presented in their work. Other authors, including Michael Parkinson[11] and Michael J. Brennan and Eduardo S. Schwartz,[12] use a discrete-time approach to the option pricing formula based on the methods of numerical analysis.

CONCLUSION

As with any mathematical construct, the option pricing formula must be carefully adapted to the realities of the marketplace and, further, must be empirically tested to assess its accuracy and to

---

[5] "The Pricing of Options and Corporate Liabilities," *Journal of Political Economy,* May 1973, pp. 637-54.
[6] "Option Pricing: A Review," *Journal of Financial Economics,* March 1976, pp. 3-51.
[7] "Theory of Rational Option Pricing."
[8] "Option Pricing: A Simplified Approach."
[9] "Two-State Option Pricing."
[10] *Investments* (Englewood Cliffs, N.J.: Prentice-Hall, 1978).
[11] "Option Pricing: The American Put," *Journal of Business,* January 1977, pp. 21-36.
[12] "The Valuation of American Put Options," *Journal of Finance,* May 1977, pp. 449-62.

illuminate any of its shortcomings. To be a practical tool, the option pricing formula must be generalized to meet a number of factors that are assumed away in its derivation—factors, such as variable interest rates and stock price changes induced by dividend payments.[13] When the proper generalizations and adjustments are made, the formula becomes a useful tool for finding mispriced options.[14]

The journey from the derivation of the formula to its application is marked not only by adjustments to meet "real world" behavior but more importantly by its proper use in constructing knowledgeable option strategies. It must be remembered that while the formula is an indispensable tool or input in selecting and executing profitable strategies, it must be combined with a good understanding of the nature of option strategies to be employed most effectively.

---

[13] The modification of the option formula for taxes is presented by Myron Scholes, "Taxes and the Pricing of Options," *Journal of Finance,* May 1976, pp. 319-32. Dividends are considered by Merton, "Theory of Rational Option Pricing"; R. Geske, "A Note on an Analytical Valuation Formula for Unprotected American Call Options on Stocks with Known Dividends," *Journal of Financial Economics,* December 1979, pp. 375-80; and Cox, Ross, and Rubinstein, "Option Pricing: A Simplified Approach." Merton also considers the effects of variable interest rates. The effect of different stochastic processes on the stock prices is discussed in John C. Cox and Stephen A. Ross, "The Valuation of Options for Alternative Stochastic Processes," *Journal of Financial Economics,* March 1976, pp. 145-66; and in Merton's two papers, "Theory of Rational Option Pricing" and "Option Pricing When Underlying Stock Returns Are Discontinuous," *Journal of Financial Economics,* March 1976, pp. 125-44.

[14] There is an increasing number of empirical papers that test the accuracy of the option formula or the existence of profit opportunities through the hedging strategy. See Dan Galai, "Pricing of Options and the Efficiency of the Chicago Board of Options Exchange," unpublished doctoral dissertation, University of Chicago, 1975, and "Tests of Market Efficiency of the Chicago Board of Options Exchange," *Journal of Business,* April 1977, pp. 167-97; D. Chiras and S. Manaster, "The Information Content of Option Prices and a Test of Market Efficiency," *Journal of Financial Economics,* March 1978, pp. 213-34; and Robert R. Trippi, "A Test of Option Market Efficiency Using a Random-Walk Valuation Model," *Journal of Economics and Business,* Winter 1977, pp. 93-98.

Financial Futures: Hedging Interest-Rate Risk*

13   ALLAN M. LOOSIGIAN
President, A. M. Loosigian & Co.
Stamford, Connecticut

INTRODUCTION

Commodity futures and fixed income securities traditionally have been regarded as widely disparate financial markets. But since the advent of the interest rate, or financial futures, market in early 1976, seasoned commodity traders have had to master the intricacies of various types of debt instruments, and corporate financial executives and institutional investment managers have been thrust for the first time into what was for most of them the alien world of futures trading. The futures men and women and the securities people have since then endeavored to create a common language and become accustomed to doing business with one another.

THE DEVELOPMENT OF INTEREST RATE FUTURES

The impetus to this new, hybrid market was the sharp increase during the 1970s and early 1980s in the volatility and absolute level of interest rates. Reacting to the debilitating effect of the 1973-74

---

*This chapter is adapted from Allan M. Loosigian, *Interest Rate Futures* (Homewood, Ill.: Dow Jones-Irwin, 1980).

credit crunch on the California—indeed the nationwide—thrift and construction industries, a group of faculty members at the University of California at Berkeley in cooperation with representatives of several of that state's large savings and loan associations sought relief from the next and subsequent squeezes in the futures market. They reasoned that the type of forward hedging that had long been practiced in the commodity and foreign exchange markets could be adapted to serve the needs of financial institutions and other organizations adversely affected by precipitous interest-rate swings. What was then lacking were instruments to accomplish such hedging and specific markets in which to trade them.

Ever receptive to new ideas that offer the prospect of increased business, the two principal Chicago futures exchanges separately developed and introduced what were generally referred to as interest-rate futures contracts. The Chicago Board of Trade introduced in October 1975 contracts for the future delivery of Government National Mortgage Association certificates, or Ginnie Maes. Several months later, a few blocks away, the Chicago Mercantile Exchange launched its first interest-rate futures contract on 90-day U.S. Treasury bills.

The next several years saw a proliferation of futures contracts on other financial instruments at the two Chicago exchanges and at other commodity and securities exchanges eager to participate in what was heralded as a potential business bonanza. Some of the new contracts, notably those on U.S. Treasury bonds and large bank 90-day certificates of deposit, flourished and attracted a wide trading interest. Others, such as 30- and 90-day commercial paper and assorted Treasury note contracts, were largely ignored. Meanwhile, a so-called second generation of financial instrument contracts, put and call options on fixed income securities, were being developed by various exchanges amid a dispute as to whether these new vehicles were securities or commodities and which regulatory agency—the SEC or the Commodity Futures Trading Commission—therefore had the primary responsibility for supervising their trading.

Exhibit 1 presents the currently traded futures contracts on financial instruments and relevant information for each contract.

WHAT IS HEDGING?

A standard textbook definition of *futures hedging* is the assumption of a futures market position, equal in size and on the opposite side of the market (i.e., long versus short or vice versa) to a related cash position for the purpose of reducing exposure to price change. An ancillary definition is the purchase or sale of futures contracts as temporary substitutes for an intended transaction in the actual com-

Exhibit 1
Currently Traded Futures Contracts on Financial Instruments

	COMEX[1]	Treasury Bills		Intermediate-Term Treasury Coupon Securities		Treasury Bonds CBT[3]
		IMM[2]	IMM[2]	CBT[3]	IMM[2]	
Deliverable items	$1 million par value of Treasury bills with 90, 91, or 92 days to maturity	$1 million par value of Treasury bills with 90, 91, or 92 days to maturity	$250,000 par value of Treasury bills due in 52 weeks	$100,000 par value of Treasury notes and noncallable bonds with 4 to 6 years to maturity	$100,000 par value of Treasury notes maturing between 3½ years and 4½ years	$100,000 par value of Treasury bonds with at least 15 years to first call or to maturity
Initial margin[4] (per contract)	$800	$1,500	$600	$900	$500	$2,800[5]
Maintenance margin (per contract)	$600	$1,200	$400	$600	$300	$1,600[5]
Daily limits[6]	60 basis points	50 basis points	50 basis points	1 point (32/32)	¾ point (48/64)	2 points (64/32)
Delivery months (each year)	February, May, August, November	March, June, September, December	March, June, September, December	March, June, September, December	February, May, August, November	March, June, September, December
Total open interest (December 31, 1979)	913	36,495	435	715	265	90,676
Date trading began	October 2, 1979	January 6, 1976	September 11, 1978	June 25, 1979	July 10, 1979	August 22, 1977

Exhibit 1 *(concluded)*

	CBT (old)[3]	Government National Mortgage Association (modified pass-through mortgage-backed certificates)	
		CBT (new)[3]	COMEX[1]
Deliverable items	Collateralized depository receipt covering $100,000 principal balance of GNMA certificates	$100,000 principal balance of GNMA certificates	$100,000 principal balance of GNMA certificates
Initial margin[4] (per contract)	$2,000	$2,000	$1,500
Maintenance margin[4] (per contract)	$1,500	$1,500	$1,125
Daily limits[6]	1½ points (48/32)	1½ points (48/32)	1 point (64/64)
Delivery months (each year) . . .	March, June, September, December	March, June, September, December	January, April, July, October[7]
Total open interest (December 31, 1979)	88,982	4,478	64
Date trading began	October 20, 1975	September 12, 1978	November 13, 1979

All specifications are as of year-end 1979.
[1] Commodity Exchange, Inc.–New York.
[2] International Monetary Market (Chicago Mercantile Exchange)
[3] Chicago Board of Trade.
[4] The speculative margin is shown where margins vary according to whether the contracts cover speculative, hedged, or spread positions.
[5] For all contracts but those that mature in current month. Then initial margin is increased to $2,500, and maintenance margin is raised to $2,000.
[6] Exchanges frequently have rules allowing expansion of daily limits once they have been in effect for a few days (margins may change also).
[7] Principal trading months; rules allow trading for current plus two succeeding months.

Source: Marcelle Arak and Christopher J. McCurdy, "Interest Rate Futures," *Federal Reserve Bank of New York Quarterly Review*, Winter 1980.

modity. The popular expression "to hedge one's bets" is a readily understood reference to this process of risk reduction.

Organized futures markets were developed more than a century ago to afford farmers and other dealers in agricultural products an alternative to relying on Providence to ensure that prices would remain unchanged or move in their favor by the time the crops were harvested, moved to market, and processed. A bond portfolio manager is essentially exercising the same option when selling Treasury bond futures as a hedge against the price depreciation that higher interest rates would inflict on bond values. Both the farmer and the portfolio manager are placing *short hedges* by selling futures to offset any potential reduction in the cash value of their respective commodities, be it wheat or 20-year Treasury bonds.

A *long hedge* is undertaken by a prospective purchaser—for example, a flour miller who buys futures to fix the cost of the wheat he plans to acquire for processing at a later date (the wheat futures are hence a temporary substitute for the actual wheat), or a corporate treasurer who buys 90-day Treasury bill futures to lock in a specific yield on a three-month investment she anticipates making when the cash earmarked for it becomes available.

In each instance, the farmer, portfolio manager, miller, and treasurer would assume equal and opposite positions in the cash (actual) and futures markets. And in each case, the futures transaction would anticipate a projected cash purchase or sale. When the farmer harvests his wheat, he will cover his short futures position by repurchasing the contracts he sold earlier, and at the same time sell the crop through his customary marketing channels. By the same token, the portfolio manager will buy in her short bond futures contracts when she is ready to sell the bonds out of her portfolio or decides that interest rates are more likely to decline than to continue rising. The miller and corporate treasurer would follow the reverse procedure, selling their long futures positions when their operating requirements and cash flow make it timely to buy the wheat or Treasury bills.

Using the popular phrase, all four "hedge their bets" in the futures market to protect themselves against adverse price changes in wheat or interest rates. But, as a result, they also forego any benefit from favorable fluctuations.

TEXTBOOK HEDGING VERSUS BASIS TRADING

Most descriptions of hedging start with at least one example of a hypothetical "perfect" hedge to illustrate the objective of recouping in one market the amount lost in another. Exhibit 2 summarizes the arithmetic of such a perfect short hedge in the case of the bond portfolio cited above. Notice that futures and cash prices declined by identical amounts—$7^{24}/_{32}$—between June 1 and December 1, satisfying the conditions of a perfect hedge, so that the $77,500 paper loss incurred in the bond portfolio was offset precisely by an equivalent profit before brokerage commissions on the short futures position.

Another way to describe the situation is that the hedge was initiated on June 1 at a $^{30}/_{32}$ difference (69-02 minus 68-04) and was "unwound" on December 1, again at $^{30}/_{32}$ (61-10 minus 60-12). This difference between cash and futures prices, called the basis, is the controlling factor in determining the outcome of all hedged positions. In the Treasury bond short hedge example, if the basis on December 1 between the 7⅞s of 1995 and the December T bond contract was less than $^{30}/_{32}$, signifying that the futures price had declined by less than the cash bonds, the futures gain on the short position would not have matched the decline in market value of the 7⅞s of 1995. If, on the other hand, the basis on December 1 was greater than $^{30}/_{32}$, the futures gain would have exceeded the cash

Exhibit 2
Perfect Short Hedge in U.S. Treasury Bonds

Cash Market	Futures Market
June 1:	
Owns $1 million U.S. Treasury 7⅞s of 1995 at 68-04* to yield 12.329 percent.	Sells 10 December bond contracts at 69-02 to yield 12.152 percent.
No transaction.	
December 1:	
U.S. Treasury 7⅞s of 1995 are at 60-12 to yield 13.870 percent.	Buys 10 December bond contracts at 61-10 to yield 13.705 percent.
No transaction.	
Unrealized loss:	Realized profit (before commissions)
7$^{24}/_{32}$ or $77,500	7$^{24}/_{32}$ or $77,500

*In futures quotations 68 $^{4}/_{32}$s is abbreviated 68-04, 69 $^{2}/_{32}$s as 69-02, and so on.

market loss. In either instance, we would have gone beyond the textbook case of a perfect hedge and entered the "real world" condition of a changing basis. The overriding question then becomes: Did the basis grow wider or narrower between June 1 and December 1, and to what extent? A synopsis of real-world conditions during 1980 is contained in Exhibit 3, where the first-of-month yields on 20-year Treasury bonds and bond futures are listed among other cash and futures market yields for that year.

The perfect short hedge summarized in Exhibit 2 is also a straight, or pure, hedge in the sense that securities are hedged by futures contracts for which they are deliverable. In such an instance, the cash-futures basis is determined by variations from the specified coupon rate and the remaining time to the contract delivery date.

Exhibit 3
1980 Selected Cash and Futures Market Yields (beginning of month, 1980)

First of Month	90-Day Bills (discount)	One-Year Bills (discount)	Three-Month CDs (discount)	90-Day Commercial Paper (discount)	GNMA 8 Percent (yield)	20-Year 8 Percent Treasury Bonds (yield)	Federal Funds (closing bid)	Prime Rate
January	12.10%	11.04%	13.25%	13.50%	10.92%	10.25%	14¼%	15%
February	12.03	11.31	13.25	13.35	11.70	11.24	13¾	15¼
March	15.13	13.73	15.55	15.75	12.65	12.17	16½	16¾
April	15.03	13.90	18.00	17.35	12.88	12.31	19	19½
May	10.78	10.05	12.00	12.15	10.59	10.47	15½	19
June	8.03	8.20	8.65	9.65	10.61	10.43	10¾	14
July	8.15	7.90	8.15	8.75	10.40	9.98	9	12
August	8.22	8.64	9.40	9.85	11.06	10.70	10	11
September	10.12	10.10	11.00	11.50	11.96	11.33	9	11½
October	11.52	11.05	12.65	12.85	11.89	11.82	14½	13
November	13.34	12.46	14.50	14.25	12.59	12.24	13¾	14½
December	14.65	13.51	17.25	17.35	13.03	12.39	17	18
Average	11.59	10.99	12.80	13.02	11.69	11.27	13½	15

Exhibit 3 *(concluded)*

First of Month	90-Day Bill Futures		GNMA 8 Percent Futures		8 Percent Treasury Bond Futures	
	Nearby	One-Year	Nearby	One-Year	Nearby	One-Year
January	11.35	9.26	11.46	11.29	10.27	10.05
February	11.99	9.96	12.48	12.22	11.46	11.09
March	14.59	12.39	13.46	13.30	12.55	12.01
April	14.04	12.16	13.38	12.91	12.25	11.81
May	10.21	9.20	11.60	11.50	10.63	10.52
June	7.77	8.53	11.65	11.78	10.60	10.67
July	7.91	8.83	11.69	11.80	11.13	11.22
August	8.79	9.35	12.32	12.41	11.02	11.05
September	10.14	10.86	12.65	12.60	11.26	11.15
October	11.86	11.61	13.17	13.07	11.89	11.69
November	13.14	12.35	13.54	13.48	12.32	12.07
December	14.38	12.62	13.71	13.45	12.53	11.97
Average	11.34	10.59	12.59	12.48	11.49	11.27

Although a straight hedge is the most satisfactory sort, interest-rate futures are often employed to hedge securities that are not deliverable under the terms of the contract being used. This so-called *cross-hedging* introduces an additional (and greater) degree of basis risk, that of the price/yield variations between the instrument being hedged and the security to be delivered according to the contract specifications. In addition to Treasury issues, Treasury bond futures might, for example, be sold to hedge long positions in corporate or government agency bonds. The effectiveness of such cross-hedges depends for the most part on the price correlation between Treasury bonds of contract grade and the bonds being hedged.

Futures contracts on 90-day commercial paper were introduced in 1977, followed two years later by contracts on 30-day commercial paper, on the supposition that they would provide a better hedge than a cross-hedge between commercial paper of varying maturities and 90-day Treasury bill futures. Yet the commercial paper futures languished and were finally discontinued because most users apparently were satisfied with the cross-hedge and did not feel a need to change. On the other hand, contracts on large bank certificates of deposit were well received when they were launched in 1981 because a cross-hedge between CDs and Treasury bill futures was not considered adequate.

Hedging, therefore, be it of a wheat crop or of a government bond portfolio, is not the automatic cut-and-dried type of operation suggested by the perfect hedge example. A closer look at Exhibit 3 shows that between June and December 1980, or during any other period for that matter, there were times when a hedge, short or long, would have proven to be more advantageous to the hedger than at other times. *Basis trading* is the attempt to profit from correct judgments concerning the optimum time to initiate and close out a hedge. Experienced hedgers know that although the futures market affords them an opportunity to substitute the lesser risk of a changing cash-futures price relationship for that of an exposed long or short position, that does not eliminate the need for careful planning and seasoned market judgment. Even so, after all of the critical factors have been weighed and due diligence exercised, the importance of sheer luck should not be minimized.

THE CASH-FUTURES PRICE STRUCTURE

An informed judgment regarding the basis (in other words, an opinion concerning the most favorable time to place and then to lift a hedge) begins with a study of the cash-futures price structure. In the case of the interest-rate futures complex, the structure is a representation of the yield equivalent of contract prices for successive delivery dates.[1] Until futures and cash yields start to converge as a contract's expiration approaches, futures prices often display a life of their own that can deviate sharply from cash market interest rates, a phenomenon we can identify as a variation in the basis.

As has always been true in the case of tangible commodities, the semi-independent behavior of interest-rate futures prices vis-à-vis cash market yields stems chiefly from differences in time and delivery grade. The pattern of successive delivery-month prices is generally one of increasingly greater discounts from, or premiums over, the cash price/yield, a sequence that depends in large part upon the absolute trend in interest rates and the relationship between short- and long-term rates. Moreover, as is demonstrated in Exhibit 4, the cash to futures and futures to futures relationships are in a continual state of flux due to ever-changing money market conditions.

So long as the consensus of market participants is that interest rates will continue to rise (as embodied in an upward-sloping yield curve), the contract price for each successive delivery month is lower than the one preceding it. As the expectation spreads that the cyclical peak in interest rates is within sight (as embodied in a flattening or downward-sloping yield curve), prices of contracts with deferred-delivery dates become progressively higher, reflecting the anticipation of lower yields with the passage of time. As time elapses and each contract in turn approaches its delivery date, bringing the indicated yield for that contract closer to the comparable cash market rate, these structural discounts and premiums diminish, giving the basis an upward or downward bias.

Hedgers must take the premium or discount structure of futures markets into account when making their market decisions. A short hedge ordinarily will fare better in a premium market (cash prices below futures) as futures prices decline relative to cash. Other considerations being equal, a discount market (cash above futures) normally favors a long hedge with futures rising toward the spot price as the contracts approach delivery date. The progression from premium or discount to parity with cash prices/yields is not always a smooth one, since imbalances occur in the current or anticipated supply and demand for deliverable securities, technical analysts respond to chart signals, and Fed watchers speculate on a change in monetary policy. All or any one of these events would cause significant, even if only temporary, changes in the basis.

---

[1] It is not the familiar cash yield curve per se that we are dealing with here, but the yield on securities of the same grade and maturity spaced at quarterly intervals over a two- to three-year period that spans a series of contract delivery dates.

Exhibit 4
Cash and Futures Discounts and (Spreads) 90-Day Treasury Bills (International Monetary Market beginning-of-month settlement discounts based on IMM Index)

Month 1980	Cash Discount First of Month	March 1980	June 1980	September 1980	December 1980	March 1981
Jan.	12.10	(−75) 11.35	(−3) 10.32	(−68) 9.64	(−29) 9.35	(−9) 9.26
Feb.	12.03	(−4) 11.99	(−61) 11.38	(−71) 10.67	(−45) 10.22	(−26) 9.96
March	15.13	(−54) 14.59	(−58) 14.01	(−75) 13.26	(−51) 12.75	(−36) 12.39
April	15.03		(−99) 14.04	(−96) 13.08	(−58) 12.50	(−27) 12.23
May	10.78		(−57) 10.21	(−57) 9.64	(−38) 9.26	(−14) 9.12
June	8.03		(−26) 7.77	(24) 8.01	(16) 8.17	(18) 8.35
July	8.15			(−24) 7.91	(27) 8.18	(26) 8.44
August	8.22			(57) 8.79	(8) 8.87	(14) 9.01
Sept.	10.12			(2) 10.14	(33) 10.47	(17) 10.64
Oct.	11.52				(34) 11.86	(10) 11.96
Nov.	13.34				(−20) 13.14	(−21) 12.93
Dec.	14.65				(−27) 14.38	(−73) 13.65

WHO SHOULD HEDGE?

The basic determination by corporate management concerning any futures market involvement should be whether there is sufficient interest-rate exposure to make hedging a necessary, or desirable undertaking. What would be the impact on corporate earnings, say, of a 2 percent increase or decline in short- and long-term interest rates? What is the company's present or anticipated position in fixed income securities or, in the case of banking institutions, fixed-rate loans? What is the amount of projected borrowing and/or investment over the coming year or two, and what will be the likely net position, the so-called asset/liability "gap." Would any foreseeable adverse change in rates be an acceptable cost of doing business? If the perceived risks are insignificant, or fall within tolerable limits, and are likely to average out over time, management may see no compelling incentive to embark upon interest-rate hedging operations.

On the other hand, should the wide swings in rates that have become the norm over the past decade persist and continue to have a marked effect on portfolio values, investment income, and/or borrowing cost, the company is vulnerable and may consider itself a hedge candidate. If such be the case, management should establish a set of policies guiding the firm's activity in this area and determine the type of hedging strategy it wishes to adopt. Should it regard itself as a straight hedger in the textbook sense, estimating its risk exposure as closely as possible and taking the prescribed action in the futures market to offset it? Or should it assume a more aggressive

June 1981	September 1981	December 1981	March 1982	June 1982	September 1982
(3) 9.29	(5) 9.34	(−2) 9.32			
(−6) 9.90	(−5) 9.85	(−4) 9.81			
(−21) 12.18	(−8) 12.10	(−2) 12.08			
(−7) 12.16	(−5) 12.11	(5) 12.16	(−1) 12.15		
(8) 9.20	(5) 9.25	(−5) 9.20	(−) 9.20		
(18) 8.53	(19) 8.72	(25) 8.97	(34) 9.31		
(18) 8.62	(21) 8.83	(21) 9.04	(28) 9.32	(21) 9.53	
(14) 9.15	(20) 9.35	(20) 9.55	(17) 9.72	(28) 10.00	
(14) 10.78	(8) 10.86	(9) 10.95	(12) 11.07	(11) 11.18	
(−12) 11.84	(−14) 11.70	(−9) 11.61	(−4) 11.57	(−11) 11.46	(−4) 11.42
(−27) 12.66	(−22) 12.44	(−9) 12.35	(−8) 12.27	(−13) 12.14	(−3) 12.11
(−58) 13.07	(−28) 12.79	(−17) 12.62	(−16) 12.46	(−12) 12.34	(−9) 12.25

posture, placing a hedge when the basis appears to offer a profit opportunity over and above straight price or rate protection, and closing it out when that profit is attained?

The strategy that is selected will influence (and in turn be influenced by) the organizational fit of the hedging operation within the business structure. Some firms regard their hedge activity as a distinct profit center and expect it to be self-sustaining. Those who favor a protective, or defensive, approach usually see hedging as a support function and do not look to it to show profits per se.

CASE ONE—A BOND PORTFOLIO HEDGE

The collapse of bond prices during 1980-81 as a consequence of soaring interest rates has been amply chronicled and does not need to be recounted here. The immediate question is: How may Treasury bond futures have been employed during those years—or indeed at any time—to offset the deleterious effect on bond portfolios of such severe price declines?

As is noted in Exhibit 1, the Chicago Board of Trade U.S. Treasury bond contract specifies the delivery of $100,000 face value Treasury bonds bearing an 8 percent coupon and a call or maturity date 15 years or more beyond the delivery month of the futures contract. To execute a short hedge, therefore, a portfolio manager would sell one futures contract for every $100,000 face value of bonds held in the portfolio. If, for example, the portfolio contained $100 million of U.S. Treasury 8s of 1996-01, the manager would sell 1,000 contracts (i.e., 1,000 contracts times $100,000 contract size = $100 million Treasury 8s in portfolio).[2]

For every futures contract sold (or bought in the case of a long hedge) the hedger must deposit initial margin of approximately $2,000 with the broker carrying the futures account. The figure is approximate because the amount required varies from broker to broker and is changed from time to time by the exchange on which that particular futures contract is traded. To hedge a $100 million bond position with the sale of 1,000 futures contracts, therefore, the hedger must deposit with the broker cash or actual U.S. Treasury bills (not bill futures) on the order of $2 million.

After once establishing a short futures position, the hedger profits by $31.25 per contract for each "tick," or minimum fluctuation of 1/32nd of a point, the Treasury bond contract drops in price. That minimum price fluctuation in turn amounts to $31,250 per 1/32nd of a point on a 1,000 contract position. To the extent that interest rates decline and the contract price rises, the hedger loses money on the short futures position at the same rate. Should the contract price move against the hedger by 25 percent of the initial margin on deposit with the broker, the hedger is required to deposit additional (maintenance) margin to his or her account.

Severe tightening of monetary policy by the Federal Reserve Board to contain inflation and suppport the U.S. dollar in foreign exchange markets—the so-called Saturday massacre at the Fed—commenced on October 8, 1979. The U.S. Treasury 8s of 1996-01 were then quoted at 88¼ bid, giving a hypothetical $100 million portfolio consisting solely of that issue a market value of about $88.25 million at the then prevailing price. (See Exhibit 5.) On the same date, September 1980 Treasury bond futures contracts traded at 87¾ on the Chicago Board of Trade. Had it been possible to sell 1,000 contracts at that price, it would have been necessary for the short hedger to deposit with a broker initial margin of about $2 million. So long as the basis—the half-point spread between cash bonds at 88¼ and futures at 87¾—remained constant, the portfolio would effectively have been locked into a value per bond of 88¼. That constant basis would have provided a perfect hedge.

Such was not the case. By October 25, 1979, the 8s of 1996-01 had dropped to 79, subjecting the hypothetical portfolio to a loss of 9¼ points, or $9.25 million; and the September 1980 bond futures fell 8 points to 79¾. The $9.25 million loss in the bond portfolio was only offset, therefore, by an $8 million gain on the futures side. Another way of saying the same thing is that futures (the September

---

[2] For clarity of illustration, a portfolio holding of U.S. Treasury bonds is assumed in this example. A similar hedge might be employed in the case of corporate, agency, or municipal bonds. Such cross-hedging, however, exposes the hedger to a greater degree of basis variation of the sort described earlier in this chapter.

Exhibit 5
Treasury Bond Portfolio Hedge, 1979-80

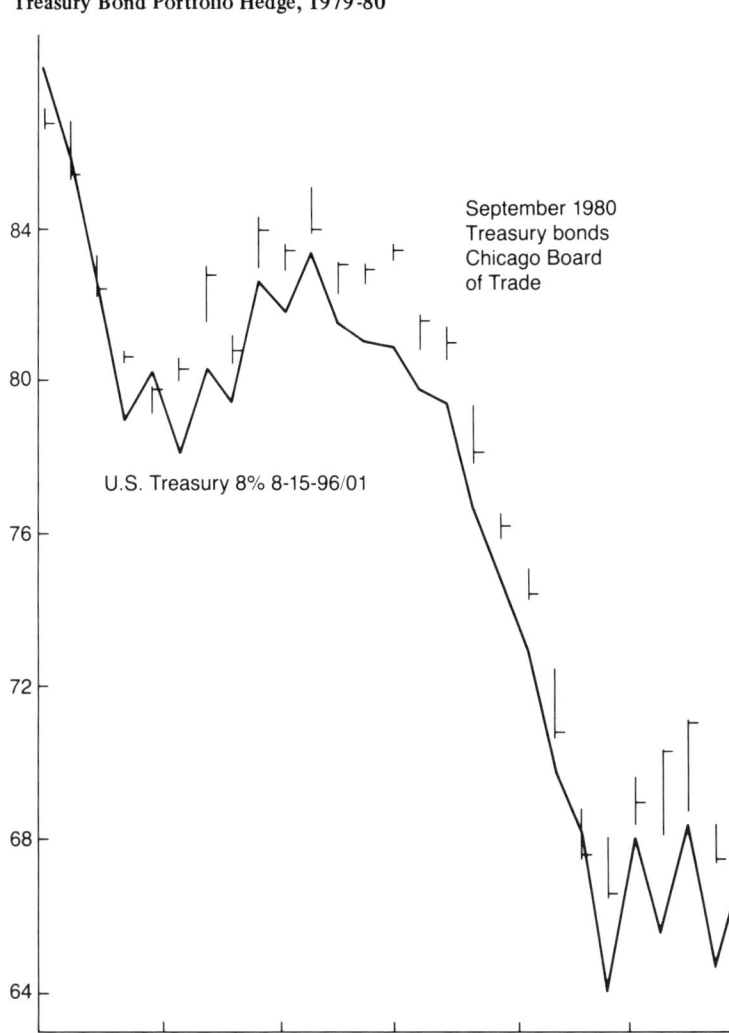

1980 contract at any rate) actually went *up* relative to the cash bonds from one-half point below to three-fourths point above. That 1¼-point swing, the equivalent of $1.25 million on 1,000 contracts, is referred to as a change in the basis and is a good illustration of hedging in practice. In this instance, the hedger substituted for the risk (as it turned out) of bonds dropping 9¼ points, the appreciably smaller risk of the basis changing by 1¼ points.

The bond market staged a modest rally during November and early December. The 8s of 1996-01 moved up to about 83¼ in the first week of December, bringing the hypothetical portfolio back to within 5 points, or $5 million, of its October 8 market value. The September 1980 contract rose during the same period to 85, causing the basis to shift further to 1¾ points above cash bonds. In total, between October 8 and December 6, there was a shift against the hedger of 2¼ points, or $2.25 million inasmuch as cash bonds were 5 points below their earlier level while the short futures position showed an unrealized gain of 2¾ (87¾ minus 85). This disparity developed as the market turned up because futures prices moved up faster than those of cash bonds. Not only are futures inherently more volatile than cash, but in early December 1979 they were anticipating a further drop in long-term interest rates by the September 1980 contracts-delivery date.

The six-week rally proved to be a false start. By mid-December the market had resumed its downward course; the 8s of 1996-01 fell in the ensuing 11-week period between December 10, 1979, and February 26, 1980, from 83 to 64. From its October 8 level, the sample portfolio had lost more than $24 million, or 27 percent of its market value, an unprecedented decline within such a brief span. During the same interval, September 1980 bond futures slid to 66½, widening the cash-futures basis further to 2½ points above cash. Under normal bond market conditions, a basis shift of one or two points is considered a substantial change. But in a crisis environment such as the first two months of 1980 clearly were, the hedger in the example would even so have managed to offset more than $22 million, or 90 percent of the $24 million decline in bond values, by means of an unrealized gain on his or her short position in futures.

Like any market operation, futures hedging is not a one-way street. So long as bond prices continue to drop, hedgers are something like heros, avoiding significant losses in their portfolios. But when a rally gets under way and unrealized losses begin to mount in the futures account, the situation is not so comfortable for them. Top managers and directors are frequently unimpressed by the argument that whatever the company is losing on its futures position, it is recouping—apart from any change in the basis—on the cash side.

As was noted earlier, initial margin is in effect the price of establishing a futures hedge. Once short hedgers deposit with the broker the required initial margin, they receive no calls for additional funds so long as the market continues to decline. The hedgers are making money on their futures position, and the equity in their trading account is thereby increasing. They are even entitled to withdraw profits from the account as profits accrue, but must subsequently replace the profits when the market turns against them.

Futures contracts are limited in the extent to which they are permitted to advance or decline from the prior day's settlement price during the course of a single trading session. These daily price limits are the futures market equivalent of a stock exchange suspending trading in a particular issue in ancitipation, or in the wake of, a significant news announcement and are intended to give traders an opportunity to assess the situation before the contract price is inordinately affected. The daily price limit also circumscribes the amount of loss (and profit) individual traders and the exchange clearing house may suffer on any given day.

If buying pressure forces a contract price "up the limit" without attracting corresponding sell orders at or below the limit price, trading ceases in that particular contract until there are offers to sell within the specified limit. The same procedure is observed each succeeding day until sell orders do materialize.

The opposite sequence occurs in a declining market wherein no buyers can be found before the contract price is offered "down the limit." The daily limits that were in effect as of December 1979 are listed in Exhibit 1. Futures exchanges have the authority to reduce or increase existing limits in the event that a change in market conditions causes a change in a contract's normal price volatility.

If, in the case of the foregoing example, the short hedge had been initiated at the end of October 1979 instead of at the beginning, repeated calls for additional margin would have been issued by the broker during the November rally. Had September 1980 Treasury bond futures contracts been sold at or near the October 29 settlement price of 79¾, the hedger would have received maintenance margin calls on his or her 1,000 short contracts of about $2 million by November 15 as the contract price rallied to 81¾. By December 6 the contract price had moved yet higher to 84¾, at which point the hedger would be called for another $3 million margin.

To be sure, as interest rates once again turned upward and bond futures prices resumed their decline, these funds were recouped. But there is a point after which the burden of repeated margin calls becomes onerous and the likelihood increases that the market will not in fact reverse itself and in the process alleviate the short hedger's distress. At some juncture the hedger should determine that market conditions dictate that it is better to remain unhedged and act to preclude further losses by liquidating the futures position (i.e., by buying the short contracts in).

If, under the worst of circumstances, a portfolio manager had elected to initiate a short hedge at the February 26 market trough and accordingly sold 1,000 September 1980 bond contracts at 66½, and if the manager had not acted to reverse this decision, the manager's futures losses would have assumed staggering proportions. During the subsequent rally of spring 1980, cumulative margin calls on a 1,000 contract short position would have amounted to more than $20 million. Once again, a market reversal would have erased those unrealized losses had the short position been maintained through the rally's peak. Prudent managers would in all likelihood have removed their hedges during the early stages of the spring rally and sought to reinstate them after it had become clear that interest rates had resumed their upward trend.

CASE TWO—A COMMERCIAL PAPER HEDGE

Just as in the preceding case, in which a bond portfolio manager would sell futures to protect the portfolio against price decline as a consequence of rising interest rates, so too would a corporate borrower sell financial futures to limit the interest cost of prospective borrowings. In the case of a commercial paper issuer, a corporate hedger would want to sell futures at a price equivalent to a discount, say, of 10 percent to recoup the additional interest cost should commercial paper rates rise to a 20 percent discount. In that event, the hedger would accrue a gain on the short futures position substantially equal to the incremental borrowing cost between 10 percent and 20 percent. That is what is referred to as locking-in a rate. If interest rates instead declined, the short hedger would instead lose money on the short futures position as the contract price moved in inverse relation to yield. That loss would in turn be offset by a lower actual borrowing cost at the time of the commercial paper sale. As in the case of a short portfolio hedge, a perfect hedge in which the two sides are exactly matched is theoretically possible, but it is seldom realized in practice.

The contract specifications for 90-day U.S. Treasury bill futures contracts traded at the International Monetary Market affiliate of the Chicago Mercantile Exchange stipulate the delivery of $1 million face value 13-week bills on a predetermined date. A buyer of 10 December contracts, for example, will receive delivery in the third week of that month of $10 million face value in bills that mature at par the third week of the following March. The seller of those 10 contracts assumes an obligation to deliver the same amount and maturity of bills on the specified delivery date.

Treasury bill futures are quoted on an index basis to reflect the 90-day discount of the deliverable bills. The index is 100 less the applicable discount, so that the purchase or sale of contracts at an 85 index fixes the delivery price of actual Treasury bills at a 90-day discount of 15 percent. A trader would buy a contract at 85 when he or she believed the cash (actual) 90-day discount on the contract delivery date would be less than 15 percent. In that case, the contract price would have risen above the trader's purchase price by the dollar equivalent of the basis-point decline in yield. The trader would sell at 85.00 when he or she believed the discount would ultimately be greater than 15 percent. As with bond futures, a corporate hedger must deposit with its brokerage house initial margin of about $2,000 per contract and will be called by the broker for additional margin in the event of adverse price movement.

The dotted line in Exhibit 6 is an inverted chart of the highest quality, 90-day dealer commercial paper rate during 1980. The pur-

Exhibit 6
Basis Chart: Treasury Bill Futures versus 90-Day Commercial Paper Rates (inverted)

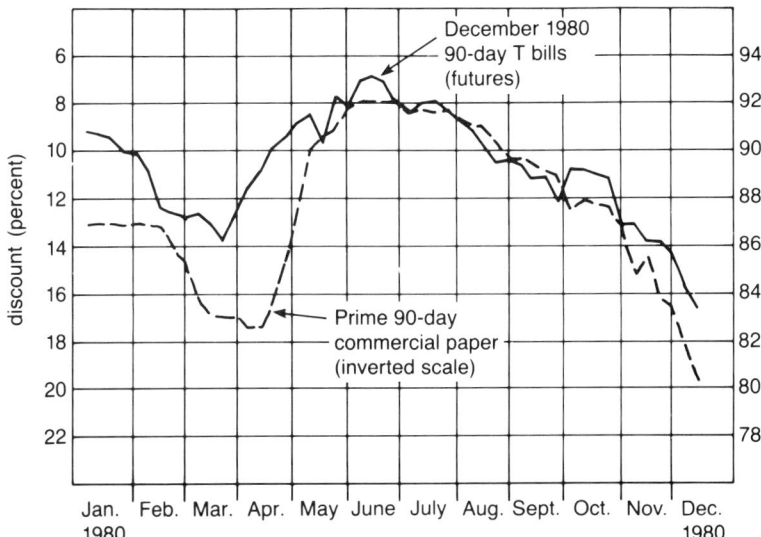

pose of inverting the scale of the chart is to compare the dollar consequences of a changing commercial paper discount with the index movement of December 1980 Treasury bill futures (solid line) throughout the year.[3]

The year opened with the 90-day dealer commercial paper discount tracing a plateau at 13 percent through January and the first half of February. There followed a rapid rate rise (shown as a price decline on the inverted scale) that peaked in mid-April at about 17½ percent and then an even sharper drop to the 8 percent level by the end of May. The third quarter witnessed a gradual rate rise, and in the fourth quarter an accelerating rate of increase exceeding the April

---

[3] The Chicago Board of Trade introduced futures contracts on both 90-day and 30-day commercial paper, but discontinued trading in the two contracts because they failed to gain acceptance by market participants. The participants preferred the more liquid Treasury bill futures contracts as hedging vehicles, even though there is some disparity between the two rates.

peak in late November and went on to end the year at about the 20 percent level.

Obviously, a corporation that sold commercial paper during the May-June 1980 period obtained a far lower rate (about 800 basis points) than a corporation that sold its paper in November and December. The question to be answered is: How may the futures market have been used to avoid paying commercial paper rates of 16 percent and above in March-April, and again during November and December?

To begin with a favorable case, a commercial paper issuer would have been able to sell futures during the final week of January at about 90, an index price reflecting a Treasury bill discount of 10 percent. By the third week of March, after the prime commercial paper rate had risen 400 basis points from 13 percent to 17 percent, it was possible to buy in (liquidate) the short futures position at an index equivalent of about 13½ percent for a gain of 350 basis points. The corporation would at that point sell its commercial paper at 17 percent, but after taking the 350-basis-point futures profit into account, it would have established an effective hedged rate of 13½ percent.

The same futures contracts, had they been sold in mid-June at 93, or 7 percent, would have realized a 950-basis-point gain when repurchased in mid-December at 83.50, or 16½ percent. For a corporation selling its commercial paper in December at 20 percent, that gain would have served to reduce its hedged borrowing cost to 10½ percent. In that instance, the basis expanded during the six-month period, so the hedge would have been in force from about 100 basis points (7 percent T bill futures to 8 percent commercial paper) to about 350 basis points (16½ percent T bill futures to 20 percent commercial paper). The net result for a corporation observing such a scenario would have been to substitute for the unhedged risk of the commercial paper rate climbing 1,200 basis points from 8 percent to 20 percent, the considerably smaller risk of the basis changing adversely by 250 basis points.

Such a strategy is by no means a surefire formula for reducing borrowing cost. The market can always go the other way; that is to say, interest rates might decline. In that case, as was noted above, a hedger would incur a loss on the short futures position and in so doing lock in a hedged rate higher than the market rate prevailing when it became time to issue its commercial paper. A corporation that sold December 1980 Treasury bill futures at 87, or 13 percent, just before the Spring 1980 market rally would, if it sold commercial paper in mid-June, have covered its short futures position at about 93, or 7 percent, for a 600-basis-point *loss*. Adding that loss to the 8 percent prime 90-day commercial paper rate in mid-June would impose a hedged borrowing cost of 14 percent at a time when nonhedgers were borrowing at 8 percent.

The moral of this story, as with that of the bond portfolio hedge, is that there are times to hedge and times not to hedge. Hedging decisions should be taken with a view of the market. The objective is to take advantage of what are perceived as temporarily low interest rates (in absolute terms as well as in terms of the cash-futures basis), applying them to prospective borrowings at a time when interest rates are expected to be significantly higher. A similar approach may be taken with respect to long-term bond financing. A major drawback in the long-term sector, however, is the relatively low correlation between corporate bond yields and the prices/yields on U.S. Treasury bond or Ginnie Mae futures contracts traded at the Chicago Board of Trade.

Another drawback in both the short- and long-term markets is the need to deposit additional margin money in the hedger's brokerage account when interest rates decline and a loss is incurred on a short futures position. Barring an abnormal shift in the basis, any losses registered in the futures account will be substantially recouped on the cash side. Nevertheless, until such time as the hedged position is terminated and the commercial paper or bonds are issued at a lower rate, cash maintenance margin deposits must be made for as long as losses are incurred in the futures account. The interest income foregone on such deposits should be included when calculating the cost of hedging.

The reverse of this strategy—a long hedge—may be employed to lock in what is judged to be an acceptable rate of return on a prospective short-term investment. In this instance, Treasury bill futures are purchased at a lower index price than the price that is expected to prevail at the time the planned investment is to be made. If the hedger's expectations are realized, the lower discount on the cash investment will be substantially offset by price appreciation of the futures contract. As with the short hedge, the actual trend of interest rates may run contrary to the long hedger's expectations. In such an event, the hedger might be advised to sell out the long futures position and attempt to capture the higher yield that would result if the upward movement in interest rates were to persist until the date of the projected investment.

ORGANIZING FOR HEDGING

A corporation, fund, or financial institution that plans to implement a hedging program should follow several basic steps:

1. A plan should be committed to writing. It should explain what the hedging function is intended to accomplish and how. It should

set down limits with regard to the size of positions (number of contracts), maximum acceptable losses (in basis points and dollars), and so on. Everyone involved with the hedging program from the board of directors to its executors should understand the plan, have input to it, and be in accord with its methods and objectives.

2. A hedge manager should be designated to execute the plan. The manager may have the title of assistant treasurer, portfolio or cash manager, or some other, but an important part of the job should be to monitor hedge positions on a daily basis and be responsible for initiating and terminating such positions.

3. The hedge manager and, to a lesser extent, everyone else involved with the plan should become thoroughly familiar with the behavior of the basis—what we have defined as the relationship between futures prices and actual interest rates—under a variety of money market conditions. The basis, after all, is the real (net) price with which a hedger is concerned.

4. A corporation's brokers, bankers, and accountants should be advised of the hedge plan, and their respective areas of expertise should be utilized as circumstances dictate.

5. It is important to develop a simple system of reporting and recordkeeping that everyone concerned has access to and can understand.

6. Above all, it is virtually imperative to initiate the hedging program on a limited scale. Financial futures are still an unknown quantity for most managers, and the learning process to master them can be costly if losses are not controlled. It usually is advisable to begin with a pilot position of 10 contracts or less. As the hedge manager and associates become more familiar with and adept in the futures market, the size of positions may be progressively increased.

ACCOUNTING CONSIDERATIONS

The accounting for hedge transactions is relatively straightforward. Inasmuch as futures contracts are regarded as commitments rather than investments, they are booked as a memorandum entry rather than entered in the general ledger. The initial margin deposit for a long or short position is debited to a margin debit account, and cash is credited by a like figure. Similar entries are made when adverse market action necessitates additional maintenance margin deposits. Realized profits and losses are posted to the deferred profit or loss account and accumulated or written off over the average life of the securities that were hedged.

Any unrealized gains or losses on open futures positions at the end of the accounting period are entered as maintenance margin deposits, matching the gains and losses against their related cash market transactions. When an anticipated cash transaction does not occur, the futures position is treated as a speculation, with the ensuing profit or loss reflected in the current income statement. Initial and maintenance margin deposits are carried as "other assets," and any related amounts due to or from brokers are shown as miscellaneous receivables or payables.

A major obstacle to interest-rate hedging by banks and savings and loan associations is the regulatory requirement that unrealized gains and losses on outstanding futures positions be "marked to the market" (i.e., priced daily and included in current income), while the offsetting cash market position being hedged continues to be carried at cost. This discrepancy in accounting treatment distorts the economic status of a hedge and renders it ineffective for reporting purposes. At the end of 1981 the accounting standards board was considering proposals to correct this anomaly.

WHAT IS A SPREAD?

The term *spread* has somewhat different meanings in the money and commodity markets, a cause for some initial confusion to newcomers to financial futures. An interest-rate spread is the basis-point difference between yields on similar fixed income securities, or various maturities of the same instrument. A futures market spread entails concurrent long and short positions in related futures contracts. The hedged positions discussed in the previous sections make up a particular type of spread, in which one of the two "legs" is a position in the cash market. Another source of confusion is the indiscriminate use of the terms *spread, straddle,* and *arbitrage* to describe the same thing. The first two terms are functionally synonymous; the word spread is favored in the grain trade, and straddle is heard more frequently in other futures markets within the United States and abroad. Arbitrage is in the strictest sense a different type of operation.

For the same reason that hedgers consider basis risk to be less than that of a fully exposed position, futures spreaders regard their specialty as a more conservative method of trading than speculating on outright long or short positions. The key element in both instances is the tendency of cash instruments and futures contracts with successive delivery dates to move up and down in price/yield more or less in tandem. An intermonth spread consists of simultaneous long and short positions in different delivery months of the same contract. An intermarket spread is placed between similar contracts, again long and short, traded on different futures exchanges. An example of such a spread would be contrary positions in U.S. Treasury note contracts traded at the Chicago Mercantile Exchange and at the

Commodity Exchange (Comex) in New York. Interinstrument spreads are taken between contracts for different maturities of like securities (i.e., 90-day versus one-year T bills) or between different securities, such as T bills and certificates of deposit or bonds and Ginnie Mae contracts.

Exhibit 4 traces the dynamics of spread relationships among the International Monetary Market's 90-day Treasury bill contracts during 1980. The data for selected dates throughout the year are presented graphically in Exhibit 7. A comparison between the two exhibits reveals that as the curve of yields for successive contract deliveries assumes a sharper upward slope, the price/yield spreads between delivery months tend to expand. But as the nearby deliveries move higher up the yield axis, causing the curve to flatten out and even-

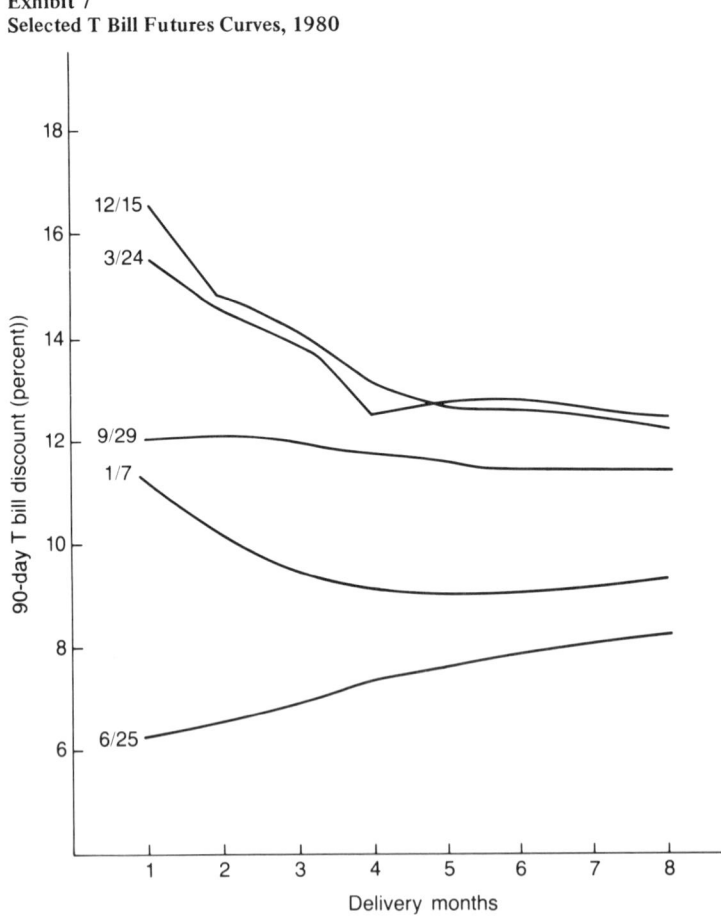

Exhibit 7
Selected T Bill Futures Curves, 1980

tually to turn into a negative or humped configuration (indicating the market's belief that short-term interest rates are at or near a peak), the spreads begin to contract, at which point the distant contracts begin moving to a price premium (yield discount) over the near and intermediate deliveries.

It is possible to reconstruct from the figures in Exhibit 4 a hypothetical 90-day T bill intermonth spread initiated in April 1980, when a short position in the December 1980 contract could have been taken at a 34-basis-point discount under a long position in December 1981 T bills (87.84 minus 87.50).[4] By the following November, the spread between the nearby and distant December contracts had widened to 79 basis points (87.65 minus 86.86), allowing the position to be "unwound" at a 45-basis-point, or $1,125, profit before commission charges on an initial margin commitment of $500. If the reverse spread had been placed in April—long December 1980, short December 1981—the position would have incurred a loss of the same magnitude during the seven-month holding period (assuming the trader made the mistake of not closing the contracts out before that point); the described situation is a demonstration that spread trading is not without its risks. An up-to-date record on the order of Exhibit 4 should be maintained by futures traders and should be studied as assiduously as traders who carry outright positions scrutinize their trend charts. Moreover, once a spread position has been established, price protection in the form of stop orders should be utilized.

WHAT IS ARBITRAGE?

The conventional definition of an arbitrage is the purchase of an asset in one market against its immediate resale at a profit in another. One example would be buying General Motors common stock on the New York Stock Exchange and selling it on the Pacific Coast Exchange. Another is the purchase of Swiss francs in Zurich against their simultaneous resale in London. A futures spread between like or different contracts is based upon an anticipated change over a period of time in the relationship between two prices, such as the short (December 1980) and long (December 1981) 90-day T bill spread described in the previous section. Since its outcome is not immediately realizable, therefore, a spread contains an element of risk that a classic arbitrage does not entail. Occasional disparities be-

---

[4] Although Exhibit 4 lists futures yields to afford ease of comparison with the cash 90-day T bill discount, the contract, as noted above, is actually quoted and traded in terms of the IMM index.

tween yields prevailing in the cash money and bond markets and related futures do, however, provide opportunities to engage in so-called quasiarbitrage.

One of these quasiarbitrages is known as the "hedged yield curve ride." Riding the yield curve is a commonplace money market operation wherein investors endeavor to improve their rate of return by purchasing a fixed income instrument with a maturity running beyond the intended term of the investment. A frequently cited illustration involves purchasing a 180-day Treasury bill with the intention of reselling it after 90 days in lieu of buying and holding to maturity an original 90-day bill. The advantage of buying the longer maturity issue is the incremental return it provides as the passage of time carries its discount down the steepest part of the yield curve. The risk implicit in this gambit is that any increase in short-term rates during the holding period would eradicate the anticipated yield advantage. If rates rose sharply enough, the investor unable to hold them to maturity might even be forced to sell the bills at a loss.

The investment trade-off made by a yield curve rider is one of accepting exposure to interest-rate risk and possible capital depreciation in return for the chance of earning a higher rate. The sale of an appropriate futures contract(s) at the time the longer term instrument is purchased serves to offset this risk. The combined transactions contain some elements of an arbitrage in that they provide for the sale of an asset at a firm price in the futures market at the same time that it is purchased in the cash market. In other words, the profit or return on the bills is fixed at the time they are bought.

Another type of interest-rate arbitrage between cash and futures markets involves the short sale of Treasury bonds and the purchase of comparable futures contracts to assure coverage of the short position at a known price. If, for example, $1 million U.S. Treasury 8¾s of 2003-08 were sold short at 65 (assuming the bonds could be borrowed to make delivery on the short sale), and at the same time 10 New York Futures Exchange Treasury bond futures contracts were purchased at 63, the bonds deliverable on the futures long position could be used to reimburse the lender of the borrowed bonds. And the two-point, or $20,000, difference less interest expense and brokerage commissions would provide a virtually riskless profit on the transaction.

Apart from the problem of borrowing appropriate bonds to deliver against the original short sale, a money manager who contemplates this type of arbitrage must take into account the price adjustment required to convert to its delivery value the market price of a Treasury bond bearing a coupon other than the specified 9 percent futures contract grade. The manager should also be aware that he or she is likely to receive from the futures short seller the cheapest bond eligible for delivery under the terms of the contract, which will be the least desirable issue from the manager's perspective. In other words, before embarking upon such an operation the would-be arbitrageur must become thoroughly familiar with the delivery terms and other futures contract specifications. Neglecting to do so, may cause the manager to be confronted with an unpleasant surprise instead of the anticipated assured profit.

HOW WELL DO FUTURES FORECAST ACTUAL INTEREST RATES?

For futures prices to forecast invariably and accurately the interest rate on a particular financial instrument as of the date it is to be delivered from the short to the long position holder, expectations must remain unchanged over a 24- to 36-month period, and market participants would need to possess perfect prescience. Both assumptions are manifestly unrealistic. If they were not, there would be no justification for futures markets in interest rates, since investors and borrowers would make their decisions on the basis of complete foreknowledge. It is precisely because short- and long-term rates have become so volatile, hence even more predictable than they were in the past, that such markets were established and very quickly became a success.

The nature of the futures delivery process requires that cash and futures prices converge to identity by the delivery date because the two are at that point interchangeable. As the element of futurity elapses during the last month or two of a contract's existence, its price becomes more closely linked to the cash counterpart.

The history of the December 1980 90-day Treasury bill contract charted in Exhibit 6 illustrates the broad swings futures prices can exhibit relative to cash rates during the life of a contract. The cash 90-day bill rate at the close of 1980 was about 15.75 percent, and the "spot" (delivery month) contract accordingly went off the board two weeks earlier on December 18 (its final trading day) at 83.5, reflecting a 16.5 discount. But throughout its 18-month life, or the approximately 360 market sessions during which the December 1980 contract was traded, it changed hands at a price of 84.25 (15.75 percent discount) on only one trading day. Between the time trading in that particular contract began in June 1979 and its expiration, the price ranged from 75 basis points below (83.5) to 875 basis points above (93) the price at which it was closed out.

The curves depicted in Exhibit 7 represent the distribution of yields on 90-day Treasury bill contracts for eight successive delivery months on five selected dates throughout 1980. The first quarter of the year saw a rise in the cash 90-day T bill discount from about 12 percent to 15 percent, a second-quarter dip to a 7 percent discount, and then a steady and ultimately accelerating climb to close the year at about the 15.75 percent level.

The T bill futures curve remained inverted during the first quarter of the year, projecting a decrease in the discount over a 24-month period of approximately 225 basis points, at a rate of about 9 basis points a month. The first marked change in the curve during 1980 took place by March 24, when it retained the same approximate slope relative to January 7 but moved about 400 basis points up the yield axis. By June 16, at the peak of the spring rally, the futures yield curve turned positive, reflecting a steadily rising discount from about 6.25 percent to 8.25 percent. By September 29 the curve had risen and turned virtually flat in the 11.5 percent to 12 percent range, and by mid-December it resumed its inverted shape from about 16.5 percent in the nearby contract to 12.5 percent in the most distant.

Evidently, the futures forecast that prevailed at the outset of 1980 underwent a continual revision throughout the year as the market responded to the same factors that shaped the course of cash market yields.

ARE FUTURES SUITABLE INVESTMENT TOOLS?

The issue of suitability of futures trading in an institutional context comes down to the matter of risk. The overriding question should be whether the use of futures increases or reduces risk under a given set of circumstances. This chapter has stressed that there are a variety of applications to which these instruments may be put. Some of them are well suited to, and can in fact contribute materially to, the realization of conservative investment objectives. Other applications are patently inappropriate. It is the responsibility of corporate financial officers or portfolio managers to acquaint themselves with the possibilities and limitations of the various trading techniques in deciding which, if any, of them are best fitted to the situation with which they are confronted.

The experience of recent years has repeatedly confirmed that we occupy a risk-ridden world, in the financial sphere as elsewhere. If it can be demonstrated that the economic risk of entering into a futures contract is measurably less than the risk of not doing so, the determination of suitability should go beyond a knee-jerk reaction that futures are highly speculative, hence beyond the pale so far as prudent money management is concerned.

Market Index Futures Contracts

14   VICTOR NIEDERHOFFER, Ph.D.
Chairman, Niederhoffer, Cross & Zeckhauser
and NCZ Commodities

RICHARD ZECKHAUSER, Ph.D.
Professor of Political Economy, Harvard University
and Founder of Niederhoffer, Cross & Zeckhauser, Inc.

OVERVIEW

Investors may soon be able to trade futures contracts in stock market averages. The Chicago Mercantile Exchange plans a contract based on the Standard & Poor's 500 stock index. The Chicago Board of Trade has proposed several market index futures contracts, including one based on an index of its own construction. The Kansas City Board of Trade plans to trade a contract based on the Value Line Composite Index.

The Kansas City contract (VLF) based on the Value Line Composite Index (VLCI) is fairly typical. Each VLF contract would constitute a promise to buy or sell 500 units of the VLCI, measured in dollars. The underlying value of one VLF contract would be roughly $50,000, since the VLCI currently hovers around 100. Initial margin requirements would be $2,000 for hedgers and $4,000 for speculators. Six contracts will trade at any one time, with delivery in March, June, September, and December.

Reprinted with permission from the January-February 1980 issue of *Financial Analysts Journal*, pp. 49-55.

Regular commissions on a round-trip transaction in one VLF contract are anticipated to be $60—only 13 percent of the cost of buying and selling a reasonably diversified stock portfolio of comparable value. Since the average monthly change in the VLCI is about 5.2 points, the corresponding change in the value of a VLF contract would be $2,600 (500 × 5.2)—about 65 percent of the initial investment of an investor speculating on margin.

Market index futures contracts will provide the margin speculator with a vehicle for participating in general market movements. He will enjoy both a high degree of leverage and low commission costs. In addition, he will know that the contract—being based on the prices of a large number of securities—will be difficult to manipulate and impossible to corner. But market index futures contracts will also be invaluable to investors (including institutions) who desire to protect themselves against such market movements; the contracts will allow them to take either a long or short position in the shares of a specific company without incurring the commensurate market-related risks.

Spurred on by the enormous success of the existing futures contracts in bonds and bills, various exchanges are promoting new market index futures contracts that offer a wide array of products of potential interest to anyone whose financial well-being is affected by the performance of common stocks. The Kansas City Board of Trade has proposed a futures contract based on the Value Line Composite Index. The Chicago Mercantile Exchange has developed a contract based on the Standard & Poor's 500 stock index. The Chicago Board of Trade has prepared one contract based on an index of their own construction that reflects the stock market as a whole, and several others based on specific industry groups. Overseas, Pierson, Helding & Pierson, N.V., a Dutch investment banking firm, is actually trading a contract based on the Dow Jones Industrial Average. In Maryland, Computer Directions Advisors is developing a market for call option writing by pension funds and call option purchasing by speculators based on the Standard & Poor's 500 contract.

Naturally, the agencies, boards, and commissions of the federal bureaucracy have been wrangling among themselves over jurisdiction of these contracts, and potential competitors, such as options exchanges, have raised substantial opposition. Thus, three years after the first contract was proposed, no definite date for the start of trading has yet been set. Because of the potential profitability of this market for both promoters and customers, however, it is hard to believe that that date is far off.

This chapter describes the mechanics of market index futures contracts and explores their potential uses and impact. For the sake of conciseness, it focuses on the Kansas City Board of Trade's contract based on the Value Line Composite Index, although most of what it says is applicable to the other contracts as well.[1] This represents the oldest proposal, dating from 1976, and appears nearest to trading, having already been formally proposed to the Commodity Futures Trading Commission.

THE VLF CONTRACT

Each Value Line Futures (VLF) contract will represent a promise to buy or sell 500 units of the Value Line Composite Index (VLCI), measured in dollars. Since the VLCI hovers around 100, the underlying value of the stocks covered by the contract will be roughly $50,000. The initial margin requirements will be $2,000 for hedgers and $4,000 for speculators; as with any commodity contract, participants will be able to post this earnest money in cash or in interest-earning Treasury bills. There will be no daily trading limit.

The minimum fluctuation in the contract's value will be $5.00, which represents a change of 0.01 percent of the value of the underlying stocks. The change in value of participants' positions will be credited or debited to their equity each day. In case of a profit, participants will be able to remove the increase in equity from their account. In case of a loss, they will have to put up additional capital.

Contracts of 3, 6, 9, 12, 15, and 18 months will trade, with delivery in March, June, September, and December. If trading opened in March 1980, for example, the longest contract would be delivered at the end of September 1981. As of July 1, 1980, the December 1981 contract would become available, and all buyers and sellers of March contracts who had not closed out their positions would settle with each other. The delivery mechanism calls for all open contracts to be settled at a price of 500 times the VLCI two days before the expiration of trading in the contract.

The average daily absolute fluctuation in the VLCI is approximately 0.6. Thus the mean change in the equity of a player long or short one contract will be $300 (500 × 0.6). This represents a profit or loss of 15 percent ($300/$2,000) for a hedger posting minimum margins. But the change represents only 0.6 percent of the value of the underlying stocks.

The contract's sponsors anticipate that regular commissions on a round-trip transaction will total $60. This represents a cost of only 0.12 percent of the underlying value of the contract, or roughly 13 percent of the cost of buying and selling a reasonably diversified stock portfolio of comparable value. It is also substantially less than an option commission. Even a 0.12 percent commission can become

---

[1] A comment by the present authors describing a DJIA contract appeared in *The Chicago MBA* 3, no. 1, and is available on request from the authors.

substantial, however, if turnover over the course of a year rivals that of the typical commodity trader; while the average stock market investment may turn over once every few years, commodity speculators frequently look to a turnover of once every week.

Movements in the VLCI

Table 1 summarizes statistics on the distribution of changes in the VLCI for the 13 years from 1966 to 1978, inclusive. For all intervals except the yearly period, the distribution of changes is roughly symmetric about zero. Apparently, yearly rises tend to be more frequent than yearly declines, but the declines tend to be larger than the rises.

Table 1
Changes in the Value Line Composite Index

	Each Day	Each Week	Each Month	Each Quarter	Each Year
Average absolute change in points	0.64	1.93	5.22	10.66	24.74
Average change on rises	0.62	1.77	5.44	10.64	17.41
Average change on declines	−0.69	−2.09	−5.06	−10.69	−39.39
Percentage of all rises	52.1	53.1	46.7	48.0	66.6
Percentiles of changes					
5 percent	1.29*	3.54	9.76	19.41	23.5
25 percent	+0.51	+1.6	+4.53	+8.18	+11.17
50 percent	+0.05	+0.17	−0.64	−1.5	+0.19
75 percent	−0.47	−1.56	−3.93	−11.22	−17.348
95 percent	−1.54	−4.24	−12.1	−20.77	−56.8

*Five percent of the daily closes in the VLCI were +1.29 points or more above the previous close.
Source: Based on all observations from January 3, 1966 to December 31, 1978. Between 1926 and 1966, Value Line computed its index only yearly.

The mean daily change in the VLCI is 0.64 points. For a week of five trading days, the mean change is 1.93—roughly three times as great. The mean weekly change would be five times as great as the daily change if daily movements were always in the same direction, and only twice as great if consecutive daily movements were completely independent. Thus, consecutive daily changes are positively correlated (a fact confirmed by the serial correlation coefficient of 0.16). With the passage of a month, the average change is about 5.2 points; the speculative investor in the contract, who "owns" 500 times the index, would thus incur an average monthly profit or loss of $2,600 (500 × 5.2), representing 65 percent of his initial investment.

These swings, while precipitous, are comparable to swings in the actively traded grain futures contracts. Corn futures contracts, the most widely traded, experience an average daily change of approximately 0.6 percent; the 0.64 point mean daily change in the VLCI represents about 0.6 percent of its average value.

Table 2 illustrates another way of using historical data to gauge the likely rapidity of change in the VLCI: How long, on average, will it take a hedger to double or lose his initial stake of $2,000—that is, how many trading days will it take the VLCI to gain or lose a cumu-

Table 2
Past Duration of Doubling or Wipe-Out (fully levered trading on Value Line Industrial Index futures market) Hedgers' Margin: $2,000

Dates		Number of Days	VLCI		Rise
From	To		From	To	
Gain of Money					
10/11/76	12/06/76	38	83.50	87.98	+4.48
12/06/76	12/30/76	17	87.98	92.53	+4.55
10/09/77	11/11/77	17	88.27	92.34	+4.07
11/11/77	4/10/78	101	92.34	96.45	+4.11
4/10/78	4/24/78	10	96.45	100.92	+4.47
4/24/78	5/12/78	14	100.92	105.15	+4.23
5/12/78	7/31/78	54	105.15	109.73	+4.58
7/31/78	8/09/78	7	109.73	113.85	+4.12
8/09/78	9/07/78	20	113.85	118.00	+4.15
10/27/78	1/04/79	46	97.44	102.00	+4.56
1/04/79	1/25/79	15	102.00	106.20	+4.20
2/27/79	3/13/79	10	101.71	105.94	+4.23
3/13/79	4/03/79	15	105.94	110.08	+4.14
4/03/79	6/22/79	56	110.08	114.14	+4.06
Average		30 days			+4.28
Loss of Money					
6/30/76	10/11/76	76	87.83	83.50	−4.33
12/30/76	10/09/77	203	92.53	88.27	−4.26
9/07/78	9/20/78	9	118.00	113.54	−4.46
9/20/78	10/19/78	21	113.54	108.00	−5.54
10/19/78	10/23/78	2	108.00	103.70	−4.30
10/23/78	10/27/78	4	103.70	97.44	−6.26
1/25/79	2/27/79	22	106.20	101.71	−4.49
Average		48			−4.81

Note: The first transaction was considered to have started at the close on 6/30/76. Daily losses were noted until a closing price showed a change of at least 4.0 points from the opening transaction. At this point, the transaction was closed out and a new opening transaction undertaken at the current close.

lative four points? During the period from June 30, 1976 to June 22, 1979, the VLCI gained 26.3 points, going from 87.83 to 114.14. It experienced six more cumulative rises of four points than cumulative losses. (In a period during which the index declined overall, of course, losses would be more frequent.)

Over the three-year period, a hedger could have doubled his stakes 21 times, with the average time for a cumulative change of plus or minus four points being 36 trading days. The fastest doubling came in the seven trading days between July 31, 1978, when the VLCI closed at 109.73, and August 9, 1978, when it closed at 113.85. The fastest total losses took two and four days in October 1978. The longest period without a doubling was the 9⅓-month period between December 30, 1976, and October 9, 1977, when the index hovered around 90. On the other hand, during the five-month period between April 10, 1978 and September 7, 1978, a fully levered hedger buyer could have doubled his entire stake five times. But this period was followed by 1½ months during which the hedger would have lost his entire stake on four consecutive occasions.

The major swings in the VLCI show considerable momentum. It also appears that volatility in the stock market, as reflected in the VLCI, is increasing. During the two years ending June 30, 1978 the futures hedger could have lost or doubled his money nine separate times. During the following year, there were 12 such occasions.

A speculator in the VLF contract has to put up twice as much as a hedger; the VLCI must thus change a cumulative eight points to double his money or wipe him out. This futures contract would be substantially less volatile than most active futures contracts. The fluctuations in the VLCI have been such that speculators would have experienced only five doublings or wipe-outs during the entire three-year period. This lack of action for speculators may dampen their willingness to provide liquidity for those on the hedging side of the market.

While hourly figures on the VLCI are not available, the average absolute Dow Jones Industrial Average (DJIA) change has been running about 1.5 points an hour. This works out to an hourly profit or loss to the hedger of four percent.

Features of the VLCI

Most averages and indexes of the stock market tend to move together, since all share many of the same individual stocks. Other things equal, the correlation between a part and the whole is positive. The correlation between two stock market averages is stronger still because the moves of the stocks included in only one average are highly correlated with the moves of the stocks contained in both averages. During the two-year period from December 31, 1976 to December 31, 1978 for example, the VLCI and the DJIA moved in opposite directions on only 69 days of the 500. Interestingly, for 45 of these 69 days, the DJIA moved down and the VLCI up. Over the same period, the two indexes moved in opposite directions in only 14 out of the 105 weeks.

Because of the high correlation between various averages, speculators and hedgers in market index futures should be able to achieve their goals regardless of the index used. Nevertheless, each average has certain unique features, and participants should be aware of them. The VLCI represents the most broadly based of the major security indexes. It now comprises 1,695 stocks—1,499 industrials, 177 utilities, and 19 rails. These include 85 to 90 percent of the stocks on the New York Stock Exchange and a significant sprinkling of American Stock Exchange, over-the-counter, and Canadian offerings. The VLCI includes all of the Standard & Poor's (S&P) 500 and all 30 DJIA stocks.

The VLCI is computed geometrically, relative to some base period. The percentages of base-period prices at which the different stocks now trade are first multiplied together. Then one finds the single factor, A, that, when multiplied by itself as many times as there are stocks in the index, comes to the same product. Say that a three-stock index was at one when its stocks were selling at 50, 100, and 200, and the stocks now sell at 40, 150, and 220, respectively. Multiplying the current to base percentages together yields 1.32 (0.8 × 1.5 × 1.1). Solving the equation A^3 equals 1.32 gives 1.097—the current value of the index.

Although less familiar than arithmetic indexes such as the DJIA or the S&P indexes, geometric indexes have some interesting properties. Each stock in each period, for instance, gets the same weighting regardless of its value. If the index consisted of two stocks, one at 10, which went up 5 percent, and the other at 100, which went up 50 percent, it would not matter for purposes of computing the index that the higher priced stock appreciated more. An arithmetic index would rise more if the higher priced stock appreciated more. (To increase the importance of a particular stock, of course, a geometric index could always include it more than once.) This equal-weighting feature of the VLCI, combined with its exceptional breadth, makes it a good indicator of overall market performance.

Performances of geometric and arithmetic indexes can be compared only if both indexes weight their stocks equally at the outset. If the geometric index includes each stock once, the arithmetic index must start with an equal investment in each stock. Surprisingly, so long as the stocks on each index do not go up or down by precisely the same percentage—in which case there will be no difference in performance—a geometric index will show less appreciation, or more depreciation, than an arithmetic index. The proof of this statement derives from the concavity of the logarithmic function, and is somewhat complex. As an example, consider two $100 stocks, with the index at one. One stock goes up to $160, the other drops to $40. While the arithmetic index will show a change of zero, the geometric average will be 0.8 (A × A = 0.4 × 1.6), representing a drop of 0.2.

Three factors determine how the VLCI will perform relative to the DJIA or the S&P 500—breadth of base, geometric versus arithmetic averaging and differences in content. Table 3 shows that the three indexes can diverge considerably. The geometric VLCI shows a less favorable trend over the 13-year period. In the significant upswing of 1975-76, however, its inclusion of many small, more speculative

Table 3
Percentage Changes in Indexes

	Between Year-Ends, 1965 and 1973	Between Year-Ends, 1972 and 1974	Between Year-Ends, 1974 and 1976
Dow Jones Industrials	−20%	−40%	+40%
Standard & Poor's 500	+ 2%	−43%	+43%
Value Line Composite	−30%	−52%	+80%

stocks that had sizable gains, together with the greater relative weighting it assigned to low-priced stocks, enabled it to overcome the comparative downward bias of geometric averaging. Lower-priced stocks offer a greater part of their return in the form of capital gains (as opposed to dividends) than higher-priced stocks, hence will in general appreciate more (or depreciate less) than higher-priced stocks. Thus the VLCI tends to appreciate faster than comparable arithmetic indexes. On the other hand, the more variability between the performances of individual stocks—that is, some doing well while others do poorly—the more the VLCI will suffer relative to arithmetic indexes.

Given the relatively low margin requirements of all the proposed market index futures contracts, arbitrageurs should be fairly active across all of them. It would be surprising if, in most periods, the VLF contract did not sell at a lower price relative to present value than the contracts based on the arithmetic indexes. However, a belief that small companies will outperform large ones will give a boost to the VLCI relative to the S&P 500 and DJIA.

USES AND IMPACT OF MARKET INDEX FUTURES CONTRACTS

Trading in market index futures contracts could prove beneficial to virtually everyone who invests in equities, for whatever purpose. Some traders—from the lowliest prospective pensioner to the highest flying seller of puts and calls or the corporation planning to issue additional stock—will use such contracts for hedging. These contracts also present speculators with a new opportunity that is particularly attractive because it offers significant leverage.

Hedging against Market Declines

The commonest motive for hedging is to guard against a market decline that would diminish the value of stocks already held. Selling the VLF contract short will prove a highly effective tool in this respect, since the value of the short position and the value of the stocks will move in opposite directions.

Consider the investor who feels that the market is entering a period of substantial volatility but is himself uncertain which way it will turn. (Haven't all investors found themselves in this situation at one time or another?) If the market is weak, he knows he cannot unload several thousand shares of individual stocks except at disastrous price concessions. He can reduce his risk, however, by selling a VLF contract short. He will thus insulate himself from both decreases and increases in the stocks' value, since a full hedge is roughly comparable to getting out of the market by selling one's stocks, except one retains title to the hedged stocks. When the period of uncertainty passes, the hedger may choose to buy the contract back.

Short sellers need not be sophisticated or wealthy institutions or hedgers who already own substantial pools of stock. Consider Professor Brown, who intends to retire in three months. His most significant assets are tied up in his retirement fund, the value of which is closely tied to the stock market. Professor Brown estimates the value of his nest egg at roughly $150,000 at current market prices. He wishes to purchase a condominium now under construction, and will be financially able to do so as long as his nest egg does not decline in value more than 10 percent. Consulting the type of statistics presented in Table 1, Professor Brown is understandably disturbed: The chance that the VLCI will decline more than 10 points—the critical 10 percent—in the next three months is about one in four. He decides he must put off purchase of the condominium.

A market in VLF or other market index futures contracts will give Professor Brown a new option. He can sell three contracts short. While he may, of course, still lose his $6,000, it will take a 20-point swing to put him in a position where he can no longer afford the condominium. The chances of this happening in a three-month period are only 1 in 20.

Dr. Jones, a graduate school classmate of Brown's who pursued a more lucrative career, has just sold the stock of his closely held corporation to a major food company for 100,000 shares of stock currently valued at $2.5 million. Because of Securities and Exchange Commission registration and pooling of interest requirements, Jones must hold for a period of two years. He can hedge against a market decline, however, by selling a VLF contract short. In this way, he can ensure for his beneficiaries a sizable nest egg, provided the stock of the diversified food company moves with the market as a whole. Of course, if Jones did not take this precaution for his beneficiaries, they could make the investment themselves. Any person of moderate means with the expectation of a future windfall in stocks might take a similar tack.

A brokerage house with a net long position in a number of stocks, incurred perhaps to accommodate its customers, may also wish to protect itself, since a substantial decline in the overall market could prove disastrous. The VLF contract would offer an excellent and economical hedge. In fact, once such contracts begin to trade, brokerage houses should be more willing to accept long and short positions in connection with their market making.

Hedging against Rises

Market index futures contracts, like most futures contracts, will initially be used to hedge against a decline in value more often than an increase. But some stock market participants, including those who have a current or future obligation to deliver stock or a product whose price is highly correlated with stocks, must also protect themselves against market rises. In the active grain markets, the volume of hedging against price increases frequently exceeds the volume of hedging against declines.

Many pension funds accrue contributions on a continuous basis, but receive the proceeds only periodically. A long investment in a VLF contract would assure that beneficiaries do not lose out if the market rises rapidly between the date of accrual and investment of the proceeds—an important advantage in an era when accountability in pension fund management is receiving considerably more attention.

For a firm that plans to grow by acquisition, a general market increase could carry target companies' stocks beyond the firm's ability to pay for them. But a firm that purchased a VLF contract could protect its acquisition potential. Similarly, the seller of a company whose deal is fixed in total dollars might wish to maintain future stock purchasing power by buying a VLF contract.

A firm that has committed to issue its shares on an installment basis, perhaps as part of a profit-sharing plan, might be happy to accept the risk that it will do well. But it may not want to get trapped into giving away excessive dollar value should the stock market as a whole have a favorable run. In that case, it should purchase a VLF or similar contract.

Foreign investors frequently plan to invest substantial funds in the United States, but, for one reason or another, wish to defer action—perhaps because of restrictions against liberating their funds or because they expect the price of their currency to rise relative to the dollar. In the interim, they may wish to invest in the U.S. market; it simply looks more promising than anything at home. Purchase of a VLF contract would protect them against the loss of an attractive opportunity.

Another potential beneficiary of the VLF contract is Arnold Goldbug. Believing that excessive government intervention will ruin the U.S. economy, Goldbug has purchased ample supplies of freeze-dried foods, secured his rural retreat, placed most of his funds in Swiss savings banks bearing negative real interest, and is long on hordes of gold and silver. He has only one worry: Disaster may not arrive as soon as his international advisers forecast. To maintain purchasing power until the advent of calamity, he could purchase a VLF contract, thereby also guarding against the possibility of massive inflation. On the other hand, if he believes the same set of circumstances will lead to a massive deflation similar to that of the 1930s, he could short the contract.

Speculators

In many cases, investors eager to go long or short market index futures contracts as hedges against the risks acquired in the course of their other investment activities will be accommodated by speculators in such contracts. The VLF and similar contracts are a splendid vehicle for individuals who like to bet that they can predict market movements.

Numerous speculators in the options market trade options for a lack of a better vehicle to play the market. The VLF contract will offer them the volatility they seek. As Table 1 shows, the VLCI changes 0.64 points per day on average. With the VLCI at 100, and a leverage factor of 12.5, a speculator who happens to be on the right side can achieve a return of 8 percent a day. Hourly rates of return from a correct prediction of direction should run about 5 percent; exact figures are not available, since the VLCI is not tabulated on an hourly basis. Furthermore, in contrast to the options market, the market index futures market will always be thick, quotations will always be relatively easy to secure, and there will be no danger of a short squeeze.

The market index futures contract will also enable option traders and other speculators to hedge certain aspects of their other investments. Speculators will be able to create preferred portfolios that focus their stakes on the gambles they really wish to make and eliminate the risks that were previously unavoidable byproducts of investing. The ability of option traders to hedge against the risk of market movements should improve the liquidity of the options market, hence increase public participation in that market. Market index futures contracts may also encourage activity in other speculative vehicles, since they will free up capital for speculation elsewhere.

VLF contracts offer even small-scale speculators an easy and inexpensive way to put their predictions to the market test. Such speculators will be able to get into and out of $50,000 worth of the market for a small amount—$60, at a minimum—and should save on research costs, since they will not have to inform themselves about particular stocks. In this respect, the VLF contract offers the advantages of an index fund, plus the possibility of selling short. Because of the volatility of the VLF, however, small speculators who cannot face total loss with impunity would probably be foolhardy to establish a position with the minimum margin; some may purchase the contract directly, putting up the full margin.

Furthermore, only the most astute speculators should be encouraged to trade VLF and similar contracts if they intend to turn them over as frequently as they do other commodity futures contracts. Studies of the performance of the public in commodity markets show that between 70 and 90 percent of speculators who are not brokers or dealers lose money. The main reason appears to be the high cost of commissions and bid-asked spreads relative to the absolute magnitude of gains and losses.

Tax Planning and Convenience

Ephraim Middleguy caught the market just right and has made a small killing. He would prefer to consolidate his gains by selling out now, but if he does, his tax penalties will be considerable. He wants to hold out until his profits qualify for favorable tax treatment as long-term capital gains; he would also like to hold his position until next year, thereby gaining some float from the IRS. But by doing so, he takes the chance that the value of his holdings will decline as he waits, and he is strongly risk-averse. He can protect himself by selling a VLF contract short.

Current commodities contracts offer some intrinsic tax advantages: While other capital assets must be held for a full year to qualify for long-term capital gains treatment, a long position in a futures contract requires only six months. The market index futures contract may thus offer stock market participants a unique opportunity to achieve long-term capital gains tax treatment. The potential in terms of more efficient tax planning for market participants is significant.

As noted, the market index futures contract also offers a convenient, readily monitored, readily marketable and potentially highly levered instrument for participating in market movements, and transaction costs will be relatively low. For example, an individual seeking diversification by purchasing and selling 100 shares of just 30 of the 1,700-odd companies comprising the VLCI would have to purchase 3,000 shares of stock at an average price of $45, for a total investment very close to the underlying value of three VLF contracts. In addition, the in-and-out commissions on the 30 round lots would total roughly $4,400; by contrast, the commissions on the VLF contracts would be about $180.

Even the largest institutional investors might find the purchase of a VLF or similar contract a convenience. The time and brokerage commissions required to invest in individual stocks on a continuous basis are burdensome. Purchase of VLF contracts would reduce commissions paid, tighten spreads between bid and asked prices, and save valued time of executive decision-makers. Mutual funds in particular will find that such contracts provide an economical and prudent hedge against risk; 85 percent of the variability of the returns in individual mutual fund portfolios is explained by movements in the averages.

VLF contracts may also offer significant cash flow advantages. By purchasing the contract on a regular (say, weekly) basis, a cash-short company can remain current with the market, while investing only a small fraction of the funds that would be required to achieve comparable positions through outright stock purchases. When funds become available, the company can sell the contract and purchase equivalent amounts of securities.

CONCLUSION

We have discussed only the most direct and obvious advantages of market index futures contracts. They will offer many subtle and secondary benefits as well. From the standpoint of the investor, the contract's key advantages are its low transaction costs and the fact that it can be purchased with a considerable degree of leverage. This alone should lend market index futures markets exceptional liquidity, which may even eventually exceed the liquidity of the spectacularly successful interest rate futures market. Indeed, the market in such contracts may even have a favorable impact on the liquidity of the stock market itself.

Market index contracts could drain a great deal of speculative activity away from stocks that move strongly in concert with the market, hence represent a considerable risk that cannot be hedged. The net result may be much greater stability in the markets for these securities; a whole range of volatile stocks may be expected to act in a much more orderly fashion. Any sell-off or run-up associated with market index futures contracts would involve assets whose total value would be measured in the hundreds of billions of dollars;

scared investors, or overcommitted investors, even by the thousands, could not drive these contracts into a speculative spin. The type of movements observed in the options expiration week of April 1978 and the Labor Day week of September 1978—attributed by many observers to the rush to cover by naked call writers—will not occur as frequently.

Of course, we must recognize that market index futures contracts may never realize their full potential. Continued regulatory intrusion or tie-ups due to unresolved jurisdictional disputes, for example, could keep these contracts from being traded as freely as would be desirable. It is even more difficult to predict which among the several contracts being offered will prove to be the most significant. The Kansas City contract in the VLCI has the advantage of being the broadest based and the most likely to be first on-line at a major stock or commodities exchange. The Chicago Board of Trade index, on the other hand, will enable hedgers and speculators to trade off risky positions in industries. And the Chicago Mercantile Exchange contract will use the more widely known and disseminated S&P 500 index. The DJIA contract, though limited in its availability, has the singular advantage of that venerable index as its base.

Despite seemingly interminable delays and dashed hopes, it appears likely that market index futures contracts will eventually trade. A futures contract in a market index represents an investment vehicle that can enable investors to neutralize the massive tidal movements of equities markets. Its potential economic benefits for speculators and hedgers, small and large, to those planning their taxes or securing their futures, are staggering. Most importantly, such contracts, by providing a sought-after investment vehicle with significant properties not now offered by other investment instruments, will further the primary aim of capital markets in our society—the efficient allocation of resources and risk. Significant economic benefit is not a force that can forever be denied, particularly if there are organizers who can expect fair recompense for their work. By the time you read this chapter, market index futures contracts may be a reality.*

---

*Editor's note: Indeed it is. See Reading 15.

Predictions Fulfilled: The Early Experience of Market Index Futures Contracts*

15 RICHARD ZECKHAUSER, Ph.D.
Professor of Political Economy, Harvard University
and Founder of Niederhoffer, Cross and Zeckhauser, Inc.

VICTOR NIEDERHOFFER, Ph.D.
Chairman, Niederhoffer, Cross and Zeckhauser, Inc.
and NCZ Commodities

Five years after efforts to develop a market index futures contract began, the Kansas City Board of Trade commenced trading in the Value Line Composite Index futures contract on February 24, 1982. Other exchanges quickly followed suit. The Chicago Mercantile Exchange initiated trading in a futures contract on the Standard and Poor's 500 Index less than two months later. On May 6, the New York Futures Exchange opened its futures market, using an index based on the New York Stock Exchange Composite Index. A month later, the Chicago Board of Trade, America's largest commodity exchange, won a battle against Dow Jones for the right to trade a futures contract using the Dow Jones Industrial Average Index. Because the court decision was later overturned, however, trading in that contract is on indefinite hold.

The introduction of three major contracts in less than six months—and a costly legal struggle for a fourth—indicates the great interest aroused by this new financial vehicle. Such interest was to be expected, since, as we showed in a previous article,[1] such contracts

---
*Copyright © 1982, Richard Zeckhauser and Victor Niederhoffer. All rights reserved.

[1] Victor Niederhoffer and Richard Zeckhauser, "Market Index Futures Contracts," *Financial Analyst's Journal,* January-February 1980, pp. 49-55. The article is reprinted as Reading 14 in this book.

serve useful economic functions as both hedging and speculative instruments, and have a range of beneficial uses for various classes of investors. We predicted then, that barring significant antagonistic regulation, that these contracts would gain widespread use and exceptional liquidity. In the first trading days of June 1982—less than a month after the New York Stock Exchange Composite Index futures started trading—an average of roughly 1,700 contracts traded daily in the Value Line, 7,000 in the New York Stock Exchange Composite Index, and 8,500 in the Standard & Poor's. With index prices at about $120, $65, and $110, respectively, contract values were $60,000, $32,500, and $55,000. (Each contract represents 500 units of its index.) The open interests in these contracts, indicating the amounts of capital at risk, were of the order $240 million, $130 million, and $420 million, respectively.

By any measure of user acceptance, market index futures contracts have been a remarkable success. Brokers, traders, and the exchanges are delighted with the new instrument. The estimated 10,000 or more speculators and hedgers who have entered these markets apparently feel that the market index futures contract is beneficial for them.

Because of this success, there is fierce competition among the exchanges. It is generally agreed that thicker markets will lure trading volume from thinner markets. Since the three market index futures serve nearly identical functions, it would be reasonable to speculate that the one that performs the best in terms of representing the market accurately and providing substantial liquidity will enlarge its market share. Two (or more) market index futures could simultaneously prosper only if some customers had lower transactions costs on one exchange and other customers on the other. (For example, stock investors might be regular customers of firms with seats on the New York Futures Exchange. Commodities traders, by contrast, might find it more convenient and cheaper to trade on the Mercantile Exchange.)[2] In addition, of course, useful, more specialized index funds might be developed—for example index funds in particular industries, to trade on particular exchanges.

Now that the success of the market index futures concept seems virtually assured, antagonistic regulation is a troubling prospect. Congress has shown more than a passing interest in the contract. For

---

[2] Dwight Grant usefully extended our January-February 1980 article by considering the number of contracts in a particular index that should trade at a particular time. He demonstrates that to reduce end-of-contract transactions difficulties, it will be worthwhile to have two overlapping contracts in the same market index. Ignoring the differential transactions cost argument, he concludes that contracts in more than one similar index are not desirable, for they will reduce the liquidity of the overall market in index futures. See "Market Index Futures Contracts: Some Thoughts on Delivery Dates," *Financial Analysts Journal*, May-June 1982, pp. 60-63.

example, the House Energy and Commerce Committee, chaired by Representative John Dingell of Michigan—best known in the regulatory arena as a staunch opponent of the regulation of automobiles—has questioned whether the public has been adequately protected from the dangers of these contracts. Dingell has suggested that the Securities and Exchange Commission may have erred in making the Commodity Futures Trading Commission responsible for overseeing market index futures. The hoary charge that these contracts are no more than gambling instruments has been raised once again, as have the (yet to be demonstrated) difficulties associated with delivery, supposedly due to the lack of a physical instrument. The who-should-regulate-and-how issue is part of a larger set of jurisdictional concerns. They are of particular moment now since they will establish precedents for a number of proposed new option contracts on a variety of futures.

The level of trading in market index futures indicates that the contracts play a useful role in reducing transactions costs. (In the fictitious world of zero transactions costs—a useful simplification often invoked in finance theory—investors would merely buy and sell whole portfolios of stocks when they wished to take a position in the market as a whole.) The transactions cost advantage is likely to be particularly significant for those who wish to short the market, since alternative investment vehicles—the short analogue of mutual funds—are not available. Moreover, many institutions are constrained in their ability to sell short.

Interestingly, if all markets functioned perfectly and costlessly—and if all traders in markets were fully rational—a market index future contract would not be expected to provide useful information. In this situation, the spot index itself would capture expectations with regard to future price. If a future in the index were established, arbitrage would assure that it traded in a fixed relationship to the spot price.[3]

Transactions costs may not be zero, even if arbitrage is perfect. Then, if the futures contract offers lower transactions costs for some parties—as seems reasonable to expect in the case of market index futures—the contract will capture some useful information. Through arbitrage, this information will feed back to affect the value of the spot index. Finding a fully arbitraged relationship between spot and

---

[3] The correct theoretical relationship is that $F = S(1 + r - d)^x$. Here F is the futures price, S is the spot price, r is the riskless rate of interest, d the average dividend rate for stocks in the index, and x the fraction of a year until expiration. For example, if the spot price were 100, the riskless rate of interest 14 percent, and the dividend rate 6 percent, then a future coming due in one year, i.e., $x = 1$, would trade at 108.

If interest rates are uncertain, a market projecting interest rates will also be required if perfectly functioning markets are to render market index futures redundant.

Table 1
Trading Relationship of Value Line Composite Index and Its Nearest Futures Contract:
Price of Future *Minus* Price of Spot at Closing, February 24, 1982-June 10, 1982 (cents)

	−200 and less	−150 to −200	−100 to −150	−50 to −100	0 to −50	0 to 50	50 to 100	100 to 150	150 to 200	200 and more	Total
Number of observations	8	7	7	11	14	10	3	6	4	1	71

future prices does *not* imply that the futures contract captures no information.

There is no need to dwell further on the theoretical aspects of this matter. Experience has proved that the futures contract and the index can trade well out of line. Table 1 compares spot and futures prices during the first 71 days of trading in the Value Line Composite Index futures.

Two points are worth noting. First, contrary to the predictions of finance theory, the futures contract was on the whole priced below the spot over this period. Second, the relationship between the futures price and the spot price varied quite considerably.

Two features of the Value Line Composite Index deserve particular emphasis in interpreting this evidence. First, because it is a geometric index, its performance is biased downward. In comparison to arithmetic indices, its future-to-spot price ratio will be "too low," which is consistent with the evidence.[4] Second, the very broad base of the index slows its response to market changes. If the market takes a significant move, some of the stocks in the index will not yet have traded. The index, based in part on premove prices of less actively traded stocks, will underrepresent the move. Because of this lagged effect, which we might call the *wait-to-be-traded* feature of a spot index, a future on that index—which attempts to jump to the equilibrium value of the index on each trade—provides a more accurate representation of the true value of the market.

If this formulation is correct, the spot index should possess considerable momentum, a tendency for successive price movements to be in the same direction; the futures contract should have very little. To test this conjecture, we examined half-hourly price changes for each over the period March 2 through June 10, 1982, to see how long a series of changes in one direction persisted before a reversal. Such a series is called a *run;* its length is the number of changes in

---

[4] The fact that market index futures provide the only convenient instrument for selling the market short provides a complementary reason why their price may be biased downwards, hence "too low."

Table 2
Runs in Half-Hourly Price Movements, Value Line Composite Index;
Futures Contract on Value Line Composite Index, March 2-June 24, 1982

	Spot Contract		Futures Contract	
Length of Run	Positive Change	Negative Change	Positive Change	Negative Change
1	49	39	114	118
2	28	22	58	64
3	15	15	27	28
4	5	13	12	8
5	3	10	2	5
6	9	4	–	3
7	5	2	1	–
8	1	4	3	–
9	–	3	–	–
10	2	1	–	–
11	–	2	–	–
12	1	–	–	–
13	2	–	–	–
16	–	1	–	–
20	–	1	–	–

one direction that it incorporates. Table 2 shows the observed lengths of runs.

Thus, for example, there were precisely 28 occasions when the spot price rose in precisely two successive half-hours and then turned down. Over this period, there were roughly as many up as down half-hourly movements in the spot price, and similarly for the future. If successive moves were independent, the probability of a run of length two would be half that of length one, three would be half of two, etc. A One Sample Run Test applied to the spot price rejects the null hypothesis of independence at the 0.01 level; that is, the spot index displays considerable momentum. For the futures contract, on the other hand, the null hypothesis of independence in successive half-hourly price movements is accepted.[5] This suggests that the futures price does try to jump to equilibrium.

The evidence is clear. The futures contract is not a redundant instrument for information capture. Its attempts to anticipate market movements are reflected by two facts: (1) it has no momentum and (2) it moves above and below the spot market. The central question then becomes whether movements in the futures contract

---
[5] See Sidney Siegel, *Nonparametric Statistics* (New York: McGraw-Hill, 1956), pp. 52-60. When the price was unchanged on a half-hourly basis, we treated this as a reversal, and assumed that the run was broken. A subsequent movement in the same direction would thus be treated as the start of a new run. This explains the discrepancy between the number of positive and negative runs. This treatment creates a slight bias in favor of accepting the null hypothesis.

on the index are actually valuable in predicting movements in the spot.

To address the value-in-prediction question, we divided the 71 observations on the first three months' trading in the Value Line futures contract, reported in Table 1, into two groups, depending on whether the value of the nearest future less the spot was above or below the median. (The median value for those observations was −45.) We then examined the movement in the spot price for the next hour, the next day, and the next three days. As shown graphically in Figure 1, the relationship between future and spot prices seems to have considerable predictive value.

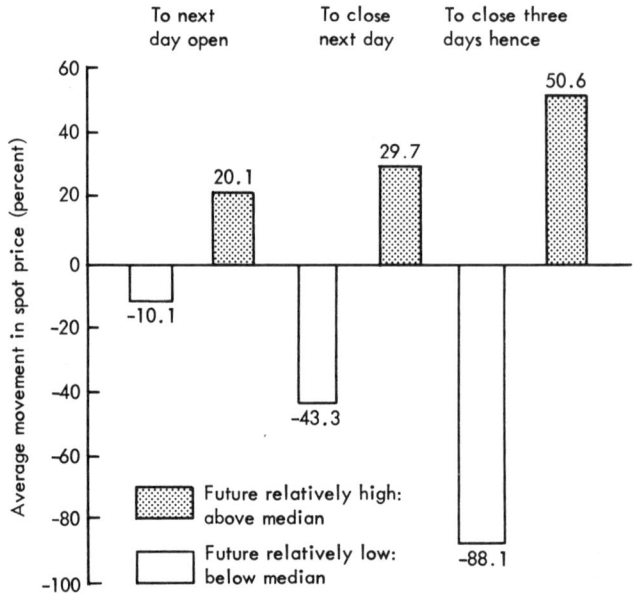

Figure 1
Movement in Spot Price as a Function of Futures Price Less Spot Price, March 2-June 10, 1982

When the future lies above the spot, the spot will tend to rise, and vice versa. We do not think that the wait-to-be-traded feature of stock indices is sufficient to explain this pattern, particularly since the effect persists far beyond the next hour. To test this effect, we ranked the movements in the spot index from close one day hence to close three days hence. The average rank for the below-median cases (future low relative to the spot) was 30.1; for the above-median cases it was 40.9. Using a one-sided test, the difference is significant at the .025 level.⁶ There is strong evidence suggesting that the futures contract captures relevant information about the movement of the spot index that is not captured by the spot index itself.⁷

CONCLUSION

Market index futures have been enormously successful trading instruments, capturing much investor and broker attention and achieving substantial trading volumes. Presumably their success is due to the lower transactions costs they offer as both hedging and speculative instruments. The advantages they offer to those who wish to be short the market are particularly significant.

More noteworthy, the market index future provides a streamlined instrument for capturing information. We have seen three kinds of evidence that support this assertion: the contract has been heavily traded; the futures price moves more rapidly than the spot price; and the futures price often lies below the spot, despite the time value of money.

The most interesting hypothesis suggested by experience to date is that the futures index may actually be of independent value in predicting movements in the spot price. The record is brief; traders may not yet have accommodated themselves to the new set of opportunities. The wait-to-be-traded bias remains to be fully assessed. But if over the long run the futures price does prove helpful in forecasting the spot price, some of the most fundamental assumptions of modern finance theory will have to be reconsidered.

---

⁶ This is a Wilcoxon Two Sample Rank Sum Test. See John W. Pratt and Jean D. Gibbons, *Concepts of Nonparametric Theory* (New York: Springer-Verlag, 1981), pp. 249-65.

⁷ Note that even if the futures index captures useful information it might not pass this test, for the captured information might be arbitraged into the spot index.

Financial futures provide an interesting illustration of this possibility. The trading volume in those markets is very large relative to that in spot markets. Traders on the spot have learned to take guidance from price movements on the futures market. If they take perfect guidance, hence arbitrage away differences, naive statistical examination might conclude that futures prices had no explanatory value. At least theoretically, however, they could be the source of all explanatory value.

section 5

Tax Shelters, Real Estate, and Venture Capital

INTRODUCTION

This section covers several topics that traditionally have not been included in investment management textbooks, although in recent years some authors have devoted space to several of the topics.

First is Reading 16, a discussion of tax shelters by Robert E. Swanson and Barbara Mardinly Swanson. The three following readings discuss real estate investments. In Reading 17, Professor Maury Seldin and Dr. Arthur M. Weimer explain how to select real estate investment opportunities, negotiating strategies, and the use of leverage in financing an acquisition. The factors that should be considered when purchasing land as an investment are discussed by Alan J. Inbinder and Roy D. Gottlieb in Reading 18. Paul Sack in Reading 19 then describes how real estate portfolios should be managed.

In 1981, an estimated $1.2 billion in venture capital was raised in the United States, slightly less than half of which was pumped into new enterprises. One reason for the recent venture capital boom was the decline in the maximum capital gains tax from 49 percent to 28 percent in 1978 and to 20 percent in 1981. In Reading 20, Alan Joel Patricof offers general guidelines that an investor should consider before investing in a new venture.

Tax Shelters*

16 ROBERT E. SWANSON, J.D.
Tax Shelter Consultant and Attorney
New York City and Ridgewood, N.J.

BARBARA MARDINLY SWANSON
Professional Writer

Despite popular belief, tax shelters were not invented late one April night in the early 1960s by an unscrupulous tax accountant in a shiny suit. They were "invented" by the members of the Congress of the United States, in their infinite wisdom (and their three-piece suits). Tax shelters are as old as the 16th Amendment to the Constitution. When, in 1913, Congress added to our Constitution the words: "The Congress shall have power to lay and collect tax on incomes, from whatever source derived, without apportionment among the several states, and without regard to any census or enumeration," and it wrote the original set of laws to implement our brand new federal income tax, Congress chose not to tax all economic activity equally. Instead, because it saw the tax laws as a means not only of collecting revenues but of achieving certain social policies as well, Congress *favored* some financial arrangements. In those first federal tax laws (and in the 70 years-worth of evolution that have rendered that 30-word amendment the leviathan it is today), Congress encouraged certain socially desirable activities by offering *tax*

---

*This selection is excerpted from Robert E. Swanson and Barbara Mardinly Swanson, *Tax Shelters: A Guide for Investors and Their Advisors* (Homewood, Ill.: Dow Jones-Irwin, 1982).

incentives to those who participate in them. So, to foster charitable giving, contributions to qualified charitable organizations are considered tax deductible. And to help people own their own homes, deductions for real estate taxes and mortgage interest payments are allowed. And, in the hopes of keeping the national economy in perpetual motion (and, in some cases, to accomplish particular social objectives at the same time), the tax laws provide businesses with a variety of tax incentives (depreciation deductions, depletion deductions, the investment tax credit, and others) designed to dollar-reward capital investment, exploration, research and development, and so on.

Under a carefully defined set of rules, individual taxpayers may buy into such a business and, without actually running or actively participating in that business, may benefit from those dollar-rewards. That is, individuals may passively invest in an enterprise and reap not only its profits but its tax advantages, too. And by law those tax advantages will extend not just to the income from that particular investment but to the individual's other income (salary, commissions, pensions, capital gains) as well.

Intentionally investing in those specific ways that will provide you with these tax advantages is perfectly legal. The deductions, credits, and other incentives need not be just the surprise bonus for having made one of the favored investments. You can shop for your incentives. Indeed, finding the most useful, most appropriate tax advantages is fundamental to educated investing today.

The tax reformer may consider sheltering to be an exploitation of a technical chink in the armor of the tax code—a game of individual taxpayers masquerading as businesses for the sole purpose of lowering their tax bills. But, in fact, investing in a business venture *in the specific ways allowed by the tax laws* is a legitimate and often effective way to protect one's income and spur the economy to boot—not opportunism at all, but a potential golden opportunity.

For example, the federal government wants to encourage the construction of low-income housing. Rather than building such apartment units itself, the government offers tax breaks to businesses that invest in them and to the individual taxpayers who *invest* in those businesses. And to sweeten the deal even more, the tax laws allow those tax breaks to apply to all of the investors' other sources of income. So if you invest in a well- and honestly run low-income housing construction project, *all* of your other sources of income can be protected by those same tax breaks. Voila! You are tax sheltering.

When an individual buys a tax shelter he or she makes a direct investment in a business. For example, when a doctor buys an interest in an oil and gas drilling program, the IRS treats him as if he is in the oil business, even though he thinks of himself as a doctor who has made a passive investment in an oil program. Because he is in the oil business, he currently deducts the drilling expenses as the wells are being drilled. These deductions are then used to reduce his other taxable income—i.e., the fees from his medical practice and income from any other sources, such as stocks, bonds, or savings accounts—all of which are in no way connected to his oil drilling venture.

How does all of this work? Tax losses and deductions are the key concepts here. Although the tax law is very complex, the principle of tax shelters is simple. The basic equation of our tax system as applied to tax shelter investments is:

Business income − Deductions = Profit or loss

A tax shelter gives you a *loss* for any year when deductions exceed income. Tax shelter investors select businesses which generate *more deductions than income* in early years in order to report tax losses in those early years. Tax shelters usually are new business enterprises. When you start up a business, there are expenses before the cash flow starts. In addition to the expenses of the new business, there are often additional tax incentives for capital investment, such as depreciation deductions, which further increase the reportable tax loss. The start-up expenses plus the additional tax incentives for investment will combine to exceed taxable income, resulting in a tax shelter loss which the investor is able to report on his or her own tax return and use to shelter other income.

You don't actually have to be losing money to report a tax loss. If you have a good investment, at the same time that you are reporting a loss on your tax return, the investment will be increasing in value. Oil drilling is a good example. Between the time an oil well is drilled and when it actually produces, there is a time lag. At the time of drilling, huge reserves of oil can be discovered that will make the well highly profitable in the long run. But in that first year of the operation, substantial drilling expenses have been incurred and no production income realized. So while you are dancing in the streets at the success of your strike, in the eyes of the IRS you have a loss that year. Your deductible expenses exceeded your income in that time period.

Cattle feeding is another example of a new business enterprise which is a tax shelter. If you own a small steer and would like to sell it to a slaughter house as a big steer, you must feed it. The cost of the feed is deductible this year as it is consumed. Next year you will sell the steer and have a profit, but this year the animal is eating, which means it is generating deductions at a time when it is not generating income. This year the steer is a tax shelter even though it is constantly increasing in value. This year you deduct the loss on your steer against your other taxable income. *Next year* when it is sold, the steer will create taxable income.

Tax shelter money gravitates to those businesses where deductions may be accelerated into the early years and where recognition of income can be put off. Let's stay with the oil and gas drilling and cattle-feeding examples to see how deductions are accelerated.

In oil and gas drilling programs, certain costs of drilling the well may be deducted in the year the well is drilled, or they may be deducted over the projected productive life of the well. A deduction today is worth more than the same deduction next year, because you have the use of the money in the meantime. So the election is made to take the deductions all in the first year. Oil and gas programs attract tax shelter money because of the option to accelerate the deduction for drilling expenses into the first year of operation.

In cattle feeding, depending on how the investment is structured, you may take a deduction this year for feed that will be consumed by your steer next year. That is, you not only get to take this year's expenses this year, but you get to turn next year's expenses into this year's deductions.

The ability to delay reporting profits is another type of tax advantage enjoyed by some businesses. If a profit can be made but the tax on it put off until a later year, you are ahead because delaying paying a tax frees up money that otherwise would have currently been paid to the government.

Real estate investment is a good example of a tax shelter offering the opportunity to delay the recognition of income. Real estate is seen as a hedge against inflation. Investors put up with low current cash yields in order to obtain current tax benefits and because they hope the value of the property will increase. That increase in value is not taxed until the property is sold or disposed of in a way to cause the gain to be realized and recognized. A significant portion of the economic profit from the investment, the appreciation value, is not currently taxed. The only part of the economic profit which is currently taxable is the rent which almost always is less than the deductions in the early years. Tax losses are available in the early years of the investment while taxation on the major portion of the profit—the appreciation—is deferred to later years. Not a bad deal.

Some businesses offer a third tax advantage—they provide the investor with current deductions which shelter *ordinary income,* and when the profit on appreciation is eventually taxed, the much lower *capital gains* rates apply. This happy phenomenon is called *converting ordinary income into capital gains.* Here, too, real estate investment is a good example. The losses from the real estate are deductible against ordinary income, and depending on how the deal is structured, the gain on the sale will be capital gains.

Some businesses are better-suited for investment than others. In considering tax shelters, look for potentially profitable businesses that offer one or more of these tax advantages:

16: Tax Shelters

1. Deductions which may be accelerated into the first year or years.
2. Situations where the recognition of income for tax purposes may be delayed or deferred.
3. Income which can be converted into capital gains.

The object of a tax shelter, then, is not to lose money. The object is to report tax losses while you are making money which is not currently taxable. You don't want your oil well to be dry or your cattle to die or your apartment building actually to decrease in value. You want lots of oil and fat cattle fetching fatter prices and runaway values for your real estate. Tax shelters produce tax losses in their early years, and if they are successful, they will generate profit—taxable profit—in subsequent years.

Assuming we have been successful in generating tax shelter losses, let's see how they work on your tax return.

HOW A TAX SHELTER LOSS REDUCES YOUR TAXES

The basic equation of our tax system as it pertains to individuals investing in tax shelters is:

Personal income − Tax shelter loss = Income subject to tax

Personal income includes salary, commissions, dividends, taxable interest, the includable portion of capital gains, rent, and royalties and so forth. The shelter results from the tax shelter loss being subtracted from personal income. The more tax shelter losses you have, the more personal income you shelter. Because tax shelter losses will shelter all types of personal income, any high-bracket taxpayer can use tax shelters, no matter what the source of his or her income is. You can use tax shelters if your income is exclusively from salary or if it is exclusively from investment or if it is a mix of the two.

TAX SHELTERS CAN ADD TO YOUR TAXABLE INCOME

Here is the bad news. Going back to our basic equation:

Personal income − Tax shelter loss = Income subject to tax

you can see that you have an *increased* tax liability when your investment starts making money. When a tax shelter loss becomes a profit, the profit is added to your personal income, thereby increasing your taxable income. Remember that for you to make money, your tax shelter must be a sound investment. Someday your sound investment will pay out, and you will have taxable income. You are likely to have cash from that investment with which to pay the tax, but we will see that in some shelters the tax liability will exceed the cash available from the shelter. Many people are unpleasantly surprised when they find that they have taxes to pay and no cash with which to pay them.

The good news is that in many tax shelters, when the loss turns into a profit, often the tax liability on the profit is less than the tax benefits gained in the early years when you were able to claim the losses.

HOW TAX SHELTERS ARE ORGANIZED

Since the key to tax shelters is losses that are made available to the investor, a business structure that will cause the tax losses to flow through to the investor is fundamental. *Most tax shelters are organized as partnerships.* The partnership form is ideally suited to tax shelters because taxable losses and gains flow directly through the partnership to the partner (here, the investor). In contrast to a partnership, the corporate form of doing business does not allow the investor to pick up the losses realized by the corporation.

A partnership is treated for tax purposes as if the investor owned the property outright. As a result, all taxable events of the partnership are picked up on the investor's tax return. The losses are reported as well as the profits. If the partnership has tax-exempt income or a capital gain, the investor receives tax-exempt income or capital gains. To use the legal terminology, the partnership is not a taxable entity; it is merely a conduit. Because it is merely a conduit, it retains no taxable income, so it does not pay taxes. The conduit is perfect for a tax-favored business like a tax shelter. On the other hand, if your business will generate a lot of ordinary income which will, in turn, be needed for reinvestment in the business, organize as a corporation. If you want to distribute money as well as tax benefits to the owners of the business, organize as a partnership.

HOW RISKY ARE TAX SHELTERS?

Tax shelters have a reputation for being very risky investments, but this notoriety may not be entirely fair. Granted, many shelter ventures fail, but careful selection, education, and interest can enhance the odds for success dramatically. Despite this logical advice to shop carefully, people who would never think of buying just any stock that comes along go through a December ritual of eagerly offering handfuls of their hard-earned dollars to any tax shelter they hear whispered about in the clubhouse locker room. Too many people take unnecessary risks in an already risky business.

Some shelters tend to be riskier than others. Here's how we rate them:

Shelters	Risk
Real estate:	
New construction	High
Existing buildings	Low
Government subsidized	Low
Rehabilitation	Low
Raw land	High
Oil and gas:	
Exploratory	High
Developmental	Medium to high
Equipment leasing	Low to medium
Cattle feeding	High
Cattle breeding	High
Research and development	High
Movies, broadway shows, books, etc.	High
Flimflam	Very high

Of course, these classifications are generalizations—what counts is how *your* tax shelter performs. A quality high-risk deal can be a lot safer than an iffy low-risk deal. Note, too, that these ratings are relative to other tax shelters—*not* to all other forms of investment. Indeed, compared to some traditional forms of investment, even the lowest-risk shelter can be a high risk. The trouble is that many of the deals offered today are (to be charitable) garbage. These are the ill-conceived business ventures which have no chance or intention of making money but which promote themselves as tax sheltering vehicles. The truth is that such "deduction mills" are frauds on the investor. Deductions alone simply cannot be enough.

In the wild and wooly days before the at-risk rules, many investors were able to make big money from deductions alone. The success or failure of the business venture was irrelevant as long as it kept churning out deductions. In fact, through quirks in the old tax laws, many of those highly leveraged deals would have fallen apart had they started to earn any money! When investors are willing to exchange their dollars for tax deductions equaling several times their investment, it's not surprising that they never see their investment dollars again. Those preform deals quickly gave tax shelters a bad reputation for being shady and risky.

If buying garbage in order to receive tax deductions made little sense back then, buying garbage today with the 1976, 1978, and 1981 at-risk rules in effect is nonsense. In all deals other than real estate, the at-risk rules limit the tax deductions an investor may claim to 100 percent of the amount invested, so if you invest $1, you can at best deduct $1. This means that even if you are in the highest, or 50 percent, tax bracket you can always lose at least 50 cents on each dollar you invest. For investing in a tax shelter to make any sense today, the shelter must be a successful business operation; it must make a profit; *it must generate for its investors some substantial amount of cash.* With the exception of a few special real estate investments, which we will discuss later, the old, straight tax deals are dead, and anyone telling you or selling you otherwise is wrong, or worse, a fraud. There are no more huge multiple write-offs, just multiple rip-offs.

Only tax shelters that are profitable businesses make sense, so invest only in shelters that look like they will be walloping financial successes. We can't stress this enough. When you consider that the impact of loss will be cushioned by the built-in tax savings, careful, informed, ungreedy sheltering can be no riskier than playing the stock market.

DEFERRAL—INTEREST-FREE LOANS

Tax shelters generate deductions (depreciation deductions, interest deductions, intangible drilling expense deductions), and when you claim these deductions, your tax bill is reduced. Reducing your tax bill means that dollars that would otherwise go to Uncle Sam stay in your pocket. (Ideally, they won't stay there long but will be sent out to work in various investment situations.)

Alas, deductions are not forever. Eventually, you must give them back. At some point, when you receive income from your investment or when you sell it, the IRS will "call in" those deductions, a process sometimes known as *recapture* and tax them.

In the meantime, however, you have had the use of that money; you have *deferred* your tax liability from one year to another. And in that sense, you have had a loan from the government. And since the IRS does not charge any interest or penalty for the time lag in payment of these tax dollars, you have had an *interest-free* loan from the government.

Of course, the government is not granting you a sum of money; you haven't had to apply for this loan nor will you have a loan, per se, to pay off at some later time. Rather, as an incentive to encourage investment in certain kinds of business activities, the government has let you keep your own money a little longer and not charged you in the interim. Since loans are normally expensive creatures, these interest-free loans are particularly valuable.

Not having to pay interest on your loan from the government and, in turn, having those dollars free to work elsewhere is one of the important benefits of deferral. The "interest" which you do not have to pay the government is money that is yours to keep. And if you turn around and invest those dollars, anything those dollars generate, less taxes, will be yours to keep as well.

Deferral's other big benefit is tied to inflation. As long as there is inflation, when the time comes for this (or any other) loan to be paid off, you will get to pay it off with Boloney (or deflated) Dollars. To understand Boloney Dollars, think of when you purchased your house. Assume that 10 years ago you bought your house for $30,000 and that you paid for it with $5,000 in cash and a mortgage of $25,000. In the 10 years since that deal was financed, inflation has played incredible games with values. Let's say that your $30,000 house is now worth $100,000. Today you're able to pay that mortgage with pieces of paper that are still called dollars but which are mere shadows of what they once were. Ten years ago, $25,000 bought most of your house (83 percent to be specific). Today, it buys only 25 percent of it! And because of inflation, 25,000 paper dollars are a lot easier to earn today than they were 10 years ago. Because of inflation, you will work a lot less to pay off your debt—hence the term, *Boloney Dollars.* (Of course, if for some reason there were *de*flation, you'd have to pay back with Filet Mignon Dollars!)

If you believe, as we do, that the government is largely responsible for inflation, then you will see poetic justice in using deferral to your advantage against the government that is so busy deflating the value of your money. You should convert your money into property. You should also become a borrower (having a negative amount of money). Who better to borrow from than the government?

REAL ESTATE

Real estate is often called the king of tax shelters, perhaps because it is by far the most popular form of tax incentive investment in the country today. Its appeal as an investment is based on several factors—real estate is *tangible,* it can be *local* (and, therefore, easy to find and easy to manage), and the concept behind the shelter is *easy to comprehend.* Indeed, the idea of property is something we pick up practically as children.

In addition, in real estate you may invest on a small scale and still make a sound profit. You are not limited to large syndicated investments. Smaller opportunities can be just as appealing, because the same economic and tax advantages enjoyed by the big investors in multimillion-dollar office buildings are also available to the individual who invests in the single-family dwelling around the corner from his home.

Real estate investment has many economic advantages:

1. Appreciation in value during inflationary times provides an inflation hedge.
2. Leverage (or the use of other people's money to make your investment) enables you to buy more property for less cash.
3. Predictability of costs and revenues in conservative real estate investments provides greater stability than in other tax shelters.
4. Government subsidies and guarantees to low- and moderate-income housing projects make them economically viable.

In addition, real estate investment offers many important tax advantages:

1. The at-risk rules do not apply. That is, deductions which are greater than the amount invested are available.
2. Ordinary income is converted into capital gains. Going into the tax shelter, deductions offset ordinary income, while coming out, much of the income is capital gains income.
3. The new 15-year write-offs give you more deductions in early years.
4. Large tax credits are available for rehabilitation of old buildings.

If you are interested in real estate shelters, you have a great many alternatives to choose from. The risk and reward possibilities vary greatly, as do the tax benefits you may receive. Such variety increases the chances of your investing in a shelter tailor-made to fit your financial and emotional needs. The major categories are:

1. Conventional New Construction. If you want a shelter that will make you feel like a real estate tycoon, go for a deal that is constructing new buildings—apartments, offices, shopping centers, warehouses, etc. When you invest in these shelters, you are in the high-risk, high-reward strata, playing the way the big boys play. Putting up a new building, as compared with buying an existing one which is completed and already rented, is a very entrepreneurial activity. You are the developer. If all goes well, you should make a good deal of money, which is your just reward for the risks you have taken. If anything goes wrong, you have problems, and more than likely, you will lose your money.

In addition to a greater potential economic reward, the tax benefits in a new construction deal are greater than they are if you purchase an existing property. Although recent legislation has reduced the tax benefits, you still receive handsome write-offs in these construction deals because during the construction period when no taxable rent is coming in, you incur fees and expenses. Some of these fees are currently deductible and others must be deducted over a period of years. But compared to most other tax shelters, the tax benefits in a new construction deal are quite attractive.

2. Government-Assisted New Construction. Of all real estate tax shelters available, government-assisted new construction deals offer the greatest tax benefits. The investor may legally obtain 3 to 1 or better write-offs and not worry that the IRS will try to throw out the whole deal. The write-offs are so large in these deals because the amount borrowed is significantly greater than it is in other investments.

There are a variety of government programs offering assistance such as rent subsidies, mortgage guarantees, and subsidies of mortgage payments. Because of these various types of assistance, very small cash investments can be leveraged to purchase big investments, which means that the tax deductions will be tremendous.

The price you pay for the government assistance is government control over how the project is run and over how much rent may be charged and, therefore, how much profit may be made. In theory, the government is supposed to allow you a modest profit, and as costs rise, rents should be allowed to rise, but often it does not work that way because of how controls actually work.

Because the economic payout is, at best, small, these deals are often strictly tax deals. Government-assisted new construction deals are the major exception to the general rule that when shopping for a shelter one should look for a deal that will provide a substantial economic profit.

3. Purchasing Existing Rental Property. These are the conservative, bread-and-butter real estate investments. Here you are buying a going concern, a known commodity. The risks are comparatively low and so are the rewards. The tax breaks are comparatively modest, too. Depreciation deductions will be spread over the life of the building, and as a consequence, you generally must wait many years before receiving tax losses equal to your equity investment.

The investor should receive an immediate and relatively constant cash flow in these deals. The cash flow should be tax free for many years, and there should be modest tax losses over and above the cash flow. Some people look on this type of investment as an alternative to municipal bonds because here, too, the investor receives a modest, tax-free current return on his money. The advantage over municipal bonds is that if the property increases in value, you benefit from the appreciation.

Lest these types of investments be categorized as uniformly humdrum, it should be noted that some of these projects can be very aggressive investments. The more venturesome investor might look for distressed properties, or properties with speculative appeal due to their locations, unusual use, or the nature of their leases, or he might look for apartments with the potential for conversion to condominiums or co-ops.

4. Rehabilitation of Old and Historic Buildings. Rehabilitation shelters are interesting, and should become quite popular as a result of the big, new tax credits provided in the 1981 Tax Act. Congress created three levels of credit based on the age of the building:

1. 15 percent credit for structures at least 30 years old.
2. 20 percent credit for structures at least 40 years old.
3. 25 percent credit for certified historic structures.

Starting in 1982 we should see an exciting new era for rehabilitation as a result of these new credits.

5. Raw Land. Speculation in raw land is as old as the territorial imperative. Raw land deals are very risky, very illiquid and, for the smart and lucky, very rewarding. The tax benefits here are comparatively few. Only the real estate taxes are deductible. Interest is also deductible—if you can obtain a loan. In most cases conventional lending institutions will not lend money on unimproved real estate.

Although interest is deductible, the amount of interest you may deduct is limited by the investment-interest limitation which provides that you may deduct interest expenses of only $10,000 plus an amount equal to your investment income.

6. Land Speculation through Farming or Timber. Many savvy investors like to do their land speculating in the form of farming or timber operations. In such deals the underlying land is part of a business which they hope will generate some cash to defray the carrying costs of the land itself. In addition to the cash, investments carried as a farming or timber operation will produce tax benefits unavailable to the holder of raw land.

OIL AND GAS

Oil and gas is our favorite tax sheltered investment. Real estate may be our first choice for *sheltering* taxes because it offers multiple write-offs. But oil and gas offers the unique and appealing combination of tax savings (smaller than those in real estate but coming all in the first year) *plus* the potential for big and fast profits.

What is so appealing about oil and gas is that you can put a hole in the ground, and, if life treats you well, a great deal of money can pour out of that hole. It is theoretically possible for a well to pay back 10 or 20 times or more what it cost. Few wells are drilled that don't have the potential to pay back five times their cost. That's the good news. The bad news is that most passive tax shelter investors have not done terribly well in these investments. Although no one keeps score (making it hard to tell just how bad the record is), the published results of the public funds over the last 10 years are very poor. Part of the problem is that the best deals never get out of Texas, Oklahoma, and Denver. And part of the problem is that the deals that do make it to Los Angeles, Chicago, or New York have extra layers of fees to middlemen, lawyers, brokers, and so forth, on top.

Despite these problems, oil and gas is still our first choice. You have to work very hard to find a good deal, but if you do and are lucky, you will be rewarded handsomely.

The terms *oil* and *gas* are used together because crude oil and natural gas are frequently found in the same geological formations. In some parts of the country, your tax shelter deal may be looking basically for oil and, in others, mostly for gas, but the two, courtesy of millions of years of nature, are often found at different levels of the same well. Although you may expect to find mostly one or the other, naturally you will exploit both if they are found. They are virtually always referred to as oil and gas shelters.

Oil and gas tax shelters are known for offering big, first-year tax deductions. Some people think that the tax benefits are so good that they don't have to worry about finding oil, or that they are worse off if they do, because the oil they halfheartedly hope to find will generate taxable income that will do them in. They are wrong. An oil deal *must* find oil. If it doesn't, you will lose money. This rule applies to every taxpayer no matter what the bracket, and it applies to both individuals and corporations.

The 1981 Tax Act brought with it a big change making oil and gas more attractive as a tax shelter to highly paid individuals. Effective in 1982 the top income tax rate is 50 percent. Before 1982 the rates went up to 70 percent, but there was a 50 percent maximum rate (called the maxi tax) on earned income (salary, commissions, etc.). The tax deductions generated by drilling for oil and gas drastically reduced the maxi tax benefits. Consequently, well-advised investors who had substantial earned income shied away from oil and gas. Starting in 1982 all income is taxed at a maximum of 50 percent. There is no longer a tax penalty on the high-income investor in oil and gas. Those investors who had stayed away from oil and gas in the past should now realize that the 1981 Tax Act makes oil and gas attractive taxwise.

EQUIPMENT LEASING

The hottest *corporate* tax shelter around is equipment leasing. When you buy equipment—railroad cars, barges, computers, executive jets, automobiles, anything from sailboats to medical laboratory equipment to cable TV systems—and rent it out to someone else, you are in an equipment-leasing tax shelter. If you buy the right kinds of equipment, these shelters have the potential of doing a lot of heavy-duty economic work for you because they combine the opportunity for substantial economic profit with very attractive tax incentives.

The economic benefits come from:

1. The rents which are collected.
2. Ownership of the equipment which you can sell ultimately.

The tax benefits come via:

1. Depreciation deductions.
2. The investment credit.

The 1981 Tax Act increased the benefits to high tax bracket corporations buying equipment and leasing it out to low tax bracket businesses. The lessor (the high-bracket corporation) receives the investment tax credit and the depreciation deductions. This technique is not new to the 1981 Tax Act, but three things are new. First, there are increased tax benefits from quicker write-offs. Second, there is a more attractive investment tax credit. Third, equipment leasing deals can be structured in a simple way that eliminates the chance that the IRS will try to disallow the tax deductions. Individual investors may enjoy the two tax benefits, but not the structure benefit. For individuals to receive the same tax benefits enjoyed by corporations, they must comply with very rigid rules which result in oddly structured deals. The reason for this preferential treatment is that Congress wants to encourage corporations to become lessors, and it wants to discourage individual tax shelter investors. Corporate fat cats are favored and individual fat cats get the shaft. Exxon can shelter its enormous income by purchasing jumbo jets and leasing them to airlines (even though Exxon's sole motivation may be to shelter income) but a high-bracket individual may not, or at least may not on the same favorable economic terms as Exxon.

Real estate, oil and gas, and equipment leasing are the three most popular tax shelters, but there are many other possibilities—some legitimate, some flimflam, some likely to succeed, some typically iffy, all tributes to American financial ingenuity. They include research and development (the "hot" shelter of the 1980s); cattle feeding (though a winner in the 1960s, a bum steer today); cattle and horse breeding (Glamorous? Possibly. Profitable? Unlikely.); art, recording, and photograph masters (usually flimflam); movies (we rate this shelter X); and Broadway shows (great fun and profits if you've got a smash hit).

THE 1981 TAX ACT

Tax shelters are still alive and well despite the tax reforms of the 1970s and the 1981 Tax Act (officially known as the Economic Recovery Act of 1981). In fact, the 1981 Tax Act has significantly helped "good" tax shelters. Many tax shelters, such as real estate and equipment leasing, offer better tax savings than ever before because deductions now come faster than before. Congress used the 1981 Tax Act to increase the appeal of certain tax shelters which Congress considers productive to the economy and beneficial to society.

Conversely, the new tax act deals out new severe penalties to those investors who put their money into "bad" tax shelters which exist to provide tax deductions, not economic profits. Before 1981, investing in a shelter of questionable legitimacy was a risk many people were willing to take. If they were audited, they would have the phony deductions disallowed and would have to pay the IRS their full tax bill plus interest. However, the interest rate assessed was well below the prime rate (it was 12 percent in 1981 compared to a prime of 20 percent or more), and audit was not inevitable. Investors who were ignorant that they were breaking the law or who willingly broke the law usually came out ahead on these deals.

Now investors in "deductions mills" and flimflam (and there will still be flimflam, there will *always* be flimflam) are taking a bigger gamble. The 1981 Tax Act included very real tax penalties for investors caught in phony tax shelters. In addition to the penalties, interest computed at the prime rate will have to be paid. Being caught in a bad tax shelter can really hurt now.

Selecting Real Estate Investment Opportunities*

17
MAURY SELDIN, DBA
Professor of Finance and Real Estate,
School of Business Administration,
The American University, Washington, D.C.

ARTHUR M. WEIMER, Ph.D., LL.D, MAI, CRE
Economic Consultant,
United States League of Savings Associations,
Washington, D.C.

Most investors consider each real estate opportunity on its own merits, whenever and however they find it. They evaluate each opportunity as it comes along. This is called an opportunistic strategy.

Such an approach requires looking over and evaluating a lot of properties. It can be very time consuming and expensive. Nevertheless, many investors opt for this approach because it seems easiest.

In order to reduce the time and expense that are required to review properties, investors may develop a set of investment policies. For example, they may decide on one or more preferred localities. They may narrow down the range of offerings to those meeting specified criteria related to price, down payment, leverage, diversification, cash flow, tax shelter, type of property, and so on.

Investors often set up the price range of the properties that they would like to consider. For those who wish to set a price policy, there are a few techniques which are quite useful. The first deals with the down payment.

A decision is needed on the amount of leverage to use. (Leverage refers to the amount of borrowed money in relation to the amount

---
*Portions of this chapter were adapted from Maury Seldin, *How to Look for Real Estate Opportunities* (Bloomington, Ind.: Weimer Business Advisory Service, 1978).

of the investor's money. The higher the percentage of borrowed money, the greater the leverage.) A high-leverage purchaser will put 10 percent of the purchase price down, or perhaps as little as 5 percent or as much as 15 percent. A typical investor who does not use high leverage will put 20-30 percent down and use only a first-mortgage.

The amount of money available for a down payment multiplied by the reciprocal of the down payment ratio gives the price range desired. If the investor has $20,000 for a down payment and wants to buy with 10 percent down, he or she can buy a $200,000 property. If the investor pays 20 percent down, a $100,000 property can be bought (0.20 = $\frac{1}{5}$; reverse the $\frac{1}{5}$ to give the multiplier of 5).

If the investor wishes to diversify, then the money available is split into down payments for a number of investments. A very high leveraged, nondiversified investor should keep substantial cash reserves. The amount of those reserves affects the amount available for a down payment.

Highly leveraged properties may produce no cash flow. If the cash flow is negative, there is a continuous requirement of providing additional funds. Unimproved land is the classic case of such an investment.

Investments with negative cash flow require reserves. Sometimes those reserves are set aside by using previously accumulated funds.

Some investors use future income as the basis for potential reserves. That is, they get more income than they spend, so the excess is available for investment. They may then program some of that excess to be used as reserves and thus to meet negative cash flow requirements.

If the investor's strategy is based upon using future personal income to meet the cash requirements, then the amount of future money may limit the size of purchase. For example, an investor with $20,000 cash may be looking for land to buy at 10 percent down. Although he or she could manage a down payment on $200,000 worth of land, the mortgage-carrying cost might be $1,800 per month. If the investor can only afford a monthly investment of half that, or $900, then the amount of the debt that could be serviced might be, say, $90,000 instead of $180,000. The property to look for would be priced at $100,000, not $200,000.

A variety of locations should be analyzed to determine which is of major interest. Investors often emphasize income-producing potential in selecting locations.

Properties go through life cycles. These life cycles are related to the physical age of structures, their maintenance and, to a great degree, their location. Investors who want the least risk select the properties that are newest but have established tenancies. Investors who want the greatest returns and are prepared to take higher risks select older properties with buildings that may not be occupied for very long before they are torn down to make way for new uses of the land. If a building is likely to be abandoned, however, and the land not reused, it should be avoided.

BROKERS

Real estate brokers are an obvious route to finding property. The foregoing policies provide the basis for telling them what the investor prefers. The opportunistic investor will chase down many ads and brokers. The systematic investor tries to identify brokers who will serve his or her interests best. The investor should qualify the agent and the property and consider those properties which seem to be reasonable candidates for acquisition.

Sometimes, the properties on the market are not attractive to the investor. Many investors with good properties find them difficult to replace. They sell only under special circumstances. Thus, much of what is on the market at a given time may be the result of an adverse selection process. This means that the properties available for purchase are generally not as good as the average investment property.

Properties may be overpriced because there are sellers who will sell, but only at very high prices. The owners of investment properties producing a good cash flow may demand outlandish prices. They can afford to wait a long time. In fact, they can make money while waiting. By way of contrast, in sales of owner-occupied houses a genuine desire to sell at acceptable prices may exist for a number of reasons, such as a transfer to another city or a change in household size and composition due to death or divorce.

Despite the problems, reading the newspaper ads, finding a responsive broker, and working with the broker is the way in which many investors proceed. Reading the newspaper ads and finding the seller is another way to proceed.

Investors typically talk to lots of people—accountants, attorneys, bankers, insurance agents, and others who have constant contact with property owners. Such people often know of property which is for sale or, better yet, property which will be on the market soon.

Property that is identified before it comes on the market is often the best kind to buy. The owner may be anxious to sell and may accept a reasonable price. A good property is frequently bought before it reaches the open market. Such property is often found through people who know of the motivations of the prospective sellers. These may be professional and business people who have the prospective sellers as clients. They may also be astute real estate brokers who know what is happening and will match up a buyer and a property even before the seller has fully decided to sell.

The opportunistic strategy is based upon responding to what is offered and picking the best property available.

SYSTEMATIC SEARCH STRATEGIES

A systematic strategy is based upon deciding what to buy and then going out to find it. Such a strategy is not widely used because it seems more difficult than the opportunistic approach. But it is likely to be more profitable.

The first step in a systematic strategy is to set objectives. This means specifying what types of property will be considered, the price range, the financing, the location, and other characteristics.

These objectives are based upon an analysis of the risks that the investor is prepared to bear and on the type of rewards desired.

For example, one investor might specify that he or she is looking for rental houses priced in the low 40s which would rent for $300 to $325 per month in a particular section that is expected to get a new freeway. The investor would look for a seller who has an assumable loan and would carry back secondary financing.

A second investor might be looking for a 12-unit apartment building with one- and two-bedroom units with rents in the $200 to $300 range. She might be looking for something priced at about $250,000, with $50,000 down, and located in a suburban community now being engulfed by metropolitan expansion.

A third investor might be looking for a 40,000-square-foot office building priced at about $1 million in a close-in community which is now a part of a metropolitan area. He may be looking for an older building which could be upgraded after a new mall is built nearby.

A fourth investor may be looking for a freestanding store that is leased to a national chain organization with a high credit standing. She may be looking for something which requires about $60,000 cash, but the amount of cash can vary substantially. The preferred location is along one of several major suburban arteries or bypasses.

In each of these instances, the investor's selection will be based on policies that the investor has established. Those policies help to define some set of properties which will qualify for the investor's purposes.

A Workable Program. If the specifications are too stringent, there will not be enough properties to choose from. If the specifications are too broad, there will be too many properties to choose from. What is necessary is to define a workable program.

The multiple listing system is an easy way to identify properties which come on the market. A real estate broker who is a member of the multiple listing service can check weekly for new listings. This is likely to be most helpful in the case of single-family houses and doubles.

For small apartment buildings the easiest technique may be to find the real estate office that does the most volume in the particular type of property that the investor is interested in.

In some cases the only way to get suitable properties is to build them. There are two basic ways to start. One is to find the right land and then build for a tenant, or in some cases to build speculatively and to look for tenants while building. The other way is to find locations that will suit a prospective tenant under an arrangement in which the investor will build and lease. This alternative means finding the tenant first and then meeting his or her needs. This is frequently done with chain and franchise operations.

The search process for land is somewhat different in that the analysis required is heavily oriented to developability, which is related to zoning and to the timing and possible location of public improvements. But a systematic approach can be used to identify what types of land may be increasing in demand, where such land is located, and who owns it.

The investor's program may utilize many sources and extend over a long period of time. Some investors advertise, which is often a good approach. It is often necessary to scout the potential locations for properties and to check the public records for ownership or to have them checked. Some investors pay brokers a fee or commission to identify desirable properties.

The acquisition process requires compromises. Thus, when a candidate property is selected, a program for acquisition is set up which includes the terms and conditions under which the investor will buy. Some of those terms and conditions will be negotiable, others not.

THE USE OF FINANCING

Leverage. Investors who want high cash flow may use leverage to increase that cash flow relative to the cash invested by borrowing at low annual constants.

The annual constant is the ratio of the annual mortgage payment (which includes principal and interest) to the original amount of the mortgage. For example, $7.50 per month per $1,000 adds up to $90 per year, including principal and interest. The interest rate might be 8 percent, with the balance devoted to the payment of principal. The annual constant, then, is 9 percent ($90 divided by $1,000).

If the annual constant is lower than the ratio of the net operating income to the purchase price, then the leverage will increase the cash flow. For example, if the property sells for $100,000 and produces a net operating income of $10,000 (that is, rents less expenses, *excluding* mortgage payments), the ratio of the operating income to the purchase price is 10 percent ($10,000 divided by $100,000). Borrow-

17: Selecting Real Estate Investment Opportunities

ing at a 9 percent annual constant will increase the cash flow relative to the cash investment as follows:

1. With no mortgage:

   Net operating income $10,000
   Less mortgage payment .... -0-
   Cash flow $10,000

   $$\frac{\text{Cash flow}}{\text{Amount invested}} = \frac{\$10,000}{\$100,000} = 10\%$$

2. With a 50 percent mortgage:

   Net operating income $10,000
   Less mortgage payment
   ($50,000 × 0.09)...................................... 4,500
   Cash flow .... $ 5,500

   $$\frac{\text{Cash flow}}{\text{Amount invested}} = \frac{\$5,500}{\$50,000} = 11\%$$

3. With a 70 percent mortgage:

   Net operating income $10,000
   Less mortgage payment
   ($70,000 × 0.09)...................................... 6,300
   Cash flow .... $ 3,700

   $$\frac{\text{Cash flow}}{\text{Amount invested}} = \frac{\$3,700}{\$30,000} = 12.3\%$$

4. With a 90 percent mortgage:

   Net operating income $10,000
   Less mortgage payment
   ($90,000 × 0.09)...................................... 8,000
   Cash flow .... $ 1,900

   $$\frac{\text{Cash flow}}{\text{Amount invested}} = \frac{\$1,900}{\$10,000} = 19\%$$

The cash flow relative to the down payment on money invested is thus increased as the amount borrowed is increased, provided that the ratio of the net operating income to the purchase price is higher than the annual constant. The more that ratio exceeds the annual constant, the more the amount of money borrowed will increase the cash flow relative to the down payment.

With interest rates high and with real estate prices high, about the only way to get a low annual constant is to borrow on a low loan-to-value ratio. Even then, it may be difficult if the price of the property is high relative to its income.

An alternative is seller financing. Many sellers who have big taxable gains will want to report their gains on an installment basis.

(*Editor's note:* The installment method permits the seller to defer payment of a portion of the gain to future tax years. In order for the seller to elect the installment basis for reporting the sale, the contract for the sale of the property must provide that at least one payment is to be received after the close of the tax year in which the sale occurs.

Many sellers will trade off lower interest rates for higher prices when providing financing for the buyer. In addition to allowing the seller to defer payment of a taxable gain, it converts interest income which is taxed at an ordinary tax rate into capital gain income which is taxed at a lower tax rate.)

Tax Shelter. Investors who want high tax shelter may use leverage to advantage.

Depreciable property, such as a building, will on a straight-line basis provide a fixed amount of depreciation each year, regardless of the type of financing. For example, a $100,000 property with $80,000 of the value in the building and $20,000 in the land has a depreciable base of $80,000. With a remaining economic life of 25 years, the depreciation is 4 percent of the $80,000, or $3,200, each year. The investor can write off that $3,200 each year, regardless of whether he or she pays all cash or borrows part of the purchase price.

If the investor pays all cash—$100,000—and the net operating income is $10,000, he or she will get $3,200 of the $10,000 in tax-sheltered income. Tax will be paid on income of $6,800, and this reduces the basis for tax purposes by $3,200 each year. Taxable income of $6,800 represents 68 percent of a $10,000 cash flow.

If the investor uses a $50,000 mortgage at 8 percent interest with a 9 percent constant, the mortgage payment will be $4,500 and the interest for the first year will be a little less than $4,000. (The interest is on the unpaid balance so that each month the amount of interest is less than the previous month. Thus, the annual interest will be a little less than 8 percent of $50,000.) The amortization will be a little over $500.

With the $50,000 mortgage the cash flow will be the $10,000 less the mortgage payment of $4,500, leaving $5,500. The taxable income, however, will be this $5,500 plus $500 amortization less the $3,200 depreciation, or $2,800. In other words, for the $50,000 down payment the investor gets $5,500 cash flow, of which the $2,800 taxable income represents about 51 percent.

The numbers will change slightly as the loan is reduced and the amount going to interest declines. But it is clear that the proportion of the cash flow which is sheltered may increase as the amount borrowed increases. For a 70 percent loan, the figures are as shown on the next page. Thus with the cash flow of $3,700 there is a taxable income of only $1,200. This $1,200 represents only 32 percent of the cash flow.

17: Selecting Real Estate Investment Opportunities

Net operating income		$10,000
Mortgage payment		
Interest (0.08 × $70,000)	$5,600	
Principal, first year (approximate)	700	
		6,300
Cash flow		$ 3,700
Plus amortization (approximate)		700
		$ 4,400
Less depreciation		3,200
Taxable income		$ 1,200

If 90 percent financing were available on similar terms (it is not likely to be), all of the cash flow would be sheltered and there would be a tax loss to write off against ordinary income. For example:

Net operating income	$10,000
Less mortgage payment	
($90,000 × 0.09 constant)	8,100
Cash flow	$ 1,900

On the $90,000 loan the interest at 8 percent is $7,200 for the year (or a little less with monthly payments). The amortization for the first year is $900.

Cash flow	$1,900
Plus amortization	900
	$2,800
Less depreciation	3,200
Tax loss	$ (400)

Thus, the entire cash flow of $1,900 is sheltered and there is a $400 tax loss which may be applied against ordinary income.

Accelerated depreciation would make these illustrations better in the earlier years of an investment but worse in the later years.

Many investors use lots of leverage in order to get tax shelter. Using more leverage, however, tends to push up the *rate* of interest. Lenders usually get higher interest rates for loans which are 80 percent of value than they do for loans which are 70 percent of value. For some types of property, the lowest rate may be at loan-to-value ratios as low as 60 percent.

Investors in income property generally obtain high leverage by using more than one mortgage. For example, an institutional lender may provide 70 percent of value, the seller may carry back 15 percent, and the purchaser thus puts up 15 percent. That would be $15,000 down with a $70,000 first mortgage and a $15,000 second mortgage.

Favorable terms may push up the price. In the above example, the sale price might really be $105,000, with $15,000 down and a $70,000 first mortgage. The seller would then have a $20,000 second mortgage, which in the open market might sell for only $15,000.

Some investors will gladly pay extra for favorable financing. They purchase a property expecting it to rise in value quickly. Thus, if the investor thinks that he can net $130,000 on a sale without waiting too long, he would rather capture the $30,000 increase in value with a down payment of $15,000 as compared to a down payment of $30,000.

With $30,000 down, he would get the whole $30,000 increase in value, which is doubling his initial investment. With $15,000 down, he could get only $25,000 of the $30,000 increase. But getting a $25,000 gain on a $15,000 investment is more profitable than getting a $30,000 gain on a $30,000 investment.

Such benefits are obviously influenced by a number of factors, including the interest costs and the tax consequences. In addition, the use of the added leverage is risky.

The point is, however, that many investors want to use leverage to capture the increase in value and look to types of investments that can be highly leveraged.

The availability of financing is influenced by the type of property, the willingness and ability of the seller to cooperate, the existing financing, the financial strength of the borrower, and the borrower's willingness to assume liability.

LOCATION

It is hard to find good real estate investment opportunities where the local economy is on the decline. An area which is suffering from a persistent unemployment problem and is experiencing an exodus of population is usually not the most desirable place to look for profitable real estate investment opportunities. For example, many investors avoid one-industry towns if there is a danger that the industry will move elsewhere.

Growing communities, on the other hand, may provide some real opportunities. Sometimes it is difficult to pick a poor property in a rapidly growing area.

The future is not necessarily a projection of the past. But there is relative safety in investing in an area with a good solid growth rate.

Even if the future growth rate is a little worse than the past growth rate has been, the area would still be a good one to invest in. It is the marginal areas that investors may find dangerous.

Within any local economy there develops a pattern of land use. Clusters of land use make up subareas of a metropolitan area. Different subareas have different growth potentials. These potentials differ because not all localities in a metropolitan area are equally desirable.

How any particular area performs relative to other areas depends on its competitive ability. If an area is in a high-income sector, then a growth of employment among high-income professionals will help it. If a community consists mostly of blue-collar workers, then a growth of factory employment will increase real estate demand there. Look for those communities which are likely to get the lion's share of the local economic growth.

The investments which turn out best are usually those which are at locations that will benefit from increasing demand.

Zoning regulations and the potential for changes in those regulations are often critical factors. Limitations on land use through deed restrictions are another important factor.

The quality of a location changes over time. Thus, some locations get better and some worse. Some superb locations with older houses are currently the subject of renewed interest, for example. Many investors try to find the locations that are likely to improve in the future.

Monitoring Investments. Few real estate investments can be made and forgotten. Even getting into an investment often requires careful personal attention and some delicate timing.

The markets for most properties tend to be cyclical. The demand for real estate is volatile because expectations change and the cost and availability of mortgage money change. Thus, at one time there may be a great many buyers and at another time there may be very few.

The physical supply of real estate changes much more slowly than the demand for it. Building takes time. Furthermore, the stock added by building is a small percentage of the total stock. Typically, the demand intensifies before there is a change in the rate at which new properties are developed. Then the supply often overshoots the real needs and the market is overbuilt.

Careful investors try to buy in the early stages of a boom in order to avoid buying too late.

If the political leadership of an area favors slow growth or managed growth, some investments will be hurt. Land, for example, may not be developed for a long time. Slow-growth policies tend to protect present investors by slowing down competition from new developments.

Avoiding Personal Liability. Investors may consider a variety of alternatives in order to avoid personal liability on loans. They can ask to have the property as the sole security for a loan. This is sometimes arranged through what is termed an "exculpatory clause." If an existing loan is taken over, the investor may be able to take title subject to the existing loan rather than assuming and agreeing to pay the existing loan. Even if there is personal liability on the first mortgage, an investor may be able to avoid it on the second, especially if the second mortgage is provided by the seller.

Protections. There are lots of other arrangements that can be made, especially in purchases of land. But if there are too many contingencies, the seller will not accept the deal. Decide what you think you are buying, and then make sure that the contract provides for it and that the necessary contingencies are covered. Thus you will only buy if your financing is right, if the title is good, if you get the right kind of deed, and if the property is in the condition that you believe it to be.

At times the contract overlooks something or circumstances may change after the initial contract has been signed but before the closing of escrow or settlement. The buyer may be protected from losing more than the deposit if it is agreed that forfeiture of the deposit will be the sole remedy in the event of default. Otherwise the buyer is potentially liable for damages on specific performance. Unlike labor contracts, real estate contracts can be enforced exactly. This is called "specific performance."

The size of the deposit is of some importance. Bigger deposits are more impressive when negotiating. The deposit can be put in an interest-bearing savings account so that the cost of tying up the money is reduced.

In addition to looking for suitable properties, the buyer should also look for agreeable sellers. Dealing with such sellers can make the contracting and the negotiating easier.

NEGOTIATING STRATEGIES

There are numerous negotiating strategies. Some strategies take much greater risks of losing a purchase than do others. And after you have worked hard to find a suitable investment you don't want to lose it. But you don't want to be taken advantage of either.

The Offer. The negotiating process starts with an offer to purchase. You set forth the terms and conditions on which you are prepared to buy. You spell them out, sign them, and give them to the seller as an offer together with a deposit.

Your offer should fall within an acceptable range. Wild offers can kill a deal. And sometimes an offer not meant to be accepted but rather to elicit a counteroffer is actually accepted. The first offer should be a serious one.

Legal Matters. The time to get your legal counsel is before you sign, not after. Your counsel can check the contract to see that it provides what you think it provides and that the legal aspects will not cause problems.

Some attorneys get involved in the business decision, and some are even good at it. You should decide whether you want business advice from your attorney or only legal advice.

Sometimes attorneys are so protective of their clients that they protect them out of deals. It is far better to decide what you want done and then to have your attorney make sure that the contract does it. Be sure you know how to do what you want to do, and find out *before* you sign the first piece of paper.

Most of the legal considerations will be noncontroversial. You don't want the settlement date to be postponed forever. You want clear title, and if you can't get it you want out. You want a warranty deed or its equivalent. Some of the more controversial issues have more business aspects than legal aspects. You want possession at settlement and proration of taxes, insurance, rents, and so on.

Basic Provisions. There may be some controversial contract items, such as finance terms, contingencies, forfeiture provisions, and time to settlement.

For strategic purposes, however, you should decide what provisions are most important to you and then be sure that they are in the contract. You may also propose some other provisions, so that in the negotiations you have something to give away if you are pressing for something extra or if the seller is pressing not to give you a key provision.

It is easiest to start with a "standard" form. The statement "It's OK, it's a standard form" falls into the same class as the statement "The check is in the mail."

Realtor® groups and others have forms which are pretty good as starters and may need no adjustment. But read them carefully; remembering that "the big print giveth and the small print taketh away." If you don't find a form you like, have a contract typed up, preferably by your attorney's office.

As has been noted earlier, the contract may have negative points. For example, you may pay a little higher price or make a little larger down payment than you had hoped to pay. You may agree to pay the second mortgage off in 7 years, not 10, or even 8. You may agree to settle in 60 days, not 120.

You may not be willing to buy unless you get the desired new first mortgage. And you will want to limit your personal liability in certain ways as well as approve the existing leases.

Some of these things can be taken care of during the negotiation process without being part of the contract. You could be provided copies of the lease, and you could conduct your physical inspection of the property. The contract could then be silent on these matters.

The Seller's Response. The seller may respond to your offer by stating the written terms that are acceptable to him or her. You can hold firm on the important items and give in on the unimportant.

It helps to have an astute broker. You may want to be represented by an attorney who negotiates for you. Third-party negotiators make things easier because they can better see what the seller considers to be most important and work out mutually advantageous trade-offs.

Acceptance. When you finally get something acceptable, you are usually better off to take it than to push things to the hilt. A lot of work goes into finding suitable investments. You should not jeopardize a good deal in order to make it just a little better. Minor differences are just that, minor differences.

Crossing the threshold of a commitment to buy is difficult for many people. The decisions are not easy, but even making no decision is decision. The best way to handle the situation may be to build a set of policies which guide you in your decision. In this way you will get great comfort from knowing that what you are doing conforms to your general plan. Then when you must take your first step, it will not seem so big.

Plan your steps in looking for real estate opportunities. Monitor your program. If the program is not working, replan it. But take your steps one at a time, and with enough steps you'll get where you want to go.

Have a safe and successful journey.

EDITOR'S ADDENDUM TO SELECTING REAL ESTATE INVESTMENT OPPORTUNITIES

In discussing the amount of depreciation that an investor would be entitled to by acquiring a building, the authors divided the depreciable base by the economic life of the building. The Economic Recovery Tax Act of 1981 changed the number of years over which depreciable property may be recovered. The new act substitutes the Accelerated Cost Recovery System (ACRS) for the class life Asset Depreciation Range (ADR) System. The life of an asset (now referred to as the recovery period) for purposes of depreciation (now referred to as ACRS deductions or cost recovery allowances) has been established by Congress. The statutory recovery period is unrelated to the useful life of the asset and is generally shorter.

In the case of depreciable property, such as residential and commercial buildings, the recovery period is 15 years if the ADR class

17: Selecting Real Estate Investment Opportunities 361

life of the property exceeds 12.5 years. Most depreciable real property will fall into this recovery period class. Other depreciable real property may fall into the 5-year or 10-year recovery periods prescribed for personal property. Therefore, in the case of the $100,000 property with a building valued at $80,000 and an economic life of 25 years, the ACRS deduction is $5,333 ($80,000 divided by 15 years). This permits the investor a greater tax shield than was available prior to the 1981 act and makes real estate investments involving depreciable real property more attractive.

Land Investment

18   ALAN J. INBINDER, AFLM
President, The Indevco Group
Skokie, Illinois

ROY D. GOTTLIEB
President, Kenroy Inc.
Skokie, Illinois

This chapter will not give you any pat answers as to how to go about buying, selling, or developing land. Instead, it will indicate what questions you must pose to yourself or your consultants before you invest in or sell land. The underlying theme of the chapter is that a profit is made on land investment when you purchase the property, not when you sell it. You only realize the profit when you sell it.

The chapter will also demonstrate that land investment is a complex and risky procedure in which both professionals and neophytes can make or lose large amounts of money, and that leveraging makes the risks even greater. The chapter will try to convince you that you must employ the best available talent or develop your own expertise through education or partnership association before you make a decision about investment in land. You must be aware of the risk/reward ratios, or you must find some company in which you have full faith and invest with it. In order to gain that faith, however, you should investigate the company's performance and its ability to correctly analyze and apply changing circumstances to property values.

PROFESSIONAL INPUT NECESSARY FOR PRUDENT LAND INVESTMENT

Appraisals are not confined to real estate—they enter into all kinds of human activities. Whenever you buy something you make a value judgment—an appraisal—that takes into consideration your needs, your desires, your ability to pay, and your alternative uses for the funds. Appraisals also enter into your social relations—how and with whom you will spend your time are governed by value judgments. Throughout your life, consciously or unconsciously, you have been appraising alternative uses for your time, alternative interests, alternative short-term and long-range goals.

Appraisals of real estate do not require mysterious capacities but skills very similar to those you have employed in making your own appraisals. It takes a lot of time to properly put together the necessary data, and it takes logical thinking to come to a rational conclusion. It is only natural that those people whose business is real estate appraising and who spend most of their time in this endeavor should do it better than the average person. As a prospective purchaser or seller of real property, you should be able to set realistic guidelines for analyzing a prospective investment or for directing a professional appraiser or real estate consultant to evaluate your alternatives.

You should expect the appraiser to give you sufficient data to enable you, as a logical, thinking person, to follow the analysis of the appraiser and to review his procedures so as to come to the same conclusion that he did. You should insist that the appraiser, either orally or in writing, provide data on properties which have a reasonable degree of comparability with the subject property and not merely numbers from sales that are inserted without confirmation in order to support his predetermined conclusion. The appraiser should state in what respects the properties from which a conclusion is reached are comparable to the subject property and in what respects they are not comparable. He should briefly explain how he derived the indicated value of the subject property from the values of the comparable properties. The appraisal data should include a location map relating the comparable properties to the subject property and a brief description of each comparable property, together with its date of sale, its price, its zoning and utility characteristics, and if possible, the length of time that the property was on the market and the difference between the asking price and the selling price.

The appraiser must make one evaluation based on the zoning which now exists and other evaluations based on the zoning alternatives that might be accomplished. Within each zoning category other than the single-family category (and to a certain extent even within the single-family category), there are several uses to which property can be put. The as-zoned value is generally the least that you can expect for the property (except, as will be discussed below, if there is a change in administration or in the availability of utilities). The alternative use values must consider the length of time it will take to accomplish the zoning, the cost of the zoning (and of possible litigation proceedings), and the timing and the terms of sale if the zoning is accomplished.

The real estate market moves in a wavelike ebb and flow, with troughs and crests, swings from high demand to oversupply to reduced demand to scarcity to high demand. In 1974-75 buying land for speculation was perhaps the worst real estate investment you could make in the Chicago metropolitan area—unless, of course, you had the foresight and the holding power to predict and wait out the boom conditions that prevailed from 1976 through 1978. In that case, land was perhaps the best investment you could have made in real estate in 1974-75, but only if you had picked the properties which were later in demand, such as land zoned and with utilities for single-family detached housing, for three-story walk-up apartments in six-unit buildings, or for commercial property in prime locations. Suburban land for condominium high rises was a slow market commodity in 1974-75 and remained a slow market commodity through 1978, as did large tracts of industrial land for speculation.

It is difficult to predict how long high demand will continue for any one potential use of vacant land. The trend we have seen over the past 20 years, however, indicates that except during war or a deep recession, the demand starts with land for single-family houses and continues until such houses are priced at a level that is no longer affordable for the mass market. The exact price level will vary in different regions of the country and in different areas within a region, and it will certainly vary with inflation and with the average level of family income in each community. Rather than try to predict a price, you can follow the trend of house sales. In the Chicago area, for example, Bell Savings lists the number of new building permits issued for each community. Statistics can be obtained on the number of lines of house advertising.

If the seasonal sales level in a strong market is dropping for single-family houses, and that seems to be the trend, you can anticipate that the next phase of the housing market will swing more actively into attached housing, which can take the form of town houses, duplexes, and low-rise condos. These types of units reflect an attempt by the buying public to seek alternatives to a single-family home on its own individual lot because they can afford these alternatives and they cannot afford the freestanding single-family home. If the shift in demand from single-family homes to units in multifamily buildings drives the prices of the latter up, the demand for rental housing as an alternative to ownership will increase. If the land in certain suburban areas is too scarce to meet the demand for single-family housing, the demand for elevator, fire-resistant (and therefore higher priced) condominium and apartment housing will increase in those areas and demand will also leap to suburban areas that are farther out, because some people will be willing to trade off the additional driving time for the saving in money. This is not a long-lived phase in a housing cycle except in the areas of a community which are in greatest demand (these are generally areas with semi luxury-level and luxury-level housing).

The selection of land for commercial use requires analysis of the demography of an area, including its rate of population growth. Generally convenience centers of up to 80,000-100,000 square feet are built in response to a demonstrated need in the community, and which location is chosen usually depends on which developer can recognize the need first and convince the anchor tenant, generally a food/drug chain, to rent in his center. As shopping centers get larger, the preplanning period gets longer and greater dependence is placed on ease of access and prominence of location for present and anticipated future needs. Land for a major shopping center should not be acquired unless the investors have a clear working arrangement with the major anchor tenants that they will need to ensure their ability to get financing and the other tenants they will need in order to make the center a success. The acquisition of land for shopping centers should be an outgrowth of a business in commercial real estate development, not a speculation in land.

Speculative office buildings in the suburban areas move with the population trends as demonstrated by housing demand, the development of shopping centers, and ease of access on major highways. The same can be said to a certain extent of the demand for industrial land. Obviously, the development of both types of property is also conditioned by supply and demand. A major determinant of office and industrial relocation is generally the ease of reaching the new location from the homes of the key executives of the company that will be occupying the space. It is generally best to begin with expertise in developing commercial and industrial properties and then to acquire land that suits the conditions of a particular program rather than to begin by acquiring land and then trying to find a commercial or industrial use for it.

In order to properly plan land investment, you must anticipate end use. It is often said that if a certain property were worth buying, somebody would have bought it already. But you might see something in the property or in the area that the people who came before you did not see, or you may just happen to come along as someone else is getting ready to sell. Keep in mind that nobody sells property for less than he thinks it is worth. If you maintain a property in its present use you are rarely going to buy a bargain. What is going to make the difference between profit and loss is your ability to correctly assess what change might be made in the use of that property, and whether that change can, in fact, be effected, and how soon this can be done.

You must be aware that in most markets you are competing with people who spend most of their business time seeking out exactly the same thing you are looking for, namely a sound land investment that will make a lot of money in a short time with little risk. There are not very many such investments, however, and so it is nearly always a question of who will compromise what in order to make a purchase. When you are seeking property of a particular kind you should review all of the property within the market area of your property, not only to determine whether the price and terms you have been offered are reasonable (because the asking prices of every property in an area could be uneconomical), but also to determine the potential competition for as yet undeveloped sites.

It is obvious that anyone acquiring land must look both at the property itself and at what surrounds it (and at what in turn surrounds that). The influence of the surroundings are directly related to their nearness to your subject site. You should observe and anticipate what existing and potential developments on nearby property will have on the development of alternative uses for your property.

You must know values and make specific analyses of a property in order to determine its potential uses. Surveying and engineering are necessary to determine the size, topography, and soil-bearing capacity of a property as well as the availability and the likelihood of the continuing availability of all the necessary utilities. Planning consideration helps you determine what you physically can put on the property irrespective of zoning. Zoning may set limit to what you can do, but the physical constraints of a property generally limit its usability further. Community services are generally available to help you decide what to do with a property, but such services are more readily understandable to professional engineers and planners than they will be to you. Moreover, engineers and planners typically have closer rapport with community officials than do land investors, and will usually be able to get more detailed information than might be made accessible to you and to get that information with less difficulty than you might experience.

The real estate tax impact on various land is becoming a more prominent issue each year. Investment in land requires carrying costs. In addition to paying interest on borrowed capital, you have the indefinite costs of widely varying tax assessments. In the Chicago metropolitan area it is not uncommon to experience increases of

18: Land Investment

400-500 percent in a tax bill on a property that is unbuildable because it lacks utilities or zoning. Generally, only limited success can be achieved in reducing these taxes.

Unless you are ready to build on vacant land at the time you acquire it, there will undoubtedly be a change in community administration or state or county jurisdiction levels between the time that you acquire the land and the time that you can market or develop it. The likelihood is that from your point of view the attitude of the governing authorities toward land development, will change for the worse. In smaller communities, for example, many homeowners want to place more restrictions on future builders than were placed on the builders of their homes. It is therefore necessary for the prospective land investor to become strongly aware of the needs and demands of village or city officials, school boards, park districts, library districts, fire protection districts, forest preserve districts, or any other potential condemning authorities. Because many community officials are influenced by petitions and potential threats to their incumbency, you must analyze the attitude of homeowner groups toward your development plan in order to determine how easily and how soon you will be able to put the vacant land you contemplate purchasing into a marketable position for development or resale. Since it is not always possible to assess the attitudes of municipalities or homeowners before property is acquired, you should try to acquire land on a contingent basis which will enable you to work out zoning and utility problems and to determine the community's attitude to your development. If your investment and development goals are sound, you may have to "fight city hall." Your risk of loss can be minimized if you purchase property which can be resold for its minimum uses at a price close to your acquisition price.

It is obvious that you need a lawyer for legal matters. It may be less obvious that you need a lawyer who specializes in real estate. Before you buy any property, or certainly as a precondition to the purchase of a property, a thorough investigation must be made of the various ordinances and codes that determine whether you can proceed as you would like to or, for that matter, in any economically viable manner. If the four corners of an intersection are in four different municipal jurisdictions, one corner could be ten times as valuable as another corner. One property might be unbuildable because of a lack of utilities, another because of a lack of zoning, and a third because the topographic or soil conditions are unsuitable for development without extreme cost, whereas the zoning, the utilities, and a positive community attitude might make the fourth property eminently suitable for building. Your lawyer can advise you as to the restrictions of the applicable municipal building, zoning, and other codes. He can also give you guidelines for satisfying Environmental

Protection Agency requirements and utility standards and for making zoning and annexation applications to park, library, forest preserve, school, and municipal districts.

You should learn about the nature of the hearings that take place in the different communities. What is essential in one community may be superfluous in others. Some jurisdictions view school board recommendations as just another consideration. Other jurisdictions require a written agreement between the investor and the school board before they will even consider a development plan. When you go into contract for land investment, whether you build yourself or sell to a developer, your ability to pay and your holding time will be directly affected by how long it takes you to arrive at solutions for the zoning, utilities, and other problems that must be resolved before it is possible to build upon your property. As the buyer of the property, you must anticipate the problems that will arise in converting land to ultimate use. Otherwise you are a gambler, not an investor.

COORDINATING PROFESSIONAL SKILLS FOR LAND INVESTMENT

Whether you invest in land on your own or you bring other people in to invest with you, you must be able to finance the land you buy for as long as you will need to carry it. You must negotiate the acquisition, the zoning, and if necessary, the development, and you must be able to coordinate the efforts of the professionals whose skills will be necessary to you. Generally you will need to put together an investment package. This will enable you to present to potential partners the information that impelled you to acquire the property.

However, you may have decided by now that all you want to do is put up your money, make profits, and have someone else mail checks to you. If so, you can buy stock in real estate companies. A few have done well in that way, but many have lost money. Investing in the stocks of real estate companies is no different from investing in the stocks of any other public company. However, since real estate development is an entrepreneurial business that is performed most successfully by individuals with high motivation and a high degree of professionalism, the basic incentive to the entrepreneur may be considerably diluted once he has made his company public since he will probably have sold a large portion of it. His interest will be diluted much further after he has had to deal with stock analysts and regulatory agencies. Consequently, the authors do not recommend the purchase of real estate stocks as a means of getting into land investment unless you happen to know the individuals who run the company and you have confidence in them.

Public limited partnerships which are frequently marketed by stock and investment houses generally serve a specific purpose—some are cash flow ventures and some are tax shelter ventures. To an investor whose goals correspond to the objective of such a limited partnership, this may be a worthwhile investment vehicle, but it still requires a great deal of faith in the ability of the company to perform.

That faith is no less necessary in a private limited partnership. However there are generally fewer investors in such a limited partnership, and these investors are more likely to have a closer relationship with the general partner. The entrepreneurial benefits to the general partner are still there—he takes the risk and a large share of the profits. Our view—perhaps because of our past experience—is that investing in a private limited partnership with people in whom you have confidence is likely to be better than investing in a public limited partnership. Although the general partner in the private placement generally takes a larger share of the profits than does the general partner in a public placement, he also generally takes a much larger risk and smaller fees, so that he has a greater need for success.

THE REWARDS AND RISKS OF LAND INVESTMENT

Great fortunes have been made from real estate investments, including investments in vacant land. People have undoubtedly bought land whose value increased rapidly because of changing circumstances. However, very few people, regardless of their experience, have been able to do this often or even to make a profit on everything they bought.

Our approach has always been to project total costs versus anticipated selling prices for various alternative uses against a time line. Based on what we think are realistic factors in all categories, we project an investor return of at least 20 percent per year (not compounded) in addition to any profit we may be seeking for ourselves. With proper leveraging, good timing, and successful zonings, some of our investments have brought returns of 100 percent per year. In other cases—where interest rates rose to over 12 percent, taxes increased by 300-400 percent, farm rentals increased only slightly, and we had to carry the property for years longer than we anticipated—we have barely salvaged a break-even.

During the period of ownership, there are income tax deductions for interest and taxes which may be of benefit to you. Land is also an inflationary hedge, in that the price of properly located land which has zoning for realistic use or which can be rezoned for a variety of uses to meet changing market conditions will generally rise at least as much as the prices of other goods and services. Up until the last few years the price of land had been appreciating much faster than that. Now we find that in the Chicago area the appreciation depends on the use to which the land can be put.

Owning property and holding it for a long enough time for development to take place all around you or selling some of it to recoup your original investment and retaining a portion can put you in the enviable position of being able to participate in the development of buildings. In a joint venture of this kind you put in your land at a price equal to the market value, which is generally much higher than your cost, and with proper legal and accounting guidance you will be able to avoid paying an immediate tax on the increased value, thus increasing your participation in the venture. Contributing land to a venture will enable you to develop a cash flow through your participation in the ownership of buildings and to build up equity as the mortgages on the buildings are paid off.

Buying land requires money or credit, or both. Keeping land through good and bad times requires more money or credit, or both. The inability to carry the land until it can be properly zoned or until market conditions will allow you to sell it at a profit can make the difference between an excellent profit and total disaster. In our opinion, "staying power" may be even more important than location in the acquisition of land, although a prime location for anticipated use is generally regarded as the principal criterion of any land investment.

Another risk in land acquisition is buying too soon or too late. Buying too soon can be corrected by adequate staying power and the will to wait. Many people who buy land years in advance of the proper market conditions will tire of holding the property and sell it at the first opportunity to make a small profit. Buying after the market has been substantially saturated will generally be done at too high a price, so that there will be too little increase in value relative to the amount of investment that you must put at risk.

It is obvious that land is an illiquid asset. You only learn how illiquid it is when you need funds for other investments and you decide to sell a piece of land. Illiquidity is not a drawback of landownership, however, if the land owned is so-called ready-to-go land which is already developed for uses that have an immediate market. Such land can be highly liquid (a 30-90-day selling period).

Changing demand in the marketplace is another large risk of landownership. This may occur for several reasons. (1) The end use for the zoning you have may lose its demand by the time your property is ready to be developed. (2) As a result of changes in the attitude of a community, you may find it difficult to obtain approval for development, even when you propose developing your property for the uses for which it is already zoned (which brings you into costly litigation), or you may be denied zoning changes. (3) Changes in the regulations and the methods of enforcing regulations of the EPA and other agencies may restrict the development of your property.

Anyone who acquires land runs the risk of condemnation, the eminent domain right of a public body to acquire property for its anticipated needs. Normally you can expect to get the purchase price you paid or more. The rules of evidence in condemnation cases are so restrictive, however, that under certain circumstances you may not even get an amount equal to the price you paid even though the condemning authorities are required to pay fair market value. However, fair market value is a matter of interpretation, and the per acre price you get, may or may not adequately reflect the damages to the remainder of your property after the condemnation and the development of the improvements contemplated by the condemnation.

On the other hand, the condemning authorities may take your least valuable property for park or flood control or may skirt your property with roads or other developments that enhance the value of the remainder, a possibility that few property owners will admit during the course of a condemnation case. With expert legal counsel and properly prepared cases, some property owners have received far more from condemnations than they could have received had their property remained subject to the whims of the marketplace.

But condemnation in any form that takes less than all of your property will change your plans for the remainder and may complicate your development program. It is wise to investigate the potential of condemnation for any property you buy, either by inquiring or by having your attorney inquire (generally discreetly) as to the intended goals of highway departments, school districts, park districts, forest preserve districts, and other agencies that are likely to need property in your area.

Selecting Land to Meet the Future Demands of the Marketplace

You now know a number of the pitfalls of land investment, and you have guidelines for the factors which must be considered in acquiring land of any kind. The criteria of land acquisition will be discussed next. It is rarely necessary to explore all of these criteria fully, but depending upon the complexity and the amount of your investment, you will have to decide how extensive your investigation and analysis should be.

In seeking land, you start either with an anticipated use or with a site that has been offered to you. If you start with an anticipated use you will generally restrict yourself to a location that is easily accessible to you unless you are seeking a series of locations for a chain of similar uses. If the latter is the case, your criteria will have already been established by the end user. Assuming, therefore, that you have a specific use in mind, you will determine what standards must be met to have a successful use of the type you propose. You will then seek sites which fit those standards or which fit most of those standards. The people whom you will approach to find such sites for you will include real estate brokers, attorneys, and accountants whose clients may have properties of the kind you are seeking. In some areas the Farm Bureau can be helpful. Builders or maintenance suppliers relating to the industry which services your end use can also be a source of information. Home builders and organizations of real estate brokers can often refer you to people who are in the business of locating the type of site you are seeking.

If, on the other hand, a site is presented to you, and you have no end use in mind, you must go through the analysis of alternative uses that was described in previous sections and then make a financial analysis of the economic viability of the proposed investment.

Once you have determined that you wish to acquire a property, then unless you can make an immediate cash purchase, you will have to develop a financing program. The best program is to get an option or a conditional purchase agreement from the seller that gives you as much time as possible—for as many reasons as you can think of—to delay the payment of money. This chapter has spelled out many reasons why you should not put too much money at risk until you have learned a lot about the property and the market. Many of these are reasons that will not warm the heart of the seller or encourage him to give you lots of time. The most legitimate (and the most convenient) reasons relate to:

1. Soil conditions. These are normally determined in 30-60 days.
2. Engineering feasibility. Depending upon the available sources of utilities, you could ask for between 60 days and one year, but typically 60 to 120 days are requested.
3. Bank financing. This is generally not too popular with sellers, since they like to feel that you have the money to proceed, but the seller may give you from 90 to 180 days for this purpose, depending upon how anxious he is to sell.
4. Zoning, subdivision, and annexation. The time that you will be allowed for this purpose will vary widely, depending upon the state of the property when you approach the seller and upon the seller's knowledgeability concerning community attitudes. Typically zoning clauses permit six months to one year unless litigation is contemplated, in which case the time may be extended to three years and if the seller does not have a good real estate attorney, some contracts may run until all litigation opportunities are exhausted.

Some lending institutions make land loans. The criteria will vary with the institution and with your credit standing. Individuals frequently bring in partners who have limited funds and a desire to be involved in a land investment that is larger than any one of them can afford. We have had groups as large as 25 in private placement funding. You can bring in a lending institution as a cogeneral partner. Generally, you will need an excellent record of performance in order to be considered for the type of joint venture in which the lending institution puts up most of the money.

Any investors worth having will expect a financial analysis setting forth the cost of the land, the cost and timing of anticipated improvements, and a schedule of sales and anticipated selling prices together with related marketing expenses. These investors will want to know what is expected of them, what your contribution and your risk position will be, and how well you can back up the risk you are taking if the venture fails.

Don't fool yourself when you prepare your analysis. If anything, be more conservative than you think necessary. Our experience has been that we can generally predict values for various uses two or three years ahead and be fairly certain that if any of the uses we project are approved, our numbers on sales prices and selling expenses will be reasonably accurate. We have found, however, that changes in community attitudes and market conditions make it extremely hard to predict how long it will take to sell a property and what zoning we will achieve. We therefore provide investors with alternative projections on various time schedules.

MARKETING LAND INVESTMENTS

Now that you have the land, what are you going to do with it? We assume that before you bought it you developed a program which outlined the steps needed to convert the raw property into a marketable commodity. Some of the things you need to do may take you out of the category of investor, which would most likely give you capital gains income tax treatment, and into the category of developer, which would most likely give you ordinary income if you were fortunate enough to make a profit. You should get competent legal and tax guidance on what your tax position permits you to do.

Even if you don't intend to do anything more than acquire land and resell it "as is," you should make an initial analysis of the property, and you should periodically reanalyze it—alone or in consultation with others—as if you were buying it all over again. Each time the reanalysis is done (this should be at least annually), you will arrive at a value for the property. When you arrive at a value at which you would not even consider purchasing the property, then you should attempt to sell it at close to that price. There is always an area of value at which you might not buy the property but you do not wish to sell it. At this point you should either consider selling the property or you should attempt to change the zoning of the property or to convert the property from raw land to improved land. Generally, when you reach this plateau level, unless a change in use potential is likely, the increase in value thereafter will not give you an adequate additional return on the market value of the property at that time.

You should also undertake a reanalysis of your property when there is a significant change in circumstances. The acquisition or development of nearby property for major uses is one such change. Others are impending or actual changes of administrations, changes in the rules or enforcement procedures of regulatory agencies, or condemnation proccedings affecting your property.

The highest resale value will always be attributed to property which is zoned, improved, and ready to be built upon, and the lowest resale value will generally be attributed to as-is unimproved land (though such land may have a "romance" value, depending upon how good a salesperson you are and upon how well you can convince a prospective purchaser of its future potential).

To bring property to a fully improved ready-to-be-built-upon state takes a lot of time and a lot of money. It also takes a willingness to limit the number of possible end uses, since a fixed development program will generally restrict the number of uses to which a property can be put.

We have found that for most people who are not in need of cash but who wish to maximize the return on their investment, the sale of their land to a competent builder or developer on a "subject to zoning" basis will generally bring the greatest return with the least effort. However, you should have confidence in the ability and good judgment of your buyer because a buyer's efforts may not only fail but may also give rise to a hostile attitude toward your property. Moreover, selling in this way ties up your property for an extensive period of time and prohibits its sale to others.

You must also consider a term sale versus a cash sale. Most people will pay much more than just the interest difference to gain time. The risk of a term sale is one of default. Personal liability or an earnest money buffer will reduce that risk.

What you paid originally may determine whether or not you make a profit, but it does not determine the value of your property, except perhaps for purposes of condemnation. Never sell your property for too little or too much because of what you paid. The selling price of your property should relate to its value as a part of its end use, allowing for some land profit to your purchaser.

18: Land Investment

If your landholding is substantial, then it may be prudent to make several sales in acreage parcels to several builders or developers or to sell the land by zoning designations. You may also want to consider the partial improvement of the land by your ownership group. That is, you may extend the major utilities to the site and obtain an overall bulk plan approval for zoning categories, and in this way confirm the existence and the availability of the required utility services and provide the groundwork for builder efforts to obtain approval for site plans.

Another method of sale is not a sale at all. As was stated previously, you can participate with a builder or a financial institution in the development of your land, so that your profit will be based not only on the appreciation of the land but on the profits that may be reaped from the sale of the end product being developed or from the ownership of income-producing property. You can also give a builder or a developer very lenient terms, provided that he intends to proceed with end uses immediately, and you can have him pay you a bonus for having arranged matters so that he will not have to seek substantial financing for your land. That bonus can be made payable only as he sells the end product.

CONCLUSIONS

The land business brings you into contact with farmers and financiers, with promoters who have ideas and nothing more, and with highly liquid investors and investment houses. In land investment, you must deal in politics, whether you want to or not, and you must acquire a rudimentary knowledge of engineering, planning, law, and accounting in order to succeed. Unless you are extremely wealthy, your timing needs to work out well, and although luck has not been stressed here, it certainly helps. Fortunes have been made and lost in the land business. Regardless of what you hear about how the "other fellow" is doing and about how fast he is doing it, in the land business, as in any other business, a conservative approach to investment, a well-planned development program, a conscientious periodic review of all the factors that relate to the value and the marketability of your property, and thorough follow-through are the best road to continued profitability.

Land Investment Checklist

Owner's status:
1. Date of original contract
2. Common name.
3. Location and municipality.
4. Original total acreage.
5. Beneficiaries of trust agreement.
6. Remaining acreage.
7. Zoning breakdown of remaining acreage.
8. Estimated value of remaining acreage.

Municipal considerations:
1. Present zoning.
2. Summary of conditions of annexation agreement, if applicable.
3. Conditions relating to zoning or PUD.
4. Contribution requirements—land and dollars.
5. Zonings pending or contemplated.
6. Subdivisions pending or contemplated.
7. Litigations, including present or threatened condemnations.
8. If zoning or subdivisions are pending, schedule of dates for hearings and approvals.

General utility considerations:
1. Public or private—if private, list company and representative; if public, list director or village engineer.
2. Location of sanitary sewer, water, and other utilities relative to subject property.
3. Tap-on costs, if any.
4. Potential topographical or soil problems.
5. Flooding considerations.
6. Access problems, including required easements, road widening, and traffic lights.

Mortgage summary:
1. Dates of payment.
2. Interest.
3. Nonmonetary requirements.

Partnership agreement summary:
1. Requirements of limited partners for funding or refunding.
2. Requirements of general partners.
3. Nonmonetary obligations of general partners.
4. Obligations for repayment of limited partners.

Pending contracts:
1. Sales summary by specific dates, including principal and interest.
2. A reduced copy of land release planned.
3. Seller's monetary requirements.
4. Seller's nonmonetary requirements.
5. Schedule of completion for seller's nonmonetary requirements, including critical path breakdown to accomplish requirements.
6. Commission obligations and schedule of payments due and to whom.
7. Buyer's requirements.

Sources of funds to satisfy ownership requirements and contract contingencies:
1. Anticipated sources of funds with which buyer will make payment on contract.

Consultants involved in owning, developing, and selling:
1. Zoning attorney.
2. Contract attorney.
3. Special counsel, if any.
4. Tax consultant.
5. Engineer.

18: Land Investment

Land Investment Checklist *(concluded)*

Consultants involved in owning, developing, and selling (continued)
6. Surveyor.
7. Architect.
8. Planner.
9. Appraiser.
10. Traffic engineer/consultant.
11. Other.

Development:
1. Staging and breakdown.
2. Contractors and subcontractors.
3. Name of coordinator.
4. Obligations of the various parties.
5. Source of funds to pay obligations of land developer–if in mortgage, get mortgage terms.
6. Critical path breakdown on development stages and anticipated completion dates.

Negotiations pending:
1. Potential buyers.
2. Proposed price and terms.

Management of Real Estate Portfolios

19 PAUL SACK
The Rosenberg Real Estate Equity Funds
San Francisco, California

This chapter will discuss equity investment in real properties. Emphasis will be on the goals of such investment, the types of properties best suited to attaining those goals, the special problems of acquisition and selecting an investment vehicle, problems of liquidity, the interrelated problems of leverage and risk. The characteristics of specific types of properties will not be discussed in detail but will be mentioned only to illustrate the types of expertise necessary for the actual selection of properties.

This chapter will not deal with mortgages, which are better regarded as part of the fixed income portfolio. Nor will the chapter deal with the tax and tax shelter aspects of real estate, except to the limited extent that they affect tax-exempt institutions.

WHY INVEST IN REAL ESTATE?

The goals of investment in real estate are:

1. Diversification.
2. To improve the stability of income and value of the portfolio.

3. To achieve current income.
4. Protection from inflation of both income and principal.

These goals must be pursued in a manner consistent with the prudent manager's concern for safety of principal and requirements for liquidity.

   1. **Diversification.** Real estate offers an opportunity to diversify into an investment whose values and current returns do not rise and fall on the same cycle as equity or fixed income securities. Moreover, as increasing numbers of portfolio managers make substantial investments in real estate, the ERISA mandate for diversification may ultimately be interpreted as requiring diversification into real estate.

   For many years, it was believed that real estate values and yields moved with those of fixed income securities, but as investors have increasingly turned to real estate as an inflation hedge, the very forces which drive interest rates upward to build inflation into those rates have caused rates of return on real estate to decline. Investors have been willing to accept lower returns on properties offering inflation protection while they were demanding higher yields on fixed income securities. For example, 20 years ago the unleveraged return on real estate was consistently higher than the interest rate on mortgages, but the reverse is now the case. Thus rates of return on real estate equity investment and fixed income rates have moved in opposite directions over that period.

   2. **Stability of Income and Portfolio Value.** Real estate values and rates of return are much less volatile than prices of equity or fixed income securities. Price movements in real estate are difficult to detect until they have progressed for a number of months, since prices are not quoted daily in newspapers. The market therefore recognizes changes in capitalization rates (yield) very slowly; and since leases are normally written for periods of years, current income also changes slowly. Thus, correctly chosen real estate investments can add to stability of portfolio values.

   3. **Current Income.** Real estate investment can provide current income at a rate in excess of the dividend rate in most portfolios and comparable to (though currently less than) rates of return on fixed income securities. During 1978, for instance, current cash returns from real estate of investment quality and purchased on an unleveraged basis were 8-8.5 percent; returns on bonds rated Aa by Standard & Poor's averaged 8.9 percent, and dividends on the stocks which make up the Dow Jones Average represented a cash return of 6.0 percent based on prices of November 30, 1978.

   4. **Inflation Protection.** A major purpose of diversification into real estate is to achieve protection against erosion by inflation of the

real value of current income and principal. The investor in real estate hopes to achieve a current rate of return comparable with that on fixed income investments combined with significant inflation protection of that return.

Achieving inflation protection requires a careful analysis of lease maturities, favoring short-term over longer leases, and attention to the future competitiveness of the property in terms of location and design. Whereas 15 years ago, many investors considered the highest quality properties to be those leased for very long periods of time to tenants with top credit, the most highly-prized properties today are those with short-term leases which thus offer the possibility of increasing rents to offset inflation.

The Liquidity of Real Estate Investments

Real estate is essentially less liquid than most other forms of investment, and the financial structures which have been devised to give some promise of liquidity—the real estate investment trusts (REITs), for example—have almost uniformly been unsuccessful. While there is obviously a price at which a piece of property can be sold quickly to provide liquidity, the orderly exploration of the market and consummation of the sale of a property frequently take up to six months.

Portfolio managers should thus commit to real estate only that portion of the total portfolio on which liquidity is not required. For some portfolios, the need for 100 percent liquidity will totally rule out investment in real estate. For others with predictable positive cash flows, a prudent manager might well consider committing 5-20 percent of the portfolio to equity investment in real estate.

Funds invested in real estate should be considered committed for at least 5 and preferably 10 years or longer. As will be seen below, leases turn over slowly; and it may take 5 to 10 years for the increases in rental income, which were the original purpose of the investment, to materialize. Properties which promise excellent inflation protection over a holding period of 10 years may show very little movement in current return and value for the first 4 to 7 years, as the investor waits for leases to expire so that rents can be increased to reflect inflation.

Incremental Value in Real Estate

Real estate offers a highly capital-intensive investment in very durable, hard assets—bricks and mortar, etc. For several decades at least, the costs of construction have risen more rapidly than the general rate of inflation. As a result, the rents necessary to support the price of new construction have risen more rapidly than the general price indices.

Rents attainable in older buildings whose location and design allow them to compete with the new buildings have similarly risen to levels just below those commanded by the new structures. As potential rents have increased, value has increased; and as current leases expire and are rewritten at increased rents, the increments in the value of the property accrue to its owners.

Conversely, where long-term leases prevent the owner from increasing the rent to market levels, the incremental value lies with the tenant.

The properties which are most likely to yield increments in value and to provide inflation protection are clearly those whose design and location make it possible for them to compete with the new properties of the future. One of the cardinal rules in investing is thus to avoid paying for features which were built for the special purposes of the present tenant but for which future tenants might have no use—features such as walk-in refrigerators, extra-heavy electric power, etc.

Characteristics of High Quality Properties

Unfortunately, it takes an expert to recognize which properties are most readily rentable to future tenants and are therefore the most desirable investments. Some of the characteristics the experts look for will be cited in this section.

The three types of properties most sought as institutional investments are office buildings, industrial buildings, and shopping centers. To this list, some would add apartment buildings—others would not. Here is a quick catalog of what the experts look for in each of these types of property.

Office Buildings. Location should be in an area with other office buildings, convenient to transportation and highways, and close to such amenities as restaurants and at least convenience shopping.

Elevator service and air conditioning should be sufficient to serve the building, and there should be an adequate number of separate air conditioning zones so that different temperatures can be maintained in different areas of the offices. Ceiling heights of nine feet are preferred, but slightly lower ceilings are acceptable in many markets.

The configuration of the building should be such that the floors can be broken up into a great variety of shapes and sizes to suit the greatest number of possible future tenants. The distance from the hall to the window is crucial and varies from city to city as the average size of tenant varies. If the distance is too great, for instance, the average size tenant will be left with a long, thin office, with only a short frontage on the windows for executives and too much back space for clerical help. Floors with the elevators in the center core offer greater flexibility than those with elevators at one end of the floor.

Industrial Buildings. Location must be convenient to highways and, preferably, to a four-way highway interchange. Proximity to the airport and to a railway are important in most markets.

Warehouses should offer dock-high loading for trucks, with weather protection in certain climates; railroad access; good ceiling heights; automatic sprinklers; and no more than 15 percent office space.

Even though the building may now be occupied by a single tenant, the bay depths should be short enough that the building could be cut up for several tenants when the current lease runs out. There should be at least 100 to 120 feet of paved area for truck turn-arounds.

It is preferable if trucks can enter from one driveway and go out another.

In manufacturing buildings, one similarly looks for a configuration which will allow the space to be cut up for a number of tenants in the future. Mezzanine office space often has little value to a future tenant and should be heavily discounted. Adequacy of parking for present and possible future uses must be calculated.

Shopping Centers. Location must offer good access by automobile and, in some markets, public transportation. Purchasing power in the trading area is of almost equal importance, and careful attention must be paid to both present and possible future competition with which that purchasing power must be shared.

Bay depths should not be too deep for the average tenant. Most tenants prefer as much window space as possible, and small tenants can rarely make good use of a space more than 60 to 75 feet deep.

Layout of the center should make entry and exit easy for cars approaching from any direction. Every tenant's sign should be visible from the street. Parking should be laid out in such a way that cars do not back up in the main aisles as other cars enter or leave a space.

Apartment Buildings. Problems of management, fear of rent control, and competition from tax-oriented investors have caused many institutions to rule out investment in apartment buildings. Nevertheless, the ability to raise rents every year (or twice a year) gives apartment buildings the potential of better inflation protection than commercial or industrial properties whose leases are generally written for periods of years.

To be competitive, apartments should be located in good residential areas, reasonably convenient to the dominant modes of transportation and to shopping. Identification from a well-traveled artery reduces advertising costs.

One-bedroom units should contain at least 650 square feet and two-bedroom units 875 square feet; otherwise, they may have to compete on the basis of price rather than quality. Floor plans should allow for a variety of furniture arrangements, provide adequate closet space, etc.

In recent years, amenities such as landscaping (with mature trees, lakes, and streams), recreation buildings, swimming pools, saunas, whirlpools, pool tables, tennis courts, and views have become crucial to competitiveness.

Characteristics of Higher Risk Properties

One way to reduce risk is to purchase only existing properties which have already been leased and whose net income can be analyzed on the basis of actual leases, rent receipts, and operating history.

Vacant or Substantially Vacant Properties. A principal difficulty in purchasing vacant or largely vacant properties is estimating the ultimate income and expenses to determine net income and thus value. If rents are projected at $6 per square foot, and only $5.50 proves attainable, the overpayment for the property could prove substantial—particularly if expenses turn out to be underestimated. For instance:

	Projected	*Actual*	*Percent Change*
Rents on 100,000 square feet	$ 600,000	$ 550,000	− 8.3%
Expenses	200,000	225,000	+12.5
Net income	$ 400,000	$ 325,000	−
Value, capitalized at 8½%	$4,700,000	$3,800,000	−19.2%

Thus, an 8 percent overestimation of the potential rent combined with a 12.5 percent underestimation of expenses lead to an overpayment of 19 percent for the property.

To guard against such possibilities, some investors purchase only substantially-occupied properties, where rents have been proven in the open market and where expenses either are not the owner's responsibility or can be analyzed on the basis of past operating data.

Another way to protect one's self is to contract for purchase of a substantially vacant property for a price which will vary in accordance with the actual rents achieved when the property has been leased. To do this, a contract is signed calling for progressive payments by the purchaser to the developer-seller on the basis of leasing achievement. The price finally paid depends on the relationship of actual leases and rents to the original projections.

Development Deals. New developments combine the necessity of working with projected, rather than actual, rents and expenses with additional uncertainty concerning the time required to bring the project onstream.

In recent years, as the Federal Reserve has resorted to periods of tight and expensive money to control inflation, the nation has experienced several years of negative real growth in the economy, meaning zero demand for additional commercial or industrial space. The result has been a stretch-out of the time it takes to fully lease new developments. Time costs money—especially when money is tight and expensive. The result has been that new developments have oftentimes not achieved projected profits, and returns have often been particularly disappointing on a time-discounted basis.

The increased time required to lease up new properties was the cause of the difficulties of many of the REITs, who had loaned money to developers who were unable to pay the carrying costs when the economy slowed up. Clearly, the rewards do not always justify the risks in development deals.

Raw Land. While it is often possible to estimate that a given piece of raw land lies in the path of development and will improve in value, it is less easy to estimate the amount of time it will take for an increase in value to be realized; therefore, the time-discounted rate of return on raw land is extremely hazardous to forecast. The threat that environmentalists will downgrade potential uses also adds an element of uncertainty which it is difficult to measure. What, for instance, is a piece of raw land worth if it is rezoned for use as a park or "open space"? The heir to 7,200 acres in Big Sur country in California was recently advised that environmental restrictions will allow subdivision into only three lots on each of which one house can be built.

Nevertheless, in a large real estate portfolio, there is room for a component of raw land—perhaps 5-10 percent of the total real estate portfolio.

Hotels and Motels. At first look, hotels and motels seem to offer excellent potential for inflation protection, because the rent can be renegotiated every night. The problem is that hotels and motels are less highly capital-intensive than the other real estate investments cited. Operating results depend on management skills, employee productivity, union negotiation, and marketing programs. Useful life of such properties may be severely curtailed by changes in fashion within the hospitality industry, requirement of a different amenity package, etc. Thus, investing in a hotel or motel is more like investing in a business than in a capital intensive piece of real property. Nevertheless, a properly-structured deal with a competent and financially capable manager could provide an attractive investment.

Restaurants and Other Special-Purpose Buildings. The incremental value in real estate stems from the usefulness of the property to other tenants in the future. Buildings specially designed to the specifications of one tenant—such as a fast-food chain—will obviously enjoy only the narrowest of markets if the original tenant moves out or, as is highly likely, if the design specifications of the original tenant change over time. Special purpose properties should be avoided.

Determining Intrinsic Value

The intrinsic value of a property is its replacement cost and constitutes the upper limit of value. Recall that the goal is to invest in well located, well designed properties which can expect to achieve increases in rents in the future matching the increases in market rents made necessary by increases in construction costs. If one pays no more than replacement cost at the time of purchase, the potential exists to share fully in the effects of inflation on market rents. If, however, one pays more than replacement cost, one has already given away some of the potential incremental value of the property. Often, a price above replacement cost seems justified by the net income of the property—particularly if the rents reflect some special features built into the property for the current tenant. Thus, it is important to estimate replacement cost independently before purchasing real property.

Leverage

Traditionally, tax-oriented investors have purchased real estate on a highly leveraged basis with loans typically constituting 75-80 percent of the purchase price. Leverage is necessary for these investors to achieve a high ratio of depreciable assets to equity investment for tax shelter. Such investors are typically less concerned with safety of principal and stability of income than managers of institutional funds.

If one knew that rental income would always increase more rapidly than expenses, it would obviously pay to be as highly leveraged as possible. The problem is that rents do not always increase so rapidly, and leverage works both ways.

For instance, consider the case of a building which has been foreclosed by a REIT because its 25 percent vacancy factor made it impossible for the investment to cover debt service. On an unleveraged basis, the 25 percent vacancy factor would simply have reduced the operating return on equity from, say, 9.5 percent to approximately 6 percent—not the most desirable result but nothing near the disaster of a foreclosure. Real estate leveraged with 75 percent debt typically breaks even at 82 percent occupancy, while unleveraged properties break even at occupancy of 40 percent or less.

Therefore, for institutional investors greatly concerned over preservation of principal and whose goals for real estate investment include improving the stability of income and value for their portfolios, leverage in any significant degree seems inappropriate.

Moreover, even to tax-oriented investors, leverage was more attractive in the past when mortgage rates were lower than rates of return on an unleveraged basis. In these times of "reverse leverage," borrowing reduces the rate of current income and increases the speculative nature of the investment in a way that may be unsuited to the goals of the managers of the fund. Managers will also want to consider the net portfolio effect of borrowing on mortgages at rates which exceed the interest rates being realized on the fixed income portion of their own portfolio.

Furthermore, in most vehicles for investment in real estate by tax-exempt institutions—including direct ownership—leverage will result in unrelated business income subject to taxation, reducing rates of return after taxes.

It seems safe to conclude, therefore, that most managers of institutional funds will purchase real estate on an unleveraged basis or will be willing to accept only small amounts of leverage—particularly where properties can be acquired subject to old loans at low interest rates.

HOW TO INVEST IN REAL ESTATE

As should now be clear, considerable expertise is necessary to put together a real estate portfolio which will meet the goals and quality standards of institutional investors. Unfortunately, there are no rating services to label a property Aaa, A, or Baa. Every property is different, because no two locations can be exactly the same.

The ideal way to invest is through direct ownership, i.e., to acquire the necessary staff and then purchase and manage the properties in-house. For reasons of diversification and the difficulty of staffing, however, only a few of the very largest institutions will find this route feasible. For instance:

Diversification. Prudence dictates diversification into at least 8 or 10 properties. In order not to compete with small, tax-oriented investors, each property should be worth at least $2-$3 million. Thus, proper diversification would require a minimum investment of approximately $25 million. If the real estate portfolio is to be 20 percent of the total, then only a fund of at least $125 million can achieve adequate diversification through direct investment; if real estate is to be 5 percent of the total portfolio, only a fund of at least $500 million can consider direct investment.

Staffing. Acquiring staff with appropriate expertise will not be easy. Such persons are highly paid within the industry, are hard to attract and not easy to hold—especially for a one-time investment of only $25 million. Moreover, different expertise is required for industrial properties, office buildings, shopping centers, etc. Several staff thus will be required. Unless an annual program is contemplated of investing approximately $25 million per year for several years, it is doubtful an appropriate staff could be assembled. While theoretically the analysis might be delegated to real estate consultants, the expertise necessary to make the final decision on consultants' recommendations is not much different from that necessary to select from offerings by brokers. Thus, staffing requirements make direct investment feasible only for funds with assets in the range of $500 million and up.

All but a very few of the larger institutions, therefore, will elect to invest in real estate in combination with other institutions with similar goals and tax status, through the vehicle of commingled funds.

Commingled Funds: Open-End versus Closed-End

The most popular commingled vehicles are open-end funds. In the same manner as with open-end mutual funds, interests are continually offered to new investors. Current income from the properties as well as funds from new investors are available to buy out those who wish to sell, appearing to give real estate a measure of liquidity not usually attainable by direct ownership. If new investment exceeds withdrawals, the fund can expand, buy ever-larger properties, and offer greater diversification. There are two caveats:

1. If requests for withdrawal exceed the sum of cash flow and new investments, liquidity can be attained only by the fund's selling properties. Thus, the appearance of liquidity may be an illusion, especially if—as is likely—the market forces which cause one investor to decide to sell out cause many to make the same decision at the same time.

2. The second problem is the knotty one of appraising real estate. It is easy to set the price at which investors buy into or sell out of commingled pools of stocks or bonds; newspapers carry the market prices daily. But appraising real estate is either an art or a very inexact science. Two appraisers, using the same data and appraising for the same purpose, can differ by 15-20 percent in their appraisal of value. As most real estate owners will attest, the only time one knows what a property is worth is when one is walking away from the title company with a check after a sale—and even then one can't be sure the price might not have been higher.

Proponents of open-end funds argue that in a large portfolio, the errors cancel each other out, but that argument is unconvincing. The appraisals could easily have a constant bias—downward in the interest of prudence and conservatism or upward in the interest of improving performance measurements for the managers of the fund (who, after all, hire the appraisers).

One example of this problem involves a highly regarded institutional fund which boasted that it is conservative in its appraisals and that the only property it had ever sold went for 20 percent more than appraised value. The appraisal process thus transferred appreciation from the early investors to those who bought in later.

In another example, fund appraisers increased the value of the portfolio by $600,000 one year and then, because of reverses in some markets, reduced the value by $1.5 million the next year. Investors had sold out both years, so the appraisal process transferred capital from those who sold out the second year to those who sold out the first year. Whether they are willing to buy into and sell out of open-ended real estate portfolios on the basis of appraised values is something institutional managers will have to weigh.

Closed-end funds can be so structured that money does not change hands on the basis of appraisals. A fixed amount of money is received into the closed-end fund and is then invested in real properties on the basis of prices arrived at by negotiations at arm's length in the open market. When all the money has been invested, each investor owns a proportionate share of a pool of properties purchased at market prices rather than buying into the fund at values set by an appraiser, as in an open-end fund.

While an open-end fund receives new money for investment and grows over a period of years, the managers of closed-end funds must periodically start a new fund—typically every year. Thus an open-end fund generally offers more diversification (more properties) than a single closed-end fund and, because the open-end fund can grow very large over time, is able to purchase larger properties than closed-end funds. However, it should be possible to achieve adequate diversification in a closed-end fund, provided it is large enough to purchase, say, a minimum of $20 million of properties; and there is no reason to believe that returns on the larger properties that lie beyond the means of closed-end funds are higher than returns on the size of property closed-end funds can buy without damage to their diversification plan.

Selecting a Real Estate Manager, Fund Manager, or Consultant

It is almost impossible to attend a one-day conference on real estate without hearing the word *entrepreneurial*. Many believe that there is an entrepreneurial component to buying, as well as to developing, real estate and that the acquisition function cannot be institutionalized, i.e. carried out by a hierarchy of committees. In such hierarchies, the field work is generally done by the least experienced operative, and written reports travel upward through a series of two or three presumably increasingly expert committees. The experience of banks with REITs is often cited as evidence that such a decision-making structure may not work well in real estate.

On the other hand, there are large institutions which have been successful in real estate—notably some of the insurance companies. The people at the top of these programs are undeniably entrepreneurial and immensely knowledgeable about real estate. While they have not been able to filter all the bad properties out of the acquisition process, they have purchased some very good ones.

Decisions in real estate are not likely to be any better than the people who make them—up and down the decision-making line. It is an essential part of the process of selecting a real estate manager, therefore, to meet with and evaluate the people at all decision-making levels in the manager's shop. Careful attention should also be paid to the decision-making procedures.

Ideally, the selecting team would also visit a representative sample of properties already purchased by the manager.

Such an evaluation will itself require some real estate expertise. If this is available within the organization with which the investing fund is associated (as in the case of the pension fund of a corporation with a real estate department), so much the better. Otherwise, it will be wise to find an adviser who is knowledgeable about real estate and in whom the selection team has confidence. The role of such an adviser would not be to evaluate the proposed real estate strategy but only the knowledgeability of the experts being hired to carry it out.

Track records should be scrutinized if available, but they are unfortunately not so easy to interpret as one might hope. In the next section, Evaluating Performance, it will be pointed out that increases in value may reflect the action of market forces over which the manager has had no control and that stabilized current income is a more meaningful measure of managers. In the cases of a closed-end fund or directly-owned properties, trends in current income are easily determined because the pool of properties is relatively fixed. On the other hand, in open-end funds where properties are continually being added to the portfolio (presumably bringing additional current income) and where portfolio values are changed quarterly on the basis of appraisals, it is not so easy to determine the track records of any single group of properties over time.

EVALUATING PERFORMANCE

Real estate is a long-term investment, because income and value change slowly. After all, one of the goals of diversifying into real estate is to add stability to the income stream and to portfolio value. Where six months seems a long time to investors in the stock market, six years is a short time in real estate.

For example, a property might be purchased because it is well located and competitively designed, its current rents are below market, and the current leases expire in six years. After six years, the investor could expect a very large increase in current income and capitalized value, including an increase in rents related to the rate of inflation over the six years following purchase. However, there would be no change in net income for six full years. Yet, it would be folly to give the manager low marks for failing to show increases in income while waiting for the current leases to expire. Real estate requires patience and cannot be evaluated on the basis of quarter-to-quarter operating results.

Most institutions, for reporting or other purposes, will want properties to be appraised independently every one or two years. Such appraisals will rely heavily on the income method of appraisal, in which current market rents will be factored in.

The formula for income value in real estate is the same as that for bonds, but the components are differently labeled:

$$\frac{\text{Stabilized net income}}{\text{Capitalization rate}} = \text{Value}$$

The *capitalization rate* is obviously akin to yield on bonds and is selected by the appraiser on the basis of her or his reading of the market. *Stabilized net income* is kin of dividends or interest payments, except that it has been adjusted for temporary aberrations in the rental market or rental program and for differences between rents received under current leases and market rents that could be achieved if those leases expired.[1] The appraisals thus can give a clue as to how the portfolio is progressing—bearing in mind, of course, that there is a 15-20 percent margin of error in appraisals.

The problem in evaluating performance on the basis of appraisals is that appraised values are heavily affected by changes in the capital-

---

[1] The appraiser handles the problem of the difference between rents under current leases and market rents which could be achieved if the current leases were not in force as follows:

Stabilized income under this method is net income which could be achieved if all rents at the property were current market rents. By the formula, stabilized net income would be divided by the capitalization rate to give the total value of the property, including both the owner's interest *and* the leasehold interests of the tenants. The appraiser would then calculate the annual estimated loss of rent resulting from the fact that rents under current leases are below market. The appraiser would then calculate the discounted present value of the stream of earnings losses resulting from the fact that rents under current leases are less than market rents, and that discounted present value would be the value of the leasehold interests. By deducting the value of the leasehold interests from the total value of the property determined by the formula, the appraiser would determine the value of the owner's fee interest in the property.

ization rate, which is a function of market forces over which the manager has no control. For the past three years, for instance, real estate has been increasing in value, because capitalization rates have been declining by ½ percent (50 basis points) per year as investors have been willing to accept lower rates of return in the short run on investments which they believe offer protection against inflation. Obviously this kind of increase in value cannot be projected indefinitely into the future, as there is some minimum return greater than zero that investors will demand under any circumstances. Changes in value based on changes in the capitalization rate reflect not the performance of the real estate manager but the evaluation of real estate as an investment by financial markets.

Changes in the numerator of the value fraction, i.e., stabilized net income, are a better measure of how well the real estate manager has done in selecting properties and managing them, as stabilized net income is based on current market rents. Therefore, for the purpose of evaluating the real estate manager, it is useful to ask the appraiser for a separate set of values based on constant (year-to-year) capitalization rates.

SUMMARY

The goals of equity investment in real estate are diversification, stability of income and value, current income, and inflation protection. Real estate is less liquid than most other forms of investment, so managers should carefully consider the proportion of funds they can actuarially afford to commit.

Incremental value in real estate lies in those properties whose high quality of design and location will allow them to compete with new properties in the future. Since the cost of construction will rise with inflation, rents in new properties and those able to compete with them will also rise.

The type of properties deemed most suitable for institutional investment are shopping centers, office and industrial buildings. Apartments rank somewhat lower, followed by hotels and motels and raw land. There is disagreement as to whether development deals and special purpose buildings are suitable.

Leverage works both ways, increasing both potential returns and potential for loss. Leverage thus increases volatility and risk.

All but the largest institutions will invest in real estate through commingled funds, and the differences between open-end and closed-end funds should be carefully considered.

Measures of comparative performance of real estate and real estate managers are just beginning to be developed and will require understanding of the nature of real estate investment.

REFERENCES

Hoagland, H. E.; L. D. Stone; and W. B. Brueggeman. *Real Estate Finance* (Homewood, Ill.: Richard D. Irwin, 1977).

Ring, A. A., and S. Passo. *Real Estate Principles and Practices* (Englewood Cliffs, N.J.: Prentice-Hall, 1977).

Wendt, P. F., and A. R. Cerf. *Real Estate Investment Analysis and Taxation* (New York: McGraw-Hill, 1979).

Wiley, R. J. *Real Estate Investment* (New York: Ronald Press, 1977).

Venture Capital

20   ALAN JOEL PATRICOF
Alan Patricof Associates
New York, New York

You are standing at a cocktail party in Palo Alto, California, sipping your Perrier, when a small fellow with long hair and glasses, looking rather serious, sidles up to you and starts a pleasant conversation about a variety of things, one being the fact that he has heard that you like to invest in promising new ventures. Somewhere along the way, he mentions a new microprocessor that he has developed. The product, described as having a multiplicity of potential applications, was used, your new friend tells you, to control the lighting in the Broadway version of *Hair*. Having seen the show and vaguely remembering that you liked the lights, you decide that this could be an interesting product, particularly when you then hear that the Playboy Club Discotheque and a newly renovated TV studio on New York City's West Side that is being turned into a discotheque to be known as Studio 54 will also be using this microprocessor. You become even more interested when he tells you that the real prospects for the company he has formed to produce his microprocessor are not in discotheque lighting but in the application of the technology to control energy use in high-rise office buildings. When you ask what discotheques have to do with energy savings, he proceeds to tell you about his MIT degrees and the broad applications of microprocessor technology that are too confusing to follow. You offer him your card, never expecting to see him again. But when you arrive at your office at 9:00 A.M. Monday, the first call you receive is from your new friend who wants to drop by to show you his business plan. In spite of the fact that his company has only three employees, is behind on its payroll taxes, and its books are a mess, a

$75,000 investment in the business would solve all his problems because it would trigger a $350,000 Small Business Administration guaranteed loan from a bank. For that investment, he is willing to give you one third of the company....

You are running counterclockwise around the reservoir in Central Park in New York City when an old acquaintance, running in the opposite direction, sees you and reverses field to run alongside. After a few minutes of chitchat, he tells you, between breaths, that he had heard you are looking for investments in interesting companies and it just so happens that there is a little piece left of a new cookie company which has been started by a literary agent whose wife developed a formula for making shortbread and whose brother-in-law had been the marketing vice president of Sara Lee, or was it Stouffer's. In any event, they produced 5,000 pounds of cookies at Christmas, which were packaged and sold through Macy's, Bloomingdale's, and a few other outlets at $10 a pound. The product has been favorably marketed in the Best Bets section of *New York Magazine,* and at least six other department stores have indicated an interest in selling it in their gourmet food departments. Your old acquaintance is buying two shares in the deal which is all sold except for the last unit....

Most of us are intrigued by a new idea and, from time to time, are offered the opportunity to make an investment in a friend's, or a friend of a friend's, or a neighbor's new company, or plan to buy out an existing company. While one should not resist the temptation entirely, it is important to recognize that this type of investment is usually very risky, highly illiquid, and should never be undertaken without a great deal of prior investigation and analysis. Once the investment has been made, you are, to one degree or another, a partner in the business. Moreover, even when sufficiently satisfied as to the validity of the project, one should restrict this type of investment to a limited portion of available funds. While it is fun to take a fling every now and then, it is also important to realize that venture capitalism is a demanding business that is best left to the professionals.

HISTORY

As an industry, venture capital took shape shortly after World War II, spearheaded to a large degree by General George Doriot and his American Research and Development Co. AR&D was fortunate to have made an early commitment in Digital Equipment Corporation, commonly known as DEC, thereby parlaying $200,000 or so into several hundred million dollars (no discotheques for them!). While that story is hard to top, the list of successful venture capital investments that have returned 50 to 100 times on the original investment grows each year.

Most such stories are focused in the electronics industry and involve names like Cray Research, Storage Technology, Qume, Tandem Computer, Four Phase Systems, Rolm, and, most recently, Apple Computer, which has risen from a mere startup in late 1977 to what will be a $150 million business in 1980. According to Steve Job, the 26-year-old cofounder and chairman of Apple, who quit his job at Atari, sold his Volkswagen, and joined forces with a friend who had just traded in his HP-55 calculator and left Hewlett-Packard, it was merely a question of "painting the bulls-eye correctly on a defined target of opportunity."

Perhaps an even greater venture capital success story is Federal Express, which was started in 1974. It has since totally revolutionized the concept of small-package delivery systems within the United States. Its fleet of red, white, and purple aircraft, which fly nightly across the country out of Memphis, Tennessee, will produce revenues of over $500 million in 1981 and make more than $40 million after taxes. This company, too, was started by a young man in his late 20s. In this case it took a substantial amount of his family's capital, together with outside investors, four rounds of financing at decreasing prices, several public offerings, and lots of senior bank financing to reach the current level of profit.

While American Research and Development is considered the first bona fide company to engage in venture capital, the business was conducted in the 1950s and 1960s on a professional basis by recognized family names, mostly from the East Coast. The roster included William Burden, J. H. Whitney, Venrock (the investment vehicle for the Rockefeller family), Bessemer Securities (the vehicle for the Phipps family), Payson & Trask, and many leading investment banking firms that devoted a certain portion of their partnership capital to imaginative risk-oriented investments outside of their general stock market activities. Such names as Armand Erpf of Loeb, Rhodes and the Loeb family; Jacob Klingenstein of Wertheim & Co.; Lazard Freres; and Lehman Brothers all participated in one way or another in investments which could be characterized as venture capital in that they involved significant equity positions in young or restructured companies.

But it was not until the booming new-issue market in over-the-counter stocks in the late 1960s, which resulted in overnight fortunes being made by original investors in early stage companies, that the industry as such actually began to take shape. For the first time, pension funds, insurance companies, and hundreds of wealthy individuals fostered the creation of investment partnerships focused entirely on venture capital. These partnerships have today become the essential means of participation by individuals and institutions into small and, for the most part, private companies that have the ultimate objective of obtaining, over a minimum 10-year period, gains substantially in excess of what the stock market and most forms of investment can be expected to produce. Warburg Pincus & Co., New Court Securities, Brentwood Associates, Sutter Hill, Heizer Group, Kleiner Perkins, and more than 200 other partnerships have sprung up in the past 10 years, located from West to East coasts, developing geographical and area specializations. While single participations in these partnerships range from as little as $100,000 to as much as $10 million, and while the pools themselves range in overall size from $3 million to $100 million, a typical partnership will have no more than 14 participants with positions ranging from $500,000 to $3 million.

The venture industry today is generally described as having $3-4 billion in capital. While individuals still account for a portion of these funds, institutional investors are the predominant factor. Because of the capital available in these groups, the size of an average investment position tends to range from $250,000 to $5 million. In other words, this is not the group that is financing your average neighborhood business.

In most investors' minds, venture capital will always refer to high technology, high-risk startups. (In addition to the names already mentioned, venture capitalists have had a major hand in the development of Evans & Sutherland, Coherent Radiation, Data General, Thermo Electron, Floating Point Systems, Measurex, Prime Computer, and a host of others.) Many of these companies took shape during the exuberant days of the late 1960s and early 1970s when a great entrepreneurial surge throughout the country resulted in the formation of companies with names that began or ended in *electronics, data, computer, onics,* or *technology.* Entrepreneurism was at its height in those days, and the tax structure was such that capital gains were taxed at 25 percent, stock options for management—as well as outright issuance of founder's stock—made it very attractive to form a new company, and there was a vibrant public market that provided a profitable exit from these investments in a very short period of time.

This environment came to an abrupt halt in the mid-1970s as a result of a dramatic decline in the public's appetite for young companies, a reflection of the collapse that had taken place in the overall public securities market. This development, coupled with the enactment of a less-favorable tax code, created a period of hibernation, both on the part of entrepreneurs and venture capitalists, that resulted in a reshaping of the venture industry and the development of a longer-term perspective to the role of venture capital.

There also emerged a more sobering awareness of the need to balance and diversify a venture portfolio, carefully mixing startups with more mature investments and the development of techniques for eventual exit other than the public market. Venture capitalists also created the so-called leveraged buyout, a new area of investment that lately has absorbed large amounts of capital. This type of investment refers to the purchase of companies or subsidiaries of companies by managements who have financed a substantial portion of the purchase price through a layer of senior bank or insurance financing, supported by a layer of subordinated debt or preferred stock provided by venture investors, plus some financing from the selling company itself.

THE VENTURE INDUSTRY TODAY

Nevertheless, the inherent instinct of the venture capitalist is to seek out the next DEC, the next Intel, or the next Federal Express. Among the areas receiving the most attention today and creating some degree of excitement are such esoteric fields as gene splitting and recombinant DNA, which have resulted in the formation of companies with valuations that stagger the imagination and which have attracted substantial corporate and institutional venture funds. Other areas of current interest include the future applications of television as a two-way vehicle for the dissemination of information. In addition, two-way TV via cable, with shopping and banking from the home, as well as accessing data bases, are bound to be a major area of interest in the 1980s. New materials for space and water, as well as everyday living, fish farming, word processing and the office of the future, microelectronics, fiber optics, new medical electronic devices (both implanted and external) for diagnosis as well as anything to do with computers or peripherals are some of the other areas that venture capitalists will be focusing on in the next decade.

In addition to the office of the future, there is much talk about the car of the future which, by 1985, will include a single microcomputer chip that will control and diagnose almost every aspect of the car's operation. But venture capital is not just high technology, and many in industry are financing new consumer products, basic industrial activities, and the restructuring of many fundamental existing enterprises.

In the past decade, most venture capitalists have achieved an impressive rate of return, ranging from 10 to 20 percent compounded annually and for shorter, more recent periods, as much as 30 percent. This is more than two to three times the gains racked up by such standard market indicators as the Dow Jones Industrials and the S&P Index. However, in a world where inflation is raging at a rate in excess of 15 percent per annum and interest rates for prime borrowers hover near 20 percent, venture investments will have to achieve even greater results to appear attractive in light of the perceived risk of illiquidity which is a meaningful barrier to overcome.

The unique aspect of venture capital is that it operates in an inefficient market where there are not an equal number of buyers and sellers. Since purchases are made privately and, to some degree, as a matter of chance based on a matching of interests and geographic location, valuations are often determined on a subjective basis. And since many of the companies are too young to determine scientifically a value at the outset, there is the opportunity for spectacular gain. A good example is Qume Corporation, which was founded in 1973 with slightly more than $1 million in equity capital. Qume is credited for broadly commercializing the "daisy wheel" printer, which has become the nucleus of most of the modern generation of typewriters and word processing machines. When ITT acquired the company in 1978 for over $17 million, investors received shares of ITT with an annual dividend of more than twice their original investment and realized 30 times their investment.

This is a perfect example of venture capital at its best. On the other hand, investors who financed the 1975 concept of splitting *Saturday Review Magazine* into four separate magazines lost $20 million before it was repurchased by its original owners and put back into its original configuration. Who could have objectively determined an appropriate valuation for investment purposes in 1973 for Qume? And for every Qume there are probably three or four complete failures and a few adequate performers where the return is good but not great. Nevertheless, the underlying elements of venture capital investing—namely, that when you lose, all you can lose is what you invested, and when you are successful, the reward can be unlimited—create a set of conditions such that, if you invest wisely and often enough and pay careful attention to details, over a period of time you should achieve impressive results.

DIVERSIFICATION

Venture investing, which typically involves young companies with new products and often untried management, has built-in features that create greater problems than investing in marketable companies that are more mature and where, when difficulties crop up, one can readily get out. The only way to hedge against venture disasters is to diversify as to the kind of portfolio companies, and to include among your investments startups, expansion financings, and turnarounds. For example, unless one were prepared to develop a high-risk profile, it would not be a good idea to invest in 10 computer startups but rather to spread the risk over different industries and to limit the number of startups to no more than three or four.

While a large source of venture capital today comes from institutions, individuals have, to a certain extent, an extra benefit in that they can sometimes structure an investment in such a form as to obtain an immediate write-off of early-stage losses through a limited partnership or a subchapter S Corporation. These structures reduce the down-side risk and, on the up-side, allow investors to obtain capital gains treatment, thereby improving the risk/reward ratio.

Regardless, for an individual to even consider participating in venture capital, it is desirable to be in the 50 percent or higher marginal tax bracket. Moreover, other than an occasional fling, one should probably not consider venture investing unless one has sufficient capital to participate in a professionally managed pool or a willingness to assume the responsibility of preliminary analysis and subsequent supervision and to make enough individual investments to spread the risk. While anyone can make an isolated investment of modest size to assist a friend or acquaintance or to back an idea that sounds particularly romantic, whether it be in microprocessors or cookies, serious venture investment should only be done by those who can allocate a meaningful amount of funds to achieve adequate diversification. Even with sufficient capital available, this segment of a portfolio, because of its higher risk profile and its lack of reliable current income, should probably not represent more than 5 or 10 percent of one's investments.

One of the appealing elements of venture investments is the psychic income that one obtains. There is a much higher degree of identification with the investment than in the stock market, and the satisfaction obtained is much greater than just seeing a stock go up. How many times have you heard someone say, "I own 10 percent of that dress company or a piece of that magazine or a share of that new restaurant?" As a matter of fact, most of the individual type of investing occurs in products or projects that are close to home and that have some consumer aspect or some degree of visibility. One of the sure ways you know you are approaching the area with a greater professional objectivity is when you can make an investment in a situation that has no identification factor associated with it.

CASE HISTORY

The following, a typical venture capital story, highlights some of the highs and lows that a venture capitalist will run into. In 1970, we were approached by an enterprising team of three Ph.D.s who had developed advanced techniques for the design of computer communications networks under the auspices of the government. They perceived that the next decade would usher in an era of computers that would talk to each other as people had become accustomed to doing. This would require both corporations and government agencies to develop new communication networks for the more efficient routing of messages at the greatest speed and the least cost.

The company operated out of a leased mansion in Long Island, located on nine acres in a pastoral setting intended to recreate the atmosphere of a university; most of the 12 initial employees held advanced mathematical or physics degrees and had come from a college or think-tank environment.

The company was founded with $150,000 of outside capital for which the investors received 15 percent of the company. One Friday evening about six months after our investment was closed, we received a phone call from the company's president indicating that the company had only enough funds to last out the month and that he was voluntarily turning over the reins to another of the founders, since he had failed as the marketing element of the team and was a drain on the survival of the business. It was readily apparent that all of the initial capital had been expended through the payment of salaries and day-to-day operating expenses. It was not that anyone had done anything wrong. It was just that the hoped-for contracts had not developed.

Rather than close down, which would have been a shattering event for both the principals and investors, it was decided to regroup, terminate six of the employees, and place three others in part-time teaching positions in the area with the two remaining founders and an assistant deferring their salaries to await the award of a particular contract on which they had placed a great deal of emphasis and which was still a few months away. That summer in Long Island, three people sat in a 30-room mansion with three desks and a telephone. It must have been a strange sight to anyone who took the time to peer behind the solemn walls of ivy.

In October the company obtained the contract it had been waiting for, rehired their brethren who had been farmed out, and, like the phoenix, rose from its ashes and grew over the next several years into a profitable enterprise. It looked as though there would be no need for additional capital. That is, until the recession of 1975, which resulted in government cutbacks and a severe drop in commercial business. At that point, the investors came up with an additional $150,000 in capital. The world was different in 1975, however, and a lot of the effervescence of valuation in 1970 had fizzled. As a result, despite the fact that the company was now an operating business with five years of history and 50 employees, this time the investors got 20 percent of the company for their $150,000, half of which was purchased by the employees.

The company pulled out of that downturn, tightened its belt, redirected its marketing efforts, and improved its pricing structure. Before long, business was booming again and space had become a problem. There was no choice but to move to a real office building with sufficient additional space for expansion. This created a temporary period of underutilized facilities and extra overhead which, as you might expect, coincided with another downturn in business. But this time, the company was agile and had diversified its business and improved its management skills sufficiently so that the downturn was hardly noticeable.

At this point in its history, the company is headed by seasoned businesspeople who have developed the necessary marketing, finance, and budgeting skills. It has an established reputation in its field and has become a leader in communications network design. It has almost 100 employees and a second office in Washington and is being noted and quoted throughout the trade press. To make things even better, it has received an offer from a major New York Stock Exchange company, which is anxious to acquire the firm at a significant multiple of the investor's cost.

The company truly has gone through all of the stages from venture capital startup, reformation, turnaround, and, finally, rapid growth. The founders have achieved a high degree of success in both a professional and business sense, and the venture investors, who have been good partners, will end up with a compound rate of return on their investment approaching 30 percent. It was not without some heartaches and some worrisome moments, but it also provided the kind of excitement and satisfaction that is possible with venture investments. At one time, we could have lost everything. At others, there was euphoric high. It did not produce a return of 50 times our investment but, on the other hand, it produced a return far in excess of what comparable market opportunities had been during the same period of time. It's a classic story—the kind that happens often enough to make venture capital a stimulating and profitable area in which to be involved.

It demonstrates, however, that the venture capital business is not for the faint of heart. And while we are all tempted as individuals to dabble in small-business investments from time to time, as an ongoing activity it is better left in the hands of professionals where risks can be minimized. The degree of attention required is such that full-time involvement is needed to improve the odds of success. Nevertheless, the next time someone calls you on the phone and asks for 30 minutes to tell you about a new concept he or she has developed for a computer, a book publishing venture, or a new type of furniture, listen. If it is a worthy idea, offer encouragement—maybe even a little money. And if you take this entrepreneur out for lunch, don't forget to pick up the check. Who knows? It may be the next Apple Computer.

DOS AND DON'TS

If, in spite of all my admonitions, you decide that venture capital is for you—and that you can afford to take the risk and cannot afford not to accept the challenge—here are a dozen rules that should be kept in mind.

1. Try to invest in companies, not products or ideas.
2. It is better to back a team of people who have had some prior

experience together, preferably in the same area that they are going into with their new project.
3. Avoid projects designed to change the world. Educating a market that it needs a product takes twice as long and costs three times as much money as expected.
4. Avoid projects that have a high critical mass for success or require approval of industry associations or political bodies. These types of deals also take more time and money than you could ever anticipate. Example: selling a material-handling system to the airline industry requires that all of the airlines agree to one similar approach. They might, but it could be costly to count on it.
5. Always invest first and foremost in people, people, people. It is as significant as location, location, location is in real estate. Talented, capable management can always improvise and redirect their strategy as to markets and products. A product without good management cannot do likewise.
6. Always make sure that a business plan has sufficient provision for a margin of error. Remember Murphy's Law: Whatever can go wrong, will go wrong.
7. Take the trouble to check the entrepreneur's references.
8. Plan the financing so that a "second round" capability is available; chances are more money will be required than originally envisioned.
9. Try to structure the financing so that your capital is returned at the earliest possible date while retaining a residual equity interest. This improves your return on investment and reduces risk.
10. Structure the financing so that after the closing the entrepreneur has both positive and negative incentives to meet and, indeed, exceed projections.
11. Ask for a cogent business plan. Generally speaking, if one can't write it down, one can't execute it.
12. Before the financing, agree upon a procedure that will provide an ongoing flow of reports between the entrepreneur and the investors.

Sources of Readings

David N. Dreman, "Psychology and Markets"
Adapted from chapter 4, "The Strange World of Reality," in *The New Contrarian Investment Strategy*, by David N. Dreman. Copyright © 1982. Reprinted by permission of Random House, Inc. This selection also appears as chapter 4 in the *Handbook of Financial Markets: Securities, Options and Futures*, ed. Frank J. Fabozzi and Frank G. Zarb (Homewood, Ill.: Dow Jones-Irwin, 1981).

Marcia Stigum, "Money Market Instruments"
Adapted from chapter 8, "Money Market Instruments," appearing in *The Handbook of Fixed Income Securities*, ed. Frank J. Fabozzi and Irving M. Pollack (Homewood, Ill.: Dow Jones-Irwin, 1983).

Kenneth J. Thygerson, "Investing in Mortgage-Backed Securities"
Appears as chapter 54 in *The Real Estate Handbook*, ed. Maury Seldin (Homewood, Ill.: Dow Jones-Irwin, 1980).

Sylvan G. Feldstein, "Guidelines in the Credit Analysis of General Obligation and Revenue Municipal Bonds"
Appears as chapter 16 in *The Handbook of Fixed Income Securities*, ed. Frank J. Fabozzi and Irving M. Pollack (Homewood, Ill.: Dow Jones-Irwin, 1983).

Robert W. Kopprasch, "Early Redemption (Put) Options on Fixed Income Securities"
Appears as chapter 24 in *The Handbook of Fixed Income Securities*, ed. Frank J. Fabozzi and Irving M. Pollack (Homewood, Ill.: Dow Jones-Irwin, 1983).

James R. Vertin, "Passive Equity Management Strategies"
Appears as chapter 8 in *Investment Manager's Handbook*, ed. Sumner N. Levine (Homewood, Ill.: Dow Jones-Irwin, 1980).

Peter L. Bernstein, "Management of Individual Portfolios"
Appears as chapter 47 in *The Financial Analysts Handbook* (Vol. 1), ed. Sumner N. Levine (Homewood, Ill.: Dow Jones-Irwin, 1975).

Martin L. Leibowitz, "Trends in Bond Portfolio Management"
Appears as chapter 17 in *Investment Manager's Handbook*, ed. Sumner N. Levine (Homewood, Ill.: Dow Jones-Irwin, 1980).

Sylvan G. Feldstein, Peter E. Christensen, and Frank J. Fabozzi, "Bond Portfolio Immunization"
Adapted from Sylvan G. Feldstein, Peter E. Christensen, and Frank J. Fabozzi, "Checking Interest Rate Volatility by Immunizing a Municipal Bond Portfolio," in *The Handbook of Municipal Bonds*, ed. Frank J. Fabozzi, Sylvan G. Feldstein, Irving M. Pollack, and Frank G. Zarb (Homewood, Ill.: Dow Jones-Irwin, forthcoming 1984).

Gary L. Bergstrom, John K. Koeneman, and Martin J. Siegel, "International Securities Markets"
Appears as chapter 12 in the *Handbook of Financial Markets: Securities, Options and Futures*, ed. Frank J. Fabozzi and Frank G. Zarb (Homewood, Ill.: Dow Jones-Irwin, 1981).

Gary L. Gastineau, "Options: Risks and Rewards"
Adapted from *The Stock Options Manual*, 2d ed., Gary L. Gastineau. Copyright © 1979. Reprinted by permission of McGraw-Hill Book Company.

Richard M. Bookstaber, "The Option Pricing Formula"
Adapted from chapter 4, "The Option Pricing Formula," in *Option Pricing and Strategies in Investing*, by Richard M. Bookstaber. Reprinted by permission of Addison-Wesley Publishing Company. Copyright © 1981.

Allan M. Loosigian, "Financial Futures: Hedging Interest-Rate Risk"
Adapted from *Interest Rate Futures*, by Allan M. Loosigian (Homewood, Ill.: Dow Jones-Irwin, 1980). Appears as chapter 38 in *The Handbook of Fixed Income Securities*, ed. Frank J. Fabozzi and Irving M. Pollack (Homewood, Ill.: Dow Jones-Irwin, Inc., 1983).

Victor Niederhoffer and Richard Zeckhauser, "Market Index Futures Contracts"
Originally appeared in the January-February 1980 issue of *Financial Analysts Journal*. Revised for inclusion as chapter 42 in the *Handbook of Financial Markets: Securities, Options and Futures*, ed. Frank J. Fabozzi and Frank G. Zarb (Homewood, Ill.: Dow Jones-Irwin, 1981).

Richard Zeckhauser and Victor Niederhoffer, "Predictions Fulfilled: The Early Experience of Market Index Futures Contracts"
Written specifically for this book. Copyright © 1982, Richard Zeckhauser and Victor Niederhoffer.

Robert E. Swanson and Barbara Mardinly Swanson, "Tax Shelters"
Adapted from *Tax Shelters: A Guide for Investors and Their Advisors,* by Robert E. Swanson and Barbara Mardinly Swanson, (Homewood, Ill.: Dow Jones-Irwin, 1982).

Maury Seldin and Arthur M. Weimer, "Selecting Real Estate Investment Opportunities"
Appears as chapter 67 in *The Real Estate Handbook,* ed. Maury Seldin (Homewood, Ill.: Dow Jones-Irwin, 1980).

Alan J. Inbinder and Roy D. Gottlieb, "Land Investment"
Appears as chapter 65 in *The Real Estate Handbook,* ed. Maury Seldin (Homewood, Ill.: Dow Jones-Irwin, 1980).

Paul Sack, "Management of Real Estate Portfolios"
Appears as chapter 10 in *Investment Manager's Handbook,* ed. Sumner N. Levine (Homewood, Ill.: Dow Jones-Irwin, 1980).

Alan Joel Patricof, "Venture Capital"
Appears as chapter 20 in *How to Make Your Money Make Money,* ed. Arthur Levitt, Jr. (Homewood, Ill.: Dow Jones-Irwin, 1981).